EQUITY SMART BETA AND FACTOR INVESTING FOR PRACTITIONERS

EQUITY SMART BETA AND FACTOR INVESTING FOR PRACTITIONERS

Khalid Ghayur

Ronan Heaney

Stephen Platt

WILEY

Library of Congress Cataloging-in-Publication Data:

Names: Ghayur, Khalid, author. | Heaney, Ronan G., author. | Platt, Stephen
 C., author.
Title: Equity smart beta and factor investing for practitioners / Khalid
 Ghayur, Ronan Heaney, Stephen Platt.
Description: Hoboken, New Jersey : John Wiley & Sons, Inc., [2019] | Includes
 bibliographical references and index. |
Identifiers: LCCN 2019011593 (print) | LCCN 2019013697 (ebook) | ISBN
 978-1-119-58345-5 (Adobe PDF) | ISBN 978-1-119-58344-8 (ePub) | ISBN 978-1-119-58322-6
 (hardback)
Subjects: LCSH: Investments. | Portfolio management. | Investment analysis.
Classification:L CC HG4521 (ebook) | LCC HG4521 .G43 2019 (print) | DDC
 332.6—dc23
LC record available at https://lccn.loc.gov/2019011593

Printed in the United States of America.
V10010041_050719

CONTENTS

CHAPTER 3
Explaining Smart Beta Factor Return Premia

PART III CAPTURING SMART BETA FACTORS

*Roger G. Clarke, Research Consultant, Analytic Investors
Harindra de Silva, Portfolio Manager, Analytic Investors/Wells Fargo
Asset Management
Steven Thorley, H. Taylor Peery Professor of Finance, Marriott School of
Business, Brigham, Young University*

ACKNOWLEDGMENTS

First of all, we wish to thank the investment practitioners who have contributed to this book. We are grateful that they took time out of their busy schedules to share their experiences relating to smart beta investing. We hope that readers will find their contributions insightful and useful.

We wish to recognize the valuable contributions and assistance provided by the following reviewers: Andrew Alford, Stephan Kessler, and Joseph Kushner.

We also wish to thank the following individuals for their insightful comments and guidance during the review process: Leyla Marrouk, Prafulla Saboo, Katie Souza, and Aicha Ziba.

Finally, this book would not have been possible without the editorial and organizational assistance of Patricia Berman and Ingrid Hanson.

DISCLAIMER

The views and opinions expressed in this book are those of the authors and do not necessarily reflect the views or position of any asset manager or entity the authors may be affiliated with. They are provided for informational and educational purposes only and do not constitute (and should not be relied upon as) any investment advice or recommendation. Views and opinions are current as of the date of publishing and may be subject to change. All investors are strongly urged to consult with their legal, tax, or financial advisors regarding any potential transactions or investments.

INTRODUCTION

Equity smart beta and factor investing has become a highly discussed and debated topic within the industry over the last few years. Indeed, investor surveys consistently highlight not only the increasing popularity but also adoption of smart beta investing. As an example, in the FTSE Russell 2018 Global Survey Findings from Asset Owners, which surveyed asset owners representing an estimated $3.5 trillion in assets across North America, Europe, Asia Pacific, and other regions, 77% of asset owners responded that they have already implemented, are currently evaluating implementation, or plan to evaluate smart beta strategies in the near future. The survey also found that smart beta adoption rates increased from 26% in 2015 to 48% in 2018. More interestingly perhaps, while FTSE Russell surveys in previous years showed a significantly higher adoption rate for large asset owners with more than $10 billion in assets, in this most recent survey, the adoption rates were more evenly distributed across small (39%), medium (43%), and large (56%) asset owners. In terms of adopted smart beta strategies, multifactor offerings showed the highest adoption rate (49%), followed by single factor low volatility (35%) and value strategies (28%). The growth in the adoption rate of multifactor offerings, most likely driven by a better understanding of the diversification benefits offered by a combination of lowly correlated equity common factors, appears to come at the expense of other smart beta strategies that have concentrated exposures to certain factors, such as fundamentally weighted strategies, which have seen adoption rates decline from 41% in 2014 to 19% in 2018.

In our opinion, smart beta is an important innovation in the field of investments, and its growing adoption across the industry is driven by many considerations. First, in our experience, many public and private pension plans have a 6% to 8% return requirement from their investment portfolio (actuarial rate of return) in order to meet their expected liabilities. In a low expected return environment, such return targets may become difficult to achieve without significantly increasing the allocation to equities. At the same time, some asset owners also have a desire to lower the volatility of the overall investment portfolio as well as the volatility in funding contributions and earnings, while retaining the equity allocation. Asset owners, therefore, appear to be confronted with conflicting objectives: (1) improve portfolio returns, but without increasing the equity allocation and/or (2) reduce portfolio volatility, but without lowering the allocation to equities. Smart beta investing may provide potential solutions to meet these goals. Certain smart beta offerings, such as multifactor strategies, offer the potential to improve expected returns, while keeping portfolio volatility at a level similar to that of the market. Certain other smart beta offerings, such as low-volatility strategies, provide the potential to lower overall portfolio risk, while seeking to generate market-like returns. As such, smart beta investing may allow investors to meet the objectives of return enhancement and/or risk reduction, without meaningfully altering the equity allocation.

Second, the introduction of smart beta investing, alongside active management, offers the potential to significantly improve the diversification benefits in a portfolio. Indeed, in combining smart beta with true alpha, investors can introduce multiple layers of diversification, which drive important efficiency gains (i.e. higher relative risk adjusted returns) in the overall portfolio.

Third, in our interactions with large asset owners, we find that, as the portfolio size grows, it may become progressively more difficult for these asset owners to find additional skilled active managers and/or increase the allocations to the best performing managers, as manager concentration may lead to capacity and/or manager risk constraints. Such asset owners are confronted with the problem of delivering a reasonable alpha on a large and growing asset base. In our experience, these asset owners have tended to look at certain smart beta strategies, mainly low tracking error multifactor offerings, as transparent and systematic strategies capable of delivering alpha (excess returns relative to the market portfolio) with high capacity and cost-efficiency.

Fourth, from an investment process point of view, the increasing popularity of smart beta investing can also be attributed to the fact that it seeks to combine the most attractive features of both active and index investing. Smart beta offerings often seek to capture the same sources of excess returns (i.e. factors) that active managers commonly emphasize, and that have depicted persistent market outperformance. But unlike active management, these sources of excess returns are now delivered in index-like approaches, which aim to mitigate investment process and transparency risks and provide meaningful implementation cost and management fee savings.

Fifth, as product structurers have more or less exhausted offerings based on capitalization-weighted indexes, their focus has shifted to smart beta indexes and associated products. According to Morningstar Research (2017), "A Global Guide to Strategic-Beta Exchange-Traded Products," strategic-beta (Morningstar's terminology for smart beta) exchange-traded products (ETPs) were introduced in the United States in May 2000. As of June 2017, strategic-beta ETPs had grown to 1,320, with aggregate assets under management of US$707 billion worldwide. In fact, the rate of growth in strategic-beta ETPs and associated assets has accelerated in the recent past. For instance, from June 2016 to June 2017, strategic-beta ETPs recorded an increase in inflows of 28.3%.

Moving forward, based on our discussions and experiences with clients, we expect growth in smart beta investing to continue. For retail investors, structured smart beta products, priced significantly below traditional active and close to traditional passive, in our opinion, are likely to attract the majority of allocations. For institutional investors, although the starting allocations to smart beta are small, we expect a typical equity portfolio structure to comprise 50% capitalization-weighted passive, 25% smart beta, and 25% active in the long run. At the same time, we also note that many investors have not yet adopted smart beta investing. According to various surveys, such as the FTSE Russell 2018 Global Survey, the need for better education on topics such as how to approach and position smart beta, how to analyze and conduct due diligence, on the large number of smart beta offerings, and how to determine the best strategy or combination of strategies for a given portfolio structure, remains the most important barrier for investors to implement smart beta investing.

The need for continued investor education provides the motivation for this book. Our hope is that investment practitioners will find the content of this book relevant and useful in understanding the theoretical underpinnings of smart beta investing, analyzing and selecting appropriate smart beta strategies that meet their specific objectives, structuring more efficient portfolios by incorporating smart beta with true alpha, and, perhaps most importantly, gaining insights from other practitioners who have successfully implemented smart beta investing in their portfolios.

OVERVIEW OF BOOK CHAPTERS

In Chapter 1, we start by reviewing the evolution of the equity smart beta space as well as some desired characteristics of smart beta offerings. This review of the evolution of smart beta investing provides useful insights in understanding the definition and current composition of the smart beta space.

Since smart beta has over time become closely aligned with factor investing, in Chapters 2 and 3 we provide an overview of equity common factors and factor investing. Chapter 2 briefly reviews the origins and theory of factor investing. We also address topics such as why investors should care about equity factors and which specific factors have become the focus of various smart beta offerings. Chapter 3 focuses on explaining smart beta factor return premia. We discuss the risk-based, behavioral, and structural explanations for why factor premia exist, why they have persisted historically, and why they can be expected to persist going forward.

The wide variety of smart beta products available in the marketplace can sometimes be overwhelming for investors, who often struggle with how to analyze and select such products. Differences in smart beta offerings can arise from many sources, such as factor specifications, weighting schemes, and methodologies used to control turnover, diversification, or capacity. The various considerations involved in capturing smart beta factors and selecting smart beta strategies are discussed in Chapters 4, 5, and 6. In Chapter 4, we propose a simple framework for understanding some of the various weighting schemes employed to capture smart beta factor returns. We also analyze the efficiency in factor capture achieved by these weighting schemes. In Chapter 5, we discuss some of the various factor signal specifications that are commonly used in the design of smart beta products. In addition to the choice of the weighting scheme, factor signal specifications can also drive differences among the various smart beta offerings. And in Chapter 6, we analyze a large number of publicly available smart beta strategies, using the factor portfolios we construct in Chapter 4. Although our focus is on smart beta strategies, we also use these factor portfolios to conduct a risk decomposition of certain active strategies. The analysis conducted in this chapter provides useful insights in understanding the drivers of performance for smart beta and active strategies as well as assessing the efficiency of factor capture or the existence of manager skill more generally.

In Chapters 7, 8, and 9, our focus shifts to understanding the performance characteristics of smart beta factor strategies. We start by analyzing the historical performance of individual smart beta factor portfolios in Chapter 7. We discuss performance across three regions, namely, US, Developed Markets ex. US, and Emerging Markets. We adjust performance for implementation costs in order to make historical simulations potentially more representative of "live" implementation. This chapter seeks to provide insights into how factors differ in terms of their total and relative risk and return attributes as well as their performance in different market regimes. In Chapter 8, we move from individual factors to factor diversification strategies. We discuss the attractive correlation attributes of smart beta factors and show how combining factors results in improved relative risk-adjusted performance, while also potentially mitigating market underperformance risk. It is often said that diversification is the only free lunch in finance. Multifactor smart beta strategies may well represent an example of the significant benefits that can be achieved through diversification. In Chapter 9, Roger Clarke, Harindra de Silva, and Steven Thorley provide an insightful discussion relating to low-volatility investing. The authors review (1) the historical performance of the low volatility factor and explanations advanced to explain it, (2) whether the anomaly is driven by systematic or idiosyncratic risk, (3) the characteristics of the low volatility factor, such as correlation with other factors, and (4) techniques commonly used for building low volatility portfolios.

With regard to smart beta implementation and portfolio structuring, Chapter 10 analyzes various potential challenges that investors face in designing multistrategy, multimanager portfolios. These challenges partially arise from current portfolio structuring practices, which, in our opinion, do not provide adequate guidance on how to implement efficient style and manager diversification. Therefore, we propose an alternative portfolio structuring framework that seeks to improve on current practices by facilitating the building of potentially more efficient overall portfolio structures that incorporate smart beta strategies alongside active management.

Investors have an increasing desire to reflect environmental, social, and governance (ESG) values and perspectives in their overall equity portfolios. In Chapter 11, we propose a framework for incorporating ESG factors as well as combining ESG factors with smart beta factor investing. The framework emphasizes customization and transparency in performance attribution, while maintaining some degree of benchmark-awareness.

Chapter 12 provides an example of the application of factor investing beyond equities. In this chapter, Oliver Bunn outlines a factor-based approach to identifying the systematic risk exposures taken by hedge funds. These economically intuitive factors based on academic research are well-defined, liquid, and can be implemented at relatively low cost. A portfolio of these systematic factors can provide investors with access to a hedge fund-like return profile.

The remainder of the book chapters comprise contributions from practitioners who have successfully implemented or are considering implementing smart beta investing in their equity portfolios. Asset owner perspectives are provided in Chapters 13 through 15. The implementation of smart beta at California Public Employees' Retirement System (CalPERS) is discussed by Steve Carden in Chapter 13. The evolution of the smart beta program at CalPERS constitutes an interesting case study because it closely mirrors the evolution of smart beta investing in the industry, in general, from an alternative beta strategy to multifactor investing. In 2006, CalPERS adopted fundamental indexation as a mean-reversion strategy that could potentially address the perceived shortcomings of a trend-following market capitalization-weighted portfolio. As fundamental indexation was implemented and monitored over the next four or five years, an understanding was gained that the excess returns of this strategy were driven by a high exposure to the value factor. This exposed the portfolio to the significant cyclicality of value returns. As a result, over time, the focus shifted toward diversifying the value exposure with other factors, such as momentum, quality, and low volatility, which have a low or negative correlation with value but independently deliver positive excess returns in the long run. CalPERS was also an early adopter of a hybrid implementation model, which combines active and index management for implementing systematic smart beta and factor strategies. In this model, external strategies are sourced from smart beta managers as a custom index through a licensing agreement and replicated in-house by CalPERS. The hybrid implementation model has resulted in meaningful trading cost and management fee savings for CalPERS. In the next case study in Chapter 14, Hans de Ruiter discusses the design and implementation of a smart beta program at the Pensionfund TNO. Historically, TNO had allocated to equities in a passive fashion using traditional index funds. The advent of smart beta offerings provided an opportunity to include additional sources of excess returns in order to potentially improve the risk-adjusted performance of the portfolio. As such, Pensionfund TNO approached smart beta as a form of enhanced indexing that would allow the fund to partially transition the portfolio from a single-beta to a multiple-beta passive strategy. In considering smart beta, Pensionfund TNO laid out the important questions that needed addressing, such as: Which smart beta factors to focus on and why? Which smart beta strategies to consider if mitigating short-term market underperformance risk is an important objective? How to address persistence of smart beta factor premiums at a practical level? How to construct multifactor smart beta strategies? How to assess and mitigate the impact of implementation costs? And which benchmark to use for the implemented smart beta strategies? This case study provides useful insights into how Pensionfund TNO addressed these questions. Another early adopter of smart beta factor investing is the Barclays Bank UK Retirement Fund (BUKRF). In Chapter 15, Ilian Dimitrov explains how smart beta over the years has contributed meaningfully to improve the risk-adjusted returns of the overall equity allocation. Initially, at BUKRF, smart beta was used for portfolio completion and exposure management purposes with the goal of achieving a diversified and balanced exposure to certain targeted factors. In recent years, the use of smart beta has broadened to include strategies that capture a specific risk premium at low cost as well as multifactor strategies that serve as an alternative to active management in highly efficient segments of global equity markets. This case study also discusses the various challenges faced by BUKRF in the implementation of their smart beta program, the criteria used in selecting appropriate smart beta strategies, the process used to determine an allocation to smart beta, and the various considerations relating to governance, monitoring, and performance benchmarking of smart beta strategies.

Chapters 16 and 17 provide investment consultants' perspectives on smart beta. Although some investment consultants have not formed a formal, public view on smart beta investing, others, such as Willis Towers Watson (WTW), have been early advocates of such strategies. In Chapter 16, James Price and Phil Tindall from WTW discuss smart beta from an asset owner's perspective. The authors argue that smart beta has resulted in a meaningful change in the investment landscape for asset owners as it shifts the emphasis from manager selection to investment strategy selection and, hence, requires a different set of skills. Smart beta requires increased up-front governance, which also means that asset owners need to form beliefs regarding smart beta, distinguish between absolute and relative return worlds, and avoid short-termism in strategy evaluation and monitoring. In this new world, asset owners also face some challenges, such as potential crowding of smart beta factors and timing allocations to strategies, which they will need to address. In the US, Wilshire Consulting have also been one of the early advocates of smart beta investing. In Chapter 17, Andrew Junkin, Steven Foresti, and Michael Rush discuss the perspectives of Wilshire Consulting with regard to smart beta. They argue that investors consider adopting smart beta as a replacement for or complement to active management, as smart beta captures many of the systematic sources of returns that active managers also implement, but does so in a systematic, transparent, and less expensive manner. Smart beta may also be appropriate as a replacement for traditional passive for those investors who are looking to improve risk-adjusted returns of their portfolios but wish to achieve that at a reasonable cost. In the end, Wilshire Consulting believes that smart beta strategies potentially represent an effective solution for those asset owners wrestling with the current low expected return environment.

Chapters 18 and 19 focus on the potential motivations for retail investors to consider smart beta investing. In Chapter 18, Lisa Huang and Petter Kolm at Fidelity Investments and Betterment, respectively, lay out the case for retail advisors to offer a complete smart beta solution to their clients. Supported by academic evidence and declining costs of implementation via exchange traded products, the authors argue that smart beta strategies represent an interesting vehicle for building more efficient and cost-effective portfolios in the retail space. In Chapter 19, Jerry Chafkin from AssetMark addresses the potential positioning of smart beta with retail investors. In his opinion, smart beta is a disciplined and systematic approach to alpha generation, which facilitates the basic objective of active management, but with greater reliability and transparency. Smart beta is a compelling proposition for retail investors because it combines the advantages of both passive (low-cost, disciplined, and transparent) and active (potential for market outperformance) investing. One of the most important appeals of smart beta investing is that as systematic strategies they help both investors and managers set appropriate expectations and maintain discipline during difficult times. This potentially significantly improves the ability to achieve investor objectives in the long run.

Finally, Chapters 20 and 21 provide some concluding remarks, including addressing some skepticisms regarding smart beta investing.

PART I

OVERVIEW OF EQUITY SMART BETA SPACE

CHAPTER 1

EVOLUTION AND COMPOSITION OF THE EQUITY SMART BETA SPACE

This chapter reviews the evolution of the equity smart beta space as well as some desired characteristics of smart beta offerings. This review of the evolution of smart beta investing provides useful insights in understanding the definition and current composition of the smart beta space.

CHAPTER SUMMARY

- The origins of smart beta investing can potentially be traced back to research investigating the shortcomings of the capitalization-weighted market indexes. These efforts and the identified shortcomings led researchers to investigate alternative non-capitalization-weighted methodologies, such as equal-weighting, minimum variance, and fundamental weighting.
- Empirical analysis of products based on these alternative weighting methodologies depicted higher risk-adjusted returns (Sharpe ratios) compared to the market index, thereby suggesting that the capitalization-weighted market index may not be as efficient as theory (the Capital Asset Pricing Model, or CAPM) would suggest.
- These products were initially referred to as alternative equity betas in the academic literature. Today, the term "smart beta" is commonly used in reference to such strategies.
- Risk decomposition analyses of alternative equity beta strategies revealed that these strategies derive much of their market outperformance through high exposures to

equity common factors, such as size, low volatility, or value, which have been well documented in the academic literature over several decades.

- As such, in our experience, investor focus shifted to capturing the equity common factors more directly and/or in a more customizable benchmark-aware implementation (an active beta perspective), which does not require replacing the capitalization-weighted market index as the policy benchmark (an alternative beta perspective).
- The composition of the smart beta space, therefore, evolved from alternative equity beta strategies to a combination of alternative beta and various factor offerings.
- The risk decomposition of alternative equity beta strategies also shows that, at least in terms of investment outcome, smart beta can be defined as mostly factor investing, as the continued success of alternative equity beta strategies critically depends on the persistence of various factor premia.
- Factor investing is not new both from a passive as well as an active implementation perspective. What is new with regard to smart beta strategies, however, is a value-adding repackaging of factor investing. Smart beta strategies create a hybrid solution that retains the attractive features of both passive and active management. Such strategies offer characteristics that emphasize efficiency, transparency, low turnover, improved diversification and capacity, and low fees.

I. INTRODUCTION

When asked about smart beta, William Sharpe's response was that the term makes him "definitionally sick."[1] Indeed, in the CAPM, Sharpe (1964) and others (Treynor (1961), Lintner (1965), and Mossin (1966)) provided a definition of the terms "beta" and "alpha." Beta is the sensitivity (regression coefficient) of an asset to the capitalization-weighted market portfolio (the factor). A stock with a beta of one behaves just like the market. A stock with a beta above (below) one is more (less) risky than the market. Alpha is the return in excess of the beta-adjusted market return. Today, however, practitioners commonly use the term beta to refer to the market portfolio or some other benchmark index. That is, for practitioners beta refers to the factor itself, rather than the exposure to the factor. A beta capture typically means a passive approach, which seeks to replicate the performance of the factor or benchmark index. Returns in excess of the benchmark are referred to as "alpha," based on the (implicit) assumption that the portfolio has a beta of one to the benchmark index.[2] But, what are practitioners referring to with regard to smart beta investing?

The definition and composition of the equity smart beta space is a source of confusion in the industry. Smart beta goes by many names, such as alternative beta, systematic beta, advanced beta, exotic beta, beta prime, or active beta, and many investment

---

[1] Authers (2014).

[2] This interpretation of the terms alpha and beta may be viewed by academics as a misuse of how these terms have been defined in the literature.

strategies with seemingly quite different characteristics are lumped into the smart beta category. At the outset, smart beta strategies were designed to address the potential shortcomings of capitalization-weighted market indexes and, as such, were positioned as a more efficient non-capitalization-weighted alternative. Over time, however, the term smart beta has become closely linked with factor investing. A review of the evolution of smart beta investing provides useful background and insights into the changing perspectives and the current composition of the smart beta space.

II. EVOLUTION OF EQUITY SMART BETA

A. Benefits of Capitalization Weighting

The CAPM (further detailed in the next chapter) demonstrates that under some simplifying assumptions the capitalization-weighted market portfolio is the most efficient portfolio on the efficient frontier, on an ex ante basis. In other words, the capitalization-weighted market portfolio is mean-variance optimal. Under the assumption of market efficiency, investors cannot do better than this portfolio. The CAPM clearly provided the theoretical motivation for the creation of capitalization-weighted equity market indexes and their widespread use in performance benchmarking and portfolio implementation. For investors, capitalization-weighted equity market indexes also offer other practical benefits, such as high capacity, high liquidity, low turnover, easy replicability, and low fees. It is no surprise, then, that capitalization-weighted equity market indexes have gained tremendous popularity with investors. Given the widespread use of such indexes around the globe, a reasonable question is whether such indexes are as efficient as theory (CAPM) would suggest. Therefore, analyzing the potential shortcomings of capitalization weighting became an important topic of research within the industry.[3]

B. Potential Drawbacks of Capitalization Weighting

Criticisms of capitalization weighting tend to center on three areas: concentration, volatility, and propensity to invest in expensive stocks.

At the individual stock level, concentration refers to a few companies having a large weight in the index, which exposes investors to significant stock-specific risk.[4]

---

[3] In the following section, we discuss the shortcomings of capitalization weighting. Another separate argument, first raised by Mayers (1976), is whether the equity market portfolio itself is a reasonable proxy for the ex ante mean-variance efficient CAPM market portfolio, which includes all marketable assets, such as equities, bonds, commodities, and real estate, as well as nonmarketable assets, such as human capital. Indeed, Stambaugh (1982) reported improved results for CAPM tests when the market portfolio included nonequity asset classes.

[4] In theory, stock-specific risk is not rewarded because it can be diversified away. Only the market risk is rewarded.

In many countries, in fact, just a handful of names may account for a large proportion of the weight of the market index. At the end of 2017, as an example, the three largest Belgian companies trading on Euronext Brussels had an aggregate market capitalization larger than that of the remaining 130 companies combined. Capitalization-weighted market indexes can also become heavily concentrated in individual industries/sectors (e.g. the technology sector in the S&P 500 Index during the technology bubble) or even countries (e.g. Japan in the MSCI EAFE Index in the mid- to late 1980s).

Another potential drawback of capitalization weighting is that it may expose passive investors to high levels of volatility. Higher volatility may be caused by the noisy nature of market prices as well as the interaction between the speculative behavior of investors and concentration. For instance, overenthusiasm of investors may lead to overpricing in individual stocks and/or industries. Rising prices for these stocks and/or industries increases their capitalization and weights in the market index, thus causing concentration. Concentration, in turn, may force passive investors, who closely replicate the market indexes, to hold more of the overpriced stocks and/or industries. As mispricing eventually corrects, investors experience significant volatility and suffer significant losses by virtue of being overly concentrated in the most overpriced stocks and/or industries of the market. The formation of bubbles, and their subsequent bursting, may imply that investors replicating the capitalization-weighted market indexes end up taking more risk than would otherwise be needed to capture the equity risk premium. One well-known example of such dynamics is the price-to-earnings (PE) ratio as well as the weight of technology stocks in the S&P 500 Index during the technology bubble. Between 1998 and 2000, as the overenthusiasm of investors led to the doubling of valuation ratios for technology stocks, their weight in the S&P 500 Index increased from 13% in 1998 to more than 30% at the start of 2000. As the technology bubble burst, the valuations and weight of technology stocks shrunk considerably, causing passive investors to experience significant portfolio volatility and losses.

Arnott et al. (2005) identified the performance drag as another potential drawback of capitalization-weighted market portfolios. Under the assumption that market prices tend to revert to underlying fundamental values, capitalization weighting tends to overweight overvalued stocks and underweight undervalued stocks, thus introducing a potential performance drag as the mispricing inevitably corrects. The performance drag may be another reason why the capitalization-weighted market portfolio may not be optimal.

C. Suggested Solutions

To address the concentration issue, weighting schemes that provide more diversification were explored. These efforts led to the development of equal-weighted indexes, capped indexes (which limit the weight of individual stocks at a certain level, such as 5% or 10%), diversity indexes (e.g. Fernholz (1998)) and maximum diversification indexes (e.g. Choueifaty and Coignard (2008)). Empirically, these portfolios were shown to outperform capitalization-weighted market indexes, on a risk-adjusted basis, thereby suggesting that concentration risk is not rewarded over time and makes capitalization-weighted indexes less efficient than those employing weighting schemes that realize more diversification. In relation to the higher volatility of capitalization-weighted market portfolios, Haugen and Baker (1991) investigated the characteristics of the minimum-variance portfolio on the efficient frontier for US stocks and found that such portfolios realized approximately 25% total risk reduction compared to the market portfolio, without sacrificing returns. Clarke et al. (2006) corroborated these results. With significant total risk reduction and market-like returns, minimum-variance portfolios realized much higher risk-adjusted returns (Sharpe ratio) relative to the market. On an empirical basis, minimum-variance portfolios, as well as other low-risk strategies, such as risk-weighting, provided another challenge to the notion that the capitalization-weighted market portfolio is mean-variance optimal. With regard to the potential performance drag embedded in capitalization weighting, Arnott et al. (2005) showed that portfolios weighted by fundamental variables of size, such as sales or cash flows, as opposed to market capitalization, outperformed the market by about 2% per annum at similar levels of risk.[5]

Figure 1.1 summarizes the challenges posed by capitalization weighting and some of the solutions that have been proposed to address them.

The non-capitalization-weighted strategies mentioned earlier, along with some others, such as EDHEC's Risk Efficient Index (Amenc et al. 2010), were positioned by their providers as an alternative for the less-efficient capitalization-weighted market portfolio. As such, these strategies were initially referred to as "alternative equity betas" (AEB) or simply "alternative betas." Over time, however, the term "smart beta" became more commonly used.

With the emergence of AEB, another important question arose: What explains the outperformance of these strategies compared to the capitalization-weighted market indexes?

D. Risk Decomposition of Alternative Equity Betas

The outperformance of AEB seemed to challenge the basic conclusions of the CAPM, but they weren't the only strategies to do so. Over multiple decades, the academic literature has also documented a number of "factors," or common characteristics of companies that were shown to explain relative risk and return differences for stocks much better than CAPM beta. For instance, Fama and French (1992) provided evidence that size and value explained the cross-section of average returns better than

---

[5] As pointed out by Arnott et al. (2005), fundamental weighting as a portfolio construction approach has been pursued by many investment managers, such as Goldman Sachs Asset Management, Global Wealth Allocation, Barclays Global Investors, and Paul Wood, at various points in time, some going back to the early 1990s.

FIGURE 1.1   Drawbacks of Capitalization Weighting and Suggested Solutions

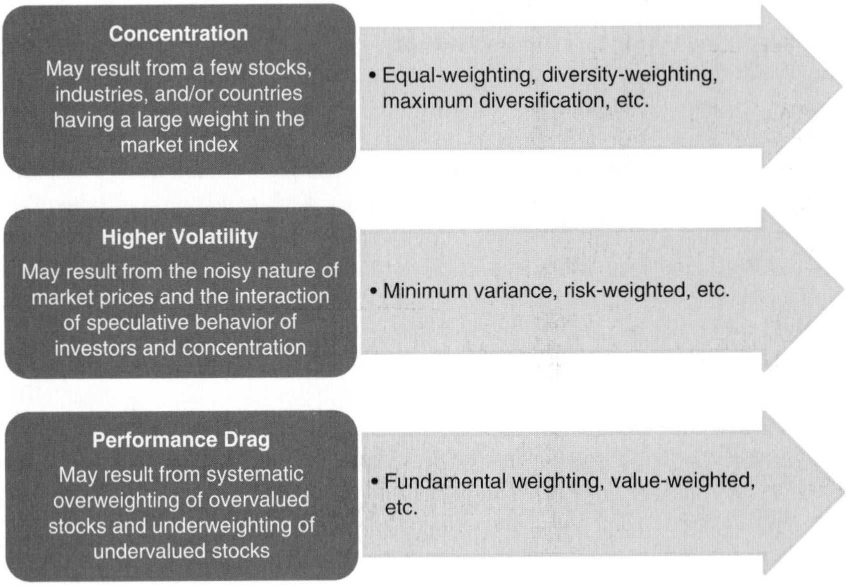

Concentration
May result from a few stocks, industries, and/or countries having a large weight in the market index

• Equal-weighting, diversity-weighting, maximum diversification, etc.

Higher Volatility
May result from the noisy nature of market prices and the interaction of speculative behavior of investors and concentration

• Minimum variance, risk-weighted, etc.

Performance Drag
May result from systematic overweighting of overvalued stocks and underweighting of undervalued stocks

• Fundamental weighting, value-weighted, etc.

market beta. Given the extensive evidence on the existence and performance of certain factors, a reasonable area of enquiry was to investigate whether the market outperformance of AEB could also be explained by these factors.

To answer this question, researchers conducted a risk decomposition analysis of various AEB. Typically, this analysis entails analyzing the exposures and efficiency of a strategy against the Fama-French 3-factor model (1992), which comprises of the market, size, and value factors, or the Carhart 4-factor model (1997), which also includes momentum. These analyses revealed that the market outperformance of various analyzed AEB strategies was explained by high and significant exposure to the considered factors, with no meaningful alpha being generated by the analyzed strategies against the 3-factor and 4-factor models (e.g. Chow et al. 2011). As an example, equal-weighted, diversity, and maximum diversification indexes outperformed the market because they had a high exposure to size (small cap). Minimum-variance and risk-weighted portfolios outperformed because they had a high exposure to low-beta, low-volatility stocks. And fundamentally weighted portfolios outperformed because they had a high exposure to value.

Although AEB strategies analyzed by Chow et al. (2011) as a group generated no meaningful alpha relative to the 3-factor and 4-factor models, another important topic to address was whether these strategies at least provided a higher efficiency capture of factor returns compared to the existing size and style indexes offered by index providers. Capitalization-weighted size (large/mid/small) and style (value/growth) indexes constitute the first attempt at capturing equity common factors in an indexing framework. Chow et al. (2011) showed that AEB, in general, represented an improvement over the existing capitalization-weighted size and style indexes as they delivered higher efficiency in factor capture. Specifically, in a risk decomposition analysis against the Fama-French 3-factor model, AEB did not generate negative alphas, while capitalization-weighted size and style factor indexes did.

If AEB derive their market outperformance through exposures to well-known equity common factors, then why wouldn't investors capture these factors more directly through methodologies that deliver higher efficiency compared to capitalization-weighted size and style indexes and more flexibility compared to AEB?

E. Renewed Focus on Factor Investing: Potential Advantages of Factor Offerings

In recent years, in our experience, investor focus has clearly shifted toward new factor products that seek to deliver the following additional value-adding features compared to capitalization-weighted size and style indexes as well as AEB.

a. Enhanced Efficiency in Factor Capture

Compared to the existing capitalization-weighted size and style indexes, many new factor offerings seek to deliver higher efficiency in factor capture through the use of non-capitalization-weighted methodologies. These include capitalization-scaled weighting, signal weighting, optimized, and other weighting schemes that seek higher levels of efficiency in factor capture. The improved efficiency may be demonstrated either in the form of higher risk-adjusted returns or, perhaps more appropriately, in the form of statistically significant factor-adjusted alphas.[6]

b. Customizable Benchmark-Aware Portfolio Construction

The alternative beta implementation perspective adopted by most AEB, which may involve replacing the capitalization-weighted policy benchmark, poses some challenges for certain investors. Some investors may not consider capitalization weighting as inefficient but may believe in the existence of extra-market factor premia. Other investors may find replacing the capitalization-weighted policy benchmark difficult for various implementation and governance reasons, even when they have reasonable doubts about the efficiency of capitalization-weighted equity benchmarks. Such investors generally would prefer to implement desired factor tilts in a benchmark-aware fashion, which does not require a respecification of the policy benchmark. Benchmark-aware means that investors can implement specific factor tilts relative to

---

[6] We review these weighting schemes and their investment efficiency in more detail in Chapter 4 and Chapter 6.

FIGURE 1.2   Implementation Perspectives

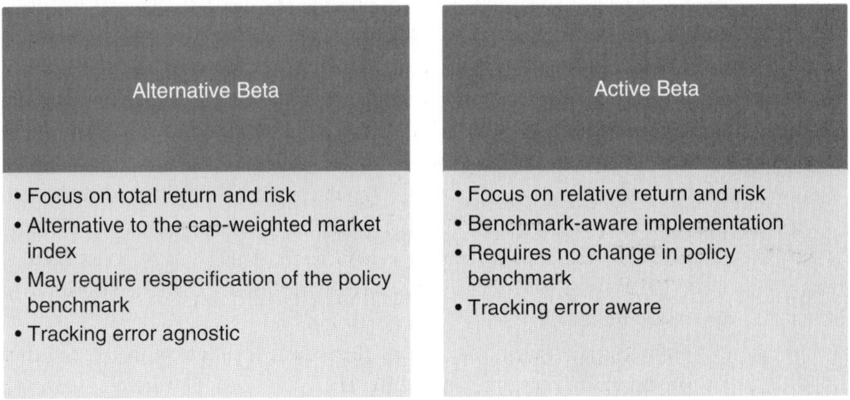

Alternative Beta	Active Beta
• Focus on total return and risk • Alternative to the cap-weighted market index • May require respecification of the policy benchmark • Tracking error agnostic	• Focus on relative return and risk • Benchmark-aware implementation • Requires no change in policy benchmark • Tracking error aware

their existing policy benchmarks, whether they are commonly used capitalization-weighted benchmarks or client-specific custom benchmarks, and at desired levels of tracking error relative to the policy benchmark. We refer to such implementations as an "active beta," as opposed to an alternative beta, perspective. As such, benchmark-aware factor strategies offer a much higher degree of "customization" and potential risk control compared to most AEB. The main features of alternative beta and active beta perspectives are summarized in Figure 1.2.

Most AEB either are not conditioned on or derived from commonly used benchmarks and/or do not provide the ability to target specific levels of tracking error relative to client-selected policy benchmarks. AEB may be used in an active beta implementation, but they are not ideal solutions. For example, the FTSE RAFI 1000 index (a fundamentally weighted index) tends to have an average long-term tracking error of about 4% to the Russell 1000 Index (e.g. Arnott et al. 2005). So, it could be implemented as a 4% tracking error active value strategy relative to the Russell 1000 Index. However, the FTSE RAFI 1000 Index is not conditioned on the Russell 1000 Index. Its starting universe is determined from a ranking based on fundamental variables of size as opposed to market capitalization. As such, the FTSE RAFI 1000 Index has a different set of constituents than the Russell 1000 Index, which raises potential benchmark mis-fit issues for investors using the Russell 1000 Index as the policy benchmark for US Large Cap. Furthermore, the tracking error of the FTSE RAFI 1000 Index to the Russell 1000 Index is not explicitly targeted. It is a by-product of the methodology used and turned out to be an average of about 4% in the long run.

c. Factor Diversification

In our experience, the benefits of factor diversification are also now well-understood by investors. Individual factors depict tremendous cyclicality in returns (e.g. value can go in and out of favor), which exposes investors to pronounced and prolonged periods of market underperformance. At the same time, factors also depict low or negative pair-wise active return (return in excess of the benchmark) correlation, which tends to deliver significant gains from diversification. As a result, factor diversification strategies tend to dominate individual factors, as documented by many studies (e.g. Asness et al. 2009, Hjalmarsson 2009, and Ghayur et al. 2013). That is, they generate higher relative risk-adjusted returns (IR), while potentially significantly mitigating market underperformance risk. Although AEB deliver exposure to multiple common factors, they are not explicitly designed for implementing balanced factor diversification strategies. Most AEBS tend to have concentrated factor exposures. As an illustration, RAFI has a much higher exposure to value than to other factors (e.g. Chow et al. 2011), while minimum-variance portfolios are composed primarily of low-volatility, low-beta stocks (e.g. Clarke et al. 2011).

As a result of the above considerations, we believe investor interest in recent years has shifted toward more efficient, customizable, and benchmark-aware single factor and factor diversification strategies. Smart beta has become closely linked with factor investing, and factor offerings now form an important component of the smart beta landscape, in addition to the various AEB.

Figure 1.3 depicts the timeline relating to the launch of some of the smart beta offerings.

III.   DESIRED CHARACTERISTICS OF SMART BETA STRATEGIES

If smart beta has become closely linked with factor investing, then what is new about smart beta? After all, factor investing has been implemented both from passive and active perspectives for a long time. Capitalization-weighted size and style indexes were introduced in 1989, and active managers, for decades, have attempted to beat the market by gaining exposure to equity common factors.

From the perspective of the source of excess return (i.e. factors), there may not be anything new in smart beta factor investing. From the perspective of how these excess return sources are captured and delivered, smart beta is creating a value-adding repackaging of factor investing. Smart beta factor strategies are a hybrid solution that seeks to harness the attractive features of both passive and active management in capturing factor returns. Compared to traditional capitalization-weighted size and style indexes, smart beta offerings deliver a more efficient exposure to factors through alternative weighting schemes, and in many cases in a benchmark-aware, tracking error-targeted fashion. Compared to traditional active management, smart beta factor strategies differ in terms of product design, product structure, and product delivery. From the perspective of product design, smart beta strategies tend to focus on factors and factor specifications that have been researched, scrutinized, and vetted in the academic literature over multiple decades. These factors, also known as rewarded factors, have been shown to retain statistical significance in multiple testing approaches that account for the problems associated with data mining and have been demonstrably

FIGURE 1.3 Timeline of Various Smart Beta Offerings

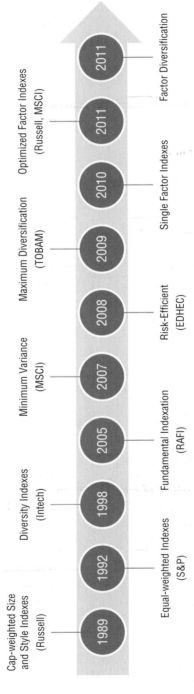

linked with persistence on an out-of-sample basis.[7] In terms of product structure, smart beta investment processes tend to be characterized by simplicity and transparency, such that the sources of risk and return embedded in the investment process are well understood by investors. Smart beta offerings seek portfolio construction and implementation methodologies that are rules-based and incorporate additional features designed to mitigate turnover and improve diversification and capacity. Finally, in terms of product delivery, smart beta strategies are offered at lower fees than traditional active management and seek to provide implementation flexibility to investors. Implementation flexibility means that the strategies are offered either in fully managed separate accounts or in various forms of index-like licensing arrangements.

IV. COMPOSITION AND DEFINITION OF EQUITY SMART BETA

In our opinion, equity smart beta could be defined in terms of investment objectives and desired characteristics of smart beta offerings. In terms of investment objectives, equity smart beta strategies seek to (1) address the potential shortcomings of capitalization weighting through alternative weighting methodologies, and/or (2) gain efficient exposure to well-documented and rewarded equity common factors.[8] Therefore, the smart beta space comprises two types of offerings: AEB and factor investing. Additionally, smart beta offerings would tend to emphasize characteristics, such as transparency, low turnover, high diversification and capacity, implementation flexibility, and lower fees.

V. TYPICAL INVESTOR QUESTIONS

1.1 Does Smart Beta Imply That the Capitalization-Weighted Market Index Is Dumb?

The smart beta terminology lends to the implication that capitalization-weighted market indexes are dumb, and some smart beta product providers have encouraged such implications. This is, of course, quite unreasonable. Smart beta products may provide improved investment efficiency, but capitalization-weighted market indexes remain the highest-capacity, highest-investability, lowest turnover, and cheapest option to capture the equity market return. That is why many practitioners, such as the consultant Willis Towers Watson, refer to the market beta as "bulk beta." Decades of academic research and practical experience of investors have provided support to the argument that minimizing implementation costs is an intelligent way of maximizing after-cost returns in the long run. There is nothing dumb about bulk beta and capitalization-weighted market indexes.

---

[7] We discuss the issues relating to multiple testing and persistence as well as the concept of rewarded factors in more detail in the next chapter.

[8] We discuss these factors in the next chapter.

1.2 Should Smart Beta Be Defined More Narrowly?

Some product providers have attempted to provide narrower definitions of smart beta arguing that the term needs a more precise meaning. As an example, Arnott and Kose (2014) write that "the way the term is bandied about, without regard for meaning, is a disservice to investors." So, they proceed to define what smart beta means to them: "A category of valuation-indifferent strategies that consciously and deliberately break the link between the price of an asset and its weight in the portfolio, seeking to earn excess returns over the cap-weighted benchmark by no longer weighting assets proportional to their popularity, while retaining most of the positive attributes of passive indexing." According to this particular definition, many perfectly reasonable smart beta products, such as those conditioned on a capitalization-sorted or weighted starting universe or price-based factors, such as size, value, or momentum, would not be viewed as smart beta. Limiting the smart beta space to valuation-indifferent strategies is, of course, not a fair depiction of the various offerings that the vast majority of industry participants would view as reasonably comprising the smart beta space.

1.3 Is Smart Beta Just Factor Investing?

On the one hand, since the market outperformance of AEB is largely explained by exposures to equity common factors, it would be reasonable to argue that smart beta is just about factor investing. On the other hand, it may be argued that investors have different investment objectives and/or philosophical beliefs, which may lead them to invest in AEB rather than seek direct exposure to well-recognized factors. In other words, non-capitalization-weighted alternatives (AEB) directly address the potential shortcomings of capitalization weighting, which may be a different investment objective than gaining an explicit exposure to certain common factors.

For example, an investor may not view market capitalization as an appropriate measure of economic size and may prefer a fundamentally weighted approach. This investment philosophy and objective may be quite different from another investor who philosophically believes in the existence and persistence of the value premium and, accordingly, seeks a direct and more pure capture of value. However, to the extent that the market outperformance of a fundamentally weighted portfolio is largely explained by value, the investment proposition for fundamental indexation becomes very closely linked with value investing. That is, to believe in the persistence of the investment performance of a fundamental index, one also has to believe in the persistence of the value premium.

Similarly, an investor concerned with the concentration inherent in capitalization weighting may consider an alternatively weighted solution, such as an equal-weighted or diversity-weighted index. Again, in such cases, even though the investor is not seeking a direct capture of size, the investment outcome is critically linked to the persistence of the size (small cap) premium.

Finally, consider the case of the minimum variance portfolio. According to finance theory, such a portfolio will have a lower risk than the market portfolio, but also lower returns. In risk-adjusted terms, the minimum variance portfolio is not expected to have a higher Sharpe ratio than the market. But in empirical studies (e.g. Haugen and Baker 1991) and in live experience (e.g. MSCI Minimum Volatility Indexes) it does, because this portfolio realizes market-like returns with lower risk. This disconnect between theory and practice is due to the low volatility premium. That is, the low volatility anomaly. As such, the investment proposition for minimum variance and other low-risk strategies is directly related to the persistence of the low volatility premium.

From an investment outcome perspective, therefore, a reasonable case can be made that smart beta is mostly about factor investing. However, from an implementation perspective, it is also true that explaining ex post performance is not equivalent to exactly replicating ex ante performance. That is, even though the ex post performance of AEB is explained by common factors (i.e. average exposures), it is quite difficult to design factor strategies that can fully replicate their ex ante performance. This is because AEB methodologies may result in time-varying factor exposures as well as some element of factor timing. As a consequence, factor strategies may be able to closely approximate, but not exactly replicate, the performance of AEB. This may lead investors to consider various AEB in the implementation of a smart beta program.

1.4 Is Smart Beta Active or Passive?

There is considerable debate in the industry as to whether smart beta strategies are active or passive. Some of the confusion in this debate stems from the fact that investors use the terms active and passive from different perspectives and meanings. We address these various perspectives below in the hope of clarifying this discussion.

Some investors argue that smart beta strategies are active because they deviate from capitalization weights. Such investors likely approach the discussion from a portfolio structuring perspective. In portfolio structuring, the process typically starts with the specification of a long-term, strategic policy benchmark, around which the entire portfolio is anchored. The replication of the policy benchmark represents the "only" passive component of the portfolio. Any strategy that deviates from the policy benchmark, with associated tracking risk, becomes active and is implemented in the active component of the portfolio. Therefore, when investors argue that smart beta is active because it deviates from capitalization-weighted benchmarks, it is because they use such benchmarks as their policy benchmarks. From the perspective of portfolio structuring, if a smart beta strategy were used as the policy benchmark, then it would become passive in the context of that portfolio, while capitalization-weighted portfolios might well be viewed as active.

Application Example 1.1

A university endowment fund uses MSCI ACWI as the policy benchmark for global equities. For this fund, the replication of MSCI ACWI is passive. Any strategy that deviates from MSCI ACWI weights would be considered active, including smart beta index approaches derived from MSCI ACWI, such as MSCI ACWI Minimum Volatility Index or MSCI ACWI Value-Weighted Index.

Now consider a family office that holds a philosophical belief that capitalization weighting is inefficient and, hence, recently changed its policy benchmark from MSCI ACWI to MSCI ACWI Minimum Volatility Index. For this investor, the replication of MSCI ACWI Minimum Volatility Index now constitutes passive investing. Strategies that deviate from this policy benchmark would be considered active, including the replication of the capitalization-weighted MSCI ACWI. In fact, a MSCI ACWI replication strategy would be considered highly active with a tracking error of more than 6% to the policy benchmark (MSCI ACWI Minimum Volatility Index).

Other investors adopt a portfolio management and implementation perspective. In this context, the replication of an index, which entails taking limited active decisions, is considered passive investing. As such, some investors may argue that smart beta is passive because many smart beta products are offered as an index, which can easily be replicated, much like the replication of a capitalization-weighted market index.

Some other investors argue that smart beta is active because, compared to capitalization-weighted market portfolios, the creation and selection of smart beta products involves taking many active decisions. For example, in the consideration of a factor diversification strategy, which factors to include, how to define them, and how to weight them would be examples of active decisions that would have to be taken.

We believe it is most helpful to approach the active versus passive debate from a portfolio structuring perspective. For a given portfolio, the replication of the selected policy benchmark is passive, and strategies that deviate from the policy benchmark are active. The fact that an active strategy can be designed and structured as an index and implemented through index replication does not make it passive. Therefore, in our view, it is helpful to distinguish between passive investing and indexing or index management. When a smart beta strategy is used as the policy benchmark in a portfolio, it becomes passive, independently of how many active decisions were taken in the creation and selection of the strategy. Otherwise, smart beta should be considered as active.

1.5 Is Smart Beta Just Active Management Implemented Passively?

This is another example of investors using the terms passive and indexing synony-mously. In this question, the term "passively" refers to an indexing approach, not passive investing, as we have defined earlier.

As discussed, an active strategy implemented through index management doesn't make it passive. Additionally, active management, broadly speaking, exploits many potential sources of excess returns, such as common factors, fundamental stock picking, market timing, factor timing, and country tactical allocation. Some of these sources, such as common factors, can indeed be captured in an indexing-type framework and that is what many smart beta factor products attempt to do. The other sources of active management excess returns cannot be captured in this manner, at least for now. Therefore, many smart beta products are an indexing-type alternative to "factor-based" active management, not all forms of active manage-ment, broadly speaking.

1.6 Can Smart Beta Be Defined as Low Tracking Error Strategies to the Market Portfolio?

It is not appropriate to define smart beta only in terms of low tracking error strate-gies to the market portfolio, as some investors do. Many quite reasonable smart beta products, such as a minimum variance portfolio, are designed and implemented as an alternative beta. Their tracking error to the capitalization-weighted market portfolio tends to be high, but that is not a consideration in an alternative beta implementa-tion. In our view, defining smart beta as low tracking error strategies limits smart beta to more or less just benchmark-aware factor investing.

1.7 A Rules-Based and Transparent Methodology Is a Desired Characteristic of Smart Beta Products. What Exactly Is Meant by These Terms and Why Are These Features Important in the Design of Smart Beta Strategies?

Rules-based and transparent means that portfolio construction (weighting scheme, rebalancing, etc.) follows prespecified and well-defined rules, which are fully dis-closed. Equal-weighting, risk-weighted, or value-weighted are examples of such construction approaches. Once the rules are specified, the interpretation of security weights at any point in time is intuitive. Rules-based approaches also imply that in the implementation of the strategy, portfolio implementers and/or traders have no discretion to deviate from the selection or weighting of securities as derived from the portfolio construction methodology.

Application Example 1.2

An investment manager offers value- and size-based portfolios, constructed using a clearly defined characteristic specification and weighting scheme. However, portfolio implementers have discretion over which trades to execute through the use of a momentum signal. A stock may not be bought in the final portfolio if the portfolio implementer considers it to have poor momentum. In this particular case, the manager's overall investment process cannot be viewed as being fully transparent and rules-based.

In our experience, one reason why rules-based and transparent approaches are preferred by investors in the assessment and selection of smart beta products is that they facilitate an understanding of the source of return and risk in the strategy. That is, investors may be able to gain a better understanding of what they are buying and what performance characteristics to expect from the strategy. A clearer understanding of the source of return and risk would also require portfolio methodologies that facilitate a fully transparent, cause-and-effect historical performance attribution of the strategy. These features make smart beta quite different from active management, where understanding the sources of risk and return may be a relatively more difficult and complex exercise.

Another important reason emphasis is placed on rules-based and transparent methodologies is that smart beta strategies are typically new products and, as such, have no or short live track records. These products are generally assessed based on a historical backtest or simulation. The main advantage of an investment process that is rules-based and transparent is that, when fully disclosed, the historical performance generated by the process can be independently replicated by investors. This provides verification and confidence to investors that, in addition to a clear understanding of the source of return and risk, the proposed strategy is actually investable and its historical performance replicable. In our experience, this is one reason why some investors approach optimized smart beta solutions with caution. In some instances, the historical backtested performance of such solutions is difficult to independently verify, as it is dependent on the specific risk-model and optimizer used, especially if it is an internally developed risk model.

Application Example 1.3

Much like active managers, index providers also often launch new products. When a new index is launched, index providers typically provide a 10- or 15-year calculated performance history (backtest) of the new index. Investors generally tend to have more confidence in the calculated history of a new index than they do in the historical simulation of a new strategy proposed by an active manager. Why?

In the case of an index provider, the launch of a new index is always accompanied by a methodology book, which details the rules of index construction and maintenance. A good and useful methodology book makes the index fully transparent, as to source of return/risk as well as construction. The methodology book allows investors to independently reconstruct the new index and replicate its historical performance. And many passive and active managers actually do that. This kind of detailed disclosure is not often provided by active managers when they launch new products.

Finally, the implementation of smart beta investing shifts the investment strategy decision making from the asset manager to the asset owner. In the context of active management, the strategy selection and implementation decisions are delegated to the active manager. That is, the active manager decides which sources of excess returns (e.g. factors) to exploit and how to exploit them. With smart beta, factor selection and portfolio implementation become the responsibility of the asset owner. Once factors are selected, in our experience, asset owners generally have a preference for transparent portfolio construction methodologies as a way to ensure that the investment process is indeed delivering a capture of the targeted or selected factors.

1.8 Low Cost Is Another Important Feature of the Smart Beta Value Proposition. What Are the Characteristics of a Low-Cost Offering?

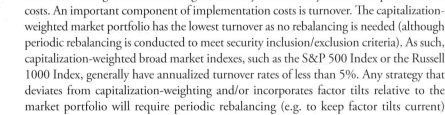

The *low-cost* feature of smart beta has many dimensions to it. One dimension is that smart beta strategies should be designed in a way that carefully controls implementation costs. An important component of implementation costs is turnover. The capitalization-weighted market portfolio has the lowest turnover as no rebalancing is needed (although periodic rebalancing is conducted to meet security inclusion/exclusion criteria). As such, capitalization-weighted broad market indexes, such as the S&P 500 Index or the Russell 1000 Index, generally have annualized turnover rates of less than 5%. Any strategy that deviates from capitalization-weighting and/or incorporates factor tilts relative to the market portfolio will require periodic rebalancing (e.g. to keep factor tilts current) and, therefore, incur additional turnover. Conventional small cap and value-growth indexes, as an example, have annual turnover of 15% to 20%. AEB and smart beta factor strategies inherently face a trade-off between keeping the portfolio current and managing turnover to a reasonable level. Delivering on the investment proposition, while keeping turnover reasonable, would clearly be a desirable feature in a smart beta offering. And this feature assumes more importance when a smart beta strategy incorporates tilts to high-turnover factors, such as momentum.

Application Example 1.4

Some strategies and factors, such as quality, value, and low volatility are relatively slow moving. Their capture can usually be implemented at reasonable levels of turnover. For example, the MSCI Quality Index series, the FTSE RAFI Fundamental Index series and the Russell Defensive Index series tend to have long-term average annual turnover of 20% or less.

More recently, smart beta managers have developed innovative turnover control techniques that allow them to offer factor diversification strategies at annual turnover rates of less than 20%, while including high turnover factors, such as momentum. This makes it possible for the strategy to incorporate the diversification benefits of factors, such as momentum, while keeping overall portfolio turnover at a reasonable level.

Application Example 1.5

Some strategies positioned as smart beta tend to have considerably higher turnover rates. The providers of such strategies argue that investors should focus on after-cost returns, not on turnover rates. However, in our experience, asset owners place a special emphasis on turnover management techniques because turnover is viewed as a given cost of implementing the strategy, whereas the possibility of excess returns is just an expectation. As a result, it is not uncommon to see (e.g. in public searches) that asset owners specify annual turnover limits (e.g. 25%) in the screening and selection process of smart beta products.

Another dimension of low cost is related to management or licensing fees. Smart beta fees generally tend to be much lower than traditional active management, whether delivered in separate accounts or structured products, and are getting closer to the fees charged for traditional passive. For instance, some recent launches of factor diversification ETFs by smart beta managers have been at fee levels similar to those charged by the largest capitalization-weighted ETFs by assets under management. These new products thus make smart beta factor investing available to investors at the price of "bulk beta."

One final dimension of low cost comes from the implementation flexibility that smart beta products provide to asset owners. Smart beta public indexes offered by index providers can be implemented much like traditional capitalization-weighted market indexes through internal replication or implementation through a passive manager. Investment managers, who may offer more advanced smart beta solutions, are also providing a variety of implementation options to asset owners. In addition to the conventional separate account structure, many managers allow asset owners to implement the strategies in-house. That is, the manager delivers a model portfolio (securities, weights, trades, etc.) at agreed-upon rebalancing dates, which the asset owner replicates (trades) using internal capabilities. The manager is paid only an asset-based licensing fee for the delivery of the model portfolio. In some instances, the asset owner may ask the manager to provide the model portfolio to an index calculation agent, who independently calculates and maintains a custom index and delivers it to the asset owner. This custom index is then replicated either by the asset owner internally or through a passive manager of their choice. Again, the manager is paid an asset-based licensing fee for the model portfolio and the index calculation agent is paid a fixed dollar amount for calculating and maintaining the custom index. These implementation options represent a significant departure from how traditional active management was delivered to asset owners and result in meaningful implementation cost savings for asset owners.

1.9 Why Is Diversification Important in the Context of a Factor Capture?

As we discuss in the next chapter, the theory of factor investing postulates that factor risk is rewarded because it cannot be diversified away, while other risks, such as stock-specific risk, which can be diversified, are not rewarded. This implies that a portfolio construction methodology that seeks to capture factor returns should also emphasize a high level of diversification in order to minimize stock-specific risk. Additionally, according to our analysis, high diversification coupled with low implementation costs improves the capacity of a given smart beta strategy. This is why a high level of diversification may also be viewed as a desired feature in the design of smart beta strategies.

Based on the earlier discussion, some of the desired characteristics of smart beta offerings are summarized in Figure 1.4.

1.10 Should Strategies Offered by Active Managers That Explicitly Target Common Factors Be Viewed as Smart Beta?

Some active managers, especially quant managers, offer investment strategies that explicitly target certain common factors, such as value, momentum, and quality. If such strategies possess some of the desired characteristics of smart beta, such as transparency, low turnover, high capacity and diversification, implementation flexibility,

FIGURE 1.4   Desired Characteristics of Smart Beta Offerings

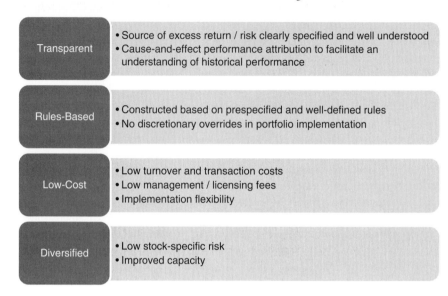

Transparent	• Source of excess return / risk clearly specified and well understood • Cause-and-effect performance attribution to facilitate an understanding of historical performance
Rules-Based	• Constructed based on prespecified and well-defined rules • No discretionary overrides in portfolio implementation
Low-Cost	• Low turnover and transaction costs • Low management / licensing fees • Implementation flexibility
Diversified	• Low stock-specific risk • Improved capacity

and low fees, then they should be viewed as smart beta. Otherwise, they may be better classified as active management, in our view. The important point here is that smart beta is not only about capturing common factor returns. It is about capturing the smart beta factor returns with methodologies and structures that emphasize certain differentiating characteristics relative to traditional active management, as we have discussed in earlier sections.

VI.   CONCLUSION

The evolution of the equity smart beta space can be traced as follows. In Stage 1, addressing the potential shortcomings of capitalization weighting led to the development of various AEB strategies. In Stage 2, risk decomposition of such strategies showed that AEB market outperformance is almost entirely explained by high and significant exposures to equity common factors. In Stage 3, investor focus shifted to capturing these factors in a more direct and/or benchmark-aware fashion. This led to the development of various single-factor and factor diversification strategies.

As a result, the equity smart beta space has evolved from AEB strategies to a combination of AEB and factor investing. In terms of investment outcome, however, smart beta is mostly about factor investing. Smart beta strategies differ from traditional passive factor investing in terms of characteristics such as higher efficiency and benchmark-aware implementation. Smart beta strategies also differ from traditional active factor investing in terms of characteristics such as better transparency, lower turnover, higher diversification and capacity, more implementation flexibility, and lower fees.

Since factor investing has become an important component of equity smart beta, in the next chapter, we provide an overview of the evolution and application of equity common factors and factor investing.

PART II

EQUITY COMMON FACTORS AND FACTOR INVESTING

CHAPTER 2

AN OVERVIEW OF EQUITY COMMON FACTORS AND FACTOR INVESTING

As discussed in the previous chapter, smart beta has, over time, become closely aligned with factor investing. In this chapter, therefore, we briefly review the origins and theory of factor investing. We also address topics such as why investors should care about equity factors and which specific factors have become the focus of various smart beta offerings and why.[1]

CHAPTER SUMMARY

- Equity common factors are stock-level characteristics that explain relative (cross-sectional) risk and return differences.
- The evolution of equity common factors and factor investing started with the Capital Asset Pricing Model (CAPM).
- The CAPM provided the basic insights that (1) the premium is earned by an undiversifiable common factor (the market portfolio under CAPM), (2) the risk of an asset is determined by its exposure to the common factor (market beta), and (3) the level of risk premium earned by an asset is driven by its diversification potential and performance during bad times (or systematic risk events).
- Attempts to empirically validate the CAPM led to the general conclusion that market beta does a poor job of explaining the cross-section of expected returns. Academic research focus, therefore, shifted to identifying other stock characteristics that might do a better job.

---

[1] For a comprehensive and illuminating discussion of common factors and factor investing, please refer to Ilmanen (2011) and Ang (2014).

- Over multiple decades, hundreds of stock characteristics, or extra-market common factors, have been identified that explain cross-sectional return differences better than market beta. But these findings may be exposed to data mining or multiple testing, which can lead to the discovery of spurious factors, that is, factors that turned out to be statistically significant just by chance and are unlikely to perform well out-of-sample.
- In order to identify truly useful factors, also known as rewarded factors, we need to assess their statistical significance in a multiple testing framework that accounts for the problems associated with data mining. Additionally, rewarded factors are those that (1) depict persistence across market segments, geography, and time, (2) better explain the cross-section of expected returns, and (3) help to identify redundant factors.
- A reasonable set of rewarded factors may comprise size, value, momentum, volatility, and quality (profitability). These factors are also the focus of various smart beta factor strategies. Therefore, we refer to them as "smart beta factors."
- Smart beta factors retain statistical significance in multiple testing approaches, depict persistence in performance on an out-of-sample basis, and better explain cross-sectional return differences as well as the performance of a large number of other factors and strategies.
- A risk decomposition analysis of various alternative beta strategies suggests that their outperformance relative to the market index can be largely explained by exposures to various smart beta factors.
- A risk decomposition of active manager performance highlights that growth managers are actually momentum players and managers also pursue other styles, such as low volatility and quality. This raises concerns regarding the relevance and usefulness of the current value-growth style paradigm.
- Investors should care about rewarded factors because (1) they have delivered persistent long-term market outperformance across market segments, countries, and time, and (2) may represent systematic influences that also help to explain the sources of risk and return in active strategies and composite portfolios.

I. INTRODUCTION: WHAT ARE EQUITY COMMON FACTORS?

Equity common factors are stock-level characteristics that explain the cross-section of expected returns and/or risk. Explaining expected returns in the "cross section" means understanding why expected returns differ across securities within a given universe and at a point in time. So, when we study the cross-section of expected returns we want to analyze and explain why stock A has a higher or lower expected return than stock B at a given point in time. Studying expected returns in the cross-section, therefore, is different from studying expected returns in the "time series," which explains how expected returns vary over time. A factor that explains the cross-section of expected returns is called a common factor because it represents a common influence in the pricing of individual securities. In the CAPM, for instance, the cross-section of expected returns is explained by the exposure (i.e. beta) that individual stocks have to the capitalization-weighted market portfolio. High beta stocks are expected to have higher expected returns and risk than the market factor and the low beta stocks.

The academic literature uses a variety of terms, such as common factors, rewarded factors, tradable factors, asset class factors, static factors, dynamic factors, style factors, or simply factors, which practitioners may find confusing. But all these terms have the same broad meaning: a common influence that explains the cross-section of expected returns.

II.   EVOLUTION OF EQUITY COMMON FACTORS AND FACTOR INVESTING

The CAPM is considered to be the first formal and coherent theory of factor investing. The work done by Markowitz (1952) on diversification and mean-variance optimization provided the impetus for Treynor (1961), Sharpe (1964), Lintner (1965), and Mossin (1966) to develop the CAPM.

A. The Capital Asset Pricing Model

Prior to the publication of the CAPM, it was generally believed that the total volatility of an asset determined its risk and return. The CAPM challenged that prevailing conventional wisdom. It provided new perspectives on what constitutes risk and how risk is rewarded. The basic insights provided by the CAPM may be summarized as follows.

a. Factor Earns the Risk Premium

Building on the concept of portfolio diversification, the CAPM shows that the capitalization-weighted market (factor) portfolio is the most efficient portfolio that investors can hold. In this portfolio, most idiosyncratic or stock-specific risk is diversified away. What we are left with is largely systematic risk associated with the factor itself. Since the systematic risk cannot be eliminated, investors have to be rewarded for bearing that risk. This implies that the factor carries the risk premium, since it also comes with a nondiversifiable risk. Further, under the CAPM assumption that investors have homogenous (identical) expectations regarding returns, risk, and correlations, the market portfolio is also shown to be mean-variance efficient and is the only common factor that matters in the pricing of individual assets.

b. Factor Exposure Defines Risk

A stock's total risk consists of two components; a systematic component, which is a function of the asset's sensitivity to the market portfolio, and a nonsystematic or idiosyncratic component, which is independent of the market (i.e. stock-specific). Since the idiosyncratic risk can be largely diversified away in a portfolio context, it is not rewarded by the market. Only the exposure to nondiversifiable, systematic risk is rewarded. In other words, the factor (market portfolio) carries the risk premium and the risk/return for an individual asset is determined by how much exposure (beta) the asset has to the factor. This is the reason why, under CAPM, total volatility of an asset is not important, or even relevant, in determining risk and expected return. What matters is the asset's co-variation (exposure) with the common factor.

c. Diversification Potential and Performance in Bad Times Drive Risk Premium

Under the CAPM, stocks that have a high exposure (i.e. high beta) to the market factor earn higher risk premium. As pointed out by Ang (2014), the intuition behind this result is that the required return on a stock is determined not by its total risk, but by the contribution that the stock makes to the risk of the overall portfolio. Since beta measures an asset's contribution to portfolio risk, high-exposure stocks have limited diversification potential. They contribute more to overall portfolio risk and, therefore, command a higher risk premium. On the other hand, low-exposure (i.e. low beta) stocks provide better portfolio diversification and risk reduction potential. Investors, therefore, are willing to hold such securities at a lower level of expected risk premium.

In more recent research, another important perspective for understanding asset pricing and factor investing is the concept of "bad times." Bad times correspond to environments when the marginal utility of wealth is high, and an additional dollar earned or lost is highly valued by investors. Examples of high-marginal-utility environments may include recessions, high unemployment, rising inflation, falling consumption, tightening monetary policy, and financial crises. Ilmanen (2011) provides examples of financial and economic bad times, which include the Great Depression of the 1930s, the postwar stagnation of 1946–1949, the stagflationary recession of 1969–1970, 1973–1975, and 1980–1982, the equity market crash of 1987, the Russian and LTCM crises of 1998, the dot-com bust and recession of 2000–2002, and the financial crisis and recession of 2007–2009. Assets that perform poorly (e.g. equities) during bad times, when marginal utility is high, require a higher risk premium to compensate generally risk-averse investors for the higher degree of risk assumed. On the other hand, investors are willing to hold less-risky assets (e.g. government bonds and bills) that provide some level of protection during economic and financial crises at lower or even negative levels of risk premium.

In the CAPM, the market portfolio is the only factor. So, bad times refer to periods of poor performance by the stock market, which may be driven by macro factors, such as low growth, high inflation, or a financial crisis. Individual assets that do even worse than the market (i.e. high beta stocks), when the market crashes, are viewed as highly risky and require a higher risk premium than the factor itself. These assets generate a higher risk premium by performing significantly better than the factor during good times. Stocks that perform well during market downturns are viewed as desirable by risk-averse investors, who are willing to own such assets for a much lower risk premium.

The above results can be summarized:

- Risk premium is associated with factors, as they embed systematic risks, which cannot be diversified away.
- The appropriate measure of risk for individual assets is their exposure to the factor, not their total volatility.
- The level of risk premium earned by an asset is a function of the diversification benefits it brings to the overall portfolio and its performance during high-marginal-utility periods (i.e. bad times).

B. Market Beta and Expected Returns

The CAPM asserts that the market beta explains the cross-section of expected returns. The publication of the CAPM, therefore, naturally led researchers to seek empirical validation of the theory. Does market beta explain the cross-section of stock returns?

Initial tests (e.g. Black et al. 1972; Fama and MacBeth 1973) found some evidence of a positive linear relationship between beta and average returns. Later studies, such as Reinganum (1981) and Lakonishok and Shapiro (1986), documented a much weaker link. Fama and French (1992) corroborated the results of later studies by reporting that no relation exists between beta and average returns for the 1963–1990 time period. Further, they found the relation to be weak for an extended 50-year sample period from 1941 through 1990.

Other articles have also highlighted the shortcomings of typical studies that have investigated the CAPM relationship. In particular, Mayers (1976) pointed out that in the CAPM, the market portfolio is defined as one that holds all assets in positive net supply, and not just equities. Therefore, studies that have rejected the CAPM based on capitalization-weighted stock market portfolios may simply be rejecting the use of the stock market portfolio as a proxy for the CAPM market portfolio. Nonetheless, despite the various issues associated with testing the CAPM, Fama and French (1992) concluded that their tests do not support the basic prediction of the CAPM model, that average stock returns are positively related to market betas. Given the stature of the authors in the marketplace, this statement was interpreted as signaling the "death of beta."

C. Extra-Market Common Factors and Smart Beta Factors

Over multiple decades, researchers have looked for stock characteristics or factors that might explain the cross-section of expected returns better than market beta. These research efforts have produced hundreds of "statistically significant" factors. These findings, however, also raise concerns relating to the validity of the reported results. In particular, how do we distinguish between factors that carry a true return premia (rewarded factors) and factors that turned out to be statistically significant in an empirical analysis just by chance ("lucky" factors)?

How can factors be statistically significant just by chance? In the context of data mining or multiple testing, it is absolutely possible. Suppose we conduct individual tests of a large number of factors, all with a true mean excess return of zero. Statistical inference tells us that we should expect to find some factors with an excess return different from zero. That is, as long as we conduct enough tests, we are likely to find some factors with statistically positive mean returns. But this result can still be attributable to luck. And these lucky factors are unlikely to perform well out-of-sample. As such, when researchers test a large number of factors, but report only the statistically significant results, their findings potentially become susceptible to multiple testing, as the reported factors may be spurious (i.e. be significant by chance). Consider flipping 10,000 fair coins 10 times and finding that one coin came up heads every time. Would you want to bet your retirement assets on that coin coming up heads again in even 6 of the next 10 flips?

In order to identify rewarded factors, we need to assess them along multiple dimensions. One dimension is that factors need to be analyzed in the context of a multiple testing framework that takes into account the problems associated with data mining. Generally speaking, this involves using higher hurdles (adjusted t-ratios) in assessing the statistical significance of the return premia associated with factors. Another dimension is persistence. Rewarded factors and factor specifications, such as book value-to-price for value, depict persistence across market segments in a given universe (i.e. work in large/mid/small segments), across geographies (i.e. work in different countries and regions, globally), and across time (i.e. work on an out-of-sample basis). In reasonable portfolio construction methods, if a common influence appears in nearly every universe and across various time periods, then we have more confidence that it is real, that is, reliable and not noise. Yet another dimension is that the set of rewarded factors creates a parsimonious multifactor model that better explains the cross-section of expected returns compared to other models, such as the CAPM. An ideal multifactor model would consist of orthogonal (independent) factors and would span the entire asset return spectrum. The final dimension is that the multifactor model of rewarded factors helps to explain other factors or identify redundant factors. That is, a large number of factors or strategies can be explained through exposures to the rewarded factors in a risk decomposition analysis.

Based on the above considerations, it is generally recognized that size, value, momentum, volatility, and profitability (an aspect of quality) constitute a reasonable set of rewarded factors. In studies that adjust significance for multiple testing, these factors remain significant at higher t-ratio thresholds. For instance, in the multiple testing framework of Harvey, Liu, and Zhu (2016), size, value, momentum, and volatility were found to be significant. Feng, Giglio, and Xiu (2017) proposed a model selection method that allows the authors to determine the contribution of new factors to an existing set of factors. They found that some recently documented factors, such as profitability, had explanatory power above and beyond the existing factors. Since smart beta factor strategies tend to focus on size, value, momentum, volatility, and quality, we also refer to these rewarded factors as "smart beta factors." Next, we briefly review the historical evidence relating to each one of the smart beta factors.

a. Size

Banz (1981) discovered that a simple characteristic, namely, Market Equity or market capitalization (i.e. price times number of shares outstanding), explained cross-sectional average returns for US stocks much better than beta. He found that smaller companies produced returns much higher than their market betas would suggest and also realized higher beta-adjusted returns than larger companies. Reinganum (1981) also reported similar results. Hawawini and Keim (1995, 1998) and Heston at al. (1995) extended the analysis to international markets and reported evidence of the size effect.

Dimson et al. (2017) studied the out-of-sample performance and persistence of various smart beta factors by analyzing the performance of the factors (1) for periods that precede the in-sample period, (2) for periods following the publication of the factor premium, and (3) in 23 countries using the longest possible data set for each country. With regard to the size premium in the US, from 1926 through 2016, they found a size premium of 2.4% per annum compared to large cap stocks. Small cap stocks, however, depicted highly cyclical performance patterns. For some time periods, for example, from 1975 to 1983, small cap stocks performed well and generated a large premium over large cap stocks. For other time periods, for example, from 1926 through 1940 (i.e. 15 years) and from 1984 through 1999 (i.e. 16 years), small cap stocks provided no premium over large cap stocks. The dismal performance of small cap stocks following the publication of Banz (1981) led some researchers to conclude that the small cap effect was either a "lucky" discovery or has been arbitraged away. The strong out-of-sample performance of small cap stocks from 2000 to 2016, however, has challenged these assertions. Over this recent period, Dimson, Marsh, and Staunton (2017) found that the small cap premium was positive across all countries, except Norway. And the average small cap premium across the 23 countries was 5.6% per annum, much higher than the average small cap premium realized over the longer term. It seems that the small cap effect, though cyclical, is alive and well, and as noted by Dimson, Marsh, and Staunton (2017), it would be hard to make a case for intentionally underweighting small cap stocks.

b. Value

Value investing needs little introduction. It is perhaps one of the most followed investment styles in the industry. Early adopters of value investing include Graham and Dodd (1934). Modern research into value characteristics originated with Williamson (1970) and Basu (1977, 1983). These authors found that in the US, stocks with low price-to-earnings multiples had much higher returns than stocks with high multiples, after adjusting for CAPM beta. Similar results were found using other valuation ratios, such as book value-to-price (e.g. Stattman 1980 and Rosenberg et al. 1985) and cash flow-to-price (e.g. Lakonishok et al. 1994). Chan et al. (1991) reported that book value-to-price plays a strong role in explaining the cross-section of average return for the Japanese stock market. Capaul et al. (1993) extended the analysis to international markets and reported that low book value-to-price stocks earned excess returns in every market they analyzed. At a global level, they documented a 1.88%

per annum return differential in favor of value stocks. Fama and French (1998) also found that the value premium was pervasive across global developed and emerging markets. They reported large value premiums in developed markets using book value-to-price, earnings-to-price, cash flow-to-price, and dividends-to-price and in emerging markets using book value-to-price and earnings-to-price.

For a long-term perspective on the performance of value stocks, Dimson et al. (2017) documented a 3.6% per annum value premium over growth stocks in the US from 1926 to 2016. The second longest history (from 1955 to 2016) is available for the UK, where the value premium has been even higher at 5.7% per year. Over the recent out-of-sample period (2000 to 2016), the value premium was positive in 19 out of the 23 countries studied by Dimson et al. (2017). At the world level, the value premium was 2.5% per annum, higher than the premium realized (2.1%) over the longer term.

A Digression: Capitalization-Weighted Size and Style Indexes

We believe investment consultants, who are typically charged with the responsibility of measuring and attributing active manager performance, were one of the first to notice that size and valuation characteristics-sorted portfolios produced portfolio exposures similar to those of large groups of active managers. This discovery gave rise to an important question: Are active managers being rewarded for characteristics selection or stock selection? Under the single-factor CAPM framework, manager skill is measured through the calculation of the CAPM alpha. However, if certain stock characteristics were shown to explain stock returns beyond the market beta, then there was a clear need to separate that characteristic selection decision from the stock selection decision. Some consultants, such as Russell Investments, determined that size and valuation characteristics appeared to be well-suited to perform this function.

It is not clear who coined the term "investment styles" to define the characteristic selection of active managers, but this term gained credence when Sharpe (1988, 1992) introduced his returns-based style analysis methodology to identify the factor exposures of a portfolio. Decades of academic research on extra-market factors and stock characteristics, along with the keen interest from investment consultants to better understand and attribute active manager performance, provided the impetus for the creation of size and style indexes and benchmarks. Capitalization-weighted size (large/mid/small) and style (value/growth) indexes, such as Russell size and style indexes, therefore, were created by index providers, and represented the first attempt at capturing equity common factors in a long-only indexing framework. Next, we briefly review the historical performance of these indexes.

We source the data for the various size and style indexes from the websites of the index providers.[2] We consider five universes, namely, the US market using Russell Indexes, and Europe, Japan, World ex. USA, and Emerging Markets using MSCI

---

[2] www.ftserussell.com; www.msci.com.

Indexes. The start date for the analysis is dictated by data availability for the indexes. The end date is June 2017 for all comparisons.

Table 2.1 shows the historical performance of size indexes for the various universes. This table presents absolute return and risk statistics for the large/midcap and small cap segments of each universe as well as relative return and risk statistics for the small cap segment versus the large/mid cap segment. In the US, the Russell 1000 Index and the Russell 2000 Index represent the large/mid cap and small cap segments, respectively. In other universes, we use the MSCI indexes. The MSCI Standard Indexes cover 85% of the float-adjusted market cap and, therefore, correspond to the large/midcap segment of the universe. The MSCI Small Cap Indexes cover securities that are between 85% and 98% float-adjusted coverage of the parent universe.

In the US market, since 1979, the Russell 2000 Index has underperformed the Russell 1000 Index by 0.21% per year. In other MSCI universes, the start date of the analysis is January 2001. Over this shorter time period, small cap indexes outperformed the Standard indexes, and the outperformance ranged from 0.36% per annum for Emerging Markets to 5.77% per annum for Europe. For comparison purposes, we also show the performance of the Russell indexes from 2001 onward. Over this recent period,

TABLE 2.1 Historical Performances of Size Indexes—Annualized Results

	Start Date	Total Gross Return (%)	Total Risk (%)	Sharpe Ratio	Active Gross Return (%)	Active Risk (%)	Infor- mation Ratio
Russell 1000 Index	Jan-79	11.84	15.05	0.49			
Russell 2000 Index	Jan-79	11.63	19.35	0.41	-0.21	10.05	-0.02
Russell 1000 Index	Jan-01	6.06	14.75	0.36			
Russell 2000 Index	Jan-01	8.17	19.14	0.42	2.11	8.84	0.24
MSCI Europe Index	Jan-01	4.58	18.79	0.25			
MSCI Europe Small Cap Index	Jan-01	10.35	21.64	0.49	5.77	7.88	0.73
MSCI Japan Index	Jan-01	2.84	15.99	0.15			
MSCI Japan Small Cap Index	Jan-01	6.52	17.12	0.36	3.68	8.36	0.44
MSCI World ex USA Index	Jan-01	4.66	16.96	0.26			
MSCI Wld ex USA Small Cap Index	Jan-01	9.00	18.27	0.48	4.35	6.12	0.71
MSCI EM Index	Jan-01	7.48	23.54	0.33			
MSCI EM Small Cap Index	Jan-01	7.84	23.44	0.34	0.36	7.36	0.05

Source: Bloomberg; GSAM; www.ftserussell.com; www.msci.com.

small cap stocks also performed well in the US, as the Russell 2000 Index outperformed the Russell 1000 Index by 2.11% per year. These performance characteristics of small cap stocks are consistent with those reported by Dimson, Marsh, and Staunton (2017). They also documented prolonged periods of poor and strong performance by small cap stocks and a large size premium from 2000 to 2016, as discussed earlier.

Table 2.2 presents the historical performance of the Russell and MSCI Value and Growth Indexes. This table reports the absolute performance numbers as well as the relative performance of the value and growth indexes compared to the parent benchmark. In the five universes studied, the value indexes have outperformed the market

TABLE 2.2 Historical Performance of Style Indexes—Annualized Results

	Start Date	Total Gross Return (%)	Total Risk (%)	Sharpe Ratio	Active Gross Return (%)	Active Risk (%)	Information Ratio
Russell 1000 Index	Jan-79	11.84	15.05	0.49			
Russell 1000 Value Index	Jan-79	12.15	14.47	0.53	0.31	4.65	0.07
Russell 1000 Growth Index	Jan-79	11.17	16.92	0.42	-0.67	4.46	-0.15
MSCI Europe Index	Jan-79	10.49	17.42	0.38			
MSCI Europe Value Index	Jan-79	10.86	18.40	0.39	0.37	3.58	0.10
MSCI Europe Growth Index	Jan-79	9.85	17.12	0.35	-0.65	3.54	-0.18
MSCI Japan Index	Jan-79	6.59	20.98	0.17			
MSCI Japan Value Index	Jan-79	8.93	20.53	0.28	2.34	5.47	0.43
MSCI Japan Growth Index	Jan-79	4.20	22.80	0.08	-2.39	5.56	-0.43
MSCI World ex USA Index	Jan-95	5.66	16.25	0.25			
MSCI Wld ex USA Value Index	Jan-95	6.43	16.85	0.29	0.77	3.36	0.23
MSCI Wld ex USA Growth Index	Jan-95	4.77	16.34	0.20	-0.90	3.35	-0.27
MSCI EM Index	Jan-98	7.48	23.54	0.33			
MSCI EM Value Index	Jan-98	7.63	23.71	0.34	0.15	3.47	0.04
MSCI EM Growth Index	Jan-98	7.20	23.86	0.32	-0.28	3.33	0.09

Source: Bloomberg; GSAM; www.ftserussell.com; www.msci.com.

and the growth indexes, over different time periods. For the universes studied, the outperformance of the value index, relative to the growth index, has ranged from 0.43% in Emerging Markets to 4.73% in Japan.

Over the years, investors have become quite familiar with size and style indexes of index providers and tend to find them a useful tool. They commonly use such indexes as policy benchmarks for subasset classes within equities, performance benchmarks for active style managers, and as the basis for structured products. Therefore, it is somewhat surprising to us that no index provider currently offers capitalization-weighted indexes for other styles, such as momentum, low volatility, and quality, which active managers typically follow, as we discuss below. It seems that it would be quite useful and instructive to create a consistent and comprehensive family of capitalization-weighted smart beta factor indexes. We construct such a family of indexes in Chapter 4.

c. Momentum

The origins of momentum research can perhaps be traced back to Levy (1967). Prior to Levy (1967), research efforts had focused on studying whether the serial correlation in individual stock prices (i.e. how stock A performs over time) could predict future returns. The general conclusion from these studies was that successive stock price changes are independent and, therefore, uphold the random walk hypothesis (RWH). However, Levy (1967) and others remarked that a large part of a stock price change co-varies with the market, that is, is driven by the market. By measuring relative strength, that is, how stock A performs relative to stock B, the effects of the overall market can be eliminated. Levy (1967) found that, in doing so, superior profits were earned by investing in stocks with high relative strength ranks. This finding challenged the basic premise of efficient markets and the RWH that past prices are not useful in explaining future returns. Since the academic profession was dominated by the proponents of efficient markets in those early years, Levy (1967), it seems, was somewhat ignored in the financial literature.

Momentum investing got another boost with the publication of a study by Jegadeesh and Titman in 1993. The authors documented that, for US stocks, past 3- to 12-month winner stocks significantly outperformed past loser stocks for holding periods of up to one year, and that the momentum effect appeared to persist across market segments, beta-based sorts, and time periods. Asness (1994) showed that momentum strategies worked even after accounting for common value factors. Rouwenhorst (1998) found evidence of medium-term return continuation in international markets, which lasted on average for about one year. Asness et al. (2012) documented the existence of a momentum effect at the asset class level for equities, government bonds, currencies, and commodities.

Taking a longer-term perspective, Dimson, Marsh, and Staunton (2017) documented a 7.4% per year premium for winner stocks over loser stocks from 1926 to 2016 for the US. Using an even longer history for the UK market, from 1900 to 2016 (i.e. 116 years), the authors reported that winner stocks outperformed loser stocks by 10.2% per annum. Across international markets, for the 2000 to 2016 time period, the momentum premium was positive in 21 of the 23 countries. The average outperformance of winner stocks over loser stocks across the 23 countries was 0.79% per month. Momentum investing has continued to generate significant excess returns on an out-of-sample basis.

Another Digression: Momentum and Active Management

It appears that active managers had discovered and exploited the benefits of momentum investing much before the publication of Jegadeesh and Titman (1993). For instance, Richard Driehaus, founder of Driehaus Capital Management, is considered by many to be the father of momentum investing and has been practicing momentum invest-ing for decades. Following the publication of Jegadeesh and Titman (1993), Grinblatt et al. (1995) also conducted a study to investigate whether the superior performance of growth-oriented funds documented in two earlier studies (Grinblatt and Titman 1989, 1993) was explained by the momentum effect. They found that to be the case. Among the various fund categories analyzed in their study, growth-oriented funds showed the highest exposure to momentum. About 89% of funds classified as aggressive-growth and 82% of funds classified as growth were momentum players. Only the income funds (value-oriented funds) showed an insignificant level of momentum exposure, but a significant level of outperformance. Grinblatt et al. (1995) also reported that 77% of all active funds in their study bought past short-term winner stocks and/or sold past short-term loser stocks, thus following a typical momentum strategy. Chan et al. (1999) also discovered that mutual funds, in general, had a preference for holding momentum stocks, thus con-firming Grinblatt et al.'s (1995) finding. Daniel et al. (1997) analyzed the stock charac-teristics chosen by active funds and found that growth-oriented funds showed statistically significant loadings to the momentum factor. Carhart (1997) documented that the "hot hands" phenomenon relating to the persistence in mutual fund performance reported by Hendricks et al. (1993) was largely explained by the momentum effect. Finally, Mulvey and Kim (2008) reported that growth-oriented institutional money managers across size segments, on average, had an excess return correlation with an industry-level momentum strategy of 40%, over the 1987–2006 time period, with the correlation rising to almost 47% for large-capitalization growth managers. Mulvey and Kim (2008) found that core institutional managers have high exposures to momentum as well.

d. Low Volatility

Given the high level of volatility experienced in stock markets globally, low-volatility in-vesting has attracted more attention and funds in recent years. But risk-based pricing anomalies have been documented in the literature for a long time. One of the first studies came from Black et al. (1972). This study found that, between 1931 and 1965, low-beta (high-beta) stocks realized a much higher (lower) return than that predicted by the CAPM. Fama and French (1992) extended the analysis to 1990 and found similar results, that is, a pattern of abnormally high returns for low-beta stocks and abnormally low re-turns for high-beta stocks. In more recent studies, Ghayur et al. (2013) observed that the lowest volatility decile of stocks within the Russell 1000 universe realized an annualized return of 13.8%, over the January 1979 to September 2012 period, with a total volatility of 11.08% compared to an annualized return of 2.95% and a total risk of 36.17% for the highest volatility decile of stocks. This corresponds to a Sharpe ratio of 0.76 for the lowest volatility decile versus 0.12 for the highest volatility decile, an astonishing difference in risk-adjusted returns. Ang et al. (2006) reported that US stocks with low idiosyncratic volatility outperformed stocks with high idiosyncratic volatility. Ang et al. (2009) then extended the analysis to global markets and discovered the low-volatility anomaly across 23 developed markets.

Many other risk-based strategies are also driven by the low-volatility, low-beta anomaly. For instance, Haugen and Baker (1991) and Clarke et al. (2006) demonstrated that minimum-variance portfolios in the US realized a 25% total risk reduction compared to the market, while delivering market-like returns. But Scherer (2010) provided analytical proof that the minimum-variance portfolio essentially invests in low-idiosyncratic and low-beta stocks. Clarke et al. (2011) also showed that low-beta stocks accounted for a large proportion of long-only, minimum variance portfolios. Along similar lines, Leote de Carvalho et al. (2011) found that long-only, minimum-variance portfolios are invested in a relatively small number of low-beta stocks. They further argued that minimum-variance and maximum diversification (Choueifaty and Coignard 2008) are essentially similar strategies that produce largely overlapping portfolios.

The low-risk anomaly reported by Black et al. (1972) for the 1931–1965 time period is one of the first documented anomalies, and it has persisted over time. For instance, French (2017) showed that, between 1963 and 2016, the lowest risk stocks outperformed the highest risk stocks by 6.8% per annum in the US. In the UK, Dimson, Marsh, and Staunton (2017) documented a 7.4% per year return advantage for the lowest risk stocks from 1984 to 2016.

e. Quality

Like value, the origins of quality investing date back at least to Graham and Dodd (1934). But unlike other common factors, there is no commonly accepted definition of quality. Quality investing may incorporate many dimensions, such as focusing on profitable companies, well-managed companies, less-risky companies, or growing companies. These various dimensions of quality have been studied in the academic literature over the years and the general conclusion is that high-quality stocks tend to outperform low-quality stocks. In a recent article, Novy-Marx (2014) studied profitability, defined as gross profits divided by total assets, and found that this measure had the same ability to predict the cross-section of expected returns as the traditional book value-to-price value measure. He also found that profitability performs better than some other measures of quality, such as Graham and Grantham's quality criteria, Sloan's (1996) earnings quality measure based on accruals, or Piotroski's (2000) F-score measure of financial strength. Asness et al. (2013) considered a comprehensive definition of quality along the dimensions of profitability, growth, safety, and payout. They reported that high-quality companies deliver much higher risk-adjusted returns than low-quality companies in the US and globally across 23 markets. (We discuss some of the various quality specifications used by smart beta providers in much more detail in Chapter 5.)

D. Multifactor Pricing Models

While each smart beta factor has been shown to work individually, a natural question arises as to whether these factors are orthogonal or independent enough to be combined in a multifactor framework to enhance explanatory power. Fama and French (1992) is an influential and celebrated article in this regard. Developing on research findings relating to size and value mentioned earlier, Fama-French constructed two zero investment, factor mimicking portfolios to capture the size and value premia. They showed that in univariate (single factor) tests the relation between market beta and average returns was weak, while the relations between size and average returns and value and average returns were strong. More importantly, the 3-factor model did a much better job of explaining the cross section of expected returns compared to the CAPM. Since the publication of the Fama-French (1992) article, the basic 3-factor model has been enhanced to incorporate other cross-sectional anomalies that were not fully explained by the 3-factor model. For instance, after the publication of Jegadeesh and Titman's (1993) momentum effect, it was noticed that the cross-sectional variation in momentum-sorted portfolios could not be fully explained by the Fama-French 3-factor model. So, Carhart (1995, 1997) extended the Fama-French model to include a momentum factor. Clarke et al. (2010) calculated a volatility factor, using the Fama-French methodology, and showed that the volatility factor was more important than the value and size factors and as important as the momentum factor in explaining the covariance structure of stock returns. They further documented that the relative importance of the volatility factor held throughout the analysis period (i.e. 1931 to 2008). Similarly, Asness et al. (2013) created a quality factor. They showed that the quality factor had negative correlation with size and value factors and a positive alpha against the Fama-French 3-factor model. That is, the performance of the quality factor was not fully explained by the 3-factor model. Multifactor pricing models are now commonly used in the industry and have replaced the CAPM in explaining the cross-section of average returns.

a. Risk Decomposition Analysis

Multifactor models are often used to explain other cross-sectional anomalies and active strategies. This application is commonly referred to as a risk or exposure decomposition analysis. In a multifactor model, the factors are considered as sources of risk (e.g. market, value, or size) and are associated with a risk premium. The idea in a risk decomposition analysis, therefore, is to determine whether a given strategy has high exposures to and, thus, can be explained by the selected risk factors. The portion of a strategy's excess returns that are not explained by the exposures to the risk factors is known as alpha, or the unexplained excess return.

With respect to an example of cross-sectional anomalies, Bhandari (1988) and Basu (1983) documented a positive relation between leverage and average returns and price-to-earnings (PE) ratios and average returns, respectively. But, Fama-French (1992) showed that the performance of leverage and PE ratios was explained by the 3-factor model, that is, the role of leverage and PE ratios was absorbed by value (price-to-book value) and size.

For an illustration of a risk decomposition of active strategies, consider Chow et al. (2011). The authors analyzed the performance of a number of alternative beta (or smart beta) strategies. The analyzed strategies included equal-weighting, risk-clustered equal-weighting, diversity weighting (e.g. Fernholz 1995), fundamental weighting (e.g. Arnott et al. 2005), minimum-variance (e.g. Haugen and Baker 1991), maximum diversification (e.g. Choueifaty and Coignard 2008), and risk-efficient (e.g. Amenc et al. 2010). The authors found that all the strategies outperformed the capitalization-weighted market portfolio. However, the outperformance was largely explained by the Fama-French 3-factor model or the Carhart 4-factor model. That is, the smart beta strategies outperformed the market index because they had high exposures to extra-market common factors. And, statistically, the strategies as a group generated no alpha relative to the 3-factor or the 4-factor model. Multifactor models are also used to analyze the performance of active managers. The general conclusion from such studies is that active managers, on average, do not generate positive factor-adjusted alpha. For instance, Fama and French (2011) found that only 3% of active funds generated a factor-adjusted alpha large enough to cover their management fees.

III.   TYPICAL INVESTOR QUESTIONS

2.1 Why Should Investors Care About Smart Beta Factors?

Investors should care about smart beta factors for the following reasons. First, much like the market factor, smart beta factors may represent systematic sources of risk, which cannot be diversified away and, hence, command a premium. Indeed, these factors have been demonstrably linked with persistent market outperformance across market segments, countries, and time. These factor payoffs may represent the first layer of active returns in structuring equity portfolios, and, with the advent of smart beta factor products, investors may be able to capture them through transparent, diversified, and low-cost offerings. Second, the risk and return of individual securities is also determined by their exposure to these extra-market rewarded factors. As such, multifactor models do a much better job of explaining return differences across individual securities than CAPM. That is, smart beta factors play a critical role in explaining the cross-section of expected returns. Third, since security pricing is influenced by exposure to smart beta factors, most active portfolios are likely to also have exposures to smart beta factors through the held securities, and their performance is likely to be driven by the magnitude of these exposures. Therefore, it is important for investors to understand these factor exposures if they wish to better understand and manage the sources of risk and return in their portfolios. Finally, multifactor models have proven to be extremely useful, through a risk decomposition analysis, in analyzing and understanding the performance of active strategies. Such models allow investors to potentially identify skill (i.e. factor-adjusted alpha) and, as a result, in combination with smart beta factors, create much more efficient overall portfolio structures. (We discuss these topics in more detail in Chapter 10.)

2.2 Is There Concensus on a Recognized Set of Common Factors?

The CAPM establishes a theoretical rationale for why the capitalization-weighted market portfolio is a rewarded common factor. But many other rewarded factors lack such theoretical backing. These extra-market factors are empirical findings. And empirically priced common factors are not theory-motivated. This makes the widespread acceptance of empirical factors across the industry rather difficult. But this should not be a cause for concern. In the field of finance, there are few topics where one could argue that the industry as a whole has reached a consensus. At a very basic level, in the context of the low volatility anomaly, for example, academics as well as practitioners cannot even agree on the exact relationship between risk and return.

At a practical level, however, for extra-market common factors to be truly useful, they should at a minimum (1) carry a CAPM-adjusted return premium, (2) depict persistence, (3) explain the cross-section of expected returns in a given universe, and (4) be able to explain a variety of other cross-sectional anomalies and active strategies.

Persistence may be assessed along multiple dimensions. One dimension is persistence across market segments. This means that the performance of a given factor and factor specification is similar in different market segments, such as large, mid, and small, so that an argument can be made that the factor works across a given universe. Another dimension is geographical persistence. This means that a given factor is shown to perform similarly across global equity markets, including developed and emerging markets, so that an argument can be made that the factor works in a systematic manner across global equities and is not linked to specific markets or economic environments. Yet another important dimension is persistence over time. This means that, on an out-of-sample basis, the factor has performed similarly to how it was shown to have performed in-sample, when it was first documented. As discussed in this chapter, smart beta factors have been shown to depict persistence along these various dimensions.

With regard to explaining the cross-section of expected returns as well as other stock anomalies and active strategies, the Fama-French 3-factor model and the Carhart 4-factor model have become the industry standard. It is important to highlight that the Fama-French 3-factor model was extended to include momentum because it was unable to fully explain the performance of momentum-sorted portfolios. Along similar lines, the 4-factor model also does not fully explain volatility- and quality-based strategies. As such, as argued by many other researchers, as well as in our perspective, it would be reasonable to extend the set of accepted common factors to include the volatility and quality factors.

Based on these considerations, there is some level of agreement in the industry that size, value, momentum, volatility, and profitability constitute a reasonable set of extra-market rewarded factors and, as such, have become the focus of smart beta factor strategies.

2.3 If Momentum Is an Important Factor in Explaining Active Manager Performance (e.g. Growth Managers), Shouldn't it Be Considered a Style Along with Value and Growth?

The existence of momentum and its ability to explain the performance of many active managers, as discussed earlier, do raise serious concerns regarding the applicability and relevance of the current value-growth style paradigm. For a stock characteristic to be useful in defining a broad investment style, it should represent the actual characteristic selection and, hence, portfolio exposures of a large group of active managers. In the current style paradigm, the growth investment style is defined in terms of high valuation ratio and/or high earnings growth characteristics. If value works, then these growth characteristics are not associated with market outperformance in the long run. Why would a large number of active managers invest in such characteristics then? Alternatively, why would managers follow a growth investment style when it is well-known that the long-term premium has been on value? Well, most of the so-called growth managers don't. All the evidence points toward the fact that growth managers are actually momentum players (e.g. Grinblatt et al. 1995, Ghayur et al. 2010). Momentum is also a much better diversifier of value than growth, as it generates independent market outperformance, while exhibiting negative active return correlation with value. It is clear that value and momentum much better define the styles of active managers than value and growth. Yet, no index provider currently offers capitalization-weighted momentum indexes, as they do for value and growth. Similar arguments can also be made for other styles, such as low volatility and quality investing. These are styles that active managers commonly follow. If the goal of style categorization is to help investors structure better portfolios and/or create more appropriate benchmarks for style managers, then the current value-growth style paradigm, in our opinion, is oversimplified, incomplete, and maybe even a dis-service to the industry.

2.4 What Is the Difference Between Smart Beta and Traditional Quant Management?

Traditional quant strategies are typically multifactor approaches. The smart beta space comprises a variety of product offerings, some of which, such as fundamental indexation, maximum diversification portfolio, or single factor strategies, are quite different from traditional quant management. Smart beta factor diversification strategies may come the closest to traditional multifactor quant management. Smart beta factor diversification strategies, however, may differ from traditional quant management along several dimensions, such as selection of factors and factor specification, portfolio construction methodologies, other investment process features, and implementation.

Smart beta strategies tend to focus on factors and factor specifications that have been researched, scrutinized, and vetted by numerous researchers over multiple decades. These factors, known as rewarded factors, retain statistical significance in studies that account for data mining or multiple testing and depict persistence in performance on an out-of-sample basis. Many quant strategies, on the other hand, may include various new proprietary factors and/or include proprietary enhancements to conventional rewarded factor specifications, such as using different value metrics for different countries or industries or combining traditional momentum with short-term momentum and/or reversals. To the extent that these proprietary factors and/or factor specifications are not in the public domain, they have not been subjected to public scrutiny in the same way that smart beta factors have been.

Smart beta factor diversification strategies may also differ from traditional quant management in terms of portfolio construction methodologies. Smart beta offerings tend to use construction methodologies that are simple, rules-based and transparent, and facilitate an understanding of the sources of risk and return embedded in the strategy. Many smart beta strategies are also delivered in the form of a public index, with a fully disclosed index methodology. Active quant strategies typically use more complex portfolio construction techniques and may not fully disclose their proprietary investment processes.

Some other investment process features may also distinguish smart beta from active quant. For instance, smart beta offerings may employ methodologies designed to deliver improved diversification, lower turnover, and increased capacity. Finally, in terms of implementation, smart beta may represent a lower cost option to capture rewarded factors in terms of both management fees and implementation flexibility. To the extent that smart beta strategies can be offered as indexes, asset owners can replicate them either internally or through their passive managers, in a variety of licensing agreements to lower implementation costs.

These distinctions between smart beta and traditional quant mentioned earlier should not be interpreted as constituting an edge for smart beta. For instance, all else being equal, a thoroughly vetted factor specification may be preferred to a proprietary one. However, it is also important to remember that currently accepted smart beta factors were once proprietary factors used by active managers (e.g. momentum). Simplicity and transparency in portfolio construction may be desired, but it may also come with loss of flexibility and ability to better manage risk. Lower turnover may be preferred, but it may also lead to a less frequent updating of portfolios to reflect changes in factor signals.

IV. CONCLUSION

From a practitioner perspective, a reasonable set of rewarded factors may consist of size, value, momentum, low volatility, and quality. Academic research has thoroughly documented the existence and significance of these factors, and practical experience of investors as well as the performance of public indexes has shown that these factors have persisted over time, some over multiple decades.

So far, however, our focus has been to review the documented empirical evidence relating to the rewarded smart beta factors. At a conceptual level, we still have to answer two important questions: Why do these factors work? And why can we expect them to persist going forward? We address these questions in the next chapter.

CHAPTER 3

EXPLAINING SMART BETA FACTOR RETURN PREMIA

In this chapter, we review the various theories and rationalizations that have been proposed in the academic literature to explain the existence and persistence of smart beta factors.

CHAPTER SUMMARY

- The CAPM provides a theoretical rationale for why the market portfolio earns its risk premium. But what explains the existence and persistence of smart beta factor premia?
- There is a general consensus in the industry today that smart beta factor excess returns are not a result of data mining or data snooping. As analyzed in the previous chapter, for these factors, we have multiple decades of out-of-sample persistence in excess returns.
- There are two primary schools of thought to explain the excess returns associated with smart beta factors: risk-based and behavioral. A third perspective, referred to as structural, which includes market frictions and other impediments, is also sometimes used to explain the excess returns of some of the smart beta factors.
- Risk-based explanations argue that factor payoffs represent risk premia arising from (1) additional risk sources, such as distress for value and illiquidity for size, or (2) exposure to factor-specific bad times, or (3) high risk of market underperformance. Since extra-market sources of risk, in equilibrium, also need to be compensated by extra return, factor risk premia can be expected to persist over time.
- Behavioral explanations argue that biased preferences and beliefs of investors cause mispricing that leads to factor excess returns. These factor (or macro)-level mispricings are difficult to fully arbitrage away, which explains why factor premia persist over time.

- Structural explanations are also sometimes used to explain the existence and/or persistence of smart beta factor premia. These generally refer to market frictions, investment management structures, and constraints or impediments that potentially cause relative mispricings and/or limit the ability to fully arbitrage away anomalous excess returns.
- Potential issues with risk-based explanations include lack of agreement on what the additional sources of risk might be for each factor, lack of agreement on what constitutes factor-specific bad times, and lack of ability to explain the simultaneous existence of multiple factors, such as value and momentum.
- Potential issues with behavioral explanations include lack of agreement on which specific biased preferences and beliefs drive factor mispricing for each factor and lack of agreement on a theory or framework that seeks to predict asset pricing in the context of factor investing.
- In the absence of strong philosophical beliefs on why smart beta factors work, practitioners may find it useful not to take a rigid stance in the risk premium versus behavioral mispricing debate, as both explanations are somewhat lacking. The truth may well be that smart beta factor premia are driven by a combination of risk and mispricing as well as structural impediments.
- The good news is that various explanations have reasonable arguments relating to the persistence of smart beta factor premia. As such, although debate continues on what explains existence of factor premia, there appears to be some degree of agreement on perhaps the more practically relevant issue of persistence.

I. INTRODUCTION

The CAPM is a theoretical model and its usefulness lies in the fact that, under certain assumptions, it provides a clear rationale for why the capitalization-weighted market portfolio is the only factor that matters and why it is rewarded over time. However, as discussed in the previous chapter, the CAPM is not validated in empirical tests. In addition to theoretical models, the financial literature also comprises empirical models, which look for factors that have historically been rewarded. Once the factors have been discovered, academics then look for an economic rationale for why the factors might have worked historically and may continue to work going forward. Smart beta factors, that is, size, value, momentum, volatility, and quality are all empirically motivated factors. From an empirical standpoint, the excess returns of these factors are shown to be statistically significant and depict persistence across market segments, geographies, and time. As such, these factors are often called rewarded factors, as opposed to spurious or lucky factors, whose performance may not persist on an out-of-sample basis. From a conceptual/theoretical perspective, however, how do we explain the existence and persistence of smart beta factors? In this chapter, we discuss various plausible explanations that have been offered.

II. DATA MINING

Following the publication of Fama and French (1992), Black (1993) became a vocal critic of their work. He voiced concerns that their findings might be subject to data mining, also referred to as data snooping by Lo and MacKinlay (1990). Black (1993) defined data mining as follows: "When a researcher tries many ways to do a study, including various combinations of explanatory factors, various periods, and various models, we often say he is 'data mining.' If he reports only the more successful runs, we have a hard time interpreting any statistical analysis he conducts. We worry that he selected, from the many models tried, only the ones that seem to support his conclusions. With enough data mining, all the re-sults that seem significant could be just accidental." When an empirical anomaly is documented without an economic theory to support its existence, concerns regarding data mining become more pronounced. This is what solicited Black's (1993) criticism of Fama-French (1992). Black (1993) argued that Fama and French (1992) showed a relation between size and average returns but provided no reason as to why such a relation could be expected to exist. Fama and French (1992) also documented a relation between book value-to-price and average returns. They speculated that this accounting ratio may capture some kind of a rationally priced risk, but did not elaborate further on what the actual risk might be and why it should be priced. Lack of reasonable explanations led Black (1993) to write: "Lack of theory is a tipoff: watch out for data mining!"

Black's criticism notwithstanding, it is important to realize that the search for rewarded factors tends to be empirically driven and, in that sense, is often theory-free at the onset. As argued by Ilmanen (2011), both theoretical and empirical models may be very useful. The latter may do a better job of explaining expected returns in the cross-section and in the time series. The former may better explain why a factor earns its return premium. The bottom line is that, with respect to empirical models, the research process tends to first focus on documenting existence and then shifts toward explaining existence, and potentially persistence. So, when an empirical anomaly is first documented, it raises concerns of data mining, as it often lacks a well-vetted theory to support it. However, over time, as economic theories are developed to explain the anomaly, and as performance persists on an out-of-sample basis, the anomaly starts to gain more credibility. This is why the acceptance and recognition of rewarded common factors is a slow process. With regard to the smart beta factors, after multiple decades of out-of-sample persistence, across market segments, geographies, and time, in our opin-ion, it would be fair and reasonable to say that there is now some level of agreement in the industry that they are not spurious factors arising from data mining.[1]

---

[1] In Chapter 2, we discussed the significance of smart beta factors in multiple testing frameworks as well as their out-of-sample performance.

III.   RISK-BASED EXPLANATIONS

Risk-based arguments offer the following general perspectives on explaining the existence and persistence of smart beta factor returns.

A. Multidimensional Nature of Risk

Fama and French, among others, are proponents of the risk-based explanations for the existence of rewarded common factors. In Fama and French (1992), they argued that if investors price assets rationally, then their findings would suggest that stock risks may be multidimensional. In addition to the market risk being captured by the capitalization-weighted market portfolio, size and value factors may well capture other dimensions of rationally priced risk. Value may be a compensation for bearing a higher level of distress risk as argued by Chan and Chen (1991). Value companies, with high book value-to-price ratios, may have poor growth prospects and their returns, therefore, may be associated with higher levels of risk, such as bankruptcy risk. Similarly, small companies are less liquid than large companies, and their return premium may well be a compensation for bearing a higher level of illiquidity risk. So, size may just be a proxy for a liquidity effect (e.g. Brennan and Subrahmanyam 1996, Crain 2011).

B. Factor-Specific Bad Times

In modern asset pricing theories, risk is also defined as covariance with bad times, or periods when the marginal utility of wealth is high (e.g. Cochrane 2001). As mentioned in the previous chapter, in addition to severe market downturns, high-marginal-utility environments may include recessions and rising unemployment, high inflation, declining consumption, and financial crises. At the asset class level, the concept of performance during bad times appears to explain differences in excess returns much better than the relation between total risk and excess return (e.g. Illmanen 2011, and Ang 2014). Assets that perform poorly during bad times (e.g. equities) command higher risk premium. Assets that provide some degree of protection during bad times (e.g. government bonds) command low or even negative risk premium.

This notion of risk (covariance with bad times) also can be extended to multifactor equity models. Recall that in the single-factor CAPM, bad times are defined as periods of low or negative returns for the market portfolio. This single perspective of bad times is of course limiting. Multifactor models approach risk from a more comprehensive perspective, as each factor potentially defines its own set of bad times. So, the return premia observed for common factors may be a compensation for bad times that go beyond just poor performance of the equity market. In the case of value, for instance, some examples of considered bad times include firm investment risk (e.g. Berk et al. 1999), luxury consumption risk (e.g. Parker and Julliard 2005), housing risk (e.g. Lustig and Van Nieuwerburgh 2005), labor income risk (e.g. Santos and Veronesi 2006), and production technology risk (e.g. Zhang 2005).

C. Market Underperformance Risk

Another risk-based perspective for explaining the return premia of rewarded common factors, which may be linked to the notion of factor-specific bad times, is that factors are highly risky as they tend to experience prolonged and pronounced periods of poor performance or underperformance relative to the market (e.g. Ang 2014). Value, as an illustration, can go in and out of favor. When value is out of favor, investors can experience large losses (e.g. during the bull market of the late 1990s). Along similar lines, momentum is well known to expose investors to periodic crashes (e.g. Daniel and Moskowitz 2014). These crashes occur over short periods and can result in large losses. Investors have to bear these high risks of factors (i.e. stay invested during difficult times) if they wish to earn the factor premia in the long run.

D. Persistence

Under risk-based explanations, smart beta factor premia may be expected to persist as they represent compensation for bearing additional extra-market sources of risk. So, in summary, the risk-based explanations argue that factor excess returns are actually risk premia arising from exposure to additional sources of risk (e.g. distress or illiquidity), and/or exposure to factor-specific bad times, and/or potential risk of large losses and market underperformance over extended periods of time. If assets are rationally priced, then as compensation for extra risks, factor premia can be expected to persist over time.

IV.   BEHAVIORAL EXPLANATIONS

In contrast to risk-based theories, which tend to offer general explanations for explaining factor excess returns, behavioral explanations tend to focus on specific investor biases and preferences that might drive the abnormal returns associated with smart beta factors.

A. Value

Following the publication of Fama and French (1992), Lakonishok et al. (1994) challenged Fama and French's argument that value stocks deliver higher returns because they are fundamentally riskier. Lakonishok et al. (1994) documented that value stocks do not possess higher risk, as measured by traditional risk metrics, such as market beta and standard deviation of returns. They further argued that if value stocks are subject to some other sources of risk, which are not captured by the traditional measures of risk, then the performance of value and growth stocks should depict that in periods when investors become highly risk-averse (i.e. bad times). However, Lakonishok et al. (1994) found that value stocks outperformed growth stocks during market downturns and during economic contractions, while delivering similar returns as growth stocks in up markets and economic expansions. These findings led

Lakonishok et al. (1994) to conclude that the value premium is not a result of higher risk of value stocks, but a result of irrational behavior of investors, which gives rise to a relative mispricing between value and growth stocks. Some behavioral biases that may lead to relative mispricing of value and growth securities include (1) the assumption of a trend in stock prices, (2) an overreaction to good or bad news, (3) simply a belief that a good company equates to a good investment, irrespective of its price, and (4) the tendency of investors to extrapolate past earnings growth too far into the future. Value companies tend to be companies that have experienced low earnings growth in the past. Growth companies tend to have experienced high growth rates. Investors tend to assume that past earnings growth rates will continue far into the future and price value and growth stocks accordingly. However, the growth rate of earnings tends to mean revert much sooner than investors expect (i.e. there is little persistence in growth rates). The duration of earnings growth is, therefore, mispriced by investors and that leads to higher returns for value stocks versus growth stocks, as subsequent earnings shocks occur. Chan et al. (2003) provided some evidence of this behavior by showing that current valuations (book value-to-price ratios) are driven by past earnings growth, as opposed to future realized growth. That is, the value premium may be attributed to investor overreaction.

B. Momentum

There are also many behavioral explanations for the existence of the momentum effect. For example, one behavioral trait known as "anchoring and adjustment" (e.g. Kahneman and Tversky 1974) may explain momentum returns. According to this bias, investors update their views only partially when new information becomes available. As a result, new information is discounted only slowly over time, which creates momentum in prices. As such, the momentum effect may be attributed to investor underreaction. Other studies, such as Grinblatt et al. (1995), have also linked the momentum returns to the herding behavior of investors, who often invest in recent winners, thus creating a bandwagon effect.

C. Simultaneous Existence of Value and Momentum

In the risk framework, the simultaneous existence of value and momentum excess returns is sometimes hard to explain. From a behavioral perspective, however, Chen et al. (2009) offered a myopic extrapolation explanation for the simultaneous existence of short-term trend (momentum) and long-term reversal (value) in prices. The long-term price reversal was documented by De Bondt et al. (1985). This finding refers to the observation that stocks with lower relative returns in the past five years tend to outperform, over the next five years, stocks with higher historical relative returns. Long-term price reversal is closely linked to value as stocks with lower relative returns in the past five years also tend to have lower valuation ratios. Chen et al. (2009) attempted to reconcile the main behavioral biases identified for momentum (short-term underreaction) and for value (long-term overreaction) through a myopic extrapolation hypothesis. The authors argued that the short-term trend and long-term reversal in prices can be explained by earnings shocks to future cash flows in all horizons. That is, there is momentum and then reversal in cash flow shocks, which causes momentum and then reversal in prices. This behavior is attributable to investors' tendency to revise future cash flows period-by-period, implying that current cash flow shocks are expected to last for a long time. Chen at al. (2009) stated: "investors overweight current earnings shocks but underweight their predictable trends." They refer to this behavior as myopic extrapolation.

D. Other Factors

More behavioral explanations are also offered to explain the existence of other anomalous returns. For instance, lottery mentality and preferences of investors is often cited as the reason for the low-volatility anomaly. According to this explanation, investors have a preference for high-volatility, high-beta stocks, which bids up their prices and lowers their expected returns relative to low-volatility, low-beta stocks. Hou and Loh (2012) analyzed various explanations for the low-volatility anomaly and found that lottery mentality of investors was a major contributor in explaining the low volatility anomaly, although almost half of the anomalous returns still remain unexplained.

Other contributing influences may include extrapolation and overconfidence biases. Indeed, Karceski (2002) pointed out that mutual fund investors tended to chase returns across asset classes over time and across funds within an asset class that had performed well. According to Karceski (2002), these biases may lead fund managers to worry more about outperforming in rising markets, then outperforming in falling markets, which may result in a preference and overpricing of high-beta, high-volatility stocks.

E. Persistence

If factor excess returns arise from mispricing attributable to the irrational behavior of investors, then why aren't such mispricings arbitraged away by investors? Numerous research articles, generally referred to as limits-to-arbitrage literature, cite many constraints to implementing arbitrage trades in real life (e.g. Shleifer and Vishny 1997, and Shleifer 2000). Arbitrage activities tend to be highly risky (i.e. can move against the arbitrageur) and costly. The Long-Term Capital Management failure is a good example in this regard.[2] At a micro level, arbitrage trades may be less risky to implement as assets can be substituted in relative value and hedging trades. For example, an individual stock may be substituted with another stock in the same industry and

---

[2] Long-Term Capital Management was a hedge fund management firm founded in 1993 that engaged in highly leveraged arbitrage trading strategies and sustained huge losses following the 1997 Asian financial crisis and the 1998 Russian financial crisis.

with similar performance characteristics. At a macro level, such as overall stock market and other common factors, highly correlated substitute assets are hard to find, which makes the arbitrage potentially highly risky. In addition, in many instances, arbitrageurs need to have long investment horizons and significant staying power, as a given mispricing can persist and even become more pronounced before it corrects. This is very hard to do, especially when the arbitrage is implemented with other people's money, people who may assess performance over shorter time periods. Other considerations may also serve as an impediment to arbitrage activities. For instance, in the case of the low volatility anomaly, borrowing restrictions (e.g. Black 1972) and benchmarks (e.g. Baker et al. 2011) are often cited as limits to arbitrage, as we discuss later.

Even though factor excess returns cannot be fully arbitraged away, presumably some portion of those excess returns can be. In this regard, McLean and Pontiff (2016) analyzed the out-of-sample and postpublication performance of a large number of factors shown to predict cross-sectional stock returns. They documented a 26% decline in out-of-sample returns and a 58% decline in postpublication returns, relative to in-sample published performance, on average, which implied a decline of 32% (58%–26%) attributable to "publication-informed" trading. These results do not suggest a complete disappearance of cross-sectional anomalous returns. Specifically, with regards to the smart beta factors, it is also worthwhile to note that these return regularities were documented decades ago, as highlighted in the previous chapter. As such, any portion of their return premia that could have been arbitraged would have disappeared by now. Yet, smart beta factors have continued to generate out-of-sample and post-publication return premia.

In summary, we believe behavioral explanations make two main arguments. First, the irrational behavior (i.e. biased preferences and beliefs) of investors causes mispricing. Second, such mispricing can potentially persist because it cannot be fully arbitraged away (i.e. there are limits to arbitrage).

V. STRUCTURAL EXPLANATIONS

For some smart beta factors, such as volatility, structural explanations have also been offered to explain the existence and/or persistence of their anomalous returns. Structural explanations typically refer to market frictions, investment management structures, or other impediments or constraints that cause mispricings and/or limit arbitrage activities. As an example, Black (1972) identified borrowing restrictions as a potential reason for the higher risk-adjusted returns observed for low beta stocks. Similarly, Baker et al. (2011) identified delegated portfolio management structures, in general, and the use of fixed benchmarks, in particular, as another reason why the low volatility anomaly persists. Baker et al. (2011) argued that conventional delegated fixed-benchmark mandates with leverage constraints create an incentive for investment managers to prefer high-beta stocks and shy away from low-beta stocks. The use of benchmarks in this manner essentially results in benchmarks themselves becoming a potential limit to arbitrage. Finally, we note an interesting study by

Asness et al. (2016) that investigated whether the low-risk anomaly was driven by leverage constraints, and hence should be measured by systematic risk, or by behavioral biases, and hence should be measured by idiosyncratic or stock-specific risk. To address this problem, the authors created new factors or signals that could be used to test one theory at a time. They found that signals that attempt to capture the leverage constraint perspective produced significant risk factor-adjusted alpha as well as depicted persistence on an out-sample basis across geographies and time. The signals that attempt to capture the behavioral perspective generally depicted less robust performance, with sentiment-related factors performing the best within this category. Based on the evidence presented in this study, the authors concluded that both leverage constraints and lottery mentality play a role in explaining the low-risk anomaly.

VI.   TYPICAL INVESTOR QUESTIONS

3.1 What Are Some of the Potential Issues Associated with Risk-Based Explanations?

Risk-based explanations argue that factor excess returns are actually risk premia arising from exposure to additional sources of risk (e.g. distress or illiquidity), and/or exposure to factor-specific bad times, and/or potential risk of large losses and market underperformance over extended periods of time. Let's review the merits of these arguments.

At one level, in our view, risk-based explanations seem reasonable. After all, if markets are rational and efficient, then factor return premia must be a compensation for bearing higher risk. However, the inability of the rational framework to identify those additional sources of risk presents a problem. Even if we accept that the underlying extra-market source of risk is distress for value and liquidity for size, there is no general agreement on risk sources relating to momentum, volatility, or quality. The risk-based explanations also cannot account for the simultaneous existence of factor excess returns, such as value and momentum. Fama and French (1998) themselves observe that past loser stocks have value-like characteristics, as price declines cause their valuation ratios to decline as well. This would imply that past loser stocks, and not past winner stocks (high momentum stocks), should have higher returns. This apparent contradiction led Fama and French to conclude that value and their 3-factor model cannot explain momentum returns. Fama even termed momentum as the "granddaddy" of market anomalies. If momentum is such a challenging anomaly, then what about the finding that low-volatility stocks outperform high-volatility stocks, which results in low risk being associated with higher returns? This finding poses such a problem that some proponents of efficient markets refuse to accept it even exists. Yet, the low-risk anomaly is one of the oldest documented anomalies, which has clearly persisted over time.

The notion that risk should be defined as covariance with bad times also seems quite reasonable. This concept of risk implies that factors deliver return premia because they perform poorly during bad times. The typical examples of bad times are periods of equity market downturns or economic recessions. Based on these definitions of bad times, our research does not support the assertion that all common factors perform poorly during bad times. Low-volatility and quality factors actually perform quite well during such periods and provide a high degree of downside protection. It may be that smart beta factors are characterized by bad times that are in addition to or different from those associated with the overall equity market. But again, the inability of academic researchers to reach a consensus on what those bad times might be is a source of confusion, which makes the argument less convincing in our judgment.

Smart beta factor returns clearly reflect a high degree of cyclicality, as factors do go in and out of favor. They also expose investors to severe market underperformance, which can last over a multiyear period. So, the observed factor return premia could be a compensation for bearing these extra risks, which go beyond the general performance risks associated with the market. This argument also seems reasonable, but it does not explain why certain factors are empirically and persistently rewarded and others not. For instance, Hou et al. (2015) analyzed the performance of 80 anomalies and found that almost half of them are insignificant in explaining the cross-section of expected returns (i.e. not priced or rewarded). Clearly, even factors that are not considered as rewarded common factors and typically not included in multifactor pricing models depict cyclicality and market underperformance risk.

3.2 What Are Some of the Potential Issues Associated with Behavioral Explanations?

Behavioral explanations argue that the irrational behavior (i.e. biased preferences and beliefs) of investors results in mispricing and gives rise to the empirically observed factor premia. One major issue with behavioral explanations is that some of them appear to be ex post and ad hoc rationalizations, although behavioral portfolio theories, of course, exist that provide some predictions on asset pricing (e.g. Shefrin and Statman 2000). There are so many potential investor biases and preferences that it is always possible to find one that explains a given anomaly. As discussed, value is attributed to investor overreaction, momentum to investor underreaction, low volatility to lottery mentality, and so on. In addition, there could be multiple and competing explanations for the same anomaly. Consider the case of momentum. Some argue it is caused by investor underreaction (e.g. Hong and Stein 2000), while others argue it is a result of investor overreaction (e.g. Daniel et al. 1998). What causes underreaction? Different studies point to different traits, such as anchoring and adjustment, representativeness, conservatism or bounded rationality. Overreaction could be caused by conservatism, overconfidence, or self-attribution.

Given the above, proponents of efficient markets often argue that many behavioral explanations lack rigor, theory, and discipline. There may be some degree of truth in this criticism.

3.3 Given the Vigorous Discussion and Debate, and the Confusion That It Inevitably Creates, How Should Investors Approach Two Basic Questions: Why Do Smart Beta Factors Exist? and Why Do They Persist?

There is no doubt that there is a clear lack of consensus in the academic community on what drives smart beta factor excess returns. Proponents of efficient markets argue that factor premia are a rational compensation for bearing additional extra-market risks. Proponents of inefficient markets counterargue that factor premia arise from the irrational behavior of investors. The lack of consensus is also apparent among practitioners in the investment industry. Index providers generally refer to factor returns as risk premia (without identifying the extra sources of risk that factors expose investors to), while active managers argue that factor premia represent behavioral anomalies that they can efficiently exploit (without addressing the various issues linked with limits-to-arbitrage).

   Why do smart beta factors work? In our opinion, in addressing this question, practitioners may find it helpful to keep the following considerations in mind.

a. Data Mining

In our opinion, smart beta factors are not spurious or lucky factors, whose performance is unlikely to persist out-of-sample. There is now some level of agreement in the industry that smart beta factor premia are not a result of data mining. As documented in Chapter 2, these factors remain significant in multiple testing frameworks and their performance has persisted on an out-of-sample basis over multiple decades.

b. Risk or Mispricing or Structural

Investors may have philosophical beliefs on market efficiency and on why certain factors work. These philosophical beliefs may lead to preference of certain factors over others. For example, in a recent interview at a fiduciary investors' symposium, Eugene Fama put forth the view that momentum is unlikely to be a risk factor, given its high turnover. "I have difficulty thinking about a risk factor with a turnover so high…. Momentum, in my view, is the biggest embarrassment for efficient markets," he said. He further admitted that he was "hoping it goes away."[3] Although Fama's statements are a bit hard to interpret (is his assertion that momentum is too risky to be a risk factor?), they do highlight his philosophical beliefs and preferences. Many other investors also feel more comfortable with value or quality investing, than they do with momentum. From a market efficiency perspective, these investors have a hard time understanding why momentum works, as it challenges even the weak form of market efficiency. Yet, in our experience, many of these same investors also implement low-volatility strategies in their portfolios, which challenge the basic

---

[3] Whyte (2016).

positive relation between risk and return that financial theory establishes. Holding philosophical beliefs is perfectly reasonable. But, consistency in philosophical beliefs is also important.

Irrespective of philosophical beliefs, practitioners should probably strive to comprehend the basic arguments relating to risk-based, behavioral, and structural explanations. But, in our view, it would not be a good use of investors' time to try to understand the nuances being argued in the academic literature within each school of thought. Is value a proxy for distress risk or some other form of risk? Do the extra-market bad times relating to value arise from labor risk or production technology risk? Does momentum result from investor underreaction or overreaction? It is best to let the academics argue about these topics for now, until further clarity and consensus emerges.

c. Persistence

In the risk-based explanations, smart beta factor premia are expected to persist because, in equilibrium, extra risk needs to be compensated with extra return. In behavioral and structural explanations, smart beta factor premia are expected to persist because of limits-to-arbitrage. Under various theories, therefore, there is a reasonable argument as to why smart beta factor return premia can be expected to persist over time. In this sense, there appears to be some level of agreement on the important issue of persistence of factor premia. As such, factor premia are sometimes referred to as "systematic" sources of returns. They are systematic in the sense that, whether arising from risk or mispricing, they tend to persist over time.

Another practical perspective on persistence is that strategies that are more likely to have investors on the other side of the trade are more likely to persist. For instance, many investors pursue a contrarian investment philosophy. They buy stocks that have recently fallen in price (other side of momentum). Other investors prefer stocks with high expected earnings growth and good, attractive stories (other side of value). And many investors prefer high-beta, high-volatility stocks in the hope of outperforming the market or their benchmarks (other side of low-volatility).

So, what is the bottom line?

The reality is that we do not fully understand why smart beta factors work. We have plausible explanations, but not agreement within the industry. Various offered explanations have potential shortcomings. Philosophical biases of investors may lead them to consider factor premia as arising out of either risk or mispricing or structural impediments. If no strong philosophical beliefs are held, then, in our view, it is not worth taking a rigid position in the risk versus mispricing versus structural debate. The truth may very well be that smart beta factor premia are driven by a combination of risk, behavioral, and structural considerations. That is our perspective. When pushed on the relative importance of the various explanations, we may have a slight preference for the behavioral and structural schools of thought.

There is good news, however. Various schools of thought do appear to have rational arguments as to why smart beta factor premia can be expected to persist. And from a practitioner viewpoint, persistence is clearly a key consideration.

3.4 Is Smart Beta Becoming a Crowded Trade, Ultimately Leading to the Disappearance of Smart Beta Factor Excess Returns?

With the popularity and growth of smart beta investing, some investors worry that it is quickly becoming a crowded trade. A crowded trade typically refers to a situation in which excess demand for a strategy or asset leads to overvaluation and, hence, lower or negative expected returns. Investors often point toward the large inflows experienced by smart beta offerings over the last few years as well as the valuation levels of smart beta strategies as evidence of crowding.

It is true that smart beta investing has seen increased inflows in recent years, but there may not be a dollar-for-dollar relationship between these inflows and the net increase in dollars linked to smart beta factors. For example, if smart beta assets have increased by US$500 billion, it does not necessarily mean that dollars invested in smart beta factors have also increased by that amount. The reasoning for this is as follows. At the industry level, over the last few years, we have seen a pronounced trend of outflows from active and inflows into passive and smart beta. Passive index investing, which replicates capitalization-weighted market benchmarks, has zero exposures to factors, by definition. Individual active managers typically have exposures to smart beta factors, but, as a group, they also look like the market, with no meaningful factor exposures, that is, positive and negative exposures of individual managers cancel out (e.g. Fama and French 2008). Therefore, a movement of funds from active to passive, broadly speaking, may have no impact on the net dollars linked to factor strategies. The move from active to smart beta, however, will increase the amount of dollars invested in factors, but not on a dollar-for-dollar basis. Recall that one of the primary value propositions for smart beta is the ability to deliver sources of excess returns that active managers have traditionally exploited in far more transparent investment processes and cheaper investment vehicles. Therefore, it would be reasonable to assume that some meaningful proportion of inflows into smart beta from active is coming from managers with positive factor exposures, but also high active fees. As such, net additional dollars linked to smart beta factor exposures may be quite a bit less than the total inflows into smart beta. Another perspective on increased smart beta inflows and potential crowding is provided by Blitz (2017). Using structured products (ETFs) as an example, he documented that as of December 31, 2015, US-listed funds that had at least three years of performance history amounted to US$1.2 trillion in assets, or about 5% of the US equity market. In analyzing the smart beta factor exposures across the full range of offered funds, Blitz (2017) found that, although some funds offered explicit positive exposures to smart beta factors, others pursued investment processes that resulted in implicit negative exposures. In the aggregate, across all funds, smart beta factor exposures turned out to be close to neutral or zero.

Thus, despite increased inflows into smart beta structured products, the data did not support the assertion that more dollars were chasing smart beta factor premia. These research findings, notwithstanding, crowding could, of course, become a real concern if inflows from both active and passive moved into smart beta at an increasing rate. But we are quite far from that situation at this stage. Additionally, despite the recent growth, smart beta assets remain a relatively small proportion of total equity assets.

Another argument for crowding relates to higher valuation levels of smart beta strategies. The issue of assessing the level of valuation of smart beta strategies, however, is a complicated one. Some researchers, for example, Arnott et al. (2016), argue that recent smart beta factor returns have been driven by increases in valuation, due to increased inflows. As a result, Arnott et al. (2016) state that some smart beta strategies have become very expensive, with a reasonable likelihood of factor crashes on the horizon. Others, for instance, Asness et al. (2015), counterargue that, despite increased popularity, smart beta factors are not overvalued based on value spreads. The question of assessing factor valuations is complicated because different methodologies can lead to different results. For example, our research shows that conventional profitability strategies currently look highly overvalued relative to history based on a price-to-book valuation metric. But from a price-to-earnings valuation perspective, these same strategies look slightly undervalued. In general, as of June 2017, we do not find any evidence of a structural overvaluation of factor strategies to the extent that it would lead us to seriously question the persistence of factor return premia.

VII. CONCLUSION

From a smart beta perspective, size, value, momentum, volatility, and quality typically constitute the set of rewarded factors. Although the industry has not yet reached a consensus on why these factors work, there is considerable and convincing evidence on the out-of-sample persistence of excess returns associated with these factors. Fama and French factors have been updated on Ken French's website for more than two decades. Live performance is also available for large-small and value-growth indexes published by index providers for global equity markets. And factors have depicted persistence across market segments (large, mid, small), across geographies (developed and emerging), and across time (out-of-sample).

In the next section of this book, we shift our focus from an academic review of factors to capturing smart beta factors in real-life implementations. We discuss the various portfolio construction methodologies and factor specifications used by providers to capture smart beta factor returns. We also analyze the historical performance of a large number of publicly available smart beta strategies to better understand their performance characteristics.

PART III

CAPTURING SMART BETA FACTORS

CHAPTER 4

WEIGHTING SCHEMES

The wide variety of smart beta products available in the marketplace can sometimes be overwhelming for investors and may pose a challenge with regards to analyzing and selecting such products. Differences in smart beta offerings can arise from many sources, such as factor specifications, weighting schemes, and methodologies used to control turnover, diversification, or capacity. In this chapter, we propose a simple framework for understanding the various weighting schemes employed to capture smart beta factor returns.[1] We also analyze the efficiency in factor capture achieved by these weighting schemes. In the next chapter, we discuss differences that could arise from factor signal specifications.

CHAPTER SUMMARY

- Smart beta products use a variety of weighting schemes and portfolio construction methodologies to capture factor returns.
- The various weighting schemes employed can be classified into two broad categories: (1) weighting schemes that "tilt" the benchmark capitalization weights toward the desired factor characteristics and (2) weighting schemes that "reweight" universe constituents from capitalization weighting to weights based on factor characteristics or some other construction objective.
- The first category, "Tilting," results in constituent total weights being a function of benchmark capitalization weights. Constituent active weights (i.e. overweights and underweights) may or may not be a function of benchmark capitalization weights depending on how the factor tilts are implemented.
  - Some weighting schemes, such as capitalization weighting and capitalization scaling, implement factor tilts by multiplying benchmark capitalization weights by factor attractiveness scores. As such, these schemes deliver a capitalization-

---

[1] In this chapter, we discuss the weighting schemes used to weight individual stocks in factor portfolios. The weighting schemes used to weight factors in the construction of multifactor strategies are discussed in Chapter 8.

scaled factor tilt, in which active weights also become a function of benchmark capitalization weights. These weighting schemes typically have low turnover, low implementation costs, and high capacity, but they may also depict high stock-level concentration and factor tilts that are influenced by capitalization weights.

- Other weighting schemes, such as active risk constrained optimization and signal tilting aim to implement purer factor tilts by making active weights independent of benchmark capitalization weights and only a function of factor attractiveness. These weighting schemes will typically have higher turnover and lower capacity than capitalization weighting and capitalization scaling.
- The second category, "Reweighting," which is benchmark-agnostic, seeks to reweight a given universe of securities from capitalization weights to weights determined by factor attractiveness or some other investment objective, for example, building a minimum variance portfolio. This category includes weighting schemes, such as equal weighting, signal weighting, and active risk unconstrained optimizing. These weighting schemes typically offer high diversification, but may also have high turnover, low capacity, and a small cap bias in factor capture.
- We create smart beta factor portfolios using the various weighting schemes. We analyze historical backtested performance and conduct an active return and risk decomposition against capitalization-weighted factor portfolios (cap-scaled factor tilts) and signal-tilted factor portfolios (cap-independent factor tilts). The main findings are:
  - All smart beta factor portfolios created using various weighting schemes outperformed the market benchmark (Russell 1000 Index).
  - Capitalization-scaled factor portfolios realized only marginal improvement in information ratios and generated no meaningful alpha in a risk decomposition relative to capitalization-weighted factor portfolios.
  - Signal-tilted factor portfolios produced higher information ratios than capitalization-weighted and capitalization-scaled factor portfolios, confirming that purer signal tilts tend to deliver better risk-adjusted performance.
  - Equal-weighted and signal-weighted factor portfolios performed similarly relative to the Russell 1000 Index. They realized higher information ratios compared to capitalization-weighted, capitalization-scaled, and signal-tilted factor portfolios. These portfolios also generated large and statistically significant alphas in a risk decomposition against the capitalization-weighted factor portfolios.
  - As we show in this chapter, equal-weighted and signal-weighted factor portfolios are equivalent to starting with an equal-weighted benchmark universe and then tilting toward the desired factors. As such, the significant outperformance of these factor portfolios is largely explained by the outperformance of the equal-weighted Russell 1000 portfolio over the Russell 1000 Index.
  - The performance of equal-weighted and signal-weighted factor portfolios is almost fully explained in a risk decomposition against the equal-weighted Russell 1000 portfolio and the signal-tilted value, momentum, volatility, and quality portfolios.

- In comparing the efficiency in factor capture of various smart beta methodologies, in our opinion, an active return and risk decomposition may be a more insightful method to a simple historical performance comparison based on risk-adjusted returns. This is because, given the significant variation in active returns, it is quite difficult to achieve statistical significance in evaluating differences in Sharpe ratios or information ratios. An active return and risk decomposition, on the other hand, provides insights to understanding factor exposures and contributions. In this exercise, the magnitude, statistical significance, and active risk contribution of the alpha (unexplained active return) generated is a useful indicator of the efficiency of a strategy.
- A capitalization-weighted parent universe (e.g. Russell 1000 Index) is not an appropriate performance benchmark for all smart beta strategies. Some weighting schemes, such as equal weighting and signal weighting implement factor tilts relative to an equal-weighted parent universe (e.g. Russell 1000 Equal-Weighted Index), not a capitalization-weighted parent universe. If the objective is to determine the efficiency of factor tilts, then their performance should be evaluated relative to the equal-weighted parent universe.

I.   INTRODUCTION

In the academic literature, it is customary to construct factor portfolios using a methodology similar to the one outlined in Fama and French (1992). The Fama-French portfolios are zero-investment, factor mimicking portfolios that rely on the notion of diversification to capture the size, value, or momentum effects. But these portfolios also have drawbacks. They require shorting, have high turnover, and do not have readily available investment vehicles that replicate their performance. Despite their usefulness in investment research, the Fama-French factor portfolios are not easily and cost-effectively investable and replicable.

Smart beta providers, therefore, design construction methodologies to create long-only, investable factor portfolios, whose performance investors can actually replicate at low cost. In this chapter, we discuss a simple conceptual framework for analyzing different weighting schemes used by smart beta providers, as well as gaining a better understanding of what drives their performance.

II.   WEIGHTING SCHEMES USED TO CAPTURE FACTOR RETURNS

All smart beta strategies that seek to capture factor returns have one common feature: they employ weighting schemes that deviate from benchmark capitalization weights of constituents. The deviation from benchmark capitalization weights can be implemented in two ways: (1) by tilting benchmark capitalization weights toward the desired factors, and (2) by "reweighting" benchmark constituents by the desired factors or some other construction objective, such as equal-weighting or building a minimum variance portfolio. These two broad categories of weighting schemes are shown in Figure 4.1.

FIGURE 4.1   Smart Beta Weighting Schemes: Two Broad Categories

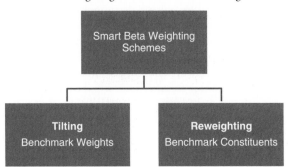

Within the Tilting category, the total weight of constituents is a function of benchmark capitalization weights. However, weighting schemes within this category may differ on how the factor tilts are determined. One approach is to multiply benchmark capitalization weights by factor attractiveness (e.g. a factor score). This multiplicative process implies that active weights of constituents also become a function of benchmark capitalization weights. We refer to such weighting schemes as "capscaled" factor tilting. The second approach determines active weights solely as a function of factor attractiveness, and independently of benchmark capitalization weights. The derived active weights are then added to capitalization weights to determine the total weight of constituents. We refer to such additive processes as delivering "capindependent" factor tilts, or purer factor tilts as the relation between factor attractiveness and active weights is improved. Therefore, within the Tilting category, total weights of constituents are always a function of benchmark capitalization weights, while active weights may or may not be.

In the Reweighting category, since benchmark constituents are reweighted based on factor attractiveness or some other construction objective, the total weight of each constituent is independent of benchmark capitalization weight, while active weight is not.

Figure 4.2 depicts an overview of the categorization of various weighting schemes and their total and active weight characteristics.

A. Tilting: Total Weights Linked to Benchmark Capitalization Weights

As a broad category, these weighting schemes seek to implement factor tilts relative to the benchmark capitalization weights of constituents. The factor tilts can be implemented by scaling benchmark capitalization weights or independently of benchmark capitalization weights.

FIGURE 4.2   Smart Beta Weighting Schemes: Total and Active Weight Characteristics

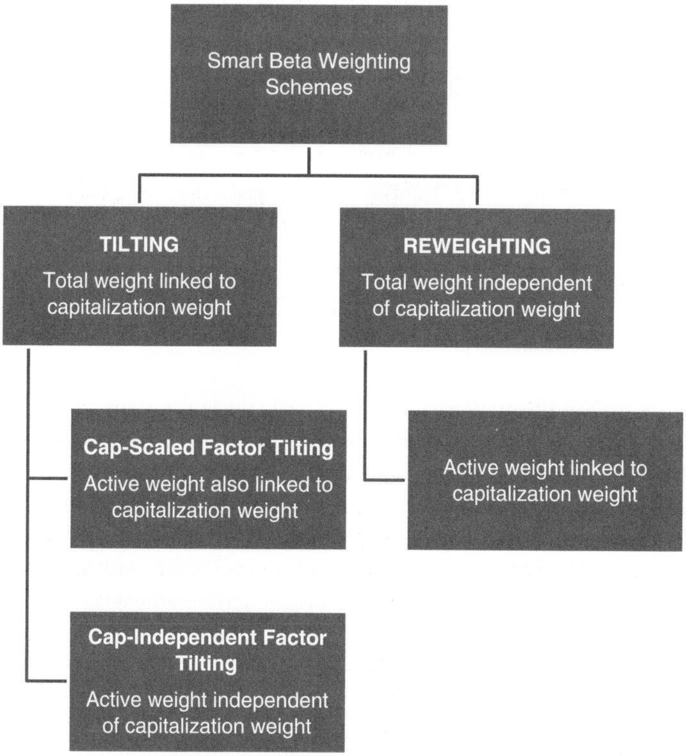

a. Cap-Scaled Factor Tilts

This category includes weighting schemes such as capitalization-weighted (CW) and capitalization-scaled (CS), in which total and active weights of constituents are a function of their benchmark capitalization weights.

i. Capitalization Weighting

Capitalization-weighted factor portfolios use a weighting scheme that is transparent and well understood by investors. Traditional style (value/growth) indexes offered by index providers are examples of CW factor portfolios. More generally, independent CW factor portfolios may be constructed using a methodology outlined in Table 4.1. The construction process starts with the specification of a benchmark universe from which the CW factor portfolios are created. All stocks in the universe are independently ranked from high to low on a factor signal, such as momentum. The highest-ranked stocks that provide a certain cumulative coverage of the benchmark universe

TABLE 4.1 Illustration of CW Factor Portfolio Construction Process

	Stock Momentum (Total Return)	Benchmark Weight (%)	Cummulative Coverage of Benchmark Weight (%)	Total Weight in Momentum Portfolio (%)	Active Weight in Momentum Portfolio (%)
Stock 1	90.20	0.50	0.50	1.00	0.50
Stock 2	85.40	1.00	1.50	2.00	1.00
Stock 3...	82.50	0.50	2.00	1.00	0.50
...Stock n...	8.20	3.00	50.00	6.00	3.00
Stock $n+1$...	7.50	0.75			-0.75

Source: GSAM.

weight (50% in this illustration) are selected for inclusion in the factor (momentum) portfolio. In this case, stocks 1 through n are selected for inclusion, as they provide 50% cumulative coverage. Then, the selected stocks are weighted by their market capitalization. Therefore, the second to last column of Table 4.1 shows that the total weight of each stock in the momentum portfolio is twice the weight the stock has in the benchmark index because we have 50% coverage of benchmark market capitalization. The active weight of each stock is equal to its capitalization weight in the benchmark (last column). If the factor index was constructed to target 25% coverage of the parent universe weight, then the total weight and active weight of constituents would be four times and three times the benchmark capitalization weight, respectively.

The construction process outlined in Table 4.1 is an approach in which constituent selection is based on factor rankings but constituent weighting is based on capitalization, whether used in the context of an independent factor portfolio (as in this illustration) or in a two-dimensional construct (e.g. traditional value-growth indexes). For the selected constituents, total weights and active weights in the factor portfolio are a function of benchmark capitalization weights and the proportion of benchmark coverage, and not a function of factor ranks or attractiveness based on the factor signal (these results are derived more formally in Appendix 4.1). For example, because Stock n in Table 4.1 is a large stock (benchmark capitalization weight of 3%), it receives the highest total weight (i.e. 6%) and the highest active weight (i.e. an overweight of 3%), despite the fact that Stock n is the least attractive security on momentum among the selected securities. Although CW factor portfolios offer high investability and capacity, their construction methodology also disturbs the link between the factor signal and the total and active weight of a constituent.

ii. Capitalization Scaling

One approach to improve the relationship between factor signals and weights is to scale benchmark capitalization weights of constituents by the factor signal. This weighting scheme is referred to as capitalization-scaled (CS) weighting. Bender and Wang (2015) provide an example of factor portfolio construction using CS weighting. More generally, the weight of a security in a CS factor portfolio is determined by multiplying the factor score of the security by its benchmark capitalization weight. In this approach, therefore, stocks with high (low) factor scores are overweighted (underweighted) relative to their benchmark capitalization weight. Within capitalization scaling, some smart beta offerings use the entire universe of benchmark constituents, while others use a subset to create more concentrated portfolios. MSCI Momentum Tilt and Quality Tilt indexes are examples of the former case. In the context of value investing, value-weighted indexes are also an example of products that capitalization-scale the entire universe. In such indexes, constituents that have high (low) value characteristics compared to the market are scaled up (down) relative to their benchmark weights. Concentrated CS offerings first select a subset of the benchmark universe, such as the top 30% of names based on a factor score, and then apply the capitalization scaling to the selected constituents. MSCI Momentum and Quality Indexes would be examples of such offerings.

CS factor portfolios improve the relationship between factor attractiveness and security weights compared to CW factor portfolios and, hence, may provide improved efficiency in factor capture. However, in such portfolios, the relation between factor signal and security weights is still not exact, as weights remain a function of capitalization weights in the benchmark index. For example, two constituents that have the same value characteristics can have different weights in the CS value factor portfolio if their capitalization weights in the benchmark index are different. More specifically, larger companies will receive a higher total and active weight, even if they have similar factor characteristics as smaller companies. Therefore, this multiplicative weighting scheme produces a cap-scaled tilt in factor portfolio construction (please see Appendix 4.1 for a derivation of these results). Finally, we note that fundamental indexation is also equivalent to a CS weighting scheme, despite the fact that fundamental indexes do not explicitly consider capitalization weights in their construction. This result is also derived in Appendix 4.1.

b. Cap-Independent Factor Tilts

This category includes weighting schemes such as active risk constrained-optimized and signal tilted (ST), where total weights are a function of benchmark capitalization weights, but active weights are not.

i. Active Risk Constrained Optimization

Active risk constrained-optimized factor portfolios offer the ability to implement factor tilts at desired levels of tracking error, while also adhering to other constraints, such as limits on turnover or sector exposures. Many smart beta managers, typically quant managers, use this construction approach. In an active risk constrained-optimized solution, the active weights are determined by a combination of alpha signal (i.e. factor signal) and active risk considerations. This significantly improves the relationship between risk-adjusted factor signals and active weights. In contrast to cap-scaled tilts introduced by CW and CS weightings, active risk constrained optimization results in purer risk-adjusted signal tilts.

ii. Signal Tilting

Some investors perceive optimized factor portfolios as opaque and as introducing a level of complexity that may not be needed in capturing smart beta factors. The basic objectives of an optimized solution, however, can also be achieved through simpler, rules-based, and more transparent weighting schemes that implement a cap-independent factor tilt. In such weighting schemes, the active weight of a constituent is determined based on the strength of a factor signal, independent of benchmark capitalization weights within the context of a long-only constraint. Then, the active weights are added to or subtracted from benchmark weights to calculate total weights. Unlike CS weighting, where the signal tilt is achieved by multiplying benchmark capitalization weights, these weighting schemes implement a purer signal tilt using an additive approach. We refer to these weighting schemes as signal tilted (ST).

ST weighting schemes seek to establish a direct relationship between a factor signal and active weights assigned to securities in the factor portfolio, subject to the long-only constraint, while targeting a specific level of active risk relative to the benchmark. A direct relationship implies that the most attractive security on a given factor signal receives the highest overweight, the second most attractive security receives the second highest overweight, and so on. Similarly, the most unattractive security is assigned the highest underweight. On the overweight side, the factor portfolios can realize a perfect correlation between factor signals and overweights, but not for underweights. The long-only constraint requires that securities cannot be underweighted by more than their benchmark weight, which limits the ability to achieve desired underweights in the case of smaller stocks. Once the active weights are determined based on factor signals, the total weight is defined as capitalization weight plus or minus the determined active weight. ST factor portfolios may provide improved efficiency in factor capture, as the active weights of securities are independent of benchmark capitalization weights, except for the long-only constraint. The FTSE Russell High Efficiency Defensive Index is an example of a ST portfolio construction process. Some smart beta managers also use ST weighting schemes in the design of their smart beta offerings. Appendix 4.1 provides a detailed example of a ST weighting scheme that establishes a linearly proportional relationship between factor scores and active weights to create ST smart beta factor portfolios.

B. Reweighting: Total Weights Independent of Capitalization Weights

This second broad category includes weighting schemes such as equal-weighted (EW), signal-weighted (SW), and active risk unconstrained-optimized.

TABLE 4.2 Illustration of EW Factor Portfolio Construction Process

	Stock Momentum (Total Return)	Benchmark Weight (%)	Cummulative Coverage of Benchmark Names (%)	Total Weight in Momentum Portfolio (%)	Active Weight in Momentum Portfolio (%)
Stock 1	90.20	0.05	0.20	0.40	0.35
Stock 2	85.40	1.00	0.40	0.40	-0.60
Stock 3...	82.50	0.25	0.60	0.40	0.15
...Stock 250...	8.20	3.00	50.00	0.40	-2.60
Stock 251...	7.50	0.75			-0.75
...Stock 500	-50.50	1.00			-1.00

Source: GSAM.

a. Equal Weighting

A popular example of an EW smart beta strategy is the EW benchmark universe, such as the Russell 1000 Equal Weight Index. Equal weighting, however, can also be used in building factor portfolios from a given benchmark universe. Capitalization-weighted and CS factor portfolios may offer higher capacity and investability, but, in addition to potentially lower efficiency in factor capture, may also expose investors to significant stock-level concentration. To introduce more diversification in factor capture, equal weighting is often employed as an alternative portfolio construction approach (e.g. Blitz 2012, Amenc et al. 2016). Table 4.2 provides an illustration of how an independent EW factor portfolio may be constructed. In this example, the starting benchmark universe consists of 500 securities. These securities are ranked on a given factor, for instance, momentum. The top 50% of securities (i.e. 250 names) are then selected for inclusion in the momentum portfolio. Finally, the selected securities are equal weighted. As such, the total weight of each security is 0.4% (1/250) and the active weight is 0.4% minus the benchmark capitalization weight (last column of Table 4.2). In this construction methodology, total weights are independent of benchmark capitalization weights, while active weights are still a function of capitalization weights, with smaller companies being overweighted and larger companies being underweighted in the final portfolio (please see Appendix 4.1 for more details). Therefore, EW factor portfolios deliver a small cap-biased factor capture.

b. Signal Weighting

In a SW scheme, the entire benchmark universe of constituents or a subset of the benchmark universe are weighted directly by the factor signal. MSCI Risk-Weighted Indexes and S&P Low Volatility Indexes are examples of SW factor portfolios. In these indexes, universe constituents are weighted by the inverse of their historical return volatility, such that lower volatility stocks receive a higher weight relative to higher volatility stocks. In this construction approach, therefore, total weights are independent of benchmark capitalization weights, as universe constituents are reweighted by the factor signal. The active weights are still a function of capitalization weights, as they are derived by subtracting capitalization weight from the total weight (refer to Appendix 4.1 for more details).

c. Active Risk Unconstrained Optimization

Many smart beta products also use an active risk unconstrained-optimization in the portfolio construction process. Minimum variance, risk-efficient, and maximum diversification portfolios are examples of smart beta strategies that employ active risk unconstrained optimization. For example, in the construction of a minimum variance portfolio, the total weight of securities is driven by total volatility and co-variances, such that low volatility stocks with high diversification potential receive a larger weight compared to high volatility stocks with low diversification potential. As such, total weights are independent of benchmark capitalization weights, while active weights are determined by subtracting capitalization weights from the total weights.

*　*　*

To summarize this section on the various weighting schemes used to construct smart beta factor offerings, we note the following:

- CW and CS weighting schemes may have low turnover, low implementation costs, and high capacity, but they potentially also expose investors to high concentration risk. CW portfolios introduce a factor tilt only in security selection, but not security weighting. CS portfolios introduce a cap-scaled (or large-cap biased) factor tilt.
- The EW and SW factor portfolios may provide more diversification, but may result in higher turnover, lower capacity, and a small cap bias in factor capture.
- Active risk constrained-optimized and ST factor portfolios seek to establish a direct relationship between factor attractiveness and active weights, and hence deliver purer factor tilts. They do so by making active weights a function only of factor signal attractiveness, and not benchmark capitalization weights (cap-independent factor tilts). Such portfolios may have lower capacity than CW and CS factor portfolios, although some smart beta managers seek to improve capacity by employing methodologies to enhance diversification and lower turnover.

In Figure 4.3, we list examples of smart beta offerings corresponding to the weighting schemes discussed in this section.

FIGURE 4.3 Weighting Schemes and Examples of Smart Beta Offerings

TILTING	TILTING	REWEIGHTING
Total and Active Weights Linked to Benchmark Capitalization Weight: Capitalization-Scaled Factor Tilts	Total Weights Linked to Benchmark Capitalization Weight, but not Active Weights: Pure Factor Tilts	Total Weight Independent of Benchmark Capitalization Weight

TILTING — Total and Active Weights Linked to Benchmark Capitalization Weight: Capitalization-Scaled Factor Tilts

- **Capitalization weighting (CW):**
  - Traditional style (value / growth) indexes
- **Capitalization scaling (CS):**
  - Value-weighted portfolios
  - Fundamental indexation
  - S&P momentum and low volatility indexes
  - MSCI momentum, quality, and low-volatility tilt indexes
  - MSCI momentum and quality indexes
  - FTSE Tilt-Tilt indexes

TILTING — Total Weights Linked to Benchmark Capitalization Weight, but not Active Weights: Pure Factor Tilts

- **Active risk constrained optimizing:**
  - Offerings of certain smart beta managers
- **Signal tilting (ST):**
  - FTSE Russell High Efficiency Defensive Indexes
  - Goldman Sachs ActiveBeta Indexes
  - Offerings of certain smart beta managers

REWEIGHTING — Total Weight Independent of Benchmark Capitalization Weight

- **Equal weighting (EW):**
  - Equal-weighted benchmarks, such as Russell 1000 Equal Weight Index
- **Signal weighting (SW):**
  - S&P intrinsic value weighted and low volatility indexes
  - MSCI risk-weighted indexes
- **Active risk unconstrained optimizing:**
  - MSCI single factor optimized indexes
  - Various multifactor optimized indexes
  - Minimum variance indexes
  - Max diversification, max decorrelation, max Sharpe ratio portfolios

III. ASSESSING THE INVESTMENT PERFORMANCE AND EFFICIENCY OF WEIGHTING SCHEMES USED TO CAPTURE FACTOR RETURNS

We now proceed to analyze the investment performance and efficiency (defined as factor-adjusted alpha) of various weighting schemes in capturing factor returns. To the extent that actual commercial products encompass a large number of decisions in their construction, it becomes very difficult to assess the performance and efficiency of just the weighting schemes using such products. For instance, two smart beta offerings that employ the same weighting scheme can depict different performance characteristics because of different signal specifications and/or methodologies used to address other areas of portfolio construction, such as diversification, turnover, or portfolio rebalancing. Therefore, in this section, we compare the performance of various weighting schemes in a controlled, internally consistent research environment, such that apples-to-apples comparisons can be facilitated.

However, before we look at the historical performance comparisons, it may be useful to lay out what we would expect to see, based on the conceptual framework presented in the previous sections. In general, we would expect:

- CW smart beta factor portfolios to outperform the market, given the existing academic evidence as well as the historical performance of some capitalization-weighted factor indexes, such as traditional value indexes,
- CS smart beta factor portfolios to realize higher IRs than CW portfolios, as they improve the link between factor attractiveness and active weights,
- ST smart beta factor portfolios as well as active risk constrained-optimized solutions to realize higher IRs than CW and CS portfolios, as they further improve the link between active weights and factor attractiveness, and
- SW and EW smart beta factor portfolios as well as active risk unconstrained-optimized solutions to also deliver higher IRs than CW and CS portfolios, as they provide a small-cap, as opposed to a large-cap, biased factor capture.

We create the smart beta factor portfolios using the rules-based weighting schemes outlined above and excluding the optimized solutions. The constructed smart beta factor portfolios are based on the same factor signal specifications. We specify the smart beta factors as follows. Size is defined as the inverse of market capitalization. Value is defined as a composite signal of three valuation ratios, namely book value-to-price, sales-to-price, and cash flow-to-price (or earnings-to-price when cash flow is unavailable). Momentum is defined as prior 11-month total return, lagged by one month. Volatility is defined as the inverse of prior 12-month standard deviation of daily total returns. Finally, profitability/quality is defined as gross profits divided by total assets. The fundamental information is sourced from Compustat and Worldscope databases and is lagged appropriately to avoid look-ahead bias. These signal specifications are well-documented in the academic literature, as discussed in Chapter 2, and should not be controversial. We also discuss these and other smart beta factor specifications in more detail in the next chapter.

After the initial construction, all smart beta factor portfolios need to be rebalanced on a periodic basis. Portfolio rebalancing involves an inherent trade-off between keeping the factor tilts current and keeping turnover low. As market prices move, keeping factor tilts or exposures current would require frequent rebalancing, such as monthly or weekly. Keeping turnover low would argue for infrequent factor index reconstitution, such as yearly. In our opinion, a quarterly rebalancing frequency provides a good balance between these two conflicting objectives.

In this chapter, we focus on the US large cap universe using Russell 1000 Index as the parent universe. The analysis period starts in January 1979, which is the start date of the Russell Indexes, and ends in June 2017. In later chapters, we extend the analysis to cover other developed and emerging markets.

A. Capitalization Weighting

The CW smart beta factor portfolios are built using the process outlined in Table 4.1, where the highest ranked stocks on a factor that provide 50% cumulative coverage of benchmark weight are selected and weighted by their market capitalization. Table 4.3 shows the historical performance of CW factor portfolios. As expected, all portfolios outperformed the Russell 1000 Index and generated a higher Sharpe ratio and a positive information ratio. However, only the active return of the CW value portfolio was statistically significant at the 5% level.

B. Capitalization Scaling

The CS smart beta factor portfolios are created by multiplying the benchmark capitalization weight by the factor score, scaled between 0 and + 1, as described in Appendix 4.1.

TABLE 4.3 Historical Performance of CW Factor Portfolios

	Total Gross Return (%)	Total Risk (%)	Sharpe Ratio	Active Gross Return (%)	Active Risk (%)	Information Ratio
Russell 1000 Index	11.84	15.05	0.49			
CW Size Portfolio	12.69	16.17	0.52	0.85	3.52	0.24
CW Value Portfolio	13.45	15.05	0.59	**1.60**	3.80	0.42
CW Momentum Portfolio	12.92	16.09	0.53	1.08	5.33	0.20
CW Volatility Portfolio	12.19	12.15	0.60	0.35	6.10	0.06
CW Quality Portfolio	12.89	15.24	0.55	1.04	3.26	0.32

Note: Figures in bold are statistically significant at the 5% level.
Source: GSAM.

TABLE 4.4 Historical Performance of CW and CS Factor Portfolios

	Total Gross Return (%)	Total Risk (%)	Sharpe Ratio	Active Gross Return (%)	Active Risk (%)	Information Ratio
Russell 1000 Index	11.84	15.05	0.49			
CW Value Portfolio	13.45	15.05	0.59	**1.60**	3.80	0.42
CS Value Portfolio	13.15	15.05	0.57	**1.31**	2.81	0.47
CW Momentum Portfolio	12.92	16.09	0.53	1.08	5.33	0.20
CS Momentum Portfolio	12.61	15.43	0.53	0.77	2.97	0.26
CW Volatility Portfolio	12.19	12.15	0.60	0.35	6.10	0.06
CS Volatility Portfolio	12.23	13.24	0.57	0.39	3.25	0.12
CW Quality Portfolio	12.89	15.24	0.55	1.04	3.26	0.32
CS Quality Portfolio	12.55	14.95	0.54	**0.71**	1.68	0.42

Note: Figures in bold are statistically significant at the 5% level.
Source: GSAM.

In creating CS factor portfolios, we do not consider size, which becomes irrelevant in this construct, as the factor signal is defined as the inverse of market capitalization. For the other factors, Table 4.4 reports the historical performance. All CS smart beta factor portfolios also outperformed the Russell 1000 benchmark, with the active returns for value and quality achieving statistical significance. As expected, CS factor portfolios produced higher information ratios compared to CW portfolios in all cases.

Assessing Investment Efficiency: Active Return and Risk Decomposition

Could the superior performance of CS portfolios simply be due to the fact that the CS weighting scheme introduces other factor biases relative to CW portfolios? To answer this question, we conduct an active return and risk decomposition exercise similar to the Fama-French risk decomposition framework, in which a strategy's excess returns are regressed against the market and other Fama-French factors. The objective of this exercise is to understand various factor exposures and to determine whether a given strategy produces a "factor-adjusted" alpha. Alpha, also referred to as unexplained return, could arise from various sources. For instance, differences in the starting universe used for portfolio construction could potentially lead to alpha. Differences in factor signal specifications could lead to alpha, such as a composite value signal as opposed to a single book value-to-price metric. A portfolio construction methodology may deliver alpha, even when the same signal specifications are used, as alpha could also arise from sector exposures, such as a sector-neutral value strategy versus a cross-sectional value capture.

In our case, we analyze the CS factor portfolios relative to the CW factor portfolios. Since all factor portfolios are similar in all respects (same starting universe, same factor signals, etc.), other than the weighting scheme, we interpret any alpha that is generated as representing a more "efficient" capture of factors driven by the weighting scheme. In other words, in our framework, a factor-adjusted alpha represents the improvement in active returns provided by a weighting scheme relative to the CW factor portfolios. The time-series regression model that we use to conduct the active return and risk decomposition is described in more detail in Appendix 4.2.

Table 4.5 shows the results of an active return and risk decomposition of CS factor portfolios against the CW factor portfolios. In each case, the CS factor portfolio had the highest exposure to the corresponding CW factor portfolio. For instance, the CS value portfolio had the highest exposure of 0.61 to the CW value portfolio. In addition, at least 80% of the active risk of the CS factor portfolios was explained by the corresponding CW factor portfolio. For example, almost 80% (2.22/2.81) of the active risk of CS value portfolio was explained by the CW value portfolio. The CS factor portfolios generated small alphas, which were statistically significant for value and quality. However, not even 10% of the active risk of CS factor portfolios was explained by the alpha terms. These results suggest that capitalization scaling is very close to capitalization weighting, and that CS smart beta factor portfolios deliver only marginal improvement in factor capture efficiency compared to CW factor portfolios.

TABLE 4.5 Active Return and Risk Decomposition of CS Factor Portfolios

	CW Size	CW Value	CW Momentum	CW Volatility	CW Quality	Alpha	Total Active Risk
CS Value Portfolio						**0.37**	
Exposure	**0.06**	**0.61**	**-0.05**	**0.03**	**-0.05**		
Contribution to Active Risk	0.07	2.22	0.17	0.06	0.08	0.20	2.81
CS Momentum Portfolio						0.16	
Exposure	**0.03**	-0.02	**0.54**	**0.02**	-0.03		
Contribution to Active Risk	-0.02	0.03	2.79	-0.01	-0.02	0.18	2.97
CS Volatility Portfolio						0.08	
Exposure	**-0.02**	**0.04**	0.01	**0.51**	**0.01**		
Contribution to Active Risk	0.01	0.05	0.00	3.08	0.00	0.10	3.25
CS Quality Portfolio						**0.23**	
Exposure	0.00	-0.02	**0.00**	0.03	**0.47**		
Contribution to Active Risk	0.00	0.04	0.00	0.02	1.47	0.15	1.68

Note: Figures in bold are statistically significant at the 5% level.
Source: GSAM.

C. Signal Tilting

We create the ST factor portfolios using the methodology outlined in Appendix 4.1. Table 4.6 reports the performance of ST factor portfolios and also compares it to CW and CS portfolios. To facilitate comparisons, and to the extent that active risk can be customized in a ST weighting scheme, the ST factor portfolios are constructed to roughly match the active risk of the CW factor portfolios. All ST factor portfolios outperformed the benchmark Russell 1000 Index and generated higher Sharpe ratios and positive information ratios. The active returns of the ST value, momentum, and quality portfolios were also statistically significant. All ST factor portfolios, except size, performed much better than CW and CS portfolios, delivering higher Sharpe ratios as well as improvements in information ratios.

To assess whether the superior performance of ST portfolios relative to CW portfolios is simply due to other factor biases, we conduct an active return and risk decomposition exercise. Table 4.7 reports the results. In each case, except for size, the

TABLE 4.6 Historical Performance of CW, CS, and ST Factor Portfolios

	Total Gross Return (%)	Total Risk (%)	Sharpe Ratio	Active Gross Return (%)	Active Risk (%)	Information Ratio
Russell 1000 Index	11.84	15.05	0.49			
CW Size Portfolio	12.69	16.17	0.52	0.85	3.52	0.24
ST Size Portfolio	12.72	16.49	0.51	0.88	3.63	0.24
CW Value Portfolio	13.45	15.05	0.59	**1.60**	3.80	0.42
CS Value Portfolio	13.15	15.05	0.57	**1.31**	2.81	0.47
ST Value Portfolio	13.84	15.31	0.60	**2.00**	3.76	0.53
CW Momentum Portfolio	12.92	16.09	0.53	1.08	5.33	0.20
CS Momentum Portfolio	12.61	15.43	0.53	0.77	2.97	0.26
ST Momentum Portfolio	13.58	16.62	0.56	**1.74**	5.04	0.34
CW Volatility Portfolio	12.19	12.15	0.60	0.35	6.10	0.06
CS Volatility Portfolio	12.23	13.24	0.57	0.39	3.25	0.12
ST Volatility Portfolio	12.86	11.69	0.67	1.01	5.94	0.17
CW Quality Portfolio	12.89	15.24	0.55	1.04	3.26	0.32
CS Quality Portfolio	12.55	14.95	0.54	**0.71**	1.68	0.42
ST Quality Portfolio	14.04	15.61	0.61	**2.20**	3.54	0.62

Note: Figures in bold are statistically significant at the 5% level.
Source: GSAM.

TABLE 4.7 Active Return and Risk Decomposition of ST Factor Portfolios

	CW Size	CW Value	CW Momentum	CW Volatility	CW Quality	Alpha	Total Active Risk
ST Size Portfolio						0.85	
Exposure	**0.28**	**0.15**	**(0.22)**	**(0.29)**	(0.01)		
Contribution to Active Risk	0.50	0.16	0.51	0.88	0.01	1.57	3.63
ST Value Portfolio						**1.02**	
Exposure	**0.19**	**0.66**	**-0.14**	0.02	**-0.07**		
Contribution to Active Risk	0.26	2.16	0.48	0.03	0.10	0.73	3.76
ST Momentum Portfolio						**0.69**	
Exposure	**0.39**	**-0.10**	**0.81**	**-0.09**	0.01		
Contribution to Active Risk	0.16	0.19	3.74	0.15	0.01	0.79	5.04
ST Volatility Portfolio						0.45	
Exposure	**0.13**	**0.09**	0.02	**0.92**	**-0.07**		
Contribution to Active Risk	-0.06	0.12	-0.01	5.26	0.01	0.63	5.94
ST Quality Portfolio						**0.79**	
Exposure	**0.44**	0.07	**-0.06**	-0.03	**0.91**		
Contribution to Active Risk	0.35	-0.04	0.00	0.02	1.92	1.29	3.54

Note: Figures in bold are statistically significant at the 5% level.
Source: GSAM.

ST factor portfolio had the highest exposure to, as well as the highest contribution to active risk from, the corresponding CW factor portfolio. All ST factor portfolios generated a positive alpha, with the alpha for value, momentum, and quality achieving statistical significance. Compared to CS factor portfolios (Table 4.5), the ST factor portfolios produced much higher alphas and a higher proportion of active risk was explained by the alpha terms. These results indicate that ST portfolios, in general, achieve higher efficiency in factor capture compared to CW and CS portfolios. This result confirms that weighting schemes that make active weights only a function of factor attractiveness, and not capitalization weights, generally tend to deliver a more efficient factor capture than capitalization-scaled factor tilts.

D. Signal Weighting

The SW factor portfolios are created using a methodology in which factor scores, scaled from 0 to + 1, are used to weight the benchmark universe of constituents. The weight of a constituent is calculated by dividing the constituent factor score by the sum of factor scores across all constituents in the universe (please refer to Appendix 4.1 for more details). In Table 4.8, we report the performance of SW factor portfolios, and compare the performance to CW, CS, and ST factor portfolios. All SW factor portfolios outperformed the Russell 1000 Index and generated active returns that were statistically significant for all factors, except size. The SW factor portfolios produced similar or higher information ratios than the other factor portfolios, except for quality.

The higher efficiency of SW factor portfolios against the CW portfolios is further highlighted by an active return and risk decomposition analysis presented in Table 4.9. All the SW factor portfolios generated large and statistically significant alphas and a high proportion of active risk was explained by the alpha terms, except

TABLE 4.8 Historical Performance of CW, CS, ST, and SW Factor Portfolios

	Total Gross Return (%)	Total Risk (%)	Sharpe Ratio	Active Gross Return (%)	Active Risk (%)	Information Ratio
Russell 1000 Index	11.84	15.05	0.49			
CW Size Portfolio	12.69	16.17	0.52	0.85	3.52	0.24
ST Size Portfolio	12.72	16.49	0.51	0.88	3.63	0.24
SW Size Portfolio	14.06	18.62	0.54	2.22	7.45	0.30
CW Value Portfolio	13.45	15.05	0.59	**1.60**	3.80	0.42
CS Value Portfolio	13.15	15.05	0.57	**1.31**	2.81	0.47
ST Value Portfolio	13.84	15.31	0.60	**2.00**	3.76	0.53
SW Value Portfolio	15.20	17.07	0.63	**3.36**	6.51	0.52
CW Momentum Portfolio	12.92	16.09	0.53	1.08	5.33	0.20
CS Momentum Portfolio	12.61	15.43	0.53	0.77	2.97	0.26
ST Momentum Portfolio	13.58	16.62	0.56	**1.74**	5.04	0.34
SW Momentum Portfolio	14.75	16.75	0.61	**2.91**	4.86	0.60
CW Volatility Portfolio	12.19	12.15	0.60	0.35	6.10	0.06
CS Volatility Portfolio	12.23	13.24	0.57	0.39	3.25	0.12
ST Volatility Portfolio	12.86	11.69	0.67	1.01	5.94	0.17
SW Volatility Portfolio	14.30	14.17	0.67	**2.46**	5.14	0.48
CW Quality Portfolio	12.89	15.24	0.55	1.04	3.26	0.32
CS Quality Portfolio	12.55	14.95	0.54	**0.71**	1.68	0.42
ST Quality Portfolio	14.04	15.61	0.61	**2.20**	3.54	0.62
SW Quality Portfolio	14.68	17.20	0.60	**2.84**	5.29	0.54

Note: Figures in bold are statistically significant at the 5% level.
Source: GSAM.

TABLE 4.9 Active Return and Risk Decomposition of SW Factor Portfolios

	CW Size	CW Value	CW Momentum	CW Volatility	CW Quality	Alpha	Total Active Risk
SW Size Portfolio						**1.46**	
Exposure	**1.26**	**0.29**	**-0.33**	**-0.43**	0.00		
Contribution to Active Risk	3.38	0.36	0.70	1.15	0.00	1.86	7.45
SW Value Portfolio						**1.85**	
Exposure	**1.05**	**0.69**	**-0.26**	**-0.09**	-0.04		
Contribution to Active Risk	2.73	1.69	0.77	0.05	0.06	1.21	6.51
SW Momentum Portfolio						**1.33**	
Exposure	**1.15**	0.04	**0.46**	-0.07	0.03		
Contribution to Active Risk	3.06	-0.01	0.85	0.14	-0.01	0.84	4.86
SW Volatility Portfolio						**0.95**	
Exposure	**1.01**	**0.26**	-0.04	**0.54**	0.01		
Contribution to Active Risk	2.09	0.55	0.07	1.73	-0.01	0.71	5.14
SW Quality Portfolio						**1.28**	
Exposure	**1.18**	**0.23**	**-0.14**	**-0.21**	**0.45**		
Contribution to Active Risk	3.41	0.21	0.22	0.46	-0.12	1.11	5.29

Note: Figures in bold are statistically significant at the 5% level.
Source: GSAM.

for momentum and volatility. We also note that all the SW factor portfolios, except size, had the highest exposure to the CW size portfolio, and not to the corresponding CW factor portfolio. For instance, the SW momentum portfolio had a higher exposure to the CW size portfolio than to the CW momentum portfolio. Additionally, at least 40% of the active risk of the SW factor portfolios was explained by the CW size portfolio. And in all cases, except size, a higher proportion of the active risk of the SW portfolios was explained by the CW size portfolio than by the corresponding CW factor portfolio.

The much higher efficiency in factor capture achieved by SW factor portfolios in Table 4.9 is somewhat surprising. This result, however, can be explained as follows. The signal weighting scheme is actually equivalent to starting with an EW universe and then tilting by the factor under consideration. This is shown graphically in Figure 4.4. For example, the SW value portfolio is a combination of an EW universe plus a value tilt. Similarly, the weighting scheme of MSCI Risk-Weighted Indexes is equivalent to starting with the EW MSCI parent universe and then tilting by the inverse of historical volatility. This explains why SW factor portfolios had such a high and significant exposure to the CW size portfolio in Table 4.9.

FIGURE 4.4 Total Weight Profile of SW Factor Portfolios

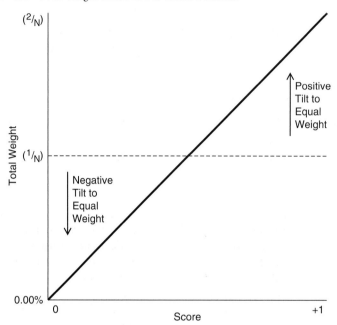

The performance of the EW Russell 1000 portfolio is shown in Table 4.10. This portfolio produced an active return of 1.71% per annum, which was statistically significant, and a higher Sharpe ratio than the Russell 1000 Index as well as an information ratio in excess of 0.3. The performance of the EW Russell 1000 portfolio is also not fully explained by the CW factor portfolios, as depicted in the risk decomposition analysis in Table 4.11. Indeed, we find a statistically significant alpha of

TABLE 4.10 Historical Performance of EW Russell 1000 Portfolio

	Total Gross Return (%)	Total Risk (%)	Sharpe Ratio	Active Gross Return (%)	Active Risk (%)	Information Ratio
Russell 1000 Index	11.84	15.05	0.49			
EW Russell 1000 Portfolio	13.55	17.23	0.54	**1.71**	5.22	0.33

Note: Figures in bold are statistically significant at the 5% level.
Source: GSAM.

TABLE 4.11 Active Return and Risk Decomposition of EW Russell 1000 Portfolio

	CW Size	CW Value	CW Momentum	CW Volatility	CW Quality	Alpha	Total Active Risk
EW Russell 1000 Portfolio						**0.90**	
Exposure	**1.06**	**0.18**	**(0.17)**	**(0.23)**	0.00		
Contribution to Active Risk	3.18	0.23	0.34	0.56	0.00	0.91	5.22

Note: Figures in bold are statistically significant at the 5% level.
Source: GSAM.

0.90%. Additionally, the EW Russell 1000 portfolio did have the highest exposure to the CW size portfolio, but only 60% (3.18/5.22) of the active risk of the EW Russell 1000 portfolio was explained by the CW size portfolio. This result may also imply that the EW Russell 1000 portfolio potentially has nonlinear size distribution properties that are not fully captured by the CW (or the ST) size portfolios.

The performance of the EW Russell 1000 portfolio largely explains the superior performance of the SW factor portfolios reported in Table 4.8 and the statistically significant alphas generated by the SW factor portfolios against the CW factor portfolios in Table 4.9. Since signal weighting essentially implements factor tilts relative to an EW universe, we could decompose the performance of SW factor portfolios against an EW Russell 1000 portfolio (substituting for the CW or ST size portfolio) and the ST value, momentum, volatility, and quality portfolios. This active return and risk decomposition is shown in Table 4.12. We note that all the SW factor portfolios had high exposures to the EW Russell 1000 portfolio and at least 50% of the active risk of SW factor portfolios was explained by the EW Russell 1000 portfolio, except for volatility. The large and statistically significant alphas reported against the CW factor portfolios have now disappeared. All the alphas in Table 4.12 were close to zero and no more than 8% of the active risk of SW factor portfolios was attributable to the alpha terms. The performance of SW factor portfolios was almost fully explained by a combination of the EW Russell 1000 portfolio and the ST factor portfolios.

E. Equal Weighting

We create the EW factor portfolios using the construction methodology outlined in Table 4.2. The historical performance of EW factor portfolios is depicted in Table 4.13, which also reproduces the performance of CW, CS, ST, and SW factor portfolios to facilitate comparisons. All EW factor portfolios outperformed the Russell 1000 benchmark and also generated higher Sharpe ratios as well as information ratios of around 0.3 or higher. The active returns of EW factor portfolios were

TABLE 4.12 Active Return and Risk Decomposition of SW Portfolios Against the EW Russell 1000 Portfolio and ST Factor Portfolios

	EW Russell 1000	ST Value	ST Momentum	ST Volatility	ST Quality	Alpha	Total Active Risk
SW Size Portfolio						-0.02	
Exposure	**1.32**	**0.10**	-0.07	-0.11	**0.06**		
Contribution to Active Risk	6.79	0.20	0.02	0.21	0.06	0.17	7.45
SW Value Portfolio						0.13	
Exposure	**0.76**	**0.91**	0.01	**0.05**	**0.03**		
Contribution to Active Risk	3.48	2.94	-0.01	0.01	0.02	0.08	6.51
SW Momentum Portfolio						0.33	
Exposure	**0.72**	-0.06	**0.69**	**0.15**	0.00		
Contribution to Active Risk	2.50	-0.01	2.30	-0.21	0.00	0.27	4.86
SW Volatility Portfolio						-0.06	
Exposure	**0.64**	**0.17**	**0.09**	**0.70**	0.03		
Contribution to Active Risk	1.71	0.42	-0.10	2.66	0.01	0.44	5.14
SW Quality Portfolio						0.13	
Exposure	**0.81**	0.09	**0.06**	-0.03	**0.47**		
Contribution to Active Risk	3.97	0.16	0.01	0.04	0.92	0.18	5.29

Note: Figures in bold are statistically significant at the 5% level.
Source: GSAM.

statistically significant, except for size. EW factor portfolios generated higher information ratios compared to CW and CS portfolios as well as ST portfolios, except for quality. Overall, the performance of EW factor portfolios was similar to SW factor portfolios and generally much better than the CW, CS, and ST portfolios.

Similar to SW factor portfolios, the EW portfolios generated large alphas in a risk decomposition against the CW factor portfolios. This is reported in Table 4.14. All the alphas were large and statistically significant, except for size.

The superior performance of EW factor portfolios that we document has also been reported by Blitz (2017). In his article, Blitz (2017) argues that many studies, such as Fama French (2012), De Groot and Huij (2011), and Asness et al. (2015), show that smart beta factors tend to deliver higher premiums within the small cap segment

TABLE 4.13 Historical Performance of CW, CS, ST, SW, and EW Factor Portfolios

	Total Gross Return (%)	Total Risk (%)	Sharpe Ratio	Active Gross Return (%)	Active Risk (%)	Information Ratio
Russell 1000 Index	11.84	15.05	0.49			
CW Size Portfolio	12.69	16.17	0.52	0.85	3.52	0.24
ST Size Portfolio	12.72	16.49	0.51	0.88	3.63	0.24
SW Size Portfolio	14.06	18.62	0.54	2.22	7.45	0.30
EW Size Portfolio	14.21	19.23	0.53	2.37	8.30	0.29
CW Value Portfolio	13.45	15.05	0.59	**1.60**	3.80	0.42
CS Value Portfolio	13.15	15.05	0.57	**1.31**	2.81	0.47
ST Value Portfolio	13.84	15.31	0.60	**2.00**	3.76	0.53
SW Value Portfolio	15.20	17.07	0.63	**3.36**	6.51	0.52
EW Value Portfolio	15.94	17.28	0.66	**4.09**	7.50	0.55
CW Momentum Portfolio	12.92	16.09	0.53	1.08	5.33	0.20
CS Momentum Portfolio	12.61	15.43	0.53	0.77	2.97	0.26
ST Momentum Portfolio	13.58	16.62	0.56	**1.74**	5.04	0.34
SW Momentum Portfolio	14.75	16.75	0.61	**2.91**	4.86	0.60
EW Momentum Portfolio	14.78	17.08	0.61	**2.94**	5.73	0.51
CW Volatility Portfolio	12.19	12.15	0.60	0.35	6.10	0.06
CS Volatility Portfolio	12.23	13.24	0.57	0.39	3.25	0.12
ST Volatility Portfolio	12.86	11.69	0.67	1.01	5.94	0.17
SW Volatility Portfolio	14.30	14.17	0.67	**2.46**	5.14	0.48
EW Volatility Portfolio	14.70	13.52	0.72	**2.86**	6.38	0.45
CW Quality Portfolio	12.89	15.24	0.55	1.04	3.26	0.32
CS Quality Portfolio	12.55	14.95	0.54	**0.71**	1.68	0.42
ST Quality Portfolio	14.04	15.61	0.61	**2.20**	3.54	0.62
SW Quality Portfolio	14.68	17.20	0.60	**2.84**	5.29	0.54
EW Quality Portfolio	15.07	17.60	0.61	**2.94**	5.73	0.51

Note: Figures in bold are statistically significant at the 5% level.
Source: GSAM.

TABLE 4.14 Active Return and Risk Decomposition of EW Factor Portfolios

	CW Size	CW Value	CW Momentum	CW Volatility	CW Quality	Alpha	Total Active Risk
EW Size Portfolio						1.50	
Exposure	**1.33**	**0.38**	**(0.34)**	**(0.03)**	(0.01)		
Contribution to Active Risk	3.43	0.48	0.72	1.21	0.01	2.46	8.30
EW Value Portfolio						**2.16**	
Exposure	**1.06**	**0.96**	**-0.27**	-0.03	-0.05		
Contribution to Active Risk	2.47	2.61	0.80	0.00	0.08	1.55	7.50
EW Momentum Portfolio						**1.13**	
Exposure	**1.14**	-0.01	**0.74**	-0.03	0.01		
Contribution to Active Risk	2.31	0.01	2.23	0.05	0.00	1.13	5.73
EW Volatility Portfolio						**1.08**	
Exposure	**1.02**	**0.30**	-0.01	**0.82**	0.07		
Contribution to Active Risk	1.48	0.61	0.02	3.53	-0.04	0.77	6.38
EW Quality Portfolio						**1.28**	
Exposure	**1.24**	**0.26**	-0.14	**-0.25**	**0.73**		
Contribution to Active Risk	3.29	0.17	0.19	0.54	0.14	1.46	5.78

Note: Figures in bold are statistically significant at the 5% level.
Source: GSAM.

of the market. For instance, the value premium tends to be stronger for small cap stocks compared to large cap stocks. These findings led Blitz (2017) to conclude that in capturing smart beta factors a small-cap tilt may be necessary "to unlock the full potential of these factor premiums."

We provide a different perspective for explaining the superior performance of EW factor portfolios. Similar to SW factor portfolios, the weighting scheme of EW portfolios is also equivalent to starting with an EW benchmark universe and then tilting by the considered factor. This is shown graphically in Figure 4.5.

The performance of the EW factor portfolios, therefore, can also be analyzed against the EW Russell 1000 portfolio and ST value, momentum, volatility, and quality portfolios, as shown in Table 4.15. The combination of the EW Russell 1000 portfolio and the ST factor portfolios almost fully explained the performance of the EW factor portfolios. The alphas for all the EW factor portfolios were close to zero and significantly smaller than those reported in Table 4.14 against the CW factor portfolios. Additionally, the proportion of active risk explained by alpha was no more than about 10%.

FIGURE 4.5   Total Weight Profile of EW Factor Portfolios

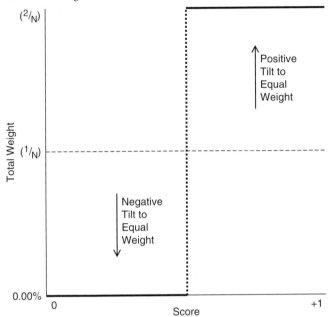

F. Summary

The important insights we gain through the analysis of various weighting schemes can be summarized as follows:

- All CW factor portfolios generated positive active returns relative to the Russell 1000 Index, but these active returns were generally not statistically significant.
- All CS factor portfolios produced only marginal improvement in IRs and modest alphas compared to CW factor portfolios.
- All ST factor portfolios achieved similar or higher information ratios compared to CW and CS portfolios. They also generated larger positive alphas, which were significant for value, momentum, and quality, in a risk decomposition analysis against the CW factor portfolios.
- The active returns of the SW and EW factor portfolios have a common component; the active return of the EW Russell 1000 portfolio over the CW Russell 1000 Index.
- The significant outperformance of the SW and EW factor portfolios relative to the CW Russell 1000 Index was largely explained by the outperformance of the EW Russell 1000 portfolio over the CW Russell 1000 Index.

TABLE 4.15 Active Return and Risk Decomposition of EW Factor Portfolios Against the EW Russell 1000 Portfolio and ST-Factor Portfolios

	EW Russell 1000	ST Value	ST Momentum	ST Volatility	ST Quality	Alpha	Total Active Risk
EW Size Portfolio						-0.26	
Exposure	**1.40**	**0.21**	(0.04)	**(0.13)**	**0.08**		
Contribution to Active Risk	7.08	0.44	0.02	0.24	0.09	0.44	8.30
EW Value Portfolio						0.10	
Exposure	**0.64**	**1.35**	**0.04**	**0.06**	**0.05**		
Contribution to Active Risk	2.67	4.63	-0.08	0.04	0.02	0.22	7.50
EW Momentum Portfolio						0.12	
Exposure	**0.59**	-0.07	**0.98**	**0.18**	-0.02		
Contribution to Active Risk	1.32	0.04	4.05	-0.22	-0.02	0.55	5.73
EW Volatility Portfolio						0.03	
Exposure	**0.52**	**0.25**	**0.10**	**0.94**	**0.09**		
Contribution to Active Risk	0.75	0.56	-0.13	4.40	0.03	0.77	6.38
EW Quality Portfolio						0.26	
Exposure	**0.78**	0.04	**0.04**	-0.07	**0.71**		
Contribution to Active Risk	3.49	0.06	0.02	0.12	1.62	0.47	5.78

Note: Figures in bold are statistically significant at the 5% level.
Source: GSAM.

- The performance of the EW Russell 1000 portfolio was not fully explained by the CW factor portfolios, as a positive and statistically significant alpha was generated, which largely explains the positive and significant alphas also generated by the SW and EW factor portfolios against the CW factor portfolios.
- The SW and EW factor portfolios can be viewed as a combination of the EW Russell 1000 portfolio and purer signal tilts delivered by the ST factor portfolios. Against this combination, the performance of SW and EW factor portfolios was almost fully explained, with no significant alpha.

IV.   TYPICAL INVESTOR QUESTIONS

4.1 How Should Investors Analyze and Compare the Performance of Various Smart Beta Strategies?

Many investors simply compare the excess or active returns of various strategies relative to a given benchmark. This is often not a meaningful comparison. To the extent that smart beta strategies have different total or active risk levels, comparing Sharpe ratios and/or information ratios may be more meaningful. However, in comparing Sharpe ratios and/or information ratios, it is also important to recognize that statistical significance in differences is difficult to realize. For instance, ST, SW, and EW smart beta factor portfolios generated higher information ratios compared to CW and CS factor portfolios, as shown in Table 4.13. The difference in information ratios, however, was not statistically significant, even in cases where the increase in information ratios was 100% or more. This highlights that the active return differences between the various factor portfolios are not large enough, given the significant variation in active returns between the various approaches, to make the differences in information ratios significant.

An active return and risk decomposition is a more insightful method for comparing the efficiency in factor capture of various smart beta strategies compared to a simple historical performance comparison. Consider the following example. The statistics in Table 4.16 suggest that the CW and ST size portfolios are similar strategies because they had almost identical performance.

However, the risk decomposition in Table 4.17 highlights that the ST size portfolio had a modest exposure to the CW size portfolio and only 14% (0.50/3.63) of

TABLE 4.16 Historical Performance of CW and ST Size Portfolios

	Total Gross Return (%)	Total Risk (%)	Sharpe Ratio	Active Gross Return (%)	Active Risk (%)	Information Ratio
Russell 1000 Index	11.84	15.05	0.49			
CW Size Portfolio	12.69	16.17	0.52	0.85	3.52	0.24
ST Size Portfolio	12.72	16.49	0.51	0.88	3.63	0.24

Note: Figures in bold are statistically significant at the 5% level.
Source: GSAM.

TABLE 4.17 Active Return and Risk Decomposition of ST Size Portfolio

	CW Size	CW Value	CW Momentum	CW Volatility	CW Quality	Alpha	Total Active Risk
ST Size Portfolio						0.85	
Exposure	**0.28**	**0.15**	**(0.22)**	**(0.29)**	(0.01)		
Contribution to Active Risk	0.50	0.16	0.51	0.88	0.01	1.57	3.63

Note: Figures in bold are statistically significant at the 5% level.
Source: GSAM.

the ST size portfolio's active risk was explained by the CW size portfolio. In addition, the ST size portfolio generated a positive alpha, approaching statistical significance with a t-stat of 1.90, which was almost as large as the ST size portfolio's active return relative to the Russell 1000 Index (Table 4.16). Also, 43% of the ST size portfolio's active risk was explained by the alpha term, or conversely unexplained by the CW factor portfolios. Clearly, it would be quite misleading to conclude, based on a simple historical performance comparison, that CW and ST size portfolios are identical strategies. They are not. They have very different factor exposures and, hence, performance patterns. In fact, the tracking error between the CW and ST size portfolios was 3.5% over the analysis period, despite the superficial similarity in performance depicted in Table 4.16. This is the reason why most academic studies use some form of a risk decomposition analysis to better understand the factor exposures and explain the performance of a given strategy. In general, the alpha generated in a risk decomposition exercise and its source, magnitude, statistical significance, and active risk contribution are a better indicator of the efficiency of a strategy.

4.2 Is a Capitalization-Weighted Parent Universe an Appropriate Performance Benchmark for Various Smart Beta Strategies?

For some weighting schemes that seek to implement factor tilts relative to benchmark capitalization weights, such as CW, CS, ST, and active risk constrained-optimized, the capitalization weighted universe is the appropriate performance benchmark. For other weighting schemes, such as EW and SW as well as some active risk unconstrained-optimized, the equal-weighted universe is a more appropriate benchmark. Recall that EW, SW, and active risk unconstrained optimized weighting schemes are equivalent to an equal-weighted universe plus a factor tilt. Therefore, analyzing their performance relative to a capitalization-weighted universe could be misleading.

To further elaborate this point, consider that the active return of an EW or SW factor portfolio relative to a capitalization-weighted benchmark universe can be decomposed into two components: (1) active return of an EW universe over the CW universe and (2) active return of the EW or SW factor portfolio over the EW universe. For instance, the active return of the EW momentum portfolio relative to the CW Russell 1000 Index is the sum of (1) the active return of EW Russell 1000 portfolio over the CW Russell 1000 Index and (2) the active return of the EW momentum portfolio over the EW Russell 1000 portfolio. Table 4.18 shows this breakdown of the active return of the EW and SW factor portfolios into the two components. Panel A shows the performance of the EW Russell 1000 portfolio relative to the CW Russell 1000 benchmark. Over the analysis period, the EW Russell 1000 portfolio outperformed by 1.71% per annum. Panel B shows the performance of the EW factor portfolios relative to the EW Russell 1000 portfolio. All EW factor portfolios delivered outperformance relative to the EW Russell 1000 portfolio and two of them, value and quality, achieved statistical significance. Using the EW momentum portfolio as an example, we can see that the total active return of 2.94%

in Table 4.13 against the CW Russell 1000 actually consists of the active return (1.71%) of the EW Russell 1000 portfolio over the CW Russell 1000 Index and the active return (1.23%) of the EW momentum portfolio over the EW Russell 1000 portfolio (i.e. 1.71% + 1.23% = 2.94%). The significant outperformance of EW and SW factor portfolios relative to the CW Russell 1000 Index in Table 4.13, therefore, is largely due to one common component, the outperformance of the EW Russell 1000 portfolio.

If the objective is to determine the efficiency with which SW or EW factor portfolios deliver factor tilts, then their performance should be compared to an EW benchmark universe, as the factor tilts in these weighting schemes are implemented relative to this universe. A comparison of Table 4.6 and Table 4.18 highlights that ST factor portfolios generated similar or higher IRs against the CW Russell 1000 Index than did the SW and EW factor portfolios against the EW Russell 1000 portfolio. Additionally, the SW and EW factor portfolios generated no alpha when decomposed relative to the EW Russell 1000 portfolio and ST factor portfolios. Therefore, the

TABLE 4.18 Historical Performance of EW Universe and EW and SW Factor Portfolios

	Total Gross Return (%)	Total Risk (%)	Sharpe Ratio	Active Gross Return (%)	Active Risk (%)	Information Ratio
PANEL A						
Russell 1000 Index	11.84	15.05	0.49			
EW Russell 1000 Portfolio	13.55	17.23	0.54	1.71	5.22	0.33
PANEL B						
EW Russell 1000 Portfolio	13.55	17.23	0.54			
EW Size Portfolio	14.21	19.23	0.53	0.67	3.49	0.19
EW Value Portfolio	15.94	17.28	0.66	**2.39**	4.55	0.52
EW Momentum Portfolio	14.78	17.08	0.61	1.23	5.86	0.21
EW Volatility Portfolio	14.70	13.52	0.72	1.16	7.01	0.16
EW Quality Portfolio	15.07	17.60	0.61	**1.53**	2.97	0.51
PANEL C						
EW Russell 1000 Portfolio	13.55	17.23	0.54			
SW Size Portfolio	14.06	18.62	0.54	0.51	2.49	0.20
SW Value Portfolio	15.20	17.07	0.63	**1.66**	3.11	0.53
SW Momentum Portfolio	14.75	16.75	0.61	1.20	4.10	0.29
SW Volatility Portfolio	14.30	14.17	0.67	0.75	5.13	0.15
SW Quality Portfolio	14.68	17.20	0.60	**1.13**	1.89	0.60

Note: Figures in bold are statistically significant at the 5% level.
Source: GSAM.

assertion that EW factor portfolios deliver higher efficiency because a small cap bias is needed to unlock the full potential of smart beta factors (Blitz 2017) is not correct. EW factor portfolios only depict higher efficiency because they are being compared to the wrong benchmark (a capitalization-weighted, as opposed to an equal-weighted, benchmark).

4.3 Are There Portfolio Construction Methodologies That May Be Viewed as Somewhat Inconsistent with What Theory Tells Us About Factor Investing?

Concentrated factor portfolios would be one example of a construction methodology that has become the subject of some debate in the industry.

Some analysts, such as Amenc et al. (2016), argue that the need for broad diversification in capturing factor returns is well-documented and well-accepted in the literature. Smart beta providers sometimes ignore this essential characteristic of factor investing in designing their offerings. For example, we have recently seen the launch of "enhanced" or "strong" factor indexes. These are highly concentrated portfolios that seek to achieve a high exposure to a given factor. The underlying premise behind such products is that, if factors work, then having a high exposure to the factor would deliver much higher returns. The high exposure is achieved by concentrating the portfolio in the highest ranked stocks on a given factor, such as investing in the top 20% of stocks ranked on value. It is true that, all else being equal, a higher exposure to a rewarded factor should lead to higher return. However, in practice, it depends on how the higher exposure is obtained. At one extreme, we could have the highest possible exposure to a given factor by investing in a single stock that ranks most attractively on that factor. In this case, the high exposure would be realized largely through stock-specific risk, which theory tells us is diversifiable and, hence, not rewarded. Even when multiple stocks are held, in some cases, the high exposure to the factor may come with significant sector or country bets. For instance, at the start of 2017, a concentrated, public momentum index had a 15% overweight in the Information Technology sector for the US index and an 18% overweight in the US plus a 15% underweight in Japan in the global index.

Proponents of concentrated factor portfolios, on the other hand, point out that diversification theory would suggest that investing in 20% of the universe might be enough to achieve adequate diversification, as uncorrelated idiosyncratic risk would be substantially reduced. Additionally, investing in the concentrated factor portfolios typically achieves the same level of IR as more diversified factor portfolios. This suggests that the potential unrewarded risks assumed are offset by the improvement in return from the increased factor exposure. As such, for capital-constrained investors, concentrated factor portfolios may offer an interesting opportunity.

In our opinion, concentrated factor portfolios are not ideal, but may represent an option for capital-constrained investors with a specific return requirement. However, such implementations should be approached with caution. The level of stock-specific, sector, or country risk assumed should be carefully assessed, and it should be well understood that such portfolios may depict high turnover, high implementation costs, and lower capacity.

V. CONCLUSION

Various smart beta offerings use weighting schemes that can be characterized as either tilting from benchmark capitalization weights or reweighting benchmark constituents away from capitalization weights. When factor tilts are implemented relative to the CW benchmark universe (e.g. Russell 1000 Index), ST factor portfolios generally deliver higher efficiency compared to CW and CS factor portfolios. When benchmark constituents are reweighted using weighting schemes, such as signal weighting and equal weighting, factor tilts are implemented relative to the EW parent universe. The performance of these weighting schemes should be assessed against the EW universe (e.g. Russell 1000 Equal Weight Index). In a risk decomposition analysis, the performance of these weighting schemes is explained by a combination of the EW parent universe and ST factor portfolios.

In the next chapter, we turn our focus to differences in smart beta offerings that could arise from various signal specifications used. We also discuss the pros and cons of potential adjustments or tweaks that are sometimes made to standard factor definitions.

APPENDIX 4.1: CONSTITUENT WEIGHTS IN VARIOUS FACTOR PORTFOLIOS

Capitalization Weighting

The process of creating CW factor portfolios entails three broad steps. First, constituents in a given parent universe are ranked on factor signals. Second, the highest-ranked constituents that cumulatively cover a certain percentage of the market capitalization of the parent universe are selected for inclusion in the portfolio. Third, the selected constituents are weighted by their market capitalization. In this methodology, constituent selection is based on factor ranks, while constituent weighting is based on market capitalization. This construction weakens the link between factor ranks and constituent weights. Among the selected constituents, large capitalization stocks will have a higher weight in the factor portfolio, irrespective of their factor ranks. More formally, the total weight (TW) and active weight (AW) of constituent i in a CW factor index are given by:

$$TW_i = \left(Cap_i / \left(\sum (Cap_i)\right)\right) * (1/p) = CapW_i * (1/p) \qquad (4.1)$$

$$AW_i = CapW_i * ((1/p) - 1) \qquad (4.2)$$

Where:

Cap_i = Market capitalization of constituent i

$\sum (Cap_i)$ = Sum of market capitalizations of all constituents in the parent index

p = Proportion of market capitalization of the parent index covered by the factor portfolio

$CapW_i$ = Capitalization weight of constituent i in the parent index

For a CW factor portfolio that covers 50% of the market capitalization of the parent index (p = 0.50), Equation (4.1) implies that the total weight of constituents will equal twice their capitalization weights in the parent index, while the active weight of constituents (Equation 4.2) will equal their capitalization weights in the parent index. This implies that the constituent active weights are only a function of capitalization weights in the parent index, and not a function of factor ranks or strength of the factor signal. This construct, therefore, results in potential lack of purity and efficiency of factor capture.

Capitalization Scaling

In order to improve the relation between active weights and factor signals or ranks, capitalization scaled (CS) weighting is typically employed. In this weighting scheme, capitalization weights are multiplied by factor scores to determine the total weight of constituents. More generally, the total weight and active weight of constituent i in a CS factor portfolio are defined as:

$$TW_i = CapW_i * S_{i,j} \qquad (4.3)$$
$$AW_i = CapW_i * \left(S_{i,j} - 1\right) \qquad (4.4)$$

Where:

$\qquad CapW_i$ = Capitalization weight of constituent i in the parent index

$\qquad S_{i,j}$ = Score of constituent i based on factor j

Value-weighted indexes and fundamentally weighted indexes are also examples of CS indexes. In the construction of value-weighted indexes, first a factor signal is specified, for example, book value-to-price (BP) for value. Then, the capitalization weights of constituents in a given universe are scaled (i.e. increased or decreased) by the ratio of a constituent's book value-to-price ratio (BP_i) to the market's book value-to-price ratio (BP_m). Thus, the total weight (TW) and active weight (AW) of constituent i in a BP CS factor portfolio are given by:

$$TW_i = CapW_i * \left(BP_i / BP_m\right) \qquad (4.5)$$
$$AW_i = CapW_i * ((BP_i / BP_m) - 1) \qquad (4.6)$$

Through the cancellation of terms, Equation (4.5) also reduces to the ratio of a constituent's book value to the market's book value, which equates to a book value-weighted construction scheme. Therefore, fundamentally weighted indexes are also a form of CS value indexes.

In a CS factor portfolio, as Equation (4.6) shows, a constituent with the same BP ratio as the market will have an active weight of zero, while the active weights of constituents with higher (lower) BP ratios than the market will be scaled up (down) relative to their capitalization weights in the parent index. As such, CS factor portfolios improve the relation between factor attractiveness and active weights compared to CW factor portfolios. However, the relation between factor signal and active weights is still not exact, as active weights remain a function of capitalization weights in the parent index. For example, two constituents with the same BP ratio can have different weights in the CS factor portfolio, if their capitalization weights in the parent index are different. More specifically, larger companies will receive a higher active weight.

Signal Tilting

In our construction, the basic objective of ST portfolios is to achieve better purity and efficiency in factor capture at given levels of active risk relative to a specified benchmark. This objective is achieved through a weighting scheme that establishes a linearly proportional relationship between factor signals, scaled between −1 and +1, and active weights of constituents in the ST portfolios, subject to the long-only constraint. Indeed, for long-only portfolios, a direct relationship between factor scores and constituent active weights can only be achieved on the overweight side, but not on the underweights. The long-only constraint imposes a benchmark weight limit on the maximum underweight that can actually be achieved in a given constituent. Therefore, for building ST portfolios, the construction process first determines the total underweight position that can actually be achieved, given the long-only constraint, and then allocates the total underweight position to the overweight side in proportion to constituent scores. This is achieved as follows.

A Cut-Off score for underweighting and overweighting securities as well as a Maximum Stock Underweight Position is specified. For example, a Cut-Off score of 0 implies that all constituents with scores less than 0 will be underweighted relative to their benchmark weights and constituents with scores greater than 0 will be overweighted. In the case of the Russell 1000 universe, a Cut-Off score of 0 means that 500 stocks will be underweighted and 500 stocks overweighted. The Maximum Stock Underweight Position determines by how much the most unattractive constituent would be underweighted. A Maximum Stock Underweight Position (MaxUW) of 1% implies that the constituent with a score of −1 will be underweighted by 1% relative to its benchmark weight (CapW$_i$). A constituent with a score of −0.5 would be underweighted by 0.5% and so on. However, given the long-only constraint, the underweight that is actually achieved for constituents with scores (S$_i$) less than the Cut-Off score is given by:

$$\text{UnderWgt}_i = \text{Max}\left(S_i * \text{MaxUW}, - \text{CapW}_i\right) \tag{4.7}$$

Once the actual underweight achieved for each constituent is calculated, these underweights are summed up to determine the Total Underweight Position ($\sum$ UnderWgt$_i$) for the factor portfolio. The Total Underweight Position is then allocated to overweight all stocks with a score greater than the Cut-Off score, in proportion to their scores, using the following formula.

$$\text{OverWgt}_i = \left(S_i / \sum S_i\right) * \sum \text{UnderWgt}_i \tag{4.8}$$

As Equations (4.7) and (4.8) highlight, the active weights of constituents in ST portfolios are directly related to factor scores, subject to the long-only constraint. Unlike CW (Equation 4.2) and CS (Equation 4.4) factor portfolios, these active weights are independent of the benchmark weights of constituents in the parent index, except for the long-only constraint. Assuming linearity in factor signal payoff, these relationships should improve the purity and efficiency of factor tilts in the ST factor portfolios. Once the active weight is determined, the total weight of constituent *i* is calculated as follows:

$$TW_i = CapW_i - UnderWgt_{i,} \text{ or} \qquad\qquad (4.9)$$

$$TW_i = CapW_i + OverWgt_i \qquad\qquad (4.10)$$

The active risk of ST portfolios may be controlled by varying the Cut-Off score and the Maximum Stock Underweight Position. These two parameters jointly determine the Total Underweight Position, or active share of the factor portfolio, and, hence, its active risk relative to the parent benchmark. For illustrative purposes, Figure 4.6 shows two portfolios constructed using a different set of values for these

FIGURE .4.6   Active Weight Profiles of Illustrative Portfolios

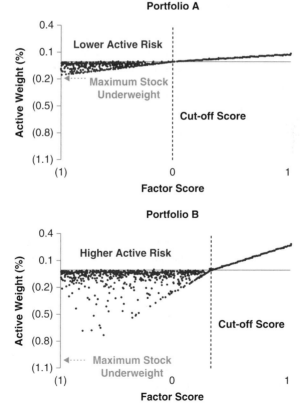

two parameters. Portfolio B uses a higher Cut-Off score and a larger Maximum Stock Underweight Position and, therefore, has a higher active risk compared to Portfolio A.

Signal Weighting

In a SW factor portfolio, benchmark constituents are reweighted by the factor score. Typically, factor scores are scaled between 0 and +1. The total weight and active weight of constituent i in a SW factor portfolio are calculated as:

$$TW_i = (Si,j / (\sum (S_{i,j}))) \tag{4.11}$$

$$AW_i = (S_{i,j} / (\sum (S_{i,j}))) - CapW_i \tag{4.12}$$

Where:

$$
\begin{aligned}
S_{i,j} &= \text{Score of constituent } i \text{ based on factor } j \\
\sum (S_{i,j}) &= \text{Sum of scores of all constituents based on factor } j \\
CapW_i &= \text{Capitalization weight of constituent } i \text{ in the parent index}
\end{aligned}
$$

In SW construction, therefore, total weights of constituents are independent of benchmark capitalization weights, while active weights are not. Risk-weighted indexes offered by index providers constitute an example of SW factor portfolios. In such indexes, the total weight of constituent i is calculated as the ratio of the inverse of constituent variance $(1 / \ell_i^2)$ to the sum of the inverse of variances of all constituents in the benchmark universe $(1 / \sum (\ell^2))$, as shown below:

$$TW_i = (1 / \ell_i^2) / ((1 / \sum (\ell^2)) \tag{4.13}$$

Equal Weighting

EW factor portfolios provide more diversification in factor capture compared to CW or CS factor portfolios. The process of creating EW factor portfolios also entails three steps. First, constituents in a given parent universe are ranked on a factor signal. Second, the highest-ranked constituents that cumulatively cover a certain percentage of the number of names in the parent universe are selected for inclusion in the portfolio. Third, the selected constituents are equal-weighted. In this construct, the total weight (TW) and active weight (AW) of constituent i in an EW factor portfolio are given by:

$$TW_i = (1/p) * (1/N) \tag{4.14}$$

$$AW_i = ((1/p) * 1/N)) - CapW_i \tag{4.15}$$

Where:

> p = Percentage of the parent index names included in the EW factor portfolio
>
> N = Number of names in the parent universe
>
> $CapW_i$ = Capitalization weight of constituent *i* in the parent index

For an EW factor portfolio that covers 50% of the names in the parent universe (p =0.50), Equation (4.15) states that the active weight of constituents will equal 2 / N minus their capitalization weights in the parent index. This implies that, similar to CW and CS factor portfolios, constituent active weights remain a function of capitalization weights in the parent index. However, unlike CW and CS factor portfolios, EW factor portfolios will underweight larger stocks, while overweighting smaller stocks. In summary, therefore, CW and CS factor portfolios introduce a large-cap bias, while EW factor portfolios introduce a small cap bias in factor capture.

APPENDIX 4.2: ACTIVE RETURN AND RISK DECOMPOSITION USING CW AND ST FACTOR PORTFOLIOS

In a Fama-French risk decomposition exercise, the excess returns of a strategy are regressed against the market factor and other Fama-French factors. The market factor in the Fama-French model is the capitalization-weighted market portfolio. The exposure to the market portfolio is centered on one, which is the beta of the market portfolio. The market portfolio is also style-neutral, that is, it has no factor tilts. The Fama-French factor portfolios take long and short positions away from the market. As such, their betas are centered on zero. This means that stocks with betas above (below) zero have positive (negative) exposure to the factors.

The methodology employed to decompose active returns of a strategy against the CW or ST portfolios is similar to the Fama-French risk decomposition framework. It is based on a time-series regression model in which a portfolio's active return (return in excess of the market or benchmark) is regressed against the active returns of the CW or ST portfolios. Since the regression is based on active returns, the beta coefficient or exposures to factor indexes or portfolios are also centered around zero. The regression is specified as follows.

$$\left(R_{Port} - R_{BM}\right) = \alpha_{Port} + \beta_{Value}\left(R_{Value} - R_{BM}\right) + \beta_{Momen}\left(R_{Momen} - R_{BM}\right)$$

$$+ \beta_{Vol}\left(R_{Vol} - R_{BM}\right) + \beta_{Qual}\left(R_{Qual} - R_{BM}\right) + \beta_{Size}\left(R_{Size} - R_{BM}\right) + \varepsilon_{Port}$$

Where

$$
\begin{array}{rl}
R_{Port} - R_{BM} = & \text{Return on the portfolio in excess of the benchmark} \\
R_{Value} - R_{BM} = & \text{Return on the CW or ST value factor portfolio in} \\
& \text{excess of the benchmark} \\
R_{Momen} - R_{BM} = & \text{Return on the CW or ST momentum factor portfolio} \\
& \text{in excess of the benchmark} \\
R_{Vol} - R_{BM} = & \text{Return on the CW or ST volatility factor portfolio in} \\
& \text{excess of the benchmark} \\
R_{Qual} - R_{BM} = & \text{Return on the CW or ST quality factor portfolio in} \\
& \text{excess of the benchmark} \\
R_{Size} - R_{BM} = & \text{Return on the CW or ST size factor portfolio in excess} \\
& \text{of the benchmark} \\
\alpha_{Port} = & \text{Portfolio's alpha (after controlling for the portfolio's} \\
& \text{exposure to factors)} \\
\beta_{Factor} = & \text{Factor loadings for the CW or ST factor portfolios}
\end{array}
$$

CHAPTER 5

FACTOR SPECIFICATIONS

In Chapter 4, we presented a framework for understanding and analyzing the performance characteristics of some of the various weighting schemes employed to capture smart beta factor returns. In this chapter, we discuss some of the various factor signal specifications that are commonly used in the design of smart beta products. In addition to the choice of the weighting scheme, factor signal specifications can also drive differences amongst the various smart beta offerings.

CHAPTER SUMMARY

- Smart beta providers typically focus on well-documented and vetted factors, such as size, value, momentum, low volatility, and quality, and often cite the underlying academic research to justify their factor selection.
- However, in designing smart beta offerings, providers also tend to deviate from the standard or conventional factor definitions used in the literature. For instance, value is routinely defined as a composite of multiple valuation ratios as opposed to just book value-to-price.
- This disconnect may arise because real-life implementation is often not the focus of academic research. Smart beta providers, on the other hand, need to pay particular attention to the replicability of their products, risk control versus a given policy benchmark, or mitigation of turnover and implementation costs.
- These considerations may naturally force providers to deviate from the academic factor specifications and implementations. And, of course, some "tweaks" to standard factor definitions may be more acceptable than others.
- With regard to value, the use of a single valuation ratio, such as book value-to-price, may raise reasonable concerns relating to diversification, active risk control, turnover, and ancillary factor exposures. The creation of a carefully designed composite valuation measure may alleviate some of these concerns.

- With regard to momentum, a commonly used tweak is to risk-adjust the conventional momentum measure to mitigate the impact of market reversals. This adjustment typically produces better information ratios, while having similar turnover and a positive active return correlation in excess of 90% with conventional momentum. The motivation for combining conventional momentum with short-term momentum is a little less clear, as short-term momentum has a 50% higher turnover and generally does not improve risk-adjusted performance.
- With regard to low volatility, providers use different risk measures, such as CAPM beta, total volatility, or idiosyncratic volatility. The various measures used, however, produce similar performance characteristics.
- With regard to quality, there appears to be significant dispersion in signal specification across providers. This dispersion also results in meaningful performance differences across the individual quality portfolios and across multifactor strategies that include quality as one of the factors.
- Some quality specifications that are used do not have performance characteristics typically associated with a defensive investment style, such as drawdown protection. Other specifications, such as quality composites, may result in duplicative exposures to component signals. And some quality measures become redundant in the presence of (or are explained by exposures to) other smart beta factors. Such measures would not be expected to provide meaningful benefits in factor diversification strategies.
- When factor specifications that are not broadly supported by the literature are used, it weakens the claim that the exploited factors are well-vetted, results in increased risk of data mining, and raises doubts concerning out-of-sample persistence in performance.
- When consistent factor definitions are not used across geographies and/or over time, it also raises concerns relating to data mining and selection bias.
- Recent research argues that the use of composites in defining factors should be avoided as it can lead to a significant overfitting bias. This bias is different from the well-known selection or multiple testing bias. The research does not imply that all composites are not useful. But, it does highlight the need for a clear rationale behind the selection and weighting of signals used to form the composite.

I. INTRODUCTION

Smart beta investing typically focuses on recognized common factors, such as size, value, momentum, volatility, and quality that have been well-documented and vetted in the academic literature by numerous researchers over multiple decades. In studies that account for data mining or multiple testing when studying a large number of factors, these smart beta factors still stand out as being significant. Most smart beta providers also focus on these same factors, often citing academic research to justify their choice. However, when it comes to designing smart beta offerings, providers may deviate from standard factor specifications or definitions used in the literature. For instance, value may be defined as a composite of several valuation ratios, as opposed to the standard book value-to-price specification often used in academic articles. Some researchers, for example, Goltz (2017), argue that such "tweaks" to standard definitions weakens the link between academic studies and how smart beta factors are defined and captured in various offerings, which also weakens the argument that academic evidence supports a given smart beta product.

It is true that there may well be a disconnect between standard definitions and implementations of factors used in the academic literature and how smart beta offerings seek to capture them. But it is also important to remember that real-life implementation is often not the primary focus of academic research. In designing smart beta products, providers have a different set of problems to address. For instance, they may pay particular attention to replicability of their products, risk control versus a given policy benchmark, or minimizing turnover and implementation costs. These considerations may force smart beta providers to deviate from academic specifications. In this chapter, we explore some of the various metrics used to define the smart beta factors and discuss the pros and cons of various methodologies and adjustments.

II.   VALUE

In 1992, the now celebrated Fama and French article investigating the cross-section of expected returns was published. At that time, the most prominent stock characteristics potentially depicting a positive relationship with average returns and risk were market beta (Black, Jensen, and Scholes 1972 and Fama and MacBeth 1973), firm size (Banz 1981), earnings-to-price ratio (Basu 1983), book-to-market equity (Stattman 1980, Rosenberg et al. 1985), and leverage (Bhandari 1988). Fama and French (1992) investigated the ability of these variables to explain the cross-section of average returns, and found that in univariate tests all variables, except market beta, had predictive power. The authors further argued that since size, earnings-to-price, book value-to-price, and leverage are scaled versions of price, they may be capturing similar information relating to risk and expected returns embedded in prices. As such, some of these variables may be redundant. In multivariate tests, Fama and French (1992), indeed, found that the ability to explain the cross-section of expected returns in a model that included size and book value-to-market was not improved by adding earnings-to-price and leverage, at least for the 1963–1990 sample period. In other words, earnings-to-price and leverage independently explained average returns, but in the presence of size and book value-to-market, they became redundant. As a result of these findings, market capitalization and book value-to-price became the standard specifications for size and value in the academic literature.

Specifically with regard to value, some smart beta managers use the book value-to-price specification. Many others deviate from this standard definition by creating a composite value specification, which may include other valuation ratios that are

TABLE 5.1 Active Return Correlation of SW Value Portfolios: Russell 1000 Universe
January 1995–June 2017

	Book Value-to-Price	Earnings-to-Price	Sales-to-Price	Free Cash Flow-to-Price	Operating Cash Flow-to-Price
Book Value-to-Price	100				
Earnings-to-Price	57	100			
Sales-to-Price	78	59	100		
Free Cash Flow-to-Price	28	40	25	100	
Operating Cash Flow-to-Price	66	67	70	31	100

Source: GSAM.

also well-documented in the academic literature. There are several reasons for making this adjustment, such as diversification, risk control, turnover reduction, and mitigating ancillary factor exposures. With regard to diversification, it should be noted that valuation ratios perform quite differently over time. This implies that they are not perfectly positively correlated, even though they scale fundamental values by the same variable: price. As an illustration, consider in Table 5.1 the active return correlations between factor portfolios created based on five commonly used valuation ratios, namely, book value-to-price, earnings-to-price, sales-to-price, free cash flow-to-price, and operating cash flow-to-price. These capitalization-weighted (CW) factor portfolios are constructed using the methodology outlined in Chapter 4. The pair-wise active return correlations across the portfolios ranged from 25% (between free cash flow-to-price and sales-to-price) to 78% (between sales-to-price and book value-to-price). The average pair-wise correlation across the five portfolios was only about 50%. As such, combining valuation ratios with relatively low active return correlations could provide some diversification benefits.

The use of a single valuation metric, such as book value-to-price, also presents a potential problem with regard to risk control relative to a given benchmark. A cross-sectional value strategy, where all stocks are ranked on a valuation metric across the whole universe, typically results in structural sector biases. That is, some industries are systematically overweighted and underweighted relative to a given policy benchmark. Additionally, individual valuation ratios tend to have different industry biases. For example, in the case of the US market, Table 5.2 shows that the book value-to-price portfolio had a large average overweight of 11.2% in Financials and a large average underweight of 8.6% in Information Technology. A valuation composite is likely to mitigate large sector active weights and, hence, allow for better active risk control. For instance, the sales-to-price portfolio had no meaningful overweight in Financials and the free cash flow-to-price portfolio had a large overweight in Information Technology. Further, the magnitudes of active weights of the free cash flow-to-price portfolio were much smaller compared to the book value-to-price portfolio.

TABLE 5.2 Russell 1000 Universe: Average Active Sector Weights of SW Value Portfolios
(January 1995–June 2017)

	Book Value-to-Price	Earnings-to-Price	Sales-to-Price	Free Cash Flow-to-Price	Operating Cash Flow-to-Price
Consumer Discretionary	-0.7	-2.3	4.8	-2.0	-1.0
Consumer Staples	-4.8	-1.1	-0.5	-3.9	-3.1
Energy	4.3	3.0	3.8	-3.5	5.1
Financials	11.2	7.6	0.2	7.2	4.7
Healthcare	-6.2	-4.2	-8.2	-1.2	-6.7
Industrials	**0.4**	**0.1**	**3.8**	**-0.3**	**0.1**
Information Technology	-8.6	-4.8	-8.5	6.4	-5.2
Materials	0.2	0.0	1.9	-1.0	0.9
Real Estate	0.7	-1.1	-1.6	-1.2	-1.0
Telecommunication Services	1.1	0.2	0.7	-1.4	3.2
Utilities	3.0	1.5	2.1	-0.2	2.0

Source: GSAM.

Valuation ratios may also have different turnover levels. For instance, sales are typically more stable than earnings, and, therefore, sales-to-price tends to have lower turnover than earnings-to-price. In fact, sales-to-price also has, on average, 20% less turnover than book value-to-price, despite the high active return correlation (Table 5.1). As such, it may be beneficial to include low-turnover valuation ratios in a value composite in order to mitigate implementation costs. Finally, valuation ratios may have quite different, and sometimes offsetting, exposures to other smart beta factors. Consider Table 5.3, which shows the active return and risk decomposition of book value-to-price and free cash flow-to-price portfolios against the other CW smart beta factor portfolios. As shown in this table, book value-to-price had high and statistically significant positive exposures to size and volatility, and negative exposures to quality and momentum, though this portfolio also delivered a statistically significant alpha of 1.37%. Free cash flow-to-price, on the other hand, had higher alpha of 2.52% and no exposure to size and volatility, a positive and significant exposure to quality, and a much lower negative exposure to momentum. These differences partially explain the low active return correlation between book value-to-price and free cash flow-to-price depicted in Table 5.1. Given the differences in ancillary factor exposures, it would be beneficial to combine free cash flow-to-price with book value-to-price, as it would mitigate the small cap and high volatility biases as well as reduce the nega-

TABLE 5.3 Active Return and Risk Decomposition of Valuation Ratios (January 1995–June 2017)

	CW Size	CW Momentum	CW Volatility	CW Quality	CW Alpha	Total Active Risk
Book Value-to-Price					**1.37**	
Exposure	**0.30**	**-0.36**	**0.16**	**-0.57**		
Contribution to Active Risk	0.56	1.36	0.15	1.31	1.19	4.57
Free Cash Flow-to-Price					**2.52**	
Exposure	-0.01	**-0.20**	0.00	**0.14**		
Contribution to Active Risk	0.00	0.41	0.00	0.01	2.41	2.83

Note: Figures in bold are statistically significant at the 5% level.
Source: GSAM.

tive exposures to quality and momentum. This, in turn, would be beneficial in the context of a multifactor strategy, in which value is combined with other factors to achieve better risk-adjusted outcomes through diversification.

In summary, there are some reasonable arguments for creating a value composite. For instance, it might be beneficial to combine free cash flow-to-price with book value-to-price, as the two ratios have low active return correlation (Table 5.1) and different industry (Table 5.2) and ancillary factor exposures (Table 5.3). However, free cash flow-to-price also has high turnover. Sales-to-price, on the other hand, has a turnover rate that is typically 20% lower than book value-to-price and 45% lower than free cash flow-to-price. As such, adding sales-to-price to a combination of book value-to-price and free cash flow-to-price could also be beneficial. This is the composite that we used in the creation of various value factor portfolios in Chapter 4.

III. MOMENTUM

The conventional definition of momentum in the academic literature, used by many smart beta providers, is last 11-month total return, lagged by one month. In terms of performance characteristics, conventional momentum strategies tend to perform well during trending markets, and poorly during market reversals. One way to potentially mitigate the impact of market reversals on the performance of momentum portfolios is to use a risk-adjusted momentum specification. The risk adjustment can be made in terms of stock-specific risk or total volatility. Table 5.4 shows the historical performance of CW conventional momentum and risk-adjusted momentum portfolios. In this case, total volatility is used to adjust conventional momentum for risk. At roughly similar levels of active risk, the risk-

TABLE 5.4 Russell 1000 Universe: Historical Performance of Momentum Portfolios
(January 1979–June 2017)

	Total Gross Return (%)	Total Risk (%)	Sharpe Ratio	Active Gross Return (%)	Active Risk (%)	Information Ratio	Annual Turnover (%)	Correlation with Conventional Momentum (%)
Russell 1000 Index	11.84	15.05	0.49					
Conventional Momentum	12.92	16.09	0.53	1.08	5.33	0.20	106	
Risk-Adjusted Momentum	13.38	15.69	0.57	1.53	4.98	0.31	106	93
Short-Term Momentum	11.79	15.50	0.48	-0.05	4.75	-0.01	157	63

Source: GSAM.

adjusted momentum produced higher active return, Sharpe ratio, and information ratio compared to conventional momentum. The two portfolios had identical annualized turnover and were highly positively correlated, with an active return correlation of 93%. As such, the risk adjustment of conventional momentum delivers slightly higher risk-adjusted returns, while remaining close to the spirit of conventional momentum investing. Some smart beta providers also combine conventional momentum with short-term momentum, defined as last five-month total return, lagged by one month, to create a composite measure. The rationale for doing this is a little less clear, as short-term momentum has no or limited market outperformance and a significantly higher turnover (Table 5.4).

IV. LOW VOLATILITY

With regard to the volatility factor, initial studies (e.g. Black et al. 1972) used the CAPM beta as the factor specification. In more recent studies, total volatility (e.g. Ghayur et al. 2013) and idiosyncratic volatility (e.g. Ang et al. 2006) specifications have also been used. Smart beta providers typically use these different definitions in their offerings to capture the volatility factor. However, Clarke et al. (2010) argued that whether the volatility signal is defined in terms of total or idiosyncratic risk makes little practical difference. Further, according to our research, the length of the estimation window used to calculate the volatility metric, such as one year or three years, does not meaningfully change the performance results either, as historical volatility is a slow-moving signal.

TABLE 5.5 Russell 1000 Universe: Historical Performance of Volatility Portfolios
(January 1981–June 2017)

	Total Gross Return (%)	Total Risk (%)	Sharpe Ratio	Active Gross Return (%)	Active Risk (%)	Information Ratio
Russell 1000 Index	11.06	14.95	0.47			
1-Year Historical Volatility	11.72	12.17	0.59	0.65	6.03	0.11
3-Year Historical Volatility	11.27	12.34	0.54	0.20	5.93	0.03
3-Year Historical Beta	11.04	12.22	0.54	-0.02	5.59	0.00
1-Year Idiosyncratic Risk	11.55	12.60	0.56	0.49	5.37	0.09

Source: GSAM.

Table 5.5 shows the historical performance of CW portfolios constructed using different volatility specifications. First, we note that increasing the estimation window from one-year to three-year historical volatility caused marginal differences in performance. Second, specifying the volatility signal as three-year CAPM beta, as opposed to three-year total volatility, also caused marginal differences in performance. Finally, whether volatility is specified as one-year total volatility or one-year idiosyncratic risk made little difference. In general, all the volatility portfolios presented in Table 5.5 realized very similar levels of total risk. Their Sharpe ratios were higher than the market and ranged between 0.54 and 0.59. Information ratios ranged from 0 to 0.11. Indeed, as pointed out by Clarke et al. (2010), various volatility specifications make little practical difference in terms of performance characteristics.

V. QUALITY

Unlike value, momentum, and volatility factors, there appears to be significant dispersion in the specification of quality. In the academic literature (e.g. Novy-Marx 2013, Fama and French 2015), quality is typically defined as profitability (gross profits over total assets) and sometimes investment (growth in total assets). Smart beta providers, however, may deviate significantly from these standard definitions in favor of characteristics such as accruals, leverage, stability, or other metrics. These differences in signal specifications can also result in significant performance differences among the various individual quality portfolios offered by smart beta providers as well as in factor diversification strategies that also use quality as one of the factors.

In our opinion, one important feature of quality investing is that, in addition to realizing reasonable IR over time, it is a defensive investment style, which mostly derives its market outperformance during periods of high risk aversion (flight to quality), such as high market drawdown periods. This dimension implies that a given quality specification should preferably result in certain performance characteristics, such as lower drawdown than the market. These performance characteristics make the quality factor quite different from other smart beta factors. For instance, value and momentum can deliver outperformance, but with similar or higher levels of drawdown compared to the market. Low-volatility investing seeks to provide drawdown protection, but with a CAPM beta much lower than one, which can lead to severe underperformance when markets are rising. Quality, on the hand, aims to deliver drawdown reduction with a CAPM beta much higher than low volatility, which may result in much better upside participation. These performance characteristics cause a well-specified quality factor to have relatively low active return correlations with other smart beta factors, which can be beneficial in the creation of factor diversification strategies. (We discuss the performance characteristics of smart beta factors in more detail in Chapter 7.)

Some quality specifications, such as leverage, depict performance characteristics that are quite different from what may be expected of a defensive investment style. Leverage portfolios typically result in CAPM beta significantly greater than one and drawdowns much higher than the market. Other quality definitions that are used may have specifications that result in duplicative exposures. For instance, consider a composite that combines return on equity (ROE) with leverage. To the extent that leverage is already included in ROE (e.g. a conventional Dupont decomposition shows that ROE = Profit Margin × Asset Turnover × Leverage), such a composite would result in a much higher weight being assigned to leverage relative to profitability.

Finally, many quality attributes that are commonly used by smart beta providers generally become redundant in the presence of other smart beta factors, that is, their performance is largely explained by the other smart beta factors. This is shown in Table 5.6, which presents an active return and risk decomposition of various CW quality portfolios against the other CW smart beta factor portfolios. We first note that Gross Profits over Total Assets generated a statistically significant alpha of 1.27% and over 80% (2.26/2.73) of its active risk was explained by the alpha term. That is, gross profitability delivered significant active return independent of other smart beta factors. More than 90% of the active risk of ROE (net income scaled by book value) was also explained by the alpha term, but this measure generated no significant alpha. All the other quality metrics depicted in this table generated small and insignificant alphas as well and at least 65% of their active risk was explained by exposures to other smart beta factors. For instance, in the case of Earnings Variability (five-year variation in operating income less interest scaled by book value), over 85% of the active risk was explained by the high exposure to the volatility factor. This implies that Earnings Variability is essentially a low-volatility strategy. Leverage showed a high positive exposure to size (i.e. a small cap bias). Growth in Assets (yearly change in total assets) was highly correlated with value, as more than

TABLE 5.6 Russell 1000 Universe: Active Return and Risk Decomposition of Various Quality Metrics (January 1979–June 2017)

	Size	Value	Momentum	Volatility	Alpha	Total Active Risk
Gross Profits over Total Assets					**1.27**	
Exposure	**0.59**	**-0.28**	0.02	**0.21**		
Contribution to Active Risk	0.53	0.06	0.01	-0.13	2.26	2.73
Return on Equity					0.27	
Exposure	**0.22**	-0.04	0.08	**0.15**		
Contribution to Active Risk	0.09	-0.02	0.02	0.05	1.72	1.86
Earnings Variability					0.05	
Exposure	**0.20**	-0.04	-0.01	**0.64**		
Contribution to Active Risk	-0.15	-0.07	0.01	2.32	0.62	2.72
Leverage					0.35	
Exposure	**0.91**	**-0.62**	**-0.23**	**-0.31**		
Contribution to Active Risk	1.39	0.97	-0.14	0.97	0.97	4.34
Growth in Assets					-0.15	
Exposure	**0.22**	**0.53**	0.04	**0.14**		
Contribution to Active Risk	0.19	1.59	-0.06	0.24	1.18	3.14
Growth in Shares Outstanding					0.05	
Exposure	**0.12**	**0.39**	**0.13**	**0.35**		
Contribution to Active Risk	0.02	1.06	-0.14	0.92	1.08	2.94

Note: Figures in bold are statistically significant at the 5% level.
Source: GSAM.

50% of its active risk was explained by this factor. Finally, Growth in Shares Outstanding (yearly change in total shares outstanding) is essentially a combination of value and low-volatility strategies, as almost 70% of its active risk was explained by these two factors.

In the context of factor diversification, the analysis shown in Table 5.6 would imply that gross profitability would be a good candidate to consider, as it is largely orthogonal to (or independent of) the other smart beta factors. The other quality metrics generated no significant factor-adjusted active return and had high loadings on other smart beta factors. Their addition and contribution in a multifactor strategy would be more questionable.

VI. TYPICAL INVESTOR QUESTIONS

5.1 What Specific Issues Are Raised When Factor Specifications and/or Adjustments Made to Standard Definitions That Are Not Fully Supported by Academic Research Are Used in Various Smart Beta Products?

In general, factor specifications, as well as adjustments to accepted factor definitions that are not well-researched and lack academic backing, may pose issues for investors. First, the use of such factor specifications and adjustments significantly weakens the claim often made by smart beta providers, that their factors are well-supported by academic research. Some factor specifications that are used may have been studied by one or two researchers, but have not been vetted in the same manner as standard definitions, by a large number of researchers across market segments, geographies, and over time. Examples would include: change in asset turnover to define quality, enterprise value-to-cash flow from operations to define value, or changes in earnings expectations to define momentum. Second, when factor specifications are not well-researched, investors have to rely on the backtests from the smart beta providers. This, of course, results in increased risk of data mining. Finally, standard factor definitions have been linked with out-of-sample persistence in performance (e.g. Dimson et al. 2017). This is generally not the case for unconventional factor definitions. As such, even though a provider's backtest may depict good performance, there tends to be a reasonable degree of doubt on whether the performance will persist on an out-of-sample basis.

5.2 Why Is Consistency Important in Defining a Given Factor Across Geographic Regions and/or Over Time?

Lack of consistency in defining a given factor across geographies and/or over time also raises serious concerns relating to data mining, in general, and selection bias and overfitting bias, in particular. In academic research, such concerns are alleviated by following a consistent definition for a factor in various markets and over time. For instance, book value-to-price as a specification for value was first researched and documented for the US market. Subsequent studies used the same factor specification to study the value effect in other markets. The results of these studies provide some degree of comfort and confidence that the book value-to-price factor is a systematic source of return (i.e. a rewarded factor) across global equities.

    Some smart beta managers use different specifications for the same factor in different geographies, primarily based on the historical performance of factors in

TABLE 5.7 Historical Performance of Various Value Portfolios (January 1988–June 2017)

	Total Gross Return (%)	Total Risk (%)	Sharpe Ratio	Active Gross Return (%)	Active Risk (%)	Information Ratio
PANEL A: US Market						
Russell 1000 Index	9.91	14.89	0.53			
Book Value-to-Price	10.23	16.00	0.52	0.33	4.57	0.07
Earnings-to-Price	11.77	14.40	0.66	1.86	4.87	0.38
Sales-to-Price	10.77	15.25	0.57	0.87	4.52	0.19
Free Cash Flow-to-Price	**12.56**	**15.46**	**0.67**	**2.66**	**2.83**	**0.94**
Operating Cash Flow-to-Price	11.41	14.99	0.62	1.50	4.75	0.32
PANEL B: Emerging Markets						
MSCI EM Index	7.48	23.54	0.33			
Book Value-to-Price	9.32	25.18	0.39	1.84	4.73	0.39
Earnings-to-Price	9.32	24.55	0.40	1.83	4.63	0.40
Sales-to-Price	10.17	25.39	0.42	2.69	4.38	0.61
Free Cash Flow-to-Price	9.04	22.55	0.40	1.55	3.55	0.44
Operating Cash Flow-to-Price	**10.81**	**24.57**	**0.45**	**3.33**	**4.11**	**0.81**

Note: Figures in bold are statistically significant at the 5% level.
Source: GSAM.

those markets. Consider the example depicted in Table 5.7. This table shows the historical performance of five CW value factor portfolios in the US and emerging markets. The table highlights the best performing portfolio, based on information ratios, in each region. Now suppose that, using this evidence, a smart beta manager defines value as free cash flow-to-price for the US market and operating cash flow-to-price for emerging markets. The smart beta manager may offer underlying fundamental reasons for the choice of the selected variables in each region, but they are unlikely to be supported by peer-reviewed academic research. In the end, the manager's specification for value in each region is likely to deliver an impressive in-sample backtest but should also raise concerns relating to out-of-sample persistence in performance.

Some other smart beta providers define the same factor, such as value, differently over time. In our view, in the context of smart beta investing, this practice is unlikely to have an underlying sound economic rationale and may raise concerns of data mining and data snooping. For example, an index provider currently offers two value indexes, launched at different points in time, which use quite different value specifications for each index. The same index provider also has multiple indexes for other factors, such as quality and momentum. These indexes were also launched at different points in time. But, what is interesting is that, contrary to value, these indexes use a consistent factor specification.

5.3 What Specific Issues Are Created by the Use of Composites in Defining Factors and/or Expected Return Signals?

In the academic literature, it is customary to use simple and single-dimensional factor specifications, such as book value-to-price for value or gross profits over total assets for profitability/quality. Smart beta providers, however, typically use composites and some can be somewhat complex in their construction. For instance, Bender and Wang (2016) define value as an equal-weighted composite of five valuation ratios, in which exponentially weighted five-year averages are used for book value, earnings, cash flow, sales, and dividend. Asness et al. (2013) consider a definition of quality that includes more than 20 stock characteristics along the dimensions of profitability, growth, safety, and payout.

The use of composites is typically avoided in the literature because it can lead to a severe overfitting bias. As pointed out by Novy-Marx (2015), the overfitting bias arises when a subset of signals, from a large number of tested signals, are combined to create a composite. The overfitting bias can lead to highly significant backtested performance, even in the case when individual signals that are combined have no real significance. The overfitting bias is also different from the commonly known selection or multiple testing bias, in which the best performing individual signal is selected from a large number of potential candidates. Novy-Marx (2015) argues that overfitting bias can be strong even in the absence of a selection bias and can get exacerbated in the presence of it.

The research does not imply that composites are not useful. As discussed in this chapter, some composites may indeed add value from a diversification as well as other implementation perspectives. However, the Novy-Marx (2015) research highlights that composites should be approached with caution. At a minimum, there should be a clear rationale for the selection and weighting of signals that form a composite. In the absence of an appropriate explanation, the historical performance of composites could well be subject to an overfitting bias.

Composite scores are also employed in the creation of factor diversification strategies. For example, the individual value, momentum and quality signals may be combined, by equal-weighting or some other weighting scheme, to construct a composite signal. The composite signal then forms the basis for building a multifactor portfolio. An interesting case in this regard is the use of a multiplicative, as opposed to an additive, composite. In a multiplicative process, the composite signal is derived by multiplying the individual factor signals. For instance, the composite signal for a value-momentum strategy is determined by multiplying the individual value and momentum signals. In our research, some multiplicative composites typically lead to multifactor portfolios that depict a high level of small cap bias and concentration, and, as such, lower capacity.

5.4 How Should Investors Approach the Variation Commonly Seen in the Specification of the Quality Factor?

As stated previously, perhaps the most significant differences between smart beta offerings relate to the specification of the quality factor. Some smart beta providers use the standard profitability measure (gross profits over total assets) studied in the academic literature. Others use more comprehensive composites designed to account for the multiple dimensions of quality investing, as determined by the provider. Smart beta providers may have reasonable arguments for preferring one definition over another. However, in our view, investors may find it useful to keep the following in mind while assessing various quality specifications.

Quality composites potentially raise some concerns. To the extent that quality composites tend to be multidimensional, they are likely to present a higher risk of an overfitting bias compared to other factor composites, such as value. Some quality composites may raise concerns relating to duplicative exposures. A combination of ROE and leverage is an example of an implicit duplicative exposure to leverage, which results in the actual weight of leverage in the composite being much higher than specified. Finally, a quality composite may include variables that are highly positively correlated with other smart beta factors. As shown in Table 5.6, earnings variability is essentially a low-volatility strategy. Leverage has a pronounced small cap bias. And growth in assets is highly correlated with value. If quality is approached as a stand-alone strategy, then high positive loadings on other smart beta factors may not be a real concern. However, in the context of multifactor strategies, it would be beneficial to have a quality specification that is largely orthogonal to the other smart beta factors.

In the end, investors would be well-advised to seek a clear rationale for the selection and weighting of metrics that comprise a given quality specification.

VII. CONCLUSION

In capturing smart beta factors, some adjustments that are made by smart beta providers to standard or conventional factor definitions may be warranted. These include risk-adjusted momentum measures to limit the impact of market reversals or value composites to better address diversification, active risk control, or ancillary factor exposures. Other adjustments that may give rise to concerns relating to selection and overfitting biases include using factor specifications that are not broadly supported by the literature, inconsistency in defining factors across geographies, changing factor definitions over time, or creating complex composites without a reasonable rationale. Investors should approach such situations with caution.

In Chapters 4 and 5, we analyzed some of the various weighting schemes and factor specifications that smart beta providers typically employ. We hope that the discussion in these two chapters will prove useful for investors in better understanding the potential differences between various smart beta offerings. In the next chapter, we use the factor portfolios constructed in Chapter 4 to conduct a risk decomposition of a large number of publicly available smart beta and active strategies. This exercise provides intriguing insights in understanding the drivers of active risk and active return of these strategies.

CHAPTER 6

ACTIVE RISK AND RETURN DECOMPOSITION OF SMART BETA AND ACTIVE STRATEGIES

In this chapter, we analyze a large number of publicly available smart beta strategies against the factor portfolios we constructed in Chapter 4. Although our focus is on smart beta strategies, we also use these factor portfolios to conduct a risk decomposition of certain active strategies. The analysis conducted in this chapter, we believe, provides useful insights in understanding the drivers of performance for smart beta and active strategies as well as assessing the efficiency of factor capture or the existence of manager skill more generally.

CHAPTER SUMMARY

- Academic studies generally show that smart beta strategies, as a group, do not produce significant factor-adjusted alpha relative to the Fama-French 3-factor or the Carhart 4-factor models.
- In order to provide another perspective, we analyzed a large number of smart beta strategies using the (long-only) factor portfolios constructed in Chapter 4, which are more easily and cost-effectively replicable compared to the Fama-French factors.
- We analyzed US large cap single factor offerings, multifactor offerings, and alternative equity beta strategies and, consistent with prior research, found that most smart beta offerings did not generate statistically significant alpha against the basic capitalization-weighted (CW) factor portfolios.
- A few highly concentrated momentum and quality indexes generated large and statistically significant alphas relative to the CW factor portfolios, which cover 50%

125

of the capitalization weight of the Russell 1000 Index. Against more concentrated CW factor portfolios that cover 25% of the Russell 1000 weight, the factor-adjusted alphas of these indexes were significantly reduced or eliminated.

- With regard to multifactor offerings, all but two strategies generated statistically significant active returns against the Russell 1000 benchmark. In a risk decomposition analysis relative to the CW factor portfolios, however, only one strategy realized an alpha that was significant at the 5% level.

- Among the alternative equity beta offerings, the equal-weighted Russell 1000 strategy realized the highest significance (*t*-statistic) in active returns. Two offerings generated significant factor-adjusted alphas, with one being the equal-weighted strategy.

- Some multifactor offerings are created by equally weighting individual factor portfolios, which are constructed using very different methodologies and have quite different active risk relative to the benchmark. Such offerings typically do not achieve balanced exposures to and active risk contributions from the targeted factors.

- Some smart beta offerings have very high and statistically significant exposure to the size factor. Given the historical evidence that US small cap stocks performed poorly from 1980 to 1999 and particularly well since 2000, the performance characteristics of such offerings are more appropriately assessed by analyzing longer-term backtests, as opposed to just post-2000 performance.

- Some active risk unconstrained optimized solutions tend to generate large alphas against the CW factor portfolios. This is because these solutions are equivalent to implementing factor tilts starting from an equal-weighted, as opposed to a capitalization-weighted, universe. As such, the large alphas of these strategies tend to disappear when active returns are decomposed against an equal-weighted Russell 1000 portfolio and ST value, momentum, low volatility, and quality portfolios.

- With regard to active strategies, academic studies, mostly based on mutual fund performance, find that active managers, in aggregate, deliver market-like returns, before fees, and underperform, after fees. Academic studies also report that active managers, as a group, look just like the market, with no meaningful factor exposures. Where market outperformance does exist, it is largely explained by exposures to smart beta factors. Factor-adjusted alpha is scarce and depicts less persistency than market outperformance emanating from positive factor exposures.

- In analyzing individual institutional asset managers, we find that a common result is net positive exposures to and active return contributions from smart beta factors, and an insignificant alpha. However, we also find a higher frequency of factor-adjusted alpha compared to academic studies, though this finding may result from selection bias in our data.

- Not all alpha in a risk decomposition exercise may represent manager skill. An alpha can arise simply due to signal, model, or construction mismatches between the analyzed strategy and factor/risk portfolios.

I. INTRODUCTION

As we have discussed in Chapter 4 and Chapter 5, smart beta offerings employ a wide variety of weighting schemes and signal specifications to capture smart beta factors. Furthermore, smart beta providers routinely make claims regarding the higher efficiency with which their methodologies deliver smart beta factor payoffs. So, a natural question is: How do the various smart beta strategies fare in a risk decomposition based on relatively simple factor portfolios? To answer this question, we first conduct a brief review of the existing literature on this topic and then proceed to discuss the results of our analysis. We follow a similar structure in analyzing active strategies.

II. RISK DECOMPOSITION OF SMART BETA STRATEGIES

A. Literature Review

In general, studies that conducted risk decomposition analyses of smart beta strategies found that such strategies, as a group, did not generate a significant alpha relative to the Fama-French factors.

For example, Chow et al. (2011) analyzed the performance of a number of smart beta strategies, which included equal-weighting, risk-clustered equal-weighting, diversity weighting (e.g. Fernholz 1998), fundamental weighting (e.g. Arnott et al. 2005), minimum-variance (e.g. Haugen and Baker 1991), maximum diversification (e.g. Choueifaty and Coignard 2008), and risk-efficient (e.g. Amenc et al. 2010). The authors replicated these strategies using methodologies that were disclosed in the public domain, such as journal articles and other research papers. In an effort to conduct an apples-to-apples comparison of the various strategies, the authors generated backtested performance in a controlled research environment, rather than using the actual performance or the published backtests of the commercial products, which incorporate numerous implementation subtleties. The authors found that all the strategies outperformed the capitalization-weighted market portfolio. However, the outperformance was almost fully explained by the Fama-French 3-factor model or the Carhart 4-factor model. That is, the smart beta strategies outperformed the market index because they had high exposures to size and value smart beta factors. And statistically, the strategies as a group generated no significant alpha relative to the 3-factor or the 4-factor model. These findings led the authors to draw the following conclusions. To the extent that various smart beta strategies are explained by the same factors or return sources (i.e. market, size, and value), they can be combined to replicate each other's performance. Further, to the extent that a simple equal-weighted portfolio also derives its market outperformance through exposures to size and value factors, the analyzed strategies, some of which use highly complex methodologies, become directly related to naive equal weighting. Finally, if strategies can be carefully combined to replicate other strategies, then investors should focus on those smart beta strategies that are characterized by lower turnover and better diversification, liquidity, and capacity.

If the smart beta strategies are explained by simple size and value factors, with no meaningful additional active return (i.e. alpha), then what is their value add? Chow et al. (2011) argued that these strategies still represent useful innovations as they allow investors to capture the size and value premia more cost-effectively compared to the Fama-French factors and more efficiently compared to the capitalization-weighted size and style indexes. Indeed, the Fama-French factors are not easily and cost-effectively replicable. And the existing capitalization-weighted size and style indexes are less efficient than the analyzed smart beta strategies because they tend to generate negative Fama-French alphas, as shown by Arnott et al. (2005) and Hsu et al. (2010).

Other studies document that various low-risk strategies are explained by the volatility factor. Scherer (2010) derived an anlytical result showing that the minimum-variance portfolio largely invests in low-beta and low-idiosyncratic risk stocks. Along similar lines, Clarke et al. (2011) and Leote de Carvalho et al. (2011) found that long-only minimum-variance portfolios are dominated by low-beta securities. Further, Leote de Carvalho et al. (2011) also documented that minimum-variance and maximum diversification are similar strategies that produce largely overlapping portfolios.

Following the publication of Chow et al. (2011), some analysts argued that, although their general conclusions relating to the lack of a significant Fama-French factor-adjusted alpha for the analyzed strategies may hold, their research design favored certain strategies over others. For example, Amenc et al. (2012) pointed out that the Chow et al. (2011) analysis is biased against optimization-based methodologies, which tend to perform poorly in universes containing a large number of securities (also known as the "curse of dimensionality"). They also argued that the implementations used by Chow et al. (2011) deviated significantly from the actaul index construction rules, which resulted in higher concentration and turnover for some strategies. For example, EDHEC-Risk Efficient indexes typically have a turnover of about 25%, whereas Chow et al. (2011) reported a turnover level of around 75% for the replicated risk-efficient strategy.

B. Our Analysis

Although analyzing various strategies in an internally consistent, controlled research environment may be a useful exercise, it is unlikley to lead to an exact replication of the performance of considered strategies. Actual products incorporate many implementation subtleties, which may be hard to mimic fully. Therefore, in our analysis, we have opted to use the actual performance of various strategies, which we obtain from publicly available sources, rather than replicating their performance in a research environment using publicly disclosed methodologies.

Academic studies also generally conduct a risk decomposition against the Fama-French factors. As previously mentioned, the Fama-French factors are impractical, as they are not easily and cost-effectively replicable. Another option in a risk decomposition exercise would be to use (long-only) passive alternatives or factor portfolios that are replicable at low cost and that cover all smart beta factors. We developed such factor portfolios in Chapter 4, such as the CW and ST factor portfolios. In our view, these factor portfolios represent useful passive alternatives, as no index provider currently offers a consistent family of CW indexes that cover all smart beta factors. Therefore, we use these factor portfolios to analyze the exposures and efficiency (alpha) of various smart beta strategies.

a. General Findings

We analyzed 30 publicly available US large cap smart beta indexes, including some that are listed in Chapter 4, Figure 4.2. These strategies consisted of value, momentum, volatility, and quality single factor offerings, multifactor offerings, and alternative equity beta strategies. We conducted an active return and risk decomposition of these strategies relative to the CW and ST factor portfolios discussed in Chapter 4. Consistent with prior research, we found that most offerings did not generate a statistically significant alpha against the basic CW factor portfolios.

In relation to single factor offerings, the evaluated indexes use a variety of signal specifications for each factor as well as different weighting schemes including, capitalization weighting, capitalization scaling, signal weighting, and optimizing. When analyzed against the CW factor portfolios, none of the considered value strategies generated a statistically significant alpha. Momentum offerings generally produced positive alphas, but they were statistically significant only for one highly concentrated index. Volatility strategies realized no meaningful alpha. And two concentrated quality indexes depicted large and statistically significant alphas. Recall that the CW factor portfolios used in this analysis cover 50% of the Russell 1000 capitalization weight. We can also report that when the concentrated momentum and quality indexes were analyzed against more concentrated CW factor portfolios, that cover 25% of the Russell 1000 capitalization weight, their alphas were significantly reduced or eliminated.

With regard to multifactor offerings, some of the products we analyzed combine individually constructed factor portfolios that use a variety of weighting schemes. For instance, one offering combines six factor indexes, namely, value (capitalization-scaled), momentum (capitalization-scaled), quality (capitalization-scaled), minimum volatility (optimized), dividend yield (capitalization-weighted) and size (equal-weighted). Other offerings construct a combination multifactor solution consisting of various optimized weighting schemes in order to mitigate model risks through model diversification. For instance, one offering equally weights maximum Sharpe ratio, minimum variance, maximum decorrelation, maximum deconcentration, and diversified risk parity weighting schemes. And some offerings combine individual factor signals into a composite signal, which is then used to construct a multifactor strategy using either active risk unconstrained optimization or simply capitalization scaling. All the multifactor strategies we analyzed outperfomed the Russell 1000 Index over the sourced period, and all but two offerings realized statistically significant active returns. However, in a risk decomposition relative to the CW factor portfolios, only one strategy generated an alpha that was significant at the 5% level.

In the analysis of alternative equity beta strategies, such as equal weighted, minimum volatility, and fundamental indexation all strategies outperformed the Russell 1000 index, with the most significant active return being realized by the equal-weighted strategy. Against the CW factor portfolios, two offerings generated statistically significant alphas, with one being the equal-weighted strategy.

b. Additional Insights

In this section, we present some examples of analyzed strategies to highlight additional useful insights that can potentially be gained from a risk decomposition exercise.

i. Factor Exposures in Diversification Strategies

Smart beta providers create multifactor strategies by combining individual factor portfolios or individual factor signals. Depending on the process used, the multifactor strategy may not depict diversified and balanced exposures across the considered factors. Table 6.1 provides an example. Multifactor Strategy 1 is a public index, which equally combines independently constructed value, volatility, and quality indexes to create a factor diversification strategy. The value index is value-weighted based on sales, book value, earnings, and cash earnings. The volatility index is a minimum volatility portfolio. And the quality index uses a composite of Return on Equity, Leverage, and Earnings Variability as the quality signal and capitalization scaling as the weighting scheme. When analyzed against the CW factor portfolios, the Multifactor Strategy 1 showed no exposure to value, despite the fact that the CW value portfolio also defines value as a composite of sales, book value, and cash flow. More interestingly, this strategy had a high exposure to the volatility factor and almost 63% of the active risk was explained by this factor. This finding may be explained by the fact that (1) the minimum volatility portfolio has a much higher active risk (about 6%) to the Russell 1000 benchmark than the value and quality portfolios (about 3%), and (2) the quality specification uses earnings variability as a metric, which is essentially a low-volatility strategy, as shown by Table 5.6 in Chapter 5. This example highlights that in creating multifactor strategies, some form of active risk parity in combining factor portfolios or factor signals would be beneficial in achieving more balanced exposures across the considered factors. This example also highlights that in selecting various signal specifications and individual components of composite signals, careful analyses should be conducted to assess their exposures and correlations with other included smart beta factors.

ii. Size Exposure of Smart Beta Strategies

Generally speaking, because smart beta strategies deviate from capitalization weights, they will tend to have a positive size exposure, that is, a small cap bias. However, some strategies may have a very high and statistically significant exposure to size. Consider Multifactor Strategy 2, which uses a multiplicative composite signal to emphasize stocks that rank well on all the targeted factors, and Alternative Equity Beta Strategy

TABLE 6.1 Example of a Smart Beta Strategy: Active Return and Risk Decomposition Against CW Factor Portfolios (Russell 1000 Universe, July 1994–June 2017)

	CW Size	CW Value	CW Momentum	CW Volatility	CW Quality	Alpha	Total Active Risk
Multifactor Strategy 1						0.21	
Exposure	**-0.16**	0.00	**-0.21**	**0.54**	**0.16**		
Contribution to Active Risk	0.23	0.00	0.24	2.09	0.05	0.71	3.33

Note: Figures in bold are statistically significant at the 5% level.
Source: GSAM.

1, which is a maximum Sharpe ratio strategy, in Table 6.2. Between July 2002 and June 2017, Multifactor Strategy 2 outperformed the Russell 1000 Index by 1.37% per annum with an active risk of 3.09%. This strategy had a very high and significant exposure to size, which contributed 0.96% to active return. The size factor also explained 37% of the active risk of the strategy. Similarly, almost 57% of the active risk of Alternative Equity Beta Strategy 1 was explained by size. The general point here is that the assessment of the historical performance characteristics of smart beta strategies that have a high exposure to small cap stocks should be approached with caution. We know from the academic studies reviewed in Chapter 2 and the size portfolios discussed in Chapter 4 that US small cap stocks performed poorly between 1980 and 1999 and particularly well since 2000. Therefore, if such strategies are assessed on the basis of backtests that depict performance only post-2000, then it would not be a complete representation of the potential performance characteristics of the strategy. In such cases, analyzing longer term backtests would be much more meaningful.

TABLE 6.2 Examples of Smart Beta Strategies: Active Return and Risk Decomposition Against CW Factor Portfolios (Russell 1000 Universe, July 2002–June 2017)

	CW Size	CW Value	CW Momentum	CW Volatility	CW Quality	Alpha	Total Active Risk
Multifactor Strategy 2						0.40	
Exposure	**0.81**	0.04	**0.19**	**0.38**	**0.16**		
Contribution to Active Risk	1.15	-0.04	0.44	0.76	0.08	0.69	3.09
Alternative Equity Beta Strategy 1						0.37	
Exposure	**0.87**	-0.08	0.09	**0.22**	**0.23**		
Contribution to Active Risk	1.21	0.09	0.11	0.15	0.05	0.51	2.13

Note: Figures in bold are statistically significant at the 5% level.
Source: GSAM.

Application Example 6.1

In 2016, an index provider launched a multifactor smart beta family of indexes. The launch of the index family was accompanied by a description of the methodology used to create the indexes as well as a simulation of the historical performance of the indexes. For US large cap, the historical performance was provided from 2001 to 2015. Over this time period, the index outperformed a US large cap benchmark by 5.4% per year with a tracking error of 4.5%, thus generating an impressive information ratio of 1.19. An active return and risk decomposition of the newly launched index conducted by us showed a very strong small cap bias, with the size factor explaining almost 47% of the active risk.

Using the index construction and maintenance rules disclosed by the index provider, the historical performance of the new index could be independently verified. When we conducted such an exercise, the historical performance of the US large cap index was replicated within 0.5% of tracking error and 0.5% of return (i.e. 90% return replication). This is not exact replication of historical performance, but it would be considered a close independent approximation, in our view. The replicated index realized an information ratio of 0.96, which is close to the reported information ratio of 1.19.

Given the strong small cap bias, as an additional step, we extended the historical performance of the replicated US large cap index to 1980. For the time period between 1980 and 2015, the replicated index generated an information ratio of only 0.53, which is about half the information ratio from 2001 to 2015. In other words, the information ratio of the replicated index for the post-2001 period (the reported period) was 0.96, while it was close to zero for the 1980–2000 period. These longer-term performance characteristics should not be surprising, as they are consistent with what we know about the historical performance of small cap stocks. However, these results do highlight the importance of reviewing the performance of smart beta strategies that load heavily on the size factor for the pre-2000 time period. This issue is potentially less of a concern for diversification strategies that have a much lower exposure to size and are more appropriately diversified, as they would also include factors that have done relatively poorly in the recent past, such as value and momentum, but had strong performance pre-2000.

iii. Active Risk Unconstrained Optimized Solutions

As mentioned in Chapter 4, some active risk unconstrained optimized solutions may result in portfolios that are almost equivalent to starting with an equal-weighted benchmark universe and then tilting toward the smart beta factors. Such strategies may generate significant alphas when decomposed against the CW factor portfolios, but not against a combination of an equal-weighted parent universe and ST factor portfolios. One example of this situation is depicted in Table 6.3. The Alternative Equity Beta Strategy 2 is an active risk unconstrained maximum diversification strategy. Between November 2002 and June 2017, this strategy generated an active return of 3.22% per year relative to the Russell 1000 index with an active risk of 4.74% (IR of 0.68). Against the CW factor portfolios, Panel A of Table 6.3, the strategy realized a large alpha of 2% per annum. The alpha term also explained over 70% of the active risk. The strategy had a factor loading of 0.81 to size, which resulted in 1.33% active return contribution from the CW size factor. However, against a combination of the equal-weighted universe (substituting for size) and ST value, momentum, volatility, and quality factor portfolios, the strategy's alpha completely disappeared, and the proportion of active risk explained by alpha dropped to about 47%. The exposure of 0.69 to the equal-weighted universe contributed 2.60% to active return, which is over 80% of the total active return of 3.22%. Despite a rather complex optimized

TABLE 6.3 Example of Smart Beta Strategy: Active Return and Risk Decomposition: Russell 1000 Universe, November 2002–June 2017

	CW Size	CW Value	CW Momentum	CW Volatility	CW Quality	Alpha	Total Active Risk
PANEL A							
Alternative Equity Beta Strategy 2						**2.00**	
Exposure	**0.81**	0.04	**0.19**	**0.38**	**0.16**		
Contribution to Active Risk	0.73	-0.01	0.04	0.44	0.11	3.43	4.74

	EW Universe	ST Value	ST Momentum	ST Volatility	ST Quality	Alpha	Total Active Risk
PANEL B							
Alternative Equity Beta Strategy 2						-0.08	
Exposure	**0.69**	-0.19	-0.10	**0.58**	**0.47**		
Contribution to Active Risk	1.13	-0.03	-0.02	0.91	0.50	2.25	4.74

Note: Figures in bold are statistically significant at the 5% level.
Source: GSAM.

construction methodology used by the Alternative Equity Beta Strategy 2, this strategy may be roughly equivalent to implementing factor tilts starting with an equal-weighted benchmark universe.

c. Summary

From the preceding analysis, we draw the following broad observations.

- All smart beta strategies that we analyzed outperformed the Russell 1000 Index over the longest possible time period for which historical performance for these strategies could be sourced publicly.
- Many smart beta strategies generated active returns that were statistically significant.
- Many smart beta strategies did not produce positive or meaningful factor-adjusted alphas against the CW factor portfolios, and only a few realized positive alphas that were significant at the 5% level.
- Some concentrated momentum and quality factor indexes produced significant alphas against the CW factor portfolios, which cover 50% of the capitalization weight of the Russell 1000 Index. However, when analyzed against more concentrated CW factor portfolios that cover 25% of the benchmark weight, the alphas were meaningfully reduced or eliminated.
- Some multifactor smart beta strategies combine individual factor portfolios or factor signals in ways that do not lead to diversified and balanced exposures across the considered factors.
- Some smart beta strategies have a very high exposure to the size factor and a large proportion of their active return is attributable to this factor. A proper understanding of the performance characteristics of such strategies cannot be gained by analyzing only post-2000 time periods.
- Some active risk unconstrained optimized solutions result in factor tilts being implemented relative to an equal-weighted benchmark universe. Such solutions may generate an alpha against the CW factor portfolios, but not against a combination of EW Russell and ST value, momentum, volatility, and quality portfolios.

III.   RISK DECOMPOSITION OF ACTIVE STRATEGIES

A. Literature Review

Given the debate around market efficiency and active versus passive, analyzing the performance of actively managed mutual funds has been a focus area for researchers and has produced a significant body of literature over the years. The general conclusions emerging from these studies may be summarized as follows.

Active managers, in aggregate, deliver similar returns as the market, before fees, and underperform, after fees (e.g. Treynor 1965, Sharpe 1966, and Jensen 1969). Active managers, as a group, also appear to be factor-neutral. For instance,

Fama and French (2011) found that active managers, in aggregate, do not have major factor exposures relative to the market, that is, they look very much like the market. Further, the authors documented that, although some active funds generated a factor-adjusted alpha, only 3% of funds realized a factor-adjusted alpha that was large enough to cover their fees.

Other studies have documented that where market outperformance did exist, it was largely explained by the smart beta factors. For example, Grinblatt and Titman (1989, 1993) found evidence of superior performance for growth-oriented funds. However, following the publication of Jegadeesh and Titman (1993), Grinblatt et al. (1995) discovered that the superior performance was explained by the momentum effect. Similarly, Hendricks et al. (1993) found persistence in performance for some mutual funds, which they termed as the "hot hands" phenomenon. Carhart (1997), however, documented that the hot hands phenomenon was also explained by the momentum factor. Studies that analyzed the stock holdings of actively managed mutual funds have found that, before costs, stocks held by active managers did outperform their benchmarks, on average (e.g. Grinblatt and Titman 1989, 1993, and Wermers 1997). Most of this outperformance, however, was attributable to the style characteristics of the stocks held. In particular, the held stocks depicted high exposure to size, value, and momentum characteristics.

In contrast to these findings, other studies have found evidence of skill, beyond characteristic selection. For example, Wermers (2000) reported positive before-fee alpha for the average fund, after adjusting for factor exposures. With regard to persistence in skill, Carhart (1997) found that persistent market outperformance was largely explained by exposures to factors and investment costs. Factor-adjusted outperformance or skill depicted less persistency over time.

B. Our Analysis

To conduct a risk decomposition of active strategies, we use the ST factor portfolios, as opposed to the CW factor portfolios employed for the smart beta strategies, for the following main reasons. First, as we discuss in more detail in Chapter 10, in structuring portfolios that also include an allocation to smart beta, in our opinion, the assessment of factor-adjusted alpha should be conducted relative to the smart beta solutions that are actually implemented. ST factor portfolios generally depict higher efficiency in factor capture, as they produce alphas relative to the CW factor portfolios. Within our framework, they represent one viable option for implementing smart beta investing in a policy benchmark-aware fashion. Second, the weighting schemes used by active managers, in general, tend to be closer to signal-tilting compared to smart beta indexes that mostly use capitalization-weighting or capitalization-scaling. Third, the ST factor portfolios may be constructed from the benchmark universe that the active manager uses at similar levels of tracking error as the active strategy, if needed. This potentially facilitates a more accurate determination of factor exposures and factor-adjusted alpha within a given universe. Also, the historical performance of ST factor portfolios is adjusted for implementation costs to make them more consistent with the historical performance of active strategies. The applied implementation cost assumptions are discussed in more detail in Chapter 7, but amount to 0.50% round-trip for the US, 0.80% for Developed Markets, and 1.5% for Emerging Markets.

In the context of incorporating smart beta with other active strategies within an overall portfolio structure, asset owners typically use commercial risk models, such as Barra or Axioma, to assess factor exposures and portfolio diversification potential. Asset owners also often provide us, on an anonymous basis, the historical performance of active managers they invest in, or are considering investing in, to get another perspective on the drivers of performance and assessment of skill. Having analyzed a very large number of institutional asset managers in this fashion, we report below some examples of the analyses that have been performed.

a. Median Return of Active Managers

To get a sense of the factor exposures of a typical active strategy, we may look at the median return of active managers over time. We calculate this return series as follows. Using Morningstar, a manager performance database, each month we identify the median return delivered by active managers within a given classification category. We then link the median return to create a return series over time. We refer to this return series as the median return of active managers. In general, we find that the median return of active managers typically has no or muted factor exposures and large negative alphas. This is depicted in Table 6.4 for the Morningstar US Large Blend Category. Panel A shows that the median return of active managers, gross of management fees, underperformed the Russell 1000 Index by 1.26% per annum over the analyzed time period, with a low active risk of 1.04%. Panel B reports that the median return of active managers had muted exposures to the smart beta factors and the total contribution to active return from exposures to these factors amounted to + 0.27% (0.14% + 0.01% + 0.09% + 0.03%). However, the large negative, and statistically significant, alpha of 1.53% resulted in an overall underperformance. The proportion of active risk explained by alpha was also almost 70% (0.72/1.04) for the US Large Blend Category.

Table 6.5 shows that similar results were obtained for the Morningstar Foreign Large Blend Category. Compared to the MSCI EAFE Index, the median return of active managers underperformed by 1.02% (Panel A). Factor exposures were insignificant, except for momentum and quality (Panel B). Smart beta factors' net active return contribution was + 0.14%, but the median return of active managers underperformed because of a large significant alpha of – 1.16%. In this case, more than 90% of the active risk was explained by the alpha term.

If the median return of active managers can be assumed to represent the typical performance characteristics of active managers, as a group, then these results may be viewed as being consistent with the findings of Fama and French (2011).

TABLE 6.4 Median Return of Active Managers: Active Return and Risk Decomposition: Morningstar US Large Blend Category, Returns in US$ Gross of Management Fees (January 1995–September 2014)

	Total Return	Total Risk	Sharpe Ratio	CAPM Beta	Active Return	Active Risk	IR
PANEL A: Historical Performance							
Russell 1000 Index	9.91	15.42	0.50	1.00			
Median Return of Active Managers	8.65	14.93	0.43	0.97	-1.26	1.04	-1.22

	ST Size	ST Value	ST Momentum	ST Volatility	ST Quality	Alpha	Total Active Risk
PANEL B: Risk Decomposition							
Median Return of Active Managers							
Exposure	0.00	**0.05**	0.01	**0.10**	0.01		
Contribution to Active Return	0.00	0.14	0.01	0.09	0.03	**-1.53**	
Contribution to Active Risk	0.00	0.09	-0.01	0.23	0.00	0.72	1.04

Note: Figures in bold are statistically significant at the 5% level.
Source: GSAM.

b. Individual Manager Analysis

We now discuss some examples of the results obtained through a risk decomposition of individual active strategies. The historical performance of the active strategies we analyzed, relative to their corresponding benchmarks, was typically provided to us by asset owners. To the extent that asset owners have conducted some level of screening to identify the managers that they wish to evaluate further, our results may be subject to a selection bias. As such, our analysis is not a characterization of active strategies, in general, but rather a depiction of a subset of active managers typically considered by institutional asset owners.

i. Market Outperformance

A large number of active institutional managers we have analyzed did outperform their respective benchmarks. Generally speaking, the outperformance was more prevalent and more pronounced for less efficient segments of global equities, such as Emerging Markets, compared to more efficient segments, such as US large cap.

TABLE 6.5 Median Return of Active Managers: Active Return and Risk Decomposition: Morningstar Foreign Large Blend Category, Returns in US$ Gross of Management Fees (January 1995–September 2014)

	Total Return	Total Risk	Sharpe Ratio	CAPM Beta	Active Return	Active Risk	IR
PANEL A: Historical Performance							
MSCI EAFE Index	4.59	17.94	0.24	1.00			
Median Return of Active Managers	3.57	17.78	0.18	0.99	-1.02	1.89	-0.54

	ST Size	ST Value	ST Momentum	ST Volatility	ST Quality	Alpha	Total Active Risk
PANEL B: Risk Decomposition							
Median Return of Active Managers							
Exposure	-0.02	-0.03	**0.11**	-0.09	**0.14**		
Contribution to Active Return	-0.03	-0.09	0.15	0.20	0.31	**-1.16**	
Contribution to Active Risk	0.00	0.02	0.07	-0.03	0.08	1.75	1.89

Note: Figures in bold are statistically significant at the 5% level.
Source: GSAM.

ii. Positive Factor Exposures

A common feature of analyzed active strategies was that their market outperformance was mainly driven by net positive exposures to smart beta factors, while the contribution of factor-adjusted alpha, either positive or negative, was muted. An example of this case is shown in Table 6.6 for an MSCI World manager. Over the analysis period, this manager outperformed the MSCI World Index by 2.49% with an active risk of 5.19%, thus generating a respectable IR of 0.48 before management fees (Panel A). The manager also had high exposures to value, momentum, and quality (Panel B). The contributions to active return from these three factors amounted to 2.30% (1.06% + 0.12% + 1.12%) and hence almost fully accounted for the realized total outperformance relative to the benchmark. The moderate positive contribution of alpha (0.58%) to overall active return was diluted by the negative active return contribution from size (– 0.55%).

iii. Varying Levels of Skill

Although a common result in our analysis is an insignificant alpha, many managers are able to effectively combine characteristic selection with other sources that also

TABLE 6.6 Sample Manager Historical Performance and Active Return and Risk Decomposition: MSCI World Benchmark, Returns in US$ Gross of Management (January 2003–September 2015)

	Total Return	Total Risk	Sharpe Ratio	CAPM Beta	Active Return	Active Risk	IR
PANEL A: Historical Performance							
MSCI World Index	8.29	15.14	0.50	1.00			
Sample Manager	10.77	14.17	0.68	0.88	2.49	5.19	0.48

	ST Size	ST Value	ST Momentum	ST Volatility	ST Quality	Alpha	Total Active Risk
PANEL B: Risk Decomposition							
Sample Manager							
Exposure	-0.30	**0.57**	**0.38**	0.20	**0.49**		
Contribution to Active Return	-0.55	1.06	0.12	0.20	1.12	0.58	
Contribution to Active Risk	0.07	-0.05	0.29	0.24	0.76	3.87	5.19

Note: Figures in bold are statistically significant at the 5% level.
Source: GSAM.

generate significant alpha, such as stock selection. Table 6.7 shows the example of a value manager benchmarked to the Russell 1000 Value Index. This manager outperformed the benchmark by 2.54% and generated an impressive IR of 1.04. The manager had a high exposure to value and a more moderate exposure to momentum. Factor selection contributed 1.10% to active return, with the remainder (1.43%) coming from a statistically significant alpha.

In some cases, the manager may have enough alpha-generating capability to offset any negative contribution to active return coming from characteristic selection. Table 6.8 provides an example of this situation for a growth manager benchmarked to the Russell 1000 Growth Index. This manager had moderate, but statistically significant, exposures to size, momentum, and quality. Momentum and quality contributed positively to active return, while the size exposure resulted in a negative contribution, as the size factor underperformed by 1.68% in this universe over the analyzed period. Overall, contribution to active return from smart beta factors was – 0.29%, mainly due to the poor performance of the size factor. However, a large positive and significant alpha of 2.07% contributed to a realized outperformance of 1.78% and an IR of 0.93.

TABLE 6.7 Sample Manager Historical Performance and Active Return and Risk Decomposition: Russell 1000 Value Benchmark, Returns in US$ Gross of Management Fees (October 2010–September 2015)

	Total Return	Total Risk	Sharpe Ratio	CAPM Beta	Active Return	Active Risk	IR
PANEL A: Historical Performance							
Russell 1000 Value Index	12.29	12.13	1.00	1.00			
Sample Manager	14.83	13.70	1.07	1.12	2.54	2.44	1.04

	ST Size	ST Value	ST Momentum	ST Volatility	ST Quality	Alpha	Total Active Risk
PANEL B: Risk Decomposition							
Sample Manager							
Exposure	**-0.17**	**0.69**	**0.23**	-0.16	-0.06		
Contribution to Active Return	0.13	1.18	0.01	-0.12	-0.08	**1.43**	
Contribution to Active Risk	-0.17	1.46	0.05	0.43	0.03	0.64	2.44

Note: Figures in bold are statistically significant at the 5% level.
Source: GSAM.

In some other cases, the positive influence of characteristic selection is diluted by negative skill. Table 6.9 provides an example. In this case, the high exposures to size, value, and momentum resulted in a total active return contribution from smart beta factors of 4.24%. However, the strategy only realized a total outperformance of 0.31% over the S&P 500 benchmark because the positive impact of factor selection was offset by a large negative alpha of 3.93%.

In assessing factor exposures and skill, additional analyses may also prove useful. For instance, where a reasonably long performance history is available, a rolling three-year or five-year risk decomposition may provide useful insights on the persistency of factor exposures and/or alpha across time. Where a manager offers strategies across different geographies, a regional analysis may be instructive in assessing the persistency of exposures and skill. Table 6.10 shows the historical performance and risk decomposition for a manager, who employs substantially the same systematic process across various regions. Over the analysis period, the manager outperformed the corresponding benchmark in each region and generated highly impressive IRs. The manager also realized large and statistically significant alphas in each region. In the United States, the manager had no meaningful factor exposures and the outperformance

TABLE 6.8 Sample Manager Historical Performance and Active Return and Risk Decomposition: Russell 1000 Growth Benchmark, Returns in US$ Gross of Management Fees (October 2010–September 2015)

	Total Return	Total Risk	Sharpe Ratio	CAPM Beta	Active Return	Active Risk	IR
PANEL A: Historical Performance							
Russell 1000 Growth Index	14.47	11.76	1.20	1.00			
Sample Manager	16.25	12.09	1.30	1.02	1.78	1.92	0.93

	ST Size	ST Value	ST Momentum	ST Volatility	ST Quality	Alpha	Total Active Risk
PANEL B: Risk Decomposition							
Sample Manager							
Exposure	**0.26**	-0.15	**0.26**	0.13	**0.20**		
Contribution to Active Return	-0.43	-0.10	0.10	0.06	0.07	**2.07**	
Contribution to Active Risk	0.17	0.01	0.21	-0.03	0.14	1.41	1.92

Note: Figures in bold are statistically significant at the 5% level.
Source: GSAM.

was largely driven by alpha. Outside the United States, the manager had meaningful value and momentum exposures. However, 60% or higher of the realized active returns were attributable to alpha in each region.

iv. Summary

Our analysis of a large number of individual institutional money managers produced the following findings.

• A large number of active managers actually outperformed their performance benchmarks.
• The outperformance was commonly attributable to net positive exposures to and positive active return contributions from smart beta factors.
• Another common result was that managers produced an alpha, which was statistically insignificant, that is not different from zero.
• Although factor-adjusted alpha is generally hard to find, we found more of it in our institutional analysis, in general, than do academic studies researching large number of mutual funds.

TABLE 6.9 Sample Manager Historical Performance and Active Return and Risk
Decomposition: S&P 500 Benchmark, Returns in US$ Gross of Management
(January 1999–September 2015)

	Total Return	Total Risk	Sharpe Ratio	CAPM Beta	Active Return	Active Risk	IR
PANEL A: Historical Performance							
S&P 500 Index	4.64	15.01	0.23	1.00			
Sample Manager	4.95	18.65	0.23	1.02	0.31	10.68	0.03

	ST Size	ST Value	ST Momentum	ST Volatility	ST Quality	Alpha	Total Active Risk
PANEL B: Risk Decomposition							
Sample Manager							
Exposure	0.49	**1.21**	**0.40**	0.24	-0.27		
Contribution to Active Return	0.75	3.35	0.54	0.34	-0.74	-3.93	
Contribution to Active Risk	0.70	3.62	-0.41	0.19	0.08	6.50	10.68

Note: Figures in bold are statistically significant at the 5% level.
Source: GSAM.

Our findings, which include market outperformance, net positive factor exposures, and higher frequency of factor-adjusted alpha, may be inconsistent with existing academic research. However, as mentioned previously, to the extent that the
historical performance provided to us by asset owners has been prescreened in some
way, either by the asset owners or the asset managers themselves, our results may be
subject to a selection bias.

IV. TYPICAL INVESTOR QUESTIONS

6.1 Does the Alpha in a Risk Decomposition Always Represent Manager Skill?

Not always: A risk decomposition determines alpha only relative to the factor portfolios used to conduct the exercise. In such analyses, many specification issues may
give rise to alpha, but not necessarily manager skill, which practitioners commonly
view as arising from activities, such as stock selection, market timing, factor timing.
Consider the following situations.

TABLE 6.10 Sample Manager Historical Performance and Active Return and Risk Decomposition: Various Benchmarks, Returns in US$ Gross of Management Fees (January 2013–December 2017)

	Total Return	Total Risk	Sharpe Ratio	CAPM Beta	Active Return	Active Risk	IR
PANEL A: U.S.							
Russell 1000 Index	15.71	9.59	1.53	1.00			
Sample Manager	17.39	10.12	1.60	1.05	1.68	1.38	1.22

	ST Size	ST Value	ST Momentum	ST Volatility	ST Quality	Alpha	Total Active Risk
Sample Manager							
Exposure	-0.17	0.13	0.07	**-0.20**	-0.03		
Contribution to Active Return	0.16	0.13	-0.05	0.00	-0.01	**1.46**	
Contribution to Active Risk	-0.05	0.09	-0.01	0.18	0.01	1.16	1.38

	Total Return	Total Risk	Sharpe Ratio	CAPM Beta	Active Return	Active Risk	IR
PANEL B: Europe							
MSCI Europe Index	7.98	12.80	0.63	1.00			
Sample Manager	12.49	12.59	0.97	0.97	4.51	2.21	2.05

	ST Size	ST Value	ST Momentum	ST Volatility	ST Quality	Alpha	Total Active Risk
Sample Manager							
Exposure	0.00	**0.47**	0.59	0.04	**0.21**		
Contribution to Active Return	0.00	0.75	0.29	0.01	0.33	**3.14**	
Contribution to Active Risk	0.00	0.15	0.85	0.01	0.20	0.99	2.21

(Continued)

TABLE 6.10 Sample Manager Historical Performance and Active Return and Risk Decomposition: Various Benchmarks, Returns in US$ Gross of Management Fees (January 2013–December 2017) (*cont'd*)

	Total Return	Total Risk	Sharpe Ratio	CAPM Beta	Active Return	Active Risk	IR
PANEL C: Developed Markets							
MSCI World Index	12.26	9.86	1.18	1.00			
Sample Manager	16.08	10.01	1.50	0.99	3.82	2.04	1.87

	ST Size	ST Value	ST Momentum	ST Volatility	ST Quality	Alpha	Total Active Risk
Sample Manager							
Exposure	0.09	**0.39**	**0.42**	-0.11	-0.01		
Contribution to Active Return	0.07	0.81	0.05	-0.03	-0.02	**2.95**	
Contribution to Active Risk	0.04	0.28	0.25	0.04	0.00	1.44	2.04

	Total Return	Total Risk	Sharpe Ratio	CAPM Beta	Active Return	Active Risk	IR
PANEL D: Emerging Markets							
MSCI EM Index	4.73	14.39	0.36	1.00			
Sample Manager	7.66	14.60	0.55	1.00	2.93	2.63	1.12

	ST Size	ST Value	ST Momentum	ST Volatility	ST Quality	Alpha	Total Active Risk
Sample Manager							
Exposure	-0.25	**0.35**	**0.37**	0.07	0.02		
Contribution to Active Return	0.42	-0.06	0.15	0.01	0.04	**2.95**	
Contribution to Active Risk	0.10	0.03	0.40	0.00	0.00	1.44	2.04

Note: Figures in bold are statistically significant at the 5% level.
Source: GSAM.

a. Signal Mismatch

A value strategy, which uses a composite signal specification, may show alpha relative to a factor portfolio, which uses only book value-to-price. This result would not be surprising, as value composites generally have historically performed better than book value-to-price. An alpha obtained from a simple combination of well-known valuation ratios may represent a higher efficiency value capture, but in our view would not represent true skill. On the other hand, if an active manager creates a more sophisticated value composite, such as industry-specific value composites based on unique manager insights, then that alpha may be viewed as manager skill. Similar arguments hold for signal mismatches for the other smart beta factors.

b. Model Mismatch

If a conventional momentum strategy is analyzed against the Fama-French 3-factor model, it is very likely to show an alpha. That alpha simply means that the active returns of the strategy are not fully explained by the 3-factor model. It would not be viewed as representing some form of manager skill. Similarly, low-volatility and quality strategies may generate an alpha relative to the Carhart 4-factor model. Or a quality strategy may show an alpha relative to a risk model, which does not include quality as a risk factor.

c. Factor Portfolio Mismatch

In some cases, a strategy may show an alpha simply because it is assessed against inappropriate factor portfolios. As we have discussed in Chapter 4 and in this chapter, EW and SW factor portfolios as well as certain smart beta active risk unconstrained optimized solutions are equivalent to implementing factor tilts relative to an equal-weighted benchmark universe. These portfolios may generate an alpha relative to the CW factor portfolios, but not relative to a combination of an equal-weighted universe and ST value, momentum, volatility, and quality portfolios.

   In assessing alpha and its link to manager skill, investors should make reasonable efforts to gain an understanding of its source. In a risk decomposition exercise, not all alpha may represent manager skill, as we would typically define it.

6.2 Why Do Risk Models Sometimes Show Counterintuitive Factor Exposures?

Asset owners conventionally use commercial risk models, such as Axioma, Barra, or Bloomberg to assess the factor exposures of active strategies. In many instances, the analysis reveals counterintuitive factor exposures. For instance, a strategy that seeks to explicitly deliver a capture of value, momentum, volatility, and quality factors may show a negative exposure to one or more factors, such as value, leading the asset owner to conclude that the strategy does not capture the value premium. The negative exposure to value can happen if the manager's investment process leads to a high negative correlation between value and other factors, which dilutes the exposure to value. Or, it can simply happen because of mismatches between the active strategy and the risk model. An active strategy may use factor definitions that are different from those used by the risk model. An active strategy may construct factor portfolios differently than the risk model, such as industry-neutral value versus cross-sectional value, or ordinal ranks versus z-scores used by risk models. An active strategy may use a different factor set compared to the risk model, such as noninclusion of quality as a risk factor in a risk model, or inclusion of other risk factors, such as liquidity in a risk model.

In addition, the inability of risk models to capture contextual relationships may sometimes lead to counterintuitive factor exposures. For example, an active strategy may be designed to take advantage of the finding that the low-volatility effect is stronger among small cap low-volatility stocks. Risk models generally do not capture such contextual returns. Finally, because of the reasons mentioned earlier, different risk models also often produce different exposures.

6.3 If Risk Models Can Produce Counterintuitive Factor Exposures, Which May Not Be Fully Reflective of Actual Exposures, Then What Other Alternatives Do Investors Have to Assess Factor Exposures?

Assessing factor exposures through the use of risk models is generally a good first step. However, for the reasons outlined above, investors should not use the output of such models as a definitive answer. In the presence of counterintuitive factor exposures, the analysis should be complemented by other methods for assessing exposures.

If a smart beta strategy is being analyzed, then a direct calculation of realized exposures to specified factors is a reasonable alternative in our opinion. Realized exposure to specified factors may be measured in terms of "Net Factor Scores," defined as the portfolio's weighted average score for a factor minus the benchmark's weighted average score to that factor. Table 6.11, Panel A shows an example of the realized average Net Factor Scores for individual factor portfolios. For instance, the table shows that the value factor portfolio had an average Net Factor Score (i.e. exposure) of 0.52 to the value factor, 0.23 to size, − 0.08 to momentum, − 0.03 to volatility, and − 0.06 to quality. The individual factor portfolios had the highest exposure to the corresponding factor and smaller exposures to other factors. When individual factor portfolios are combined to create a diversification strategy, we can expect some dilution in exposures because a given factor has negative exposures to other factors. Panel B of Table 6.11 provides an illustration of a diversification strategy that combines in equal proportions the individual value, momentum, volatility and quality portfolios. The Combination Portfolio realized positive average Net Factor Scores to all factors. The Combination Portfolio also had a positive size exposure (0.11), even though the size portfolio was not explicitly included in the combination. It is interesting to note that when this Combination Portfolio was analyzed using the Barra risk model, an exposure of – 0.15 to the value factor was calculated. Using the Bloomberg risk model, the exposure to value was determined to be only – 0.02. And yet, the actual realized exposure to value, as measured by the Net Factor Score, was 0.10 (Panel B of Table 6.11).

If an active strategy is being analyzed, then assessing factor exposures relative to the actual smart beta factor portfolios that are implemented is a good approach in our opinion. This is because the diversification benefits in a portfolio that includes smart beta and active strategies are driven by the correlation structure between the two components. Additionally, the diversification benefits within the active strategies component should be assessed by the correlation of factor-adjusted alphas relative to the smart beta implementations.

TABLE 6.11 Smart Beta Strategies Example: Average Net Factor Scores

	Size Factor	Value Factor	Momentum Factor	Volatility Factor	Quality Factor
PANEL A: Individual Factor Portfolios					
Size Portfolio	0.68	0.09	-0.11	-0.15	-0.12
Value Portfolio	0.23	0.52	-0.08	-0.03	-0.06
Momentum Portfolio	0.11	-0.08	0.43	-0.05	0.03
Volatility Portfolio	0.18	0.05	-0.02	0.23	-0.01
Quality Portfolio	0.11	-0.07	0.03	0.05	0.53
PANEL B: Diversification Strategy					
Combination Portfolio	0.11	0.10	0.10	0.07	0.18

Source: GSAM.

V. CONCLUSION

Our analysis of various smart beta and active strategies produced the following general results.

Most smart beta strategies were largely explained by the basic CW factor portfolios, that is, they generated no factor-adjusted alphas relative to these portfolios. Some highly concentrated single factor portfolios produced significant alphas against the broad CW factor portfolios, but not necessarily against more concentrated versions. A few smart beta strategies did produce statistically significant alphas. Out of all the analyzed smart beta offerings, the simple equal-weighted strategy realized the second-highest significance in factor-adjusted alpha, with a t-statistic of almost 3.

In analyzing a large number of institutional money managers, most of the active strategies were largely explained by the ST factor portfolios. In our sample, which may be subject to a selection bias, active managers generally outperformed their benchmarks. Their outperformance, however, was commonly realized through net positive exposures to smart beta factors, while the factor-adjusted alpha contribution is typically muted. We also found a higher frequency of statistically significant alpha compared to academic articles that have studied a large number of mutual funds.

In the next section of this book, we turn our attention to gaining a deeper understanding of the performance characteristics of smart beta factors. We discuss individual factor performance in Chapter 7, followed by the characteristics and benefits for factor diversification strategies in Chapter 8.

PART **IV**

PERFORMANCE CHARACTERISTICS OF SMART BETA FACTOR STRATEGIES

PERFORMANCE CHARACTERISTICS OF INDIVIDUAL SMART BETA FACTORS

In this chapter, we analyze the historical performance of individual smart beta factors based on implementation cost-adjusted signal-tilted factor portfolios. We discuss performance across three regions, namely, US, Developed Markets ex. US, and Emerging Markets. We adjust historical simulated performance for implementation costs in order to potentially make it more representative of "live" implementation.

CHAPTER SUMMARY

- We use the historical performance of signal-tilted (ST) factor portfolios created in Chapter 4 to understand the performance characteristics of individual smart beta factors.
- To more closely proxy live implementation, we calculate after-cost historical performance statistics.
- Based on our analysis, we estimate an implementation cost penalty of 0.5% round-trip for the US, 0.8% for Developed Markets ex. US, and 1.5% for Emerging Markets. These costs are assessed against the annual turnover of the ST factor portfolios.
- In order to mitigate turnover, we employ a buffer-based portfolio rebalancing process. This process reduces turnover by approximately 50%, without sacrificing after-cost investment performance.
- All factor portfolios outperformed their respective benchmarks, except for the size portfolio in the Developed Markets ex. US universe.

- In general, and consistent with prior academic research, the size portfolios depicted no outperformance between 1979 and 1999, while registering strong gains post-2000.
- Value portfolios produced after-cost information ratios of around 0.5 or higher across the three regions. The largest underperformances of the value portfolios mostly occurred in periods of strong market rallies.
- Momentum portfolios generally realized lower active returns and information ratios compared to the other factors across the three regions. This is largely due to the poor performance of the momentum factor since 2009. The largest underperformances for the momentum portfolios happened during market reversal years, that is, strong positive (negative) returns followed by large negative (positive) returns.
- Low-volatility portfolios, targeting a 4% active risk to the underlying benchmark, realized total risk reduction ranging from 16% in the US and Developed Markets ex. US universes, and 11% in the Emerging Markets universe. Volatility portfolios also generated positive active returns, thus producing meaningful improvements in Sharpe ratios compared to the market. These portfolios depicted a consistent pattern in active returns in up-and-down markets, outperforming during market downturns and underperforming during upswings.
- Quality portfolios produced after-cost information ratios of 0.5 or higher in the three regions. These portfolios depicted defensive characteristics, as the downside capture ratios were consistently below 100% in all universes. However, quality was differentiated from low-volatility investing in that for similar levels of active risk, quality portfolios generated much higher active returns and information ratios.
- Based on the historical performance characteristics of ST factor portfolios, we can draw the following broad observations. Size is a high-risk factor, as size portfolios consistently generated higher total risk, maximum drawdown, and CAPM betas compared to the market. Volatility is a low-risk factor, as volatility portfolios delivered significant total risk and drawdown reduction. Quality is a hybrid factor, as quality portfolios portrayed defensive characteristics but with much higher active returns and IRs compared to low-volatility portfolios. Value and momentum portfolios did not depict consistent performance characteristics across the three regions.
- All individual smart beta factors expose investors to significant market underperformance risk. Not only have these factors underperformed the market by a wide margin in a given year, the underperformances have also lasted over multiple consecutive years.
- The high market underperformance risk of individual smart beta factors implies that in order to realize the return premia associated with smart beta factors, investors must be willing and able to stay the course and keep a long-term investment perspective.

I. INTRODUCTION

In Chapter 4, we analyzed various weighting schemes that are typically used to capture smart beta factors. One important conclusion that emerged from the analysis is that signal-tilted (ST) factor portfolios tend to generate statistically significant alphas when decomposed against capitalization-weighted (CW) factor portfolios. Equal-weighted (EW) and signal-weighted (SW) factor portfolios also generate significant alphas relative to CW factor portfolios. However, EW and ST factor portfolios are equivalent to implementing factor tilts relative to an equal-weighted parent universe. As such, their performance is almost fully explained when decomposed against a combination of the equal-weighted universe (substituting for the size factor) and the ST value, momentum, quality, and low-volatility factor portfolios. Further, in Chapter 6, we discussed the finding that most smart beta strategies we analyzed did not generate a statistically significant alpha against the basic CW factor portfolios. Some smart beta strategies, such as active risk unconstrained optimized solutions, also get very close to implementing factor tilts relative to an equal-weighted universe. Such strategies may produce an alpha against the CW factor portfolios, but not relative to an equal-weighted universe and ST factor portfolios.

Therefore, based on these findings in Chapter 4 and Chapter 6, we focus our attention on the ST factor portfolios as a potential implementation option. Through these portfolios, we seek to gain an understanding of the performance characteristics of size, value, momentum, quality, and low-volatility smart beta factors. We build the ST factor portfolios using the construction methodology outlined in Appendix 4.1 of Chapter 4. We study three universes, namely, US, Developed Markets ex. USA, and Emerging Markets, to cover global equities. We use the Russell 1000 Index as the universe for the US and MSCI Standard Indexes for the other two regions. To facilitate comparisons, all ST factor portfolios are constructed to target an average active risk of about 4% to the underlying parent universe. The start date for this analysis is January 1979 for the US, which corresponds to the start date for the Russell Indexes. For the other two universes, the start dates are January 1995 for Developed Markets ex. US, and January 1998 for Emerging Markets. The choice of these start dates is mainly dictated by the availability of good quality fundamental data for these markets. The end date of the analysis is June 2017. We define the size signal as the inverse of market capitalization, value as a composite of three valuation ratios, namely book value-to-price, sales-to-price, and cash flow-to-price (or earnings-to-price when cash flow is unavailable), momentum as prior 11-month total return, lagged by one month, volatility as the inverse of prior 12-month standard deviation of daily total returns, and quality/profitability as gross profits divided by total assets. The fundamental information is sourced from Compustat and Worldscope databases and is lagged appropriately to avoid look-ahead bias. We discussed these signal specifications in some detail in Chapter 4 and Chapter 5. All ST factor portfolios presented in this chapter are rebalanced on a quarterly basis. A quarterly rebalancing frequency, in our opinion, provides a good balance between the conflicting objectives of keeping the portfolios current (that is, reflective of changes in factor attractiveness scores) and keeping turnover at a reasonable level.

II. AFTER-COST PERFORMANCE: ACCOUNTING FOR IMPLEMENTATION COSTS

The ST factor portfolios that were constructed in Chapter 4 did not incorporate implementation costs. In order to make these portfolios more representative of live implementation, we start our analysis by calculating the after-cost performance of ST factor portfolios as well as discussing the methodology we employ to mitigate turnover.

A. Determining Implementation Costs

After-cost performance is typically calculated by multiplying the estimated implementation costs by the turnover of the factor portfolios. As such, we need to determine what implementation cost assumption we should use. The costs involved in replicating CW factor portfolios (e.g. Russell 1000 Value Index) may represent a good starting point for determining the implementation costs for ST Factor portfolios. Based on our experience and on conversations with passive managers and traders, a 0.15% round-trip implementation cost assumption would be a reasonable estimate for US large cap style indexes. A higher level of implementation costs for the ST factor portfolios would also seem reasonable, given potential investability and capacity considerations. But how much higher should the estimated implementation cost be relative to CW factor portfolios?

One approach to answering this question would be to compare the Average Cap ratios of the ST and CW factor portfolios. The Average ST and CW factor portfolio Cap ratio is calculated in the following manner. At each rebalance, the weight of each security in the ST factor portfolio is divided by the weight of that security in the benchmark and a security Cap ratio is calculated. For instance, if a security has a factor portfolio weight of 5% and a benchmark weight of 2%, then the security Cap ratio would be 2.5. A ST factor portfolio Cap ratio is calculated as the weighted sum of security Cap ratios, using the security weights in the ST factor portfolio. The factor portfolio Cap ratios at each rebalance are then averaged over time to calculate the Average Cap ratio for the ST factor portfolios. The first column of Table 7.1 shows the Average Cap ratios for the five ST factor portfolios. In the case of CW factor portfolios, which we constructed to cover 50% of benchmark weight in Chapter 4, the factor portfolio Average Cap ratio is always 2, as shown in the second column. The implementation cost assumption for the ST factor portfolios could then be calculated by multiplying the ST-to-CW Average Cap ratio by the implementation cost of CW factor portfolios (i.e. 0.15%). The ST-to-CW Average Cap ratio is shown in the third column. Finally, an estimate of implementation costs for the ST factor portfolios (fourth column) is derived by multiplying the ST-to-CW Average Cap ratio by the 0.15% cost assumption used for the CW factor portfolios. For instance, for the ST quality portfolio, which had the highest ST-to-CW Average Cap ratio of 3.42, the implementation costs were estimated to be 0.51% round-trip (i.e. 0.15% times 3.42).

TABLE 7.1 Estimated Implementation Costs for ST Portfolios: Russell 1000 Universe (January 1979–June 2017)

	ST Average Cap Ratio	CW Average Cap Ratio	ST-to-CW Ratio	Estimated Implementation Cost (%)
Size Portfolio	6.60	2.00	3.30	0.49
Value Portfolio	3.22	2.00	1.61	0.24
Momentum Portfolio	2.34	2.00	1.17	0.18
Volatility Portfolio	1.96	2.00	0.98	0.15
Quality Portfolio	6.85	2.00	3.42	0.51

Source: GSAM.

We also note that we analyzed the performance of ST factor portfolios when the maximum Cap ratio for an individual stock was constrained to five. We found little difference in information ratios relative to the unconstrained factor portfolios presented in Table 7.1.

Based on this analysis, for simplicity and also to be conservative, we used a single 0.50% round-trip implementation cost assumption for all US ST factor portfolios. This cost assumption is toward the upper range of the numbers reported in the last column of Table 7.1. For Developed Markets ex. US and Emerging Markets, we followed a similar process and used a round-trip implementation cost estimate of 0.80% and 1.5%, respectively. These cost estimates were assessed against the turnover of the ST factor portfolios to calculate the after-cost performance.

Table 7.2 reports the before-cost and after-cost historical performance of US ST factor portfolios. The cost adjustment did not influence the risk profile of ST factor portfolios, but lowered returns. The largest decline in returns was registered by the ST momentum portfolio, which also had the highest annualized turnover of 92%. However, all ST factor portfolios outperformed the Russell 1000 benchmark and generated higher Sharpe ratios, on an after-cost basis.

B. Mitigating Turnover

From the perspective of real-life implementation, managing, and mitigating turnover is an important and desirable feature of a smart beta offering. Turnover is a guaranteed cost of implementing a strategy, whereas its expected return is just that; an expectation. Therefore, investors tend to prefer investment processes that deliver factor payoffs with reduced turnover. We employ a buffer-based rebalancing methodology to mitigate the turnover of ST factor portfolios without sacrificing after-cost investment performance. This process works as follows. At each rebalance, the target weight for each security is determined based on the updated factor scores. Then, a buffer is specified around the target weight of each security. The buffer is set as the maximum of (1)

TABLE 7.2 Before-Cost and After-Cost Historical Performance of ST Factor Portfolios: Russell 1000 Universe (January 1979–June 2017)

	Total Gross Return (%)	Total Risk (%)	Sharpe Ratio	Annualized Turnover (%)
Russell 1000 Index	11.84	15.05	0.49	
ST Size Portfolio—Before Cost	12.91	16.95	0.51	
ST Size Portfolio—After Cost	12.61	16.95	0.50	54
ST Value Portfolio—Before Cost	14.29	15.51	0.62	
ST Value Portfolio—After Cost	13.96	15.51	0.60	58
ST Momentum Portfolio—Before Cost	13.32	16.08	0.55	
ST Momentum Portfolio—After Cost	12.81	16.08	0.53	92
ST Volatility Portfolio—Before Cost	12.74	12.53	0.63	
ST Volatility Portfolio—After Cost	12.58	12.53	0.62	30
ST Quality Portfolio—Before Cost	14.41	15.76	0.62	
ST Quality Portfolio—After Cost	14.17	15.77	0.61	43

Source: GSAM.

20% of the Maximum Stock Underweight Position used in constructing a given ST factor portfolio or (2) 0.20%. (Refer to Chapter 4, Appendix 4.1, for details relating to the construction methodology of ST factor portfolios.) If the current weight of a security at rebalance date is within the buffer, no trade takes place. If the security weight is outside of the buffer, then a trade is conducted to bring the weight to the upper (for sells) or lower (for buys) bound of the buffer, but not all the way to the target weight. The impact of buffer-based rebalancing on the turnover of US ST factor portfolios is shown in Table 7.3. The application of buffer-based rebalancing resulted in meaningful reduction in portfolio turnover, ranging from 42% for momentum to 60% for volatility. The average turnover reduction across all ST factor portfolios was 52%.

What is the impact of the buffer-based rebalancing on the historical performance of ST factor portfolios? On the one hand, the use of buffers may interfere with the purity of factor capture, as security weights are not perfectly aligned with target weights based on current factor scores. All else being equal, this should have a negative impact on the performance of the ST factor portfolios. On the other hand, buffer-based rebalancing significantly reduces turnover, which should improve after-cost performance. The statistics reported in Table 7.4 for the US universe show that, in our construction process, the two effects approximately offset. The Sharpe ratios of ST factor portfolios constructed with the buffer are similar to those of ST factor portfolios created without buffers. In other words, turnover is reduced by approximately 50%, without any meaningful loss in after-cost investment performance. Similar results

TABLE 7.3 Impact of Buffer-Based Rebalancing on the Turnover of ST Factor Portfolios: Russell 1000 Universe (January 1979–June 2017)

	Annualized Turnover Without Buffer	Annualized Turnover With Buffer	Reduction in Annualized Turnover (%)
ST Size Portfolio	54	30	44
ST Value Portfolio	58	26	55
ST Momentum Portfolio	92	53	42
ST Volatility Portfolio	30	12	60
ST Quality Portfolio	43	18	58
Average			52

Source: GSAM.

TABLE 7.4 After-Cost Historical Performance of ST Factor Portfolios With and Without Buffers: Russell 1000 Universe (January 1979–June 2017)

	Total Gross Return (%)	Total Risk (%)	Sharpe Ratio	Annualized Turnover (%)
Russell 1000 Index	11.84	15.05	0.49	
ST Size Portfolio—Without Buffer	12.61	16.95	0.50	54
ST Size Portfolio—With Buffer	12.85	16.51	0.52	30
ST Value Portfolio—Without Buffer	13.96	15.51	0.60	58
ST Value Portfolio—With Buffer	13.73	15.18	0.60	26
ST Momentum Portfolio—Without Buffer	12.81	16.08	0.53	92
ST Momentum Portfolio—With Buffer	12.77	16.10	0.52	53
ST Volatility Portfolio—Without Buffer	12.58	12.53	0.62	30
ST Volatility Portfolio—With Buffer	12.66	12.68	0.62	12
ST Quality Portfolio—Without Buffer	14.17	15.77	0.61	43
ST Quality Portfolio—With Buffer	14.14	15.61	0.61	18

Source: GSAM.

were obtained in the World ex. USA and Emerging Markets universes. As mentioned previously, significantly reducing turnover, which is a guaranteed implementation cost, while retaining after-cost investment performance, would be viewed as a highly desirable feature in the design of a smart beta strategy.

III. AFTER-COST PERFORMANCE CHARACTERISTICS

With the implementation cost assumptions and the buffer-based portfolio rebalancing methodology outlined, we now proceed to analyze the after-cost performance of the ST factor portfolios, as presented in Table 7.5 for the three regions.

A. Size

In the US, the ST-size portfolio outperformed the Russell 1000 Index by 1% per annum, but also had higher total and systematic risk (CAPM Beta of 1.07). However, the portfolio produced a higher Sharpe ratio than the benchmark and an information ratio (IR) of 0.27, on an after-cost basis. The ST size portfolio had a higher Maximum Drawdown than the market and also depicted high market underperformance risk. The Worst Underperformance Year was 8.46% and Maximum Rolling 3-Year Annualized Underperformance was 5.61%. During up markets, the ST size portfolio performed better than the market (Upside Capture Ratio of 108, that is, rose 8% more than the market, on average), but also underperformed in declining markets (Downside Capture Ratio of 107, that is, fell 7% more than the market, on average).

Consistent with the size factor's performance patterns discussed by Dimson et al. (2017), the US ST-size portfolio also depicted long relative performance cycles. Figure 7.1 shows the cumulative active return profile of the size portfolio. Broadly speaking, the entire analyzed period can be broken down in two subperiods. The period between 1979 and 1999 was characterized by lackluster performance, in which the size portfolio did no better than the Russell 1000 Index. From 2000 onward, however, the size portfolio has produced significant outperformance. As mentioned by Dimson, Marsh, and Staunton (2017), despite long periods of lackluster performance, it would be hard to use these performance characteristics of the size factor to make a case for intentionally underweighting small cap stocks. The evidence presented here, however, does highlight the need to analyze smart beta strategies that have high and concentrated exposure to the size factor over the pre-2000 period. (Also see Application Example 6.1 in Chapter 6.)

To represent markets outside the US, the historical performance in Table 7.5 is presented from January 1995 for the MSCI World ex. USA universe and from January 1998 for the MSCI EM universe. Across the three universes, the size portfolios depicted consistent risk characteristics. These portfolios had higher total risk and CAPM betas compared to the market. Generally speaking, the size portfolios performed well in rising markets and poorly in falling markets. In the MSCI World ex. USA universe, the size portfolio generated no active return over the analysis period.

FIGURE 7.1 ST Size Portfolio: Cumulative Active Return (Russell 1000 Universe, January 1979–June 2017)

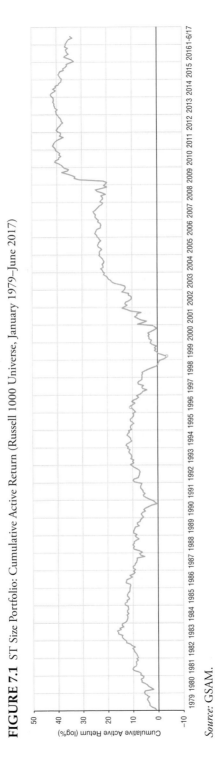

Source: GSAM.

TABLE 7.5 After-Cost Historical Performance of ST Factor Portfolios—Annualized Results (Period Ending June 2017)

	Start Date	Total Gross Return (%)	Total Risk (%)	Sharpe Ratio	CAPM Beta	Maximum Drawdown (%)	Active Gross Return (%)	Active Risk (%)	Information Ratio	Worst Under-performance Year (%)	Max Rolling 3-Year Annualized Under-performance (%)	Upside Capture Ratio	Downside Capture Ratio
Russell 1000 Index	Jan-79	11.84	15.05	0.49	1.00	−51.13							
ST Size Portfolio		12.85	16.51	0.52	1.07	−52.73	1.00	3.78	0.27	−8.46	−5.61	108	107
ST Value Portfolio		13.73	15.18	0.60	0.98	−55.97	1.89	3.92	0.48	−10.91	−7.91	102	93
ST Momentum Portfolio		12.77	16.10	0.52	1.04	−50.56	0.93	3.86	0.24	−8.35	−4.09	106	104
ST Low-Volatility Portfolio		12.66	12.68	0.62	0.82	−43.88	0.82	4.11	0.20	−13.33	−8.11	88	75
ST Quality Portfolio		14.14	15.61	0.61	1.00	−43.57	2.30	4.18	0.55	−5.38	−2.81	104	94
MSCI World ex. USA Index	Jan-95	5.66	16.25	0.25	1.00	−56.34							
ST Size Portfolio		5.66	16.79	0.25	1.01	−58.86	0.00	3.56	0.00	−11.29	−8.30	100	100
ST Value Portfolio		7.66	17.30	0.36	1.04	−60.51	2.00	4.06	0.49	−10.59	−5.96	105	97
ST Momentum Portfolio		6.64	15.99	0.31	0.95	−55.94	0.98	3.97	0.25	−11.86	−4.94	100	95
ST Low-Volatility Portfolio		7.09	13.69	0.37	0.83	−47.96	1.43	3.93	0.36	−10.72	−2.84	88	78

(*Continued*)

TABLE 7.5 After-Cost Historical Performance of ST Factor Portfolios—Annualized Results (Period Ending June 2017) (*Cont'd*)

	Start Date	Total Gross Return (%)	Total Risk (%)	Sharpe Ratio	CAPM Beta	Maximum Drawdown (%)	Active Gross Return (%)	Active Risk (%)	Information Ratio	Worst Under-performance Year (%)	Max Rolling 3-Year Annualized Under-performance (%)	Upside Capture Ratio	Downside Capture Ratio
ST Quality Portfolio		8.08	14.85	0.41	0.89	−49.78	2.42	3.54	0.68	−3.08	−3.96	95	83
MSCI EM Index	Jan-98	7.48	23.54	0.33	1.00	−61.44							
ST Size Portfolio		8.03	24.49	0.35	1.03	−63.27	0.54	3.65	0.15	−4.45	−3.04	103	101
ST Value Portfolio		10.21	24.64	0.43	1.04	−61.00	2.72	3.62	0.75	−2.89	−2.58	108	100
ST Momentum Portfolio		8.25	23.44	0.36	0.98	−66.41	0.77	4.36	0.18	−12.68	−6.71	101	98
ST Low-Volatility Portfolio		9.00	20.89	0.41	0.88	−55.24	1.51	3.56	0.43	−14.56	−0.93	92	85
ST Quality Portfolio		9.82	21.78	0.44	0.92	−56.82	2.34	3.61	0.65	−7.02	−1.74	97	88

Source: GSAM.

This is largely due to the performance of small cap stocks between 1995 and 1999. Over this period, the size portfolio experienced five consecutive years of market underperformance, registering a cumulative active return drawdown of close to 40%. Since 2000, however, the size portfolio has produced significant gains, consistent with the performance of the size factor in other regions.

B. Value

For the US universe, the ST value portfolio outperformed the Russell 1000 index by 1.89% per year with only slightly higher total risk, thus generating a much higher Sharpe ratio. The portfolio also produced a highly respectable after-cost IR of 0.48. The Maximum Drawdown was higher than the market and the portfolio also depicted high market underperformance risk, with the worst annual underperformance of 10.91% and a rolling three-year underperformance of 7.91% per year. In the other two universes, the value portfolios also generated much higher Sharpe ratios than the market as well as high IRs. These portfolios also had similar or higher total risk and drawdown compared to the market.

It is sometimes argued that value investing tends to perform well during periods of low risk aversion (good times), as proxied by rising markets, and poorly during periods of high risk aversion (bad times), as proxied by falling markets. We did not find consistent support for this argument, based on the performance of the ST value portfolios. Across the three regions, we did find that value portfolios had Upside Capture ratios in excess of 100. However, in falling markets, we found that value portfolios had Downside Capture ratios of 100 or less. In Emerging Markets, the value portfolio's outperformance largely came in up markets. But, in the US, the outperformance was mainly attributable to better performance in down markets. In fact, in analyzing periods of large underperformances, we found that, in the case of the US with the longer history, the five largest underperformances of the value portfolio came in calendar years when the market registered a gain of at least 20% in four out of the five instances. This is shown in Table 7.6. Further, as depicted in Figure 7.2,

TABLE 7.6 Five Largest Annual Underperformances of the ST Value Portfolio: Russell 1000 Universe (January 1979–June 2017)

	ST Value Portfolio—Active Return (%)	Russell 1000 Index—Total Return (%)
1999	−10.91	20.91
1998	−8.08	27.02
1980	−7.61	31.87
2007	−7.56	5.77
1989	−3.72	30.43

Source: GSAM.

FIGURE 7.2 ST Value Portfolio: Cumulative Active Return (Russell 1000 Universe, January 1979–June 2017)

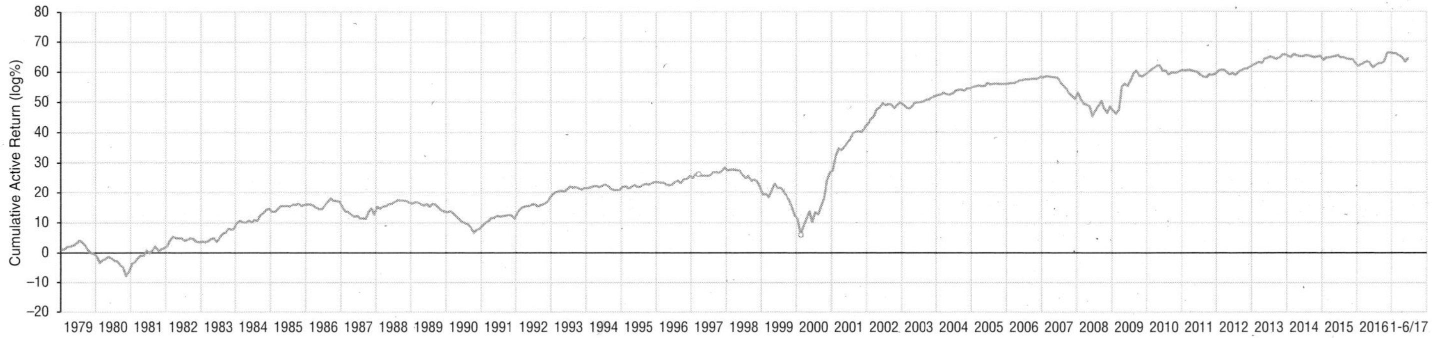

Source: GSAM.

the value portfolio's largest cumulative underperformance also came during the late 1990s, when strong market rallies were driven by large technology stocks.

C. Momentum

The ST momentum portfolios outperformed their respective benchmarks in the three regions, but generally produced lower after-cost IRs compared to the other factor portfolios. The momentum portfolios had similar or higher total risk and drawdown compared to the market in the three regions. In the US, the momentum portfolio had a CAPM beta in excess of one. In the other two regions, the momentum portfolios had a CAPM beta of less than one, which resulted in momentum working as a defensive strategy. That is, performing well during market downturns (i.e. downside capture ratios less than 100).

Momentum tends to perform well during trending markets. But, momentum is also well-known for exposing investors to periodic and significant market underperformance, especially during market reversals. These periods are characterized by rising (falling) markets followed by falling (rising) markets. Although not every market reversal causes an underperformance of the momentum strategy, the largest underperformances do tend to occur during a market reversal. Table 7.7 shows that the three largest underperformances of the momentum portfolios in each universe happened in a reversal calendar year. For instance, in the US, the sharp decline in the market in 2008 (– 37.60%) was followed by a strong rally in 2009 (+ 28.43%). In 2009, the momentum portfolio recorded a large underperformance of 8.35%. The momentum portfolios experienced extremely high and negative active returns in 2009 outside the US as well, with the largest underperformance of 12.68% in Emerging Markets. In fact, the momentum portfolios have performed relatively poorly since 2009, as shown in Figure 7.3 for the US universe, which has resulted in the low active returns and IRs reported in Table 7.5.

D. Low Volatility

Signal-tilted low-volatility portfolios overweight low-volatility, low-beta stocks and underweight high-volatility, high-beta stocks, based on one-year historical total daily return volatilities. The fact that the volatility portfolios realized lower total risk and CAPM betas than the respective market benchmarks implies that historical volatility is a good predictor of future volatility and CAPM betas, at least at a diversified portfolio level. The volatility portfolios, targeting an active risk of around 4% to the underlying benchmark, generated a total risk reduction of around 16% in the US and World ex. US universes and 11% in the Emerging Markets universe. Despite the total risk reduction, volatility portfolios realized higher returns than the market in the various universes. This resulted in meaningful Sharpe ratio improvements. The volatility portfolios also depicted a consistent pattern in up and down markets. The downside capture ratios were consistently below 100. On the other hand, the

TABLE 7.7 Market Reversals and Performance of ST Momentum Portfolios—Annualized Results

	1980	1981	1999	2000	2008	2009
Russell 1000 Index–Total Return	31.87	−5.10	20.91	−7.79	−37.60	28.43
ST Momentum Portfolio–Active Return		−7.38		−7.05		−8.35
	1999	2000	2008	2009	2015	2016
MSCI World ex USA Index–Total Return	28.27	−13.16	−42.23	34.39	−2.60	3.29
ST Momentum Portfolio–Active Return		−5.61		−11.86		−6.09
	2007	2008	2008	2009	2015	2016
MSCI EM Index–Total Return	39.82	−53.19	−53.19	79.02	−14.60	11.60
ST Momentum Portfolio–Active Return		−6.04		−12.68		−6.4

Source: GSAM.

upside capture ratios were also consistently below 100, implying that low-volatility strategies underperformed when markets were rising (because of their low CAPM betas). The market underperformance risk of volatility portfolios is also quite high. The large underperformances typically happen when markets are rising sharply. In the case of the U S, this is shown in Figure 7.4, with significant underperformances occurring in 1979–1980 and 1998–1999 when markets registered strong gains.

E. Quality

The ST quality (profitability) portfolios outperformed the market and generated after-cost IRs in excess of 0.50 across the three regions. In the US, the total risk and CAPM beta were similar to the market. However, the maximum total drawdown was 15% lower than the market and similar to that achieved by the ST volatility portfolio. Outside the US, over a shorter analysis period, the ST quality portfolios had CAPM betas significantly below one and closer to the ST volatility portfolios. This may be largely due to the high active return correlation between quality and volatility factors over the shorter analysis period, as we will discuss in more detail in the next chapter.

Quality is often considered a defensive investment style, which can be expected to perform well during periods of high risk aversion. And risk aversion tends to be high during periods of market drawdowns. During such periods, a flight to quality typically takes place, leading to superior performance of the quality portfolios.

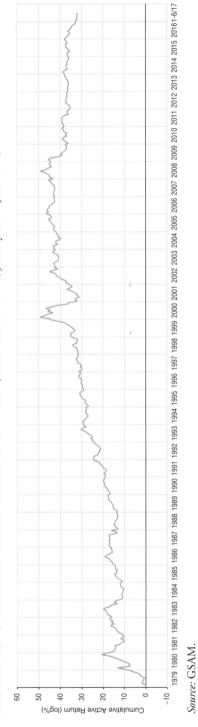

FIGURE 7.3 ST Momentum Portfolio: Cumulative Active Return (Russell 1000 Universe, January 1979–June 2017)

Source: GSAM.

FIGURE 7.4 ST Low-Volatility Portfolio: Cumulative Active Return (Russell 1000 Universe, January 1979–June 2017)

Source: GSAM.

In addition to lower total drawdown, this feature is also depicted in the downside capture ratios, which were consistently below 100% in all universes. Although quality is a defensive style, it has performance characteristics, which make it somewhat different from low-volatility investing. In particular, for similar levels of active risk (i.e. 4%), the quality portfolios have generated much higher active returns and IRs compared to low-volatility portfolios. The active returns also depict more consistency, as shown in Figure 7.5 for the US ST quality portfolio.

F. Summary of Performance Characteristics

Based on the performance characteristics of ST factor portfolios, we highlight the following general observations.

- Size is a high-risk factor. Across the three regions, size portfolios consistently realized higher total risk, maximum drawdown, and CAPM betas compared to the market. Generally speaking, the size portfolios performed well in rising markets and poorly in falling markets.
- Low volatility is, by definition, a low-risk factor. Low-volatility portfolios consistently had CAPM betas significantly lower than one. These portfolios provided significant total risk and drawdown reduction. Because of the low CAPM betas, low-volatility portfolios outperformed in falling markets and underperformed in rising markets.
- Quality is a hybrid factor. Quality portfolios delivered some form of risk reduction, such as lower drawdowns compared to the market, but also realized high active returns and IRs in the three regions. The outperformance of quality portfolios was largely driven by better performance in falling markets.
- Value and momentum portfolios did not depict consistent performance patterns across the three regions.
- All factor portfolios experienced large and prolonged underperformances, thus depicting a high market underperformance risk.

IV. TYPICAL INVESTOR QUESTIONS

7.1 Is Momentum a Profitable Strategy, on an After-Cost Basis?

Academic studies document that momentum investing has generated impressive excess returns over long periods of time. However, momentum also has very high turnover and academic studies typically do not account for implementation costs. As such, many investors rightfully wonder whether momentum is a profitable strategy once its high turnover and associated trading costs are taken into account.

It is true that amongst the smart beta factors momentum has the highest turnover, approaching 100% for 4% active risk ST momentum portfolios. This

FIGURE 7.5 ST Quality Portfolio: Cumulative Active Return (Russell 1000 Universe, January 1979–June 2017)

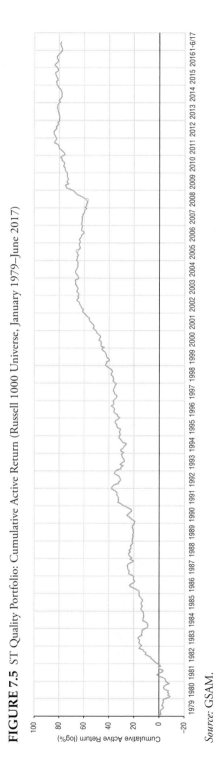

Source: GSAM.

turnover, however, can be substantially reduced through turnover mitigation techniques. For instance, we have shown that buffer-based rebalancing can potentially reduce turnover by about 50%. And assuming relatively conservative implementation costs, this reduction in turnover is achieved without sacrificing after-cost returns. According to the historical performance analysis presented in this chapter, momentum portfolios across various regions have generated reasonable after-cost active returns and IRs, despite the fact that momentum investing has encountered some headwinds since 2009.

7.2 What Important Overall Observations May Be Drawn from an Analysis of the Historical Performance of Individual Smart Beta Factors?

Individual smart beta factors, across various regions and over different time periods, have delivered respectable after-cost active returns and IRs relative to the underlying market benchmarks. However, in our opinion, investors should be mindful of the following two important considerations with regards to investing in individual smart beta factors.

a. Market Underperformance Risk

All individual smart beta factors expose investors to significant market underperformance risk. The factors can underperform the market by a significant margin in a single year. For instance, in the case of the US, the worst annual underperformance ranged from 5.38% for quality to 13.33% for volatility (Table 7.5). Additionally, not only can individual factors significantly underperform the market in a given year, the underperformance can also last over multiple years. It is quite common for individual factors to experience two, three, or even five consecutive years of market underperformance. This can lead to quite large cumulative underperformances over time. As an example, the US ST value portfolio had a cumulative underperformance relative to the Russell 1000 Index of over 25% between 1998 and 1999. Further, notice in Table 7.5 that all factors across the three regions registered annualized underperformance on a rolling three-year basis.

b. Investment Horizon

The high market underperformance risk of factors is sometimes cited as a reason why factors actually deliver a return premium (e.g. Ang 2014). That is, the observed factor premia are a compensation for bearing the high and painful risk of underperforming the market by a wide margin over extended periods of time. This argument may make conceptual sense, but it does not explain (1) why certain factors are rewarded and others not, despite having similar market underperformance risk, and (2) why certain factors are more highly rewarded than others, despite having lower market underperformance risk (e.g. quality in Table 7.5). However, one conclusion is clear. In order to earn the return premia associated with rewarded smart beta factors, that is size, value, momentum, low volatility, and quality, investors must maintain a long-term investment horizon. That is, investors must be willing to stay the course during periods of pronounced and prolonged market underperformance, if they wish to realize the full benefits of smart beta factor investing.

V. CONCLUSION

Using conservative estimates of implementation costs and techniques for mitigating turnover, we have shown in this chapter that individual smart beta factors have delivered attractive historical performance across various regions of global equities. However, one cautionary finding is that individual smart beta factors also expose investors to prolonged and pronounced underperformance relative to the market. This result implies that investors need to bear short-term pain in order to harvest factor return premia in the long run.

The market underperformance risk associated with factor investing can, nonetheless, be mitigated. Indeed, smart beta factors have attractive correlation attributes. Combining smart beta factors to create factor diversification strategies, therefore, tends to significantly reduce the risk of underperforming the market, while also improving relative risk-adjusted returns. We address the important topic of factor diversification in the next chapter.

CHAPTER 8

PERFORMANCE CHARACTERISTICS OF FACTOR DIVERSIFICATION STRATEGIES

It is often said that diversification is the only free lunch in finance. Multifactor smart beta strategies may represent an example of such a free lunch. In this chapter, we discuss the attractive correlation attributes of smart beta factors and show how combining factors results in improved relative risk-adjusted performance, while also potentially mitigating market underperformance risk.

CHAPTER SUMMARY

- Smart beta factors depict low or negative pair-wise active return correlations in the long run, which has the potential to provide significant diversification benefits in a multifactor strategy.
- In the short run, such as rolling five-year periods, pair-wise correlations are unstable. Generally negatively correlated factors become positively correlated and moderately positively correlated factors become highly positively correlated. This finding may lead to the conclusion that factor diversification may not work as well over shorter time horizons.
- Diversification benefits in a multifactor strategy, however, are driven by the "off-diagonal average" of all the individual factor pair correlations. Over the long run, this average generally depicts correlation close to zero across the smart beta factors.
- The short-term variation in the off-diagonal average is also significantly less than the variation in individual factor pairs. Even the highest values reached by this average

on a rolling five-year basis remain quite moderate. This happens because at a given point in time positively correlated factor pairs are offset by negatively correlated factor pairs. That is, there is "diversification" within the correlation structure of smart beta factors.

- The behavior of the off-diagonal average would suggest that multifactor strategies should provide diversification benefits even in the short term, such as five-year rolling periods.
- To study the characteristics of factor diversification, we create an equally weighted combination of tracking error-matched signal-tilted (ST) value, momentum, low-volatility, and quality factor portfolios, which we refer to as the ST Multifactor Portfolio (MFP).
- In long-term simulations in the three universes we analyzed, namely the US, Developed Markets ex. US, and Emerging Markets, the ST MFP realized about 50% reduction in active risk compared to the average of the active risks across the factor portfolios. This reduction in active risk is known as "gain from diversification."
- Because of the significant reduction in active risk, the ST MFPs realized much higher IRs compared to the individual factor portfolios in all three regions.
- The improvement in IR meaningfully enhanced the statistical significance of the active return of the MFPs, with t-statistics exceeding five in the US and four in other regions.
- To the extent that all factors rarely underperformed the market at the same time, the ST MFPs also depicted lower probability of market underperformance compared to individual factor portfolios.
- Also due to the stability of the off-diagonal average, the MFPs realized consistent active risk reduction over five-year rolling periods, with an average of 56% and a minimum reduction of almost 30%.
- Based on rolling five years, the average IR of the MFPs were also significantly higher compared to individual factor portfolios.
- We also constructed MFPs using capitalization-weighted (CW), capitalization-scaled (CS), signal-weighted (SW), and equal-weighted (EW) factor portfolios to analyze the diversification benefits realized by other weighting schemes.
- The CW, CS, and ST MFPs, which form the Tilting category of weighting schemes discussed in Chapter 4, realized similar active risk reduction or gain from diversification. This implies that, within the Tilting category, the active return correlation structure is not meaningfully affected by the various weighting schemes.
- The SW and EW MFPs, which form part of the Reweighting category, produced only marginal active risk reduction and gain from diversification. This result is driven by the high positive pair-wise active return correlations across the SW and EW factor portfolios. As discussed in Chapter 4, SW and EW factor portfolios have a common influence, which is the performance of the equal-weighted universe versus the capitalization-weighted universe. As such, SW and EW MFPs realize much lower diversification benefits when assessed against a capitalization-weighted benchmark.

- CS MFP produced a small factor-adjusted alpha against the CW factor portfolios. ST, SW, and EW MFPs realized much higher, and more statistically significant, alphas. However, the alphas of SW and EW FPDs disappeared when decomposed against an equal-weighted universe and ST value, momentum, low-volatility, and quality portfolios.
- With regard to portfolio construction, two approaches to building factor diversification strategies, namely portfolio blending and signal blending, have recently become the subject of a debate within the industry.
- Some studies have argued that signal blending is a more efficient approach because it avoids securities with offsetting factor exposures, and thus realizes higher exposures to targeted factors.
- Our research, based on a comparison of exposure-matched portfolios, challenges the general dominance of signal blending. It shows that, at moderate levels of factor exposure and active risk, portfolio blending produces better IRs. At high levels of factor exposure and active risk, signal blending retains better diversification and produces higher IRs.
- Our perspective on this debate, however, is that the decision of which approach to use needs to be made in the context of a given investment process.

I.   INTRODUCTION

In the previous chapter, we highlighted that individual smart beta factors depicted different active return characteristics. For instance, generally speaking, size portfolios outperformed in up markets and underperformed in down markets. Volatility portfolios, on the other hand, depicted the opposite pattern; outperforming in down markets and underperforming in up markets. Value portfolios realized the largest outperformances when the market registered negative or moderately positive returns, while the largest underperformances happened in periods when the markets rose sharply. The largest outperformances of momentum portfolios were realized in strong trending markets, while the largest underperformances happened in mostly market reversal years. These active return characteristics imply that smart beta factors may have attractive active return correlation attributes, which could potentially deliver significant diversification benefits. In this chapter, therefore, we start by analyzing the long-term and short-term correlation attributes of factor active returns.

II.   ACTIVE RETURN CORRELATIONS

We analyze the active return correlation attributes of smart beta factors for three regions, namely, US (from January 1979 to June 2017), Developed Markets ex. US (from January 1995 to June 2017), and Emerging Markets (from January 1998 to June 2017).

A. Long-Term Correlations

Table 8.1 reports the pair-wise active return correlations of the ST factor portfolios. Across the three regions, the size portfolios had a positive active return correlation with value and negative correlation with volatility. This implies that value stocks tend to be small cap stocks, whereas low-volatility stocks seem to have a large cap bias. Value portfolios had a negative correlation with momentum, as stocks with low valuation ratios typically lack momentum and stocks with high momentum tend to see increases in their valuation ratios. Value portfolios also had a negative correlation with quality, defined as gross profits scaled by total assets. This implies that high-profitability stocks tend to have growth-like characteristics. However, profitability is not conventional growth investing per se, as growth stocks would have a much higher negative correlation (close to – 100%) with value. In general, the long-term active return correlations across the various factor pairs were low or negative. The "off-diagonal average" active return correlation across all the factor pairs in Table 8.1, was – 0.4% in the US, 3.6% in World ex. US and 2.7% in Emerging Markets. That is, there was almost zero active return correlation across all the smart beta factors, on average. These correlation attributes may be viewed as attractive, and may imply that, in the long run, multifactor strategies should deliver meaningful diversification benefits.

B. Short-Term Variation in Correlations

Table 8.1 shows the pair-wise active return correlations over long periods of time. From a portfolio implementation and monitoring perspective, however, two further questions arise: How stable are these correlations over shorter time periods? And how might they affect potential diversification benefits in the short term?

Table 8.2 shows the active return correlations over rolling five-year periods for the three universes. This table shows the average five-year rolling correlation as well as the minimum and maximum values achieved for each factor pair in each universe. Based on the reported statistics, it would be fair to say that pair-wise active return correlations have been unstable in the short term. Generally negatively correlated factors, such as, value and momentum or value and quality, became positively correlated. And lowly positively correlated factors, such as quality and momentum, became highly positively correlated, with correlations exceeding 60%.

The fact that individual pair-wise active return correlations are unstable and that factor pairs can become highly positively correlated may suggest that factor diversification may not provide meaningful benefits in the short term. However, this is not the case. In a multifactor strategy, portfolio diversification potential is largely driven by the off-diagonal average of all the individual factor pair correlations, especially when the factors are equal-weighted and matched on active risk. The variation in the off-diagonal average, based on rolling five-year periods, is shown in the last column of Table 8.2. Across all universes, the variation in the off-diagonal average was

TABLE 8.1 Average Pair-Wise Active Return Correlations of ST Factor Portfolios

	Size	Value	Momentum	Volatility	Quality	Off-Diagonal Average
PANEL A: US (Russell 1000 Universe: Jan 1979–Jun 2017)						
Size	100					
Value	29	100				
Momentum	8	–36	100			
Volatility	–39	28	–20	100		
Quality	24	–17	27	–8	100	**-0.4**
PANEL B: World ex. USA (MSCI World ex USA Universe: Jan 1995–Jun 2017)						
Size	100					
Value	55	100				
Momentum	–12	–30	100			
Volatility	–10	–16	19	100		
Quality	13	–22	18	21	100	**3.6**
PANEL C: Emerging Markets (MSCI EM Universe: Jan 1998–Jun 2017)						
Size	100					
Value	55	100				
Momentum	–7	–14	100			
Volatility	–15	–11	5	100		
Quality	–18	–35	15	52	100	**2.7**

TABLE 8.2 Average Pair-Wise Active Return Correlations of ST Factor Portfolios: Five-Year Rolling Periods

	Size–Value	Size–Momentum	Size–Volatility	Size–Quality	Value–Momentum	Value–Volatility	Value–Quality	Momentum–Volatility	Momentum–Quality	Volatility–Quality	Off-Diagonal Average
PANEL A: US (Russell 1000 Universe: Jan 1979–Jun 2017)											
1979–2017	**29**	**8**	**-39**	**24**	**-36**	**28**	**-17**	**-20**	**27**	**-8**	**-3**
Minimum	-27	-32	-75	-7	-64	-65	-62	-55	-28	-62	-12
Maximum	75	37	-16	43	0	78	15	11	59	29	12
PANEL B: World ex. U.S.(MSCI World ex U.S. Universe: Jan 1995–Jun 2017)											
1995–2017	**55**	**-12**	**-10**	**13**	**-30**	**-16**	**-22**	**19**	**18**	**21**	**6**
Minimum	14	-44	-17	12	-48	-74	-70	-7	-4	17	-10
Maximum	72	4	-9	24	-5	30	30	33	41	83	21
PANEL C: Emerging Markets (MSCI EM Universe: Jan 1998–Jun 2017)											
1998–2017	**55**	**-7**	**-15**	**-18**	**-14**	**-11**	**-35**	**5**	**15**	**52**	**1**
Minimum	43	-34	-44	-41	-62	-43	-67	-23	-5	24	-15
Maximum	57	5	1	1	19	20	4	38	47	69	16

significantly less than the variation in any individual factor pair. The maximum levels reached for the off-diagonal average were only 12% in the US, 21% in World ex. US, and 16% in Emerging Markets. Despite the fact that individual factor pairs became highly positively correlated, the off-diagonal average only achieved moderately positive levels. This implies that all the factor pairs did not become highly positively correlated at the same time. There was also "diversification" within the correlation structure of smart beta factors, as positively correlated factor pairs were offset by negatively correlated factor pairs. As an illustration, Table 8.3 shows the correlations for all the factor pairs for the first five-year subperiod across the three universes. The diversification and offsetting of individual factor pair correlations, which keeps the off-diagonal average low, is well highlighted by the reported statistics.

C. Summary of Correlation Attributes

The following general observations may be drawn from the foregoing discussion.

- Smart beta factors have exhibited attractive low or negative pair-wise active return correlations in the long run.
- Pair-wise active return correlations, however, are not stable over shorter time periods, such as, rolling five-year subperiods. Factors that are characterized by generally negative correlation, often become positively correlated. And factors that typically are moderately positively correlated often see significant increases in correlation levels.
- Nonetheless, in a multifactor strategy, portfolio diversification is driven by the off-diagonal average of individual factor pair correlations. Benefiting from offsetting pair-wise correlations, this average depicts much less variation, with even the maximum values on a rolling five-year basis remaining at highly attractive levels.

The correlation attributes outlined above suggest that combining smart beta factors to create multifactor strategies should deliver notable diversification benefits, not just in the long run, but also over shorter time periods.

III.   PERFORMANCE CHARACTERISTICS OF FACTOR DIVERSIFICATION STRATEGIES

To analyze the benefits of factor diversification, we create an equally weighted combination portfolio of ST value, momentum, volatility, and quality portfolios. Recall from Chapter 7 that the individual factor portfolios are constructed at about a 4% active risk relative to the corresponding benchmark. Therefore, our weighting scheme not only equally weights the factor portfolios on market value (and returns), but also on active risk (i.e. active risk parity). We refer to this combination portfolio as a ST Multi-Factor Portfolio (MFP). In constructing the ST MFP, we do not include the ST size portfolio. The reason for this is as follows. Since the ST factor

TABLE 8.3 Average Pair-Wise Active Return Correlations of ST Factor Portfolios: Five-Year Subperiod

	Size–Value	Size–Momentum	Size–Volatility	Size–Quality	Value–Momentum	Value–Volatility	Value–Quality	Momentum–Volatility	Momentum–Quality	Volatility–Quality	Average
PANEL A: US (Russell 1000 Universe: Jan 1979–Jun 2017)											
1979–1983	0	33	–16	43	–64	67	14	–53	10	29	**6**
PANEL B: World ex. USA (MSCI World ex U.S. Universe: Jan 1995–Jun 2017)											
1995–1999	68	–44	–17	24	–38	9	30	13	–1	34	**8**
PANEL C: Emerging Markets (MSCI EM Universe: Jan 1998–Jun 2017)											
1998–2002	57	4	–5	1	19	9	–28	38	10	24	**13**

portfolios deviate from capitalization weights of securities, they already incorporate a size bias to varying degrees. As such, the MFP also has an ancillary exposure to the size factor. The MFP, therefore, provides exposure to all five factors, even though the size portfolio is not explicitly included in its construction.

A. Potential Diversification Benefits

Before we look at the historical performance of the MFP, it might be useful to lay out what we would expect to see. In general, combining lowly correlated assets provides the following primary diversification benefits.

a. Active Risk Reduction: Gain from Diversification

Diversification driven by attractive correlation attributes should result in meaningful risk reduction relative to the average risk of the component assets. This risk reduction is typically known as "gain from diversification." In the context of smart beta factors, the "total return" pair-wise correlations between the factor portfolios are very high because total returns include a common influence; the market factor. As a result, we would expect the MFP to realize minimal, if any, total risk reduction compared to the average total risk across the factor portfolios. In the "active return" space, however, factor portfolios have low or negative pair-wise correlations as well as low off-diagonal average correlation. This should result in significant reduction in active risk for the MFP relative to the average active risk across the factor portfolios.

b. Higher Risk-Adjusted Returns

The level of total and active return of a diversification strategy is not impacted by asset correlations. That is, the gain from diversification is primarily realized in the risk space. As such, the total and active returns of a diversification strategy would roughly equal the average return of the assets comprising the strategy. Therefore, we would expect the total and active return of the MFP to roughly equal the average of the component factor portfolios. Since we know that factor portfolios have outperformed the market, we would expect the MFP to outperform as well. If the total risk of the MFP is similar to that of the market, that is, high total-risk factors are counterbalanced by low total-risk factors, then the MFP would also generate higher Sharpe ratios than the market, because of higher expected returns. But, the MFP would not be expected to generate a higher Sharpe ratio than all of the individual factors. For instance, since low-volatility portfolios realize significant total risk reduction, while outperforming the market, their Sharpe ratios could be higher than the MFP.

On the other hand, because of the expected significant reduction in active risk, the MFP may generate higher IRs than the component factor portfolios. The improvement in IR would translate into a much higher statistical significance (*t*-statistic) for the active return of the MFP. This would also imply that the active return of the MFP can be expected to be more stable than the active return of the individual factor portfolios. Additionally, to the extent that individual factor portfolios depict different performance characteristics, that is, they may not all underperform the market at the same time, the MFP could potentially exhibit lower market underperformance risk compared to the individual factor portfolios.

B. Long-Term Historical Performance of the ST MFP

Table 8.4 reports the long-term historical performance of the four individual ST factor portfolios as well as the ST MFP for the three regions.

a. Active Risk Reduction: Gain from Diversification

As expected, the MFPs realized minimal total risk reduction relative to the average total risk of the four factor portfolios. In the US, the average total risk across the four factor portfolios was 14.9%. With a total risk of 14.5%, the MFP generated only about a 3% reduction. Similar or lower decreases in total risk were recorded in the other two regions.

Gain from diversification was much higher for the active risk of the MFPs. In the case of the US, the average active risk across the factor portfolios was 4%. Therefore, the MFP realized a 55% reduction with an active risk of 1.8%. The active risk reduction in World ex. USA and Emerging Markets universes was 47% and 48%, respectively.

b. Risk-Adjusted Returns

The MFPs realized Sharpe ratios that were about 23% higher than the market in the US and Emerging Markets and 48% higher in World ex. USA. However, the Sharpe ratio of the MFPs was not the highest achieved in a given region. For instance, the volatility portfolio realized a higher Sharpe ratio than the MFP in the US, while the quality portfolios had a higher Sharpe ratio in World ex. USA and Emerging Markets.

However, because of the significant gain from diversification in the active risk space, the IRs of the MFPs in all three regions were much higher than the IRs of the individual factor portfolios. The MFPs produced high "after-cost" IRs of above 0.85. In the US, the IR of the MFP was 134% higher than the average IR across the factor portfolios and 56% more than the highest-IR individual factor portfolio (value). In the other two regions, the IR of the MFP was about 92% higher than the average IR and 27% higher than the highest-IR individual factor portfolio (quality for World ex. USA and value for Emerging Markets). The improvement in IR meaningfully enhanced the statistical significance, and stability, of the MFP active returns. The after-cost active return of 1.55% for the US MFP was associated with a t-statistic of more than five. The active returns of the MFPs in the other regions had a t-statistic in excess of four. Thus, despite the fact that the active returns of factor portfolios were not all statistically significant individually, their combination was highly significant because of meaningful gain from diversification.

TABLE 8.4 Historical Performance of ST MFP: Annualized Results (Periods Ending June 2017)

	Start Date	Total Gross Return (%)	Total Risk (%)	Sharpe Ratio	CAPM Beta	Maximum Drawdown (%)	Active Gross Return (%)	Active Risk (%)	Information Ratio	Worst Under-performance Year (%)	Max Rolling 3-Year Annualized Under-performance (%)	Upside Capture Ratio	Downside Capture Ratio
Russell 1000 Index	Jan-79	11.84	15.05	0.49	1.00	-51.13							
Value		13.73	15.18	0.60	0.98	-55.97	1.89	3.92	0.48	-10.91	-7.91	102	93
Momentum		12.77	16.10	0.52	1.04	-50.56	0.93	3.86	0.24	-8.35	-4.09	106	104
Volatility		12.66	12.68	0.62	0.82	-43.88	0.82	4.11	0.20	-13.33	-8.11	88	75
Quality		14.14	15.61	0.61	1.00	-43.57	2.30	4.18	0.55	-5.38	-2.81	104	94
MFP		**13.40**	**14.51**	**0.60**	**0.96**	**-48.23**	**1.55**	**1.80**	**0.86**	**-2.92**	**-1.38**	**100**	**91**
MSCI World ex. USA Index	Jan-95	5.66	16.25	0.25	1.00	-56.34							
Value		7.66	17.30	0.36	1.04	-60.51	2.00	4.06	0.49	-10.59	-5.96	105	97
Momentum		6.64	15.99	0.31	0.95	-55.94	0.98	3.97	0.25	-11.86	-4.94	100	95
Volatility		7.09	13.69	0.37	0.83	-47.96	1.43	3.93	0.36	-10.72	-2.84	88	78
Quality		8.08	14.85	0.41	0.89	-49.78	2.42	3.54	0.68	-3.08	-3.96	95	83
MFP		**7.43**	**15.16**	**0.37**	**0.93**	**-53.74**	**1.76**	**2.05**	**0.86**	**-5.16**	**-0.89**	**97**	**88**
MSCI EM Index	Jan-98	7.48	23.54	0.33	1.00	-61.44							
Value		10.21	24.64	0.43	1.04	-61.00	2.72	3.62	0.75	-2.89	-2.58	108	100
Momentum		8.25	23.44	0.36	0.98	-66.41	0.77	4.36	0.18	-12.68	-6.71	101	98
Volatility		9.00	20.89	0.41	0.88	-55.24	1.51	3.56	0.43	-14.56	-0.93	92	85
Quality		9.82	21.78	0.44	0.92	-56.82	2.34	3.61	0.65	-7.02	-1.74	97	88
MFP		**9.37**	**22.50**	**0.41**	**0.95**	**-60.05**	**1.89**	**1.97**	**0.96**	**-2.23**	**0.26**	**99**	**93**

Figures 8.1 through 8.3 show the cumulative active returns for the MFPs in the three regions. Compared to similar charts for the individual factor portfolios reported in Chapter 7, the MFPs depict much less variability in active returns.

c. Market Underperformance Risk

How likely is it that all factors may underperform the market at the same time? Table 8.5 provides a perspective based on calendar year active returns. In the US, all four factors did not underperform the market simultaneously in any year over the entire analysis period. Outside the US, all four factors underperformed in only one calendar year, or 5% of the time. Two or more factors underperforming happened 59% of the time in the US and 40% and 50% of the time in World ex. USA and EM, respectively. We also note that all four factors simultaneously outperformed more often than they underperformed in all three regions. Because of these characteristics, the MFP registered a much lower probability of under-performing the market compared to the individual factor portfolios, as shown in Table 8.6.

In Table 8.4, we also note that the worst annual underperformance for the MFP was less pronounced than the individual factor portfolios, except for World ex. USA universe where quality had a smaller underperformance. The maximum three-year annualized underperformance was significantly lower for the MFP compared to the individual factor portfolios in all regions.

C. Short-Term Historical Performance of the ST MFP

As shown in Table 8.2 and Table 8.3, on a rolling five-year basis, the off-diagonal average of pair-wise active return correlations depicted much less variation than the individual correlation pairs. This would suggest that the MFP should provide mean-ingful diversification benefits even in the short run.

a. Active Risk Reduction: Gain from Diversification

This is indeed what we find in Figure 8.4 for the US universe. This chart shows the average active risk across the four factor portfolios and the active risk of the MFP on a rolling five-year basis. The MFP active risk is consistently below the average ac-tive risk across the four factor portfolios. This implies that a meaningful gain from diversification was achieved at each point in time. On a rolling five-year basis, the average reduction in active risk realized by the MFP was 56%, while the minimum reduction was 28% and the maximum 72%. Similar results were found in the other regions.

b. Risk-Adjusted Active Returns

Significant reduction in active risk, coupled with the fact that all factors typically have not underperformed at the same time, should benefit the risk-adjusted short-term

FIGURE 8.1 ST MFP Portfolio: Cumulative Active Return (Russell 1000 Universe, January 1979–June 2017)

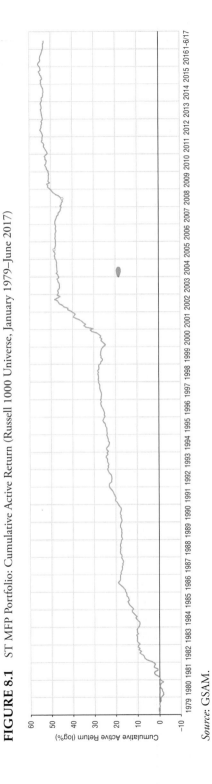

Source: GSAM.

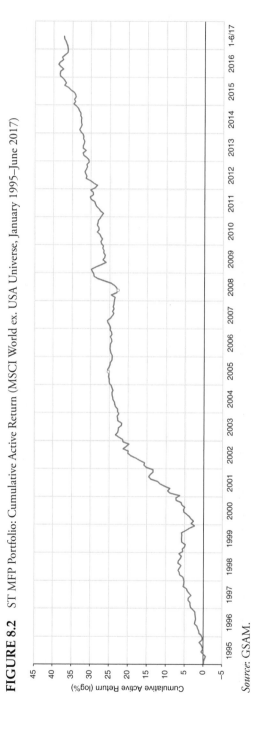

FIGURE 8.2 ST MFP Portfolio: Cumulative Active Return (MSCI World ex. USA Universe, January 1995–June 2017)

Source: GSAM.

FIGURE 8.3   ST MFP Portfolio: Cumulative Active Return (MSCI EM Universe, January 1998–June 2017)

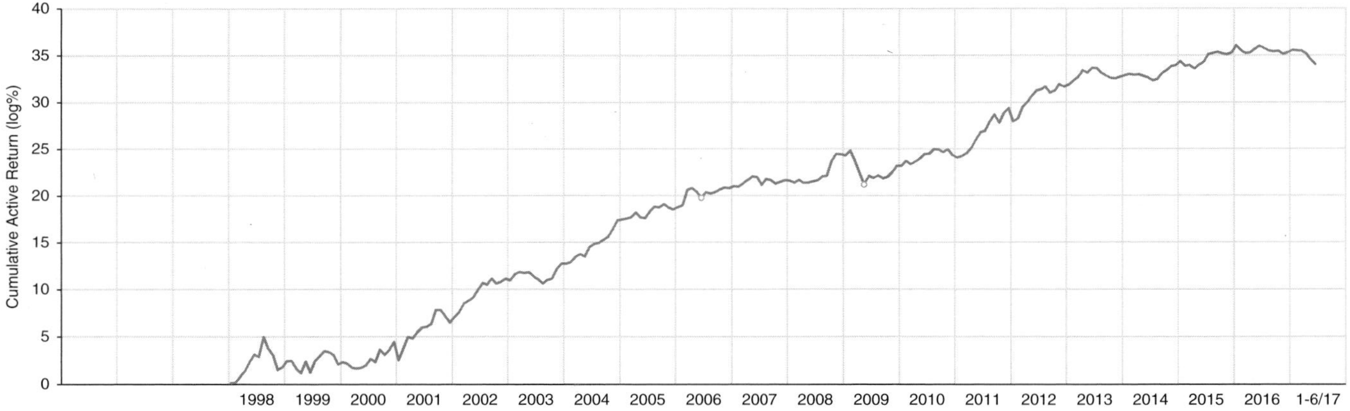

Source: GSAM.

TABLE 8.5 Probability of Simultaneous Market Underperformance in a Calendar Year: Various Time Periods

	Analysis Period	% Time	Cumulative % Time
PANEL A: Russell 1000 Universe	Jan 79–Jun 17		
Four Factors Underperformed		0	0
Three Factors Underperformed		21	21
Two Factors Underperformed		38	59
One Factor Underperformed		28	87
All Factors Outperformed		13	
PANEL B: MSCI World ex USA Universe	Jan 95–Jun 17		
Four Factors Underperformed		5	5
Three Factors Underperformed		9	14
Two Factors Underperformed		26	40
One Factor Underperformed		43	83
All Factors Outperformed		17	
PANEL C: MSCI EM Universe	Jan 98–Jun 17		
Four Factors Underperformed		5	5
Three Factors Underperformed		5	10
Two Factors Underperformed		40	50
One Factor Underperformed		30	80
All Factors Outperformed		20	

TABLE 8.6 Probability of Market Underperformance: Various Time Periods

	Analysis Period	% Time
PANEL A: Russell 1000 Universe	Jan 79–Jun 17	
Value		36
Momentum		46
Volatility		46
Quality		38
MFP		**28**
PANEL B: MSCI World ex USA Universe	Jan 95–Jun 17	
Value		35
Momentum		30
Volatility		43
Quality		30
MFP		**22**
PANEL C: MSCI EM Universe	Jan 98–Jun 17	
Value		40
Momentum		35
Volatility		35
Quality		35
MFP		**10**

FIGURE 8.4   MFP Active Risk Compared to the Average Active Risk Across Individual Factor Portfolios (Russell 1000 Universe, January 1979–June 2017)

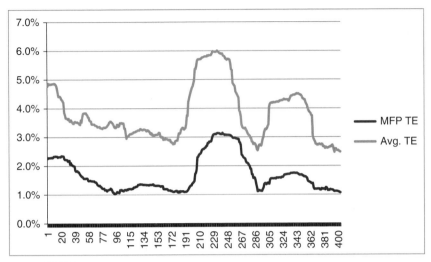

Source: GSAM.

performance of the MFP. For the US universe, this is shown in Table 8.7. For five-year rolling periods, the average IR of the MFP was much higher than the average IRs of the individual factor portfolios, while the minimum IR was larger and maximum higher, except for the IR of value. We can also report that, based on independent five-year subperiods, the MFPs did not underperform the market in any subperiod across the three regions, while individual factor portfolios did. The lowest IR realized by the MFP in an independent five-year subperiod was 0.34 in the US, 0.22 in World ex. USA, and 0.45 in Emerging Markets.

D. Enhancements

Smart beta managers also typically incorporate enhancements in order to improve the performance of their strategies. Such enhancements may include: mitigating unrewarded risks that may dilute the IR of individual factor capture, such as momentum reversals or controlling for industry or country active weights, reducing undesirable ancillary factor exposures, such as the large cap bias inherent in low-volatility investing, and seeking to improve after-cost performance by incorporating liquidity constraints and turnover mitigation methods. By way of an example, Table 8.8 shows the impact of a turnover mitigation method on individual ST factor portfolios as well as the ST MFP, for the US universe. This method applies two adjustments to control turnover. First, in the construction of individual ST factor portfolios, a trading "buffer" is used, as discussed in Chapter 7. The application of the buffer to individual factor portfolios reduced the turnover for the MFP from 56% to 27%, that is, a 52%

TABLE 8.7 Five-Year Rolling Information Ratios: Russell 1000 Universe
(January 1979–June 2017)

	Average	Minimum	Maximum
Value	0.60	−0.93	2.16
Momentum	0.26	−0.85	1.65
Volatility	0.64	−0.61	1.82
Quality	0.19	−1.08	1.66
MFP	**0.90**	**−0.41**	**2.10**

TABLE 8.8 Impact of Turnover Minimization Technique on the Turnover of ST MFPs:
Russell 1000 Universe (January 1979–June 2017)

	Annualized Turnover Without Buffer	Annualized Turnover With Buffer	Annualized Turnover with Turnover Minimization (%)
ST Value Portfolio	58	26	
ST Momentum Portfolio	92	53	
ST Volatility Portfolio	30	12	
ST Quality Portfolio	43	18	
ST MFP	**56**	**27**	**15**

reduction. Second, a Turnover Minimization Technique is applied. This technique seeks to take advantage of the low or negative cross-sectional correlations between the smart beta factors, which may result in a security being bought in one factor portfolio (e.g. value) and sold in another (e.g. momentum). Through netting of trades across individual factor portfolios, the Turnover Minimization Technique aims to reduce the turnover of factor combination portfolios. Relative to the MFP With Buffer, the application of this technique resulted in a 45% reduction in turnover for the MFP (from 27% to 15%). Overall, compared to a "naive" MFP, which simply combines individual factor portfolios, the two steps of the turnover management process decreased the turnover of the MFP from 56% to 15%, that is, a 74% reduction in annualized turnover.

As an illustration, Table 8.9 compares the performance of the ST MFP with an MFP that incorporates the above-mentioned enhancements. Across the three regions, the Enhanced ST MFPs realized higher Sharpe ratios compared to the ST MFP and registered increases in IR ranging from 17% for Emerging Markets to 26% for World ex. USA. While the downside capture profiles were similar, the enhancements marginally improved the upside capture ratios.

TABLE 8.9 Historical Performance of ST and Enhanced ST MFPs: Annualized Results (Periods Ending June 2017)

	Start Date	Total Gross Return (%)	Total Risk (%)	Sharpe Ratio	CAPM Beta	Maximum Drawdown (%)	Active Gross Return (%)	Active Risk (%)	Information Ratio	Worst Under-performance Year (%)	Max Rolling 3-Year Annualized Under-performance (%)	Upside Capture Ratio	Downside Capture Ratio
Russell 1000 Index	Jan-79	11.84	15.05	0.49	1.00	−51.13							
ST MFP		13.40	14.51	0.60	0.96	−48.23	1.55	1.80	0.86	−2.92	−1.38	100	91
Enhanced ST MFP		**13.76**	**14.70**	**0.62**	**0.97**	**−48.58**	**1.92**	**1.83**	**1.05**	**−3.59**	**−1.26**	**102**	**92**
MSCI World ex. US Index	Jan-95	5.66	16.25	0.25	1.00	−56.34							
ST MFP		7.43	15.16	0.37	0.93	−53.74	1.76	2.05	0.86	−5.16	−0.89	97	88
Enhanced ST MFP		**7.79**	**15.32**	**0.39**	**0.94**	**−54.17**	**2.12**	**1.97**	**1.08**	**−4.29**	**−0.86**	**99**	**88**
MSCI EM Index	Jan-98	7.48	23.54	0.33	1.00	−61.44							
ST MFP		9.37	22.50	0.41	0.95	−60.05	1.89	1.97	0.96	−2.23	0.26	99	93
Enhanced ST MFP		**10.02**	**22.53**	**0.44**	**0.95**	**−59.51**	**2.54**	**2.27**	**1.12**	**−3.98**	**0.41**	**100**	**92**

E. Diversification Strategies Using Other Weighting Schemes

So far, in our analysis of factor diversification, we have constructed the MFP using ST factor portfolios. We now investigate how an ST MFP compares to MFPs developed from capitalization-weighted (CW), capitalization-scaled (CS), signal-weighted (SW), and equal-weighted (EW) factor portfolios that we discussed in Chapter 4. Table 8.10 presents the after-cost performance comparison. For the US universe, Panel A and Panel B show the CW and CS MFPs, respectively. In both cases, the active risk reduction for the MFPs relative to the average active risk for the four factor portfolios amounted to about 54%, which is similar to the 55% reduction achieved by the ST MFP (Panel E). The CS MFP realized a 38% improvement in IR compared to the CW MFP. However, the ST MFP had an IR, which was 132% and 69% higher than the IR of CW MFP and CS MFP, respectively. The active risk reduction was significantly lower for the SW MFP (16%) in Panel C and EW MFP (27%) in Panel D. The limited gain from diversification resulted in only moderate increases in the IRs of the SW and EW MFPs compared to the individual factor portfolios. For instance, the IR of the SW MFP was only 21% higher than the average IR across the factor portfolios and 14% higher than the highest-IR factor portfolio (momentum). The IRs of SW and EW MFPs were also much lower than the IR of ST MFP, despite the fact that individual SW and EW factor portfolios had IRs similar or higher than the IRs of ST factor portfolios.

The limited diversification benefits realized by combining SW and EW factor portfolios are not surprising. As previously shown in Chapter 4, the SW and EW factor portfolios are equivalent to implementing factor tilts starting with an equal-weighted universe. This means that all SW and EW factor portfolios have a common influence in active returns relative to the capitalization-weighted universe. That common influence is the performance of the equal-weighted universe versus the capitalization-weighted universe. As such, the pair-wise active return correlations for these weighting schemes tend to be much higher, as shown in Table 8.11. The CW, CS, and ST weighting schemes, which form part of the "Tilting" category of weightings discussed in Chapter 4, depicted similar pair-wise correlations, which suggest that the correlation structure between factors is not affected by different weighting schemes within this category, although efficiency of factor capture is. However, the SW and EW factor portfolios, which form part of the "Reweighting" category, produced a significantly different correlation structure. All active return correlation pairs had high positive correlations because of the common influence of the equal-weighted universe in their active returns. The off-diagonal average was negative for the CW, CS, and ST factor pairs, while it was large and positive for the SW and EW factor pairs. The correlation structure of SW and EW factor portfolios, depicted in Table 8.11, explains why a combination of such portfolios delivers only moderate diversification benefits against a capitalization weighted benchmark.

TABLE 8.10 Historical Performance of Various MFPs: Annualized Results (Russell 1000 Universe: January 1979–June 2017)

	Total Gross Return (%)	Total Risk (%)	Sharpe Ratio	CAPM Beta	Maximum Drawdown (%)	Active Gross Return (%)	Active Risk (%)	Information Ratio	Worst Under-performance Year (%)	Max Rolling 3-Year Annualized Under-performance (%)	Upside Capture Ratio	Downside Capture Ratio
Russell 1000 Index	11.84	15.05	0.49	1.00	-51.13							
PANEL A: Capitalization Weighting												
Value	13.16	15.05	0.57	0.97	-54.19	1.32	3.80	0.35	-10.45	-7.30	101	94
Momentum	12.33	16.10	0.50	1.01	-50.19	0.49	5.36	0.09	-11.94	-7.91	103	101
Volatility	11.97	12.15	0.59	0.74	-39.42	0.13	6.10	0.02	-18.60	-13.84	82	68
Quality	12.72	15.24	0.54	0.99	-43.31	0.88	3.26	0.27	-7.75	-4.77	100	96
CW MFP	**12.65**	**14.09**	**0.57**	**0.93**	**-46.07**	**0.80**	**2.18**	**0.37**	**-5.68**	**-2.71**	**97**	**90**
PANEL B: Capitalization Scaling												
Value	12.96	15.05	0.56	0.98	-53.88	1.11	2.81	0.40	-8.30	-5.72	101	96
Momentum	12.26	15.43	0.51	1.00	-48.88	0.41	2.98	0.14	-6.81	-4.13	102	101
Volatility	12.12	13.24	0.56	0.86	-44.35	0.28	3.25	0.09	-10.40	-7.11	91	82
Quality	12.44	14.95	0.53	0.99	-46.55	0.60	1.68	0.36	-4.67	-2.17	100	97
CS MFP	**12.48**	**14.48**	**0.55**	**0.96**	**-48.28**	**0.63**	**1.24**	**0.51**	**-2.09**	**-1.21**	**99**	**94**

(Continued)

TABLE 8.10 Historical Performance of Various MFPs: Annualized Results (Russell 1000 Universe: January 1979–June 2017) (cont'd)

	Total Gross Return (%)	Total Risk (%)	Sharpe Ratio	CAPM Beta	Maximum Drawdown (%)	Active Gross Return (%)	Active Risk (%)	Information Ratio	Worst Under-performance Year (%)	Max Rolling 3-Year Annualized Under-performance (%)	Upside Capture Ratio	Downside Capture Ratio
PANEL C: Signal Weighting												
Value	14.88	17.07	0.61	1.05	-58.02	3.04	6.51	0.47	-18.16	-11.89	110	100
Momentum	14.32	16.75	0.59	1.07	-52.05	2.47	4.89	0.51	-12.80	-7.28	111	104
Volatility	14.09	14.17	0.66	0.89	-47.98	2.25	5.15	0.44	-19.24	-14.12	96	81
Quality	14.43	17.20	0.59	1.09	-51.60	2.59	5.30	0.49	-11.91	-8.68	112	105
SW MFP	**14.48**	**16.06**	**0.62**	**1.02**	**-52.45**	**2.64**	**4.57**	**0.58**	**-7.02**	**-8.78**	**107**	**97**
PANEL D: Equal Weighting												
Value	15.43	17.28	0.63	1.04	-60.55	3.59	7.50	0.48	-18.90	-14.34	110	97
Momentum	13.98	17.09	0.57	1.07	-52.79	2.14	5.77	0.37	-11.22	-6.14	111	106
Volatility	14.35	13.52	0.70	0.81	-44.56	2.50	6.38	0.39	-22.26	-17.18	92	71
Quality	14.67	17.60	0.59	1.11	-49.94	2.83	5.79	0.49	-10.54	-8.11	114	107
EW MFP	**14.72**	**15.86**	**0.64**	**1.01**	**-52.17**	**2.87**	**4.64**	**0.62**	**-6.98**	**-8.22**	**107**	**95**
PANEL E: Signal Tilting												
Value	13.73	15.18	0.60	0.98	-55.97	1.89	3.92	0.48	-10.91	-7.91	102	93
Momentum	12.77	16.10	0.52	1.04	-50.56	0.93	3.86	0.24	-8.35	-4.09	106	104
Volatility	12.66	12.68	0.62	0.82	-43.88	0.82	4.11	0.20	-13.33	-8.11	88	75
Quality	14.14	15.61	0.61	1.00	-43.57	2.30	4.18	0.55	-5.38	-2.81	104	94
ST MFP	**13.40**	**14.51**	**0.60**	**0.96**	**-48.23**	**1.55**	**1.80**	**0.86**	**-2.92**	**-1.38**	**100**	**91**

TABLE 8.11   Average Pair-Wise Active Return Correlations of Factor Portfolios: Russell 1000 Universe (January 1979–June 2017)

	Value	Momentum	Volatility	Quality	Off-Diagonal Average
PANEL A: Capitalization Weighting					
Value	100				
Momentum	−42	100			
Volatility	18	−1	100		
Quality	−43	18	1	100	**−9**
PANEL B: Capitalization Scaling					
Value	100				
Momentum	−47	100			
Volatility	19	−3	100		
Quality	−47	21	5	100	**−9**
PANEL C: Signal Weighting					
Value	100				
Momentum	55	100			
Volatility	67	45	100		
Quality	78	75	46	100	**61**
PANEL D: Equal Weighting					
Value	100				
Momentum	30	100			
Volatility	52	22	100		
Quality	60	58	21	100	**41**
PANEL E: Signal Tilting					
Value	100				
Momentum	−36	100			
Volatility	28	−20	100		
Quality	−17	27	−8	100	**−2**

F. Assessing Efficiency: Factor-Adjusted Alpha

Table 8.12 reports the factor-adjusted alphas of various MFPs emanating from an active return and risk decomposition. For the Russell 1000 universe, Panel A1 shows that, when analyzed against the CW factor portfolios, CS MFP produced only marginal improvements in efficiency with an annualized alpha of 0.19%. This alpha was associated with a *t*-statistic of 2.89 and contributed 30% and 8% to active return and active risk, respectively. In contrast, the ST and Enhanced ST MFPs generated higher alphas and statistical significance (*t*-statistic) and explained a higher proportion of active return and active risk. The SW and EW MFPs also delivered large alphas against the CW factor portfolios. But, as documented before in Chapter 4, these alphas disappear when decomposed against the equal-weighted universe and

TABLE 8.12 Factor-Adjusted Alpha of Various MFPs

	Annualized Alpha (%)	t-Statistic	Alpha Contribution to Active Return (%)	Alpha Contribution to Active Risk (%)
PANEL A: Russell 1000 Universe: Jan 1979–Jun 2017				
Panel A1: Against CW Factor Portfolios				
CS MFP	0.19	2.89	30	8
ST MFP	0.76	3.90	39	34
Enhanced ST MFP	1.12	5.09	58	42
SW MFP	1.31	3.61	31	18
EW MFP	1.27	3.34	32	20
Panel A2: Against EW Universe and ST Factor Portfolios				
SW MFP	–0.15	–0.78	–	4
EW MFP	–0.37	–1.23	–	8
PANEL B: MSCI World ex. USA Universe: Jan 1995–Jun 2017 Against CW Factor Portfolios				
ST MFP	0.68	2.66	39	26
Enhanced ST MFP	1.12	3.75	53	40
PANEL C: MSCI EM Universe: Jan 1998–Jun 2017 Against CW Factor Portfolios				
ST MFP	1.14	3.86	60	32
Enhanced ST MFP	1.50	3.55	59	50

ST factor portfolios (Panel A2). Panel B and Panel C document that the ST and Enhanced ST MFPs also produced large and highly statistically significant alphas in the other regions.

G. Summary

With regard to factor diversification strategies, we highlight the following broad conclusions based on the forgoing discussion.

- Smart beta factors depict low or negative off-diagonal average of pair-wise active return correlations, which gives rise to significant gain from diversification in the form of active risk reduction and IR enhancement compared to individual factor portfolios.
- Although pair-wise correlations are highly unstable in the short run, the off-diagonal average depicts less variation. As such, multifactor strategies provide diversification benefits not only in the long run, but also in the short term.
- To the extent that smart beta factors do not all underperform the market simultaneously, multifactor strategies depict a lower probability of market underperformance compared to individual factors.
- Weighting schemes with similar objectives, such as the Tilting category or the Re-weighting category, do not meaningfully affect the correlation structure between smart beta factors.
- However, weighting schemes within a given category, such as Tilting, still produce meaningfully different efficiency (i.e. factor-adjusted alpha) in capturing smart beta factor payoffs.

IV.   CONSTRUCTING DIVERSIFICATION STRATEGIES: THE PORTFOLIO BLENDING VERSUS SIGNAL BLENDING DEBATE

In our experience, as interest in multifactor strategies has grown, investor focus has shifted toward portfolio construction issues. Two construction approaches, namely portfolio blending and signal blending, have recently become the subject of debate within the industry.

The portfolio blending approach is a two-step portfolio construction process. In Step 1, individual factor portfolios are constructed. Then, in Step 2, the individual factor portfolios are combined to create the multifactor diversification strategy. The combination portfolio may use equal-weighting, risk-weighting, or an optimization process to determine the weights assigned to individual factor portfolios. The various MFPs we have constructed and discussed in this chapter follow the portfolio blending approach. Other examples of multifactor strategies that use the portfolio blending approach include the MSCI Diversified Factor Mix Indexes and the Scientific Beta Multi-Beta Multi-Strategy Indexes.

The signal blending approach is a single-step portfolio construction process. In this process, the individual factor signals (i.e. scores or ranks) are combined to create a composite signal. For instance, the value signal and the momentum signal are combined into a value plus momentum composite signal for each security in the universe. The composite signal is then used to construct the value plus momentum portfolio. Examples of multifactor offerings that follow the signal blending approach include the MSCI Diversified Multi-Factor Indexes and the FTSE Russell Tilt-Tilt Indexes.

The debate in the industry relates to which approach delivers superior investment efficiency (i.e. risk-adjusted returns).

A. Literature Review

One of the first papers on this topic came from Clarke et al. (2016), in which the authors discussed a theoretical framework for comparing the two approaches. The comparison was based on assessing the mean-variance efficiency (i.e. Sharpe ratio) of a long-only portfolio of individual securities (signal blending) and a long-only optimal combination portfolio (portfolio blending) constructed from individual factor portfolios. The authors considered four factors in their analysis, namely, low beta, small size, value, and momentum. Based on certain assumptions about the expected factor information ratios, the correlation structure and secondary exposures, the authors found the following results. Relative to an unconstrained long-short optimal combination portfolio, the long-only optimal combination portfolio realized about 50% of the potential Sharpe ratio improvement. In contrast, the long-only portfolio of individual securities realized 70% to 80% of the potential improvement, mainly due to "stronger factor exposures." Based on empirical results from a universe of the largest 1,000 US stocks, the authors also reported that the portfolio of individual securities achieved a 20% higher Sharpe ratio and IR than the optimal combination portfolio.

Bender and Wang (2016) used a rules-based weighting methodology, which scales market capitalization weights by a rank multiplier (capitalization scaling). They considered four equity factors; value, momentum, quality and volatility. The authors found that a bottom up portfolio (signal blending) produced a 20% higher IR than a combination portfolio (portfolio blending).

Fitzgibbons et al. (2016) compared the performance of active risk-matched portfolios derived from a universe similar to MSCI World from February 1993 to December 2015. They considered value and momentum factors. The authors found that, at a 4% tracking error, the integrated portfolio (signal blending) produced a 40% higher IR than the portfolio mix (portfolio blending). Additionally, the benefits of integration were shown to increase when the correlation between factors is more negative, the number of factors is increased, or the tracking error is higher. The authors argued that the integrated approach achieved higher risk-adjusted returns because it "avoided securities with offsetting exposures" (i.e. securities that rank highly on one factor, but poorly on another factor), while emphasizing securities with balanced positive exposures to the desired factors.

Leippold and Rüegg (2017) challenged the general conclusion reached by the three studies cited earlier that signal blending dominates portfolio blending. They showed that the signal-blending approach produced better risk-adjusted returns than portfolio blending for only a few factor combinations. Additionally, when they conducted robust performance tests, they found no evidence of significant differences between the two approaches; that is, the hypothesis that the two approaches are the same could not be rejected. Therefore, they concluded that the dominance of signal blending reported by earlier studies is a "statistical fluke."

Fraser-Jenkins et al. (2016) considered the value, momentum, and quality factors. They used an equally weighted benchmark of the largest 500 stocks from the MSCI World Index as the selection universe. The individual factor portfolios were defined as the top quintile of stocks by factor rank and were equal weighted. In their building block approach (portfolio blending), the individual factor portfolios were combined in equal proportions. In the combination approach (signal blending), the individual factor ranks for each stock were averaged, and the top quintile of stocks based on the composite rank were selected and equal weighted. Fraser-Jenkins et al. (2016) reported that, for the various strategies tested, both the building block and the combination approaches lie on a straight risk/return line and, hence, deliver similar levels of risk-adjusted returns.

B. Our Perspective

In order to investigate the relative merits of portfolio blending and signal blending approaches, we conducted extensive research on the topic and published our findings in Ghayur, Heaney, and Platt (2018) (GHP). In this section, we provide a brief discussion of the main results of our study.

a. Potential Methodological Biases

GHP argue that existing studies may introduce potential methodological biases that hinder an apples-to-apples comparison of the two approaches. One important bias is that differences in observed performance may arise simply from differences in achieved factor exposures under the two approaches, even when the same methodology is used. Consider the example depicted in Figure 8.5. In this illustration, a value-momentum signal blend is constructed by selecting the top 25% of the names based on the composite signal. The portfolio blend is created by combining individually constructed value and momentum portfolios that also select top 25% of the names based on individual factor signals. This methodology leads to the signal blend holding the top 25% of the names, while the portfolio blend holds a much higher proportion of names (e.g. around 40%). As a result, the signal blend achieves a much higher exposure to the targeted factors, compared to the portfolio blend, because it is a more concentrated portfolio. If factors work, then we would expect

FIGURE 8.5   Illustration of Signal Blend and Portfolio Blend Approaches: Unmatched Factor Exposures

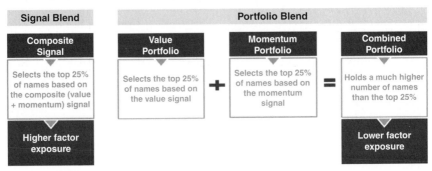

Source: GSAM.

the signal blend (higher exposure) to perform better than the portfolio blend (lower exposure). But, it is not because the signal blend is a more efficient approach. It is simply because the research methodology used resulted in the signal blend achieving higher exposures to rewarded factors and, thus, outperforming the portfolio blend. In GHP's assessment, the articles cited above are exposed to this bias to varying degrees. For instance, Clarke et al. (2016) compared a signal blend, which held 200 stocks, to a portfolio blend, which combined individual value (200 stocks), low beta (200 stocks), momentum (200 stocks), and size (800 stocks) portfolios. Comparing the two approaches based on active risk-matched portfolios, as done by Fitzgibbons et al. (2016), mitigates this bias, but does not eliminate it as active risk-matching is an indirect method for matching factor exposures. In fact, Fitzgibbons et al. (2016) argue that their signal blend outperforms the portfolio blend precisely because it achieves stronger exposure to targeted factors by avoiding securities with offsetting exposures.

In Bender and Wang (2016), we believe the methodology used also potentially introduces some bias as their portfolio blend shows no meaningful diversification benefits. Exhibit 5 of their study documents that the portfolio blend had an active risk of 4.78%, which was only 10% lower than the average active risk of 5.31% across the four considered factor portfolios. The IR of their portfolio blend (0.59) only showed marginal improvement and was actually lower than the highest-IR individual factor portfolio (momentum, with an IR of 0.61). These results are surprising and at odds with the strong benefits of factor diversification we have highlighted in this chapter using a variety of weighting schemes. Additionally, the weighting scheme used by Bender and Wang (2016) also causes implicit differences in achieved factor exposures between the two approaches. In fact, GHP show that in this weighting scheme the exposures can be matched by either reweighting the signals in the signal blend or reweighting the portfolios in the portfolio blend. When exposures are matched in this fashion, the resulting portfolio blend and signal blend are similar portfolios with no differences in performance.

b. Comparing Exposure-Matched Portfolios

The objective of comparing two portfolio construction approaches is to determine the efficiency (i.e. risk-adjusted returns) with which they deliver factor exposures. This objective is hard to achieve in a research setup that does not match the compared portfolios on factor exposures, as differences in performance can simply be due to differences in exposures. Therefore, GHP argue that a more informative framework for comparing the two approaches would be to (1) directly match the portfolio blend and the signal blend on factor exposures and then (2) assess the efficiency (e.g. IR) with which the two approaches deliver those exposures. This is the framework that GHP followed in their study.

Based on exposure-matched portfolios, GHP showed that, at low-to-moderate levels of factor exposures and active risk (typically less than 4%), the portfolio blend generated higher IRs than the signal blend for various 2-factor, 3-factor, and 4-factor combinations and across various regions of global equities. The stronger performance of the portfolio blend was largely driven by the interaction effects between the factors. At high levels of factor exposures and active risk, the signal blend achieved better diversification and realized higher IRs than the portfolio blend. The GHP study, therefore, challenges the conclusion of earlier studies that signal blending dominates portfolio blending under almost all conditions.

c. Other Advantages of Portfolio Blending

In our experience, many investors pursue a portfolio blending approach in implementing factor diversification strategies because, in addition to simplicity and transparency, it offers many additional advantages. It is an approach that may appeal to investors who wish to retain the ability to strategically or tactically change the allocations to individual factors over time, that is, some form of factor timing. It may also appeal to investors who believe that different providers, and their methodologies, have a higher level of expertise in capturing specific factors, which portfolio blending would allow to access. Portfolio blending resonates better with investors who seek transparency in performance attribution to gain a deeper understanding of the multiple sources of risk and return embedded in multifactor strategies. Investors who have governance considerations that lead them to define factors and exposures in terms of individual factor portfolios also prefer the portfolio blending approach. And finally, portfolio blending may appeal to investors who use the actually implemented factor portfolios to assess factor exposures and alpha realized by active managers, as discussed in more detail in Chapter 9.

d. Investment Process Considerations and Focus of Debate

In addition to the aspects analyzed earlier, the way managers define, construct, and implement factor investing may also influence the correlation structure and efficiency of factor capture, thus potentially impacting the favorability of one approach versus another. For example, consider the simple case of value. Fitzgibbons et al. (2016)

defined value as book value/price. Fraser-Jenkins et al. (2016) defined value as a blend of book value/price, 12-month forward P/E, and dividend yield. Bender and Wang (2016) defined value as an equally weighted combination of five valuation ratios, in which the fundamental variables are five-year exponentially weighted averages of sales, earnings, book value, dividends, and cash flow. These diverse definitions of value are likely to result in different correlations between value and other factors, such as conventional momentum. Furthermore, the methods by which factors are normalized and factor signals are constructed vary across managers. Some managers use z-scoring, others use ordinal ranking, and some use fixed multipliers. Finally, the weighting scheme employed to construct factor portfolios may also vary. Managers may use equal weighting, cap weighting, scaled cap weighting, signal weighting or optimizing schemes.

To the extent that methodological differences give rise to varying results, the focus of the current portfolio blending versus signal blending debate, which seeks to reach a general conclusion on the superiority of one approach versus another, may be misplaced, in our opinion. The way a manager defines, constructs, and implements factor strategies can have a meaningful impact on the correlation structure and the efficiency of factor capture. As such, we believe that a decision about the best way to capture factor effects is most appropriately made in the context of a given investment process.

V. TYPICAL INVESTOR QUESTIONS

8.1 In the Creation of Multifactor Strategies, Are There Portfolio Construction Methodologies That Would Provide Better Diversification Benefits Than Others?

As we have outlined in this chapter, within the Tilting category of weighting schemes, CW, CS, and ST factor portfolios as well as active risk constrained optimized solutions produce an active return correlation structure for smart beta factors, which is largely similar. These weighting schemes, therefore, will likely produce similar diversification benefits (i.e. reduction in active risk) in a multifactor strategy. However, these weighting schemes do differ in terms of realized efficiency in factor capture (i.e. factor-adjusted alpha), with ST portfolios and active risk constrained optimized solutions generally producing higher efficiency than CW and CS factor portfolios.

When a capitalization-weighted universe is used as a benchmark, the SW and EW factor portfolios depict high positive active return correlations. Their ability to provide meaningful diversification benefits is, therefore, limited. This is an important result, which suggests that investors may not fully benefit from factor diversification when they combine SW and EW factor portfolios as well as active risk unconstrained optimized solutions to implement multifactor strategies.

8.2 In a Multifactor Strategy, What Influences the Choice of Factors That Are Being Considered?

In implementing a multifactor strategy, investors may use a variety of factor combinations. The choice of selected factors may be driven by various considerations. Philosophical beliefs may influence the factor set under consideration. Some investors may not believe in the existence of the size or low-volatility premia and, hence, may not invest in these factors. Some benchmark-sensitive investors, who focus on IR, may not include the volatility factor in a multifactor strategy, as low-volatility investing typically produces low IRs. In implementing a defensive multifactor strategy, investors may only consider the volatility and quality factors, as the other smart beta factors do not depict defensive characteristics.

> **Application Example 8.1**
>
> In considering a multifactor strategy, an institutional asset owner decided not to include the volatility factor. The asset owner has a long investment horizon as well as the ability and willingness to take the equity market risk. In terms of investment objectives, therefore, the asset owner wanted to keep the CAPM beta of the multifactor strategy close to one and to target a reasonable after-cost IR. The inclusion of the volatility factor would have lowered the CAPM beta and the IR of the multifactor strategy.

Some smart beta managers do not include momentum in their multifactor offerings. They may argue that momentum has high turnover, which increases implementation costs and lowers investment capacity. Other managers highlight the diversification benefits of including momentum, as it independently produces positive active returns and is negatively correlated with some of the other smart beta factors. These managers have also developed turnover management methods, which allow them to include momentum in a multifactor strategy to benefit from its diversification potential, while significantly mitigating its natural turnover. An illustration of such a technique was provided in Table 8.8, in which the MFP produced a turnover of only 15%, despite including high turnover factors, such as momentum.

In our opinion, in the absence of philosophical beliefs and specific investment objectives, including more smart beta factors in a multifactor strategy is to be preferred. As we have discussed in this chapter, the diversification benefits of a multifactor strategy are driven by the off-diagonal average of all the correlation pairs across the considered factors. The off-diagonal average benefits from the "diversification" that takes place within the correlation structure, as positively correlated factor pairs are offset by negatively correlated pairs. All else being equal, the diversification embedded within the off-diagonal average benefits from more lowly or negatively correlated factors, rather than less.

8.3 Within the Portfolio Blending Approach, Is an Integrated Multifactor Solution a More Efficient Implementation of a Multifactor Strategy Compared to Investing in Individual Factor Portfolios?

In implementing multifactor strategies through a portfolio blending approach, investors typically have two implementation options:

1. Investing in individual factor portfolios constructed by different providers or by the same provider.
2. Investing in a single integrated solution offered by a provider, which delivers exposure to all the targeted factors.

In general, we believe investing in individual factor portfolios would be a reasonable implementation option for asset owners who:

- Wish to retain the ability to strategically or tactically time factors, and/or
- Believe that different providers have a higher level of expertise in capturing specific factors, and/or
- Have the ability to implement (i.e. replicate) the licensed individual factor portfolios from different providers at the same time through internal trading to take advantage of trade-netting.

Application Example 8.2

An institutional asset owner invests in a momentum strategy of a smart beta manager, in a fundamental indexation strategy to gain exposure to value, and in two internally developed strategies to gain exposure to quality and low volatility. The external strategies are licensed from external providers and implemented internally. The plan internally trades all factor portfolios at the same time, when portfolio rebalancing is conducted, to take advantage of trade-netting to reduce turnover and implementation costs.

In the absence of factor timing, philosophical beliefs in different methodologies, and ability to implement internally, we believe an integrated multifactor solution would generally be a more efficient implementation option for the following reasons.

- An integrated solution may, in principle, ensure that individual factor portfolios are constructed using a consistent methodology. This implies that the asset owner's investment staff and various oversight committees/boards would have to familiarize themselves with and communicate a single investment process, as opposed to multiple methodologies if multiple products/providers were used.

- An integrated solution may, in principle, also ensure that factor diversification is implemented in a manner that delivers balanced exposures to the desired factors, such as through active risk parity.
- An integrated solution may provide a better ability to target the desired tracking error of the overall multifactor strategy. Some smart beta offerings, such as the Research Affiliates' Fundamental Index or MSCI's Momentum and Quality Indexes, do not specifically target a given level of tracking error to the underlying policy benchmark, which may lead to uncontrolled variation in the tracking error of the factor portfolios as well as the tracking error of the overall multifactor strategy.
- Perhaps most importantly, an integrated solution may typically take advantage of trade-netting opportunities to reduce turnover and implementation costs. For example, the turnover mitigation technique illustrated in Table 8.8 realized a 74% reduction in turnover compared to a naive combination of individual factor portfolios.

8.4   One of the Advantages of the Portfolio Blending Approach Is a Simple and Transparent Portfolio Performance Attribution. What Does Transparency in Performance Attribution Mean? and Why Is the Portfolio Blending Approach Better Suited to Meet This Objective?

In a strategy that includes multiple factors, multiple sources of risk and return are introduced. Transparency in performance attribution simply means that the ex-post performance of the portfolio is explained in a manner that facilitates an understanding of these multiple sources of risk and return. In our experience, transparency in performance attribution has become a key objective for asset owners, especially in the implementation of multifactor strategies. The portfolio-blending approach potentially better meets this key objective than the signal-blending approach. The reason is that the building-block framework of portfolio blending facilitates cause-and-effect performance attribution, in which the overall portfolio return is directly attributed to each underlying factor portfolio.

Table 8.13, which is sourced from the GHP study, shows an illustration of the factor-level performance attribution made possible by portfolio blending. In the signal blend, the performance of the portfolio cannot be easily decomposed into the performance of the component factor portfolios. In the portfolio blend, however, the portfolio performance can be easily attributed to the underlying factor portfolios. The active return of the portfolio blend is the average of the value and momentum portfolios, with momentum performing modestly better than value (3.31% vs. 3.01%). The diversification benefits, which arise from the negative active return correlation between value and momentum, are evidenced by the significantly lower

TABLE 8.13 Factor-Level Performance Attribution: Russell 1000 Universe
(January 1979–June 2016)

	Active Return (%)	Active Risk (%)	Information Ratio
Signal Blend	2.52	4.25	0.59
Portfolio Blend	3.15	3.55	0.89
Value Portfolio	3.01	6.85	0.44
Momentum Portfolio	3.31	9.32	0.36

Source: *Financial Analysts Journal*, Spring 2018.

active risk of the portfolio blend compared with that of the individual-factor portfolios. The active risk reduction (or gain from diversification) results in a higher IR for the portfolio blend relative to the individual-factor portfolios. Note also that the momentum portfolio has higher active risk than the value portfolio (9.32% vs. 6.85%), suggesting that diversification could be improved by a better balance of active risk.

The portfolio blend and the individual-factor portfolios also lend themselves to detailed and transparent performance attribution at the levels of country markets, sectors, or individual stocks. Table 8.14, also sourced from the GHP study, illustrates a sector-level attribution in which total active return and active risk are decomposed into sector allocation and selection within sectors. First, looking at the active return of the portfolio blend, we note that using the value and momentum factors to select sectors contributed 0.67% to active returns. Stock selection within sectors using the factors contributed an additional 2.49%, for a total active return for the portfolio of 3.15%. At the individual factor level, sector selection contribution (0.47%) was lower and stock selection within sectors contribution (2.54%) was higher for value compared to momentum (0.89% and 2.43%, respectively). In terms of risk-adjusted returns, sector

TABLE 8.14 Sector-Level Performance Attribution: Russell 1000 Universe
(January 1979–June 2016)

	Active Return (%)			Active Risk (%)			Information Ratio		
	Sector	Within Sector	Total	Sector	Within Sector	Total	Sector	Within Sector	Total
Signal Blend	0.47	2.06	2.52	2.44	2.44	4.25	0.19	0.84	0.59
Portfolio Blend	0.67	2.49	3.15	2.08	2.14	3.55	0.32	1.16	0.89
Value Portfolio	0.47	2.54	3.01	3.94	4.42	6.85	0.12	0.57	0.44
Momentum Portfolio	0.89	2.43	3.31	3.95	6.11	9.32	0.23	0.40	0.36

Source: *Financial Analysts Journal*, Spring 2018.

selection IR was higher for momentum than for value (0.23 vs. 0.12), while stock selection within sectors IR was higher for value compared to momentum (0.57 vs. 0.40). These are insights that are not easily observable in a signal blending approach.

8.5 In the Portfolio Blending Versus Signal Blending Debate, the Arguments and Counterarguments Seem Complicated. At a Practical Level, How Should Investors Approach the Decision of Which Construction Methodology to Follow?

The portfolio blending versus signal blending debate has practical implications, as multifactor strategies are gaining in popularity, and the debate is about the efficiency with which such strategies are implemented. In our experience, many investors currently implement multifactor investing using the portfolio blending approach, as it may be better suited to meet certain objectives, such as simplicity and transparency in portfolio construction and performance attribution. Some studies argue, however, that signal blending is a much more efficient approach to constructing multifactor strategies and hence, when investors pursue a portfolio blending approach they do so at the expense of investment efficiency. In other words, there is a trade-off between investment efficiency and other objectives, such that the pursuit of such objectives may result in lower risk-adjusted returns.

However, as GHP have highlighted, existing studies introduce various methodological biases, which do not produce an apples-to-apples comparison. If the objective is to determine the efficiency with which the two approaches deliver factor exposures, then that determination cannot be reasonably made without matching the compared portfolios on factor exposures. For instance, Bender and Wang (2016) showed that, in their simulation setup, signal blend outperformed the portfolio blend. But, as GHP argue in their study, if the compared portfolios were matched on factor exposures using the Bender and Wang (2016) process, the two portfolios would produce identical performance.

Broadly speaking, the general dominance of the signal blending approach is challenged when exposure-matched portfolios are compared, as shown by GHP. Their findings suggest that the trade-off between investment efficiency and other objectives is only valid when high active risk multifactor strategies are considered. At the low-to-moderate levels of active risk (typically less than 4%) that asset owners generally pursue in allocating to multifactor smart beta strategies, portfolio blending and signal blending deliver similar risk-adjusted returns. As such, investors can pursue the additional objectives without concerns relating to loss of investment efficiency.

Additionally, the focus of the current debate seems misplaced to us. The studies cited previously use a "specific" methodology and investment process to establish the superiority of one approach versus the other, and then extend those results to a "general" conclusion, as if the same results would hold when looked at through the lens of other investment processes. Therefore, it is our view that investors have to approach this topic within the context of a given investment process.

8.6 Can Factor Timing Improve the Performance of a Multifactor Strategy?

Some recent articles (e.g. Arnott et al. 2016) have argued that the growing popularity of smart beta investing has resulted in many factors becoming expensive relative to history and, thus, being susceptible to crashes. The implication here, of course, is that investors should avoid such richly priced factors and double-up on the attractively priced ones. The cheapness or expensiveness of factor strategies is typically determined using current valuation spreads or valuation ratios and sometimes comparing them to historical averages and/or valuations of other factor portfolios. Changing the allocations to factors in a multifactor strategy, such as underweighting expensive factors and overweighting cheap factors, based on valuation signals is a form of factor timing. The general assumption in value timing is that, if value works, then it could prove helpful in timing factors as well.

Asness et al. (2017) did not find evidence that smart beta factors have experienced steady increases in valuations as assets have grown in such strategies. Further, they explored the use of valuation metrics to time factors and concluded that it is "deceptively difficult." They found no meaningful differences in gross returns and gross Sharpe ratios in comparing a value-timed strategy with a nontimed diversified multifactor strategy.

Our research generally supports the findings of Asness et al. (2017). We find that factor portfolio valuations do not mean-revert in a predictable manner, and current valuations only loosely predict future factor performance, at least for time horizons that matter to practitioners. Yet, factor timing has the potential to introduce additional sources of risk in the portfolio, reduce factor diversification, and significantly increase turnover. The fact that value works in certain cases, such as stock selection, does not necessarily imply that it works in all applications. For instance, for decades, investors have tried to time the market using aggregate valuation ratios, with mixed results. And that's just one factor. Trying to time multiple other factors using such techniques is an extremely difficult task, with an uncertain value add. We do not mean to imply here that all forms of factor timing should be avoided. For instance, a factor rotation strategy that seeks to take advantage of the medium-term mean reversion of factor premia has been pursued by some asset owners with some degree of success.

8.7 In Many Instances, Smart Beta Strategies Are New Products, Which Are Promoted on the Basis of Historical Backtests and Simulations. How Should Investors Assess the Representativeness of a Historical Backtest?

In our opinion, the representativeness of a backtest, in general, may be assessed along the following three broad dimensions:

1 Signal/Factor Specifications
2 Portfolio Construction
3 Implementation Costs

We discuss these dimensions in more detail below.

a. Signal/Factor Specifications

Factor specifications that have broad academic support and are simple and transparent may be viewed as more representative than those that are (1) proprietary, (2) have limited academic support or (3) are highly complex in their design, such as composite specifications that include multiple individual signals. In our opinion, an example of a signal specification that has limited academic support would be Enterprise Value-to-Cash Flow from Operations to define the value factor. An example of a complex factor specification would be the use of a quality composite that includes more than 20 individual signals along various dimensions, such as profitability, stability, leverage, and payout. Complex composites can potentially become subject to an overfitting bias (e.g. Novy-Marx 2016). This bias can result in the composite generating statistically significant results, even though most of the individual signals used in the composite are not statistically significant on a standalone basis.

b. Portfolio Construction

Portfolio construction methodologies that are not fully transparent and do not lend themselves to an independent replication of historical performance may be viewed as being more susceptible to potential data mining. An example would be a highly complex optimized solution based on an internally developed risk model.

c. Implementation Costs

Historical simulations that do not account for, or use relatively liberal assumptions relating to, turnover and implementation costs may be viewed as less representative of expected out-of-sample performance.

In our experience, investors typically apply a "discount," which involves reducing the back-tested active return and information ratio of a strategy, to make them potentially more representative for future performance. The discounts being applied generally range from 0% to 50% depending on the perceived or actual transparency and replicability of backtested performance. A 50% discount may be viewed by some investors as appropriate for backtests that are based on unsupported factor specifications, nontransparent portfolio construction methodologies, and simulations that do not account for turnover and implementation costs.

VI. CONCLUSION

Factor diversification strategies tend to produce higher relative risk-adjusted returns (i.e. IR), with potentially lower market underperformance risk, compared to individual factors. They also generally depict better risk-adjusted performance compared to alternative equity beta offerings that have concentrated exposures to specific smart beta factors. This dominance of multifactor strategies, in our experience, is now well-understood and well-accepted by investors.

CHAPTER 9

THE LOW-VOLATILITY ANOMALY

Roger G. Clarke
Research Consultant,
Analytic Investors

Harindra de Silva
Portfolio Manager,
Analytic Investors/Wells
Fargo Asset Management

Steven Thorley
H. Taylor Peery Professor of Finance,
Marriott School of Business
Brigham, Young University

I. INTRODUCTION

In this chapter we address low volatility as a factor in equity securities. The performance of low-risk securities is referred to as an anomaly in the stock market, because historically there has not been a return penalty for investing in lower risk stocks. In the first section we review the empirical data that supports the presence of a low-volatility factor, and note explanations advanced to explain the anomaly. In the second section we examine whether the low-volatility anomaly is driven by the systematic or idiosyncratic risk of individual stocks. We present the previously unpublished empirical result that the anomaly is almost completely associated with market beta and should thus be called the low-beta anomaly. In the third section we look at some of the characteristics of the low-volatility factor, including its correlation with other well-known equity market factors like value and momentum. In the fourth section we describe various techniques for building low-volatility portfolios. In the fifth section we comment on the growth of commercially available ETFs that attempt to capture the low-volatility effect and make it available to investors. We close with a short summary section and conclusion.

II. HISTORICAL MANIFESTATION OF THE LOW-VOLATILITY FACTOR

The well-known Low-Volatility Anomaly in the US and global equity markets is that low risk stocks have returns that at least equal the returns of high-risk stocks, in contrast to capital markets theory. Evidence for this anomaly was present in early academic tests of the Sharpe (1964) Capital Asset Pricing Model and has been documented in a number of more recent practitioner publications like Clarke, de, Silva, and Thorley (2006). For example, Exhibit 9.1 plots the performance of five risk-quintile portfolios and the large-cap US stock market over the last half-century, 1967 to 2016. The vertical axis in Exhibit 9.1 is the average portfolio return in excess of the contemporaneous risk-free rate, and the horizontal axis is portfolio risk as measured by the realized standard deviation of those returns. The market portfolio and risk-quintile portfolio average return and risk numbers are reported in the first two rows of Exhibit 9.2.

The market portfolio in Exhibits 9.1 and 9.2 contains the largest 1,000 US common stocks (excluding ETFs), capitalization-weighted, with dividends reinvested and rebalanced monthly, a rough proxy for the Russell 1000 Index. The market portfolio's 6.23% average excess return over 50 years, divided by the market portfolio's risk of 15.21%, gives a Sharpe ratio of 0.41, as reported in the third row of Exhibit 9.2 and shown by the slope of the Capital Market Line in Exhibit 9.1. This 0.41 Sharpe ratio verifies a substantial premium over the risk-free rate for the equity market as a whole, in accordance with basic intuition about risk and return.

The five risk-quintile portfolios plotted in Exhibit 9.1 employ a monthly sort of the 1,000 stocks in the market benchmark into five 200-stock portfolios, using the prior 36-month return standard deviation of each stock. The five risk-quintile portfolios are capitalization-weighted and rebalanced monthly, with performance numbers as given in Exhibit 9.2. Because larger stocks in the US market tend to have lower risk, the 200 stocks in Portfolio 1 (low risk) comprise about 36 rather than just 20% of total market capitalization, while the 200 stocks in Portfolio 5 (high risk) comprise only about 7% of total market capitalization. The result of this skewed cross-sectional distribution of market capitalization is that Portfolio 2 rather than the "middle risk" Portfolio 3 plots closer to the general market in Exhibit 9.1.

The results in Exhibits 9.1 and 9.2 illustrate two well-known historical facts: First, the cross-sectional variation in individual stock risk is persistent and predictable, so that stocks sorted into the lower and higher quintiles based on their historical (i.e. prior 36 month) risk, produce portfolios with reliably lower and higher realized risk. For example, the 12.34% realized risk of Portfolio 1 is less than half the 26.73% realized risk of Portfolio 5, as reported in Exhibit 9.2. Second, the average

EXHIBIT 9.1   Total Risk Quintile Portfolio Performance (1967–2016)

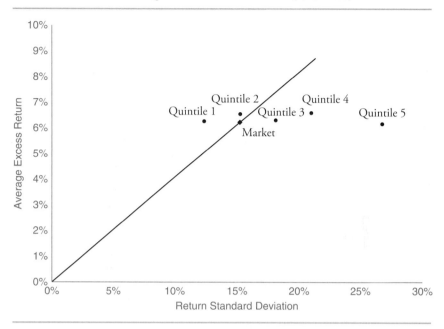

EXHIBIT 9.2   Total Risk Quintile Portfolio Performance (1967–2016)

	Market	1 Low	2	3	4	5 High	Quintile 1 –Quintile 5
Average Return	6.23%	6.27%	6.54%	6.31%	6.59%	6.17%	0.10%
Standard Deviation	15.21%	12.34%	15.23%	18.08%	20.97%	26.73%	20.99%
Sharpe Ratio	0.41	0.51	0.43	0.35	0.31	0.23	0
Market Beta	1	0.73	0.96	1.15	1.3	1.54	–0.8
Market Alpha	0.00%	1.69%	0.58%	–0.86%	–1.48%	–3.41%	5.10%
Active Risk		5.26%	4.43%	4.57%	7.16%	12.94%	17.07%
Information Ratio		0.32	0.13	–0.19	–0.21	–0.26	0.3

return to individual stocks does *not* increase with risk, in that all five risk-quintile portfolios have realized returns that are within half a percentage point of the 6.23% market return, statistically and economically indistinguishable from each other. This historical experience runs counter to what one would expect about higher return for higher risk *within* the US stock market. The same no-reward-to-risk pattern has been documented in other country equity markets, for example by Blitz and Vliet (2007), and for periods that precede 1967. We focus on the last half-century in the US equity market due to the availability of accurate and comprehensive data on a large (i.e. 1,000) set of stock returns in the CRSP database.

The portfolio performance results in Exhibits 9.1 and 9.2 run counter to the concept that investors demand higher returns for higher risk. The historical data could be a biased representation of higher investor expectations for higher risk stocks, so that investors have simply been repeatedly disappointed in the past. But the long history in the US equity market and similar results in other country markets suggests that there are probably other explanations. Researchers have proposed several theories related to either investor behavioral biases or leverage constraints. One proposal is that investor preferences for "lottery" effects represented by the upside potential of high-risk stocks may result in the prices of those stocks being bid up beyond their fair value, as suggested in Boyer and Vorkink (2014). Alternatively, high-risk stocks may be good "story" stocks whose gains selectively demonstrate skill, thereby attracting additional investors, as discussed in Frazzini and Pedersen (2014). Constraints on some investors against short selling may be an impediment to taking the mispricing out of the high-risk stocks by more sophisticated investors, as explained in Baker et al. (2011).

Another theory is that the asset management industry's focus on *market relative* return and portfolio tracking error, instead of absolute return and volatility, may lead professional fund managers to shy away from lower volatility stocks that have relatively high tracking error to the broad market. For example, the active risk of 5.26% for the lowest-risk (i.e. quintile 1) portfolio given in Exhibit 9.2 is actually higher than for quintile portfolios 2 or 3. In any event, the rationale for why the anomaly exists is important to predicting whether the same pattern will persist going forward. Specifically, a better understanding of why the public equity markets have performed the way they have in the past could provide a perspective on the conditions under which the anomaly is likely to continue.

The performance numbers in Exhibit 9.2 illustrate another characteristic of low-volatility stock returns. By design, the market beta of the lower volatility portfolios is below 1.00. This means that when the market is down, the lower volatility portfolios tend to outperform the market, but to underperform when the market is up. Low-volatility portfolios keep pace with the market on average, but the market relative returns are somewhat cyclical and less directional than the market. For example, a zero net-investment portfolio formed by subtracting the high-risk portfolio (quintile 5) returns from the low risk portfolio (quintile 1) returns in Exhibit 9.2 has an average return of just 6.27% – 6.17% = 0.10%, but a large return standard deviation of 20.99%. On the other hand, the realized market beta of this long/short portfolio is large negative value of – 0.80, suggesting a significant hedge to the market portfolio. The Q1-Q5 portfolio thus has a healthy Information Ratio of 0.30, as reported in Exhibit 9.2.

III. HOW IS "LOW VOLATILITY" DEFINED?

Three general measures of stock risk are total volatility, beta risk, and residual or idiosyncratic volatility. The three measures are linked in that the total volatility of a security can be decomposed into sensitivity to a market index (i.e. beta) and idiosyncratic risk, according to the formula

$$\sigma_i = \sqrt{\beta_i^2\, \sigma_M^2 + \sigma_{\varepsilon,i}^2} \qquad (9.1)$$

An open question among equity market observers is whether the Low Vol Anomaly is associated with beta risk, and thus more correctly called a "Low-Beta Anomaly" or with idiosyncratic risk, and thus more correctly called a "Low Idio Anomaly." The quintile sorting of individual stocks in Exhibit 9.1 is based on total risk, specifically parameter σ_i in Equation (9.1). In contrast, Exhibits 9.3 and 9.4 use the separate parameters β_i and $\sigma_{\varepsilon,i}$, respectively, to sort the 1,000 individual stocks each month into 200-stock risk-quintile portfolios.

As can be seen by visually comparing Exhibits 9.3 and 9.4, simply sorting by the security risk parameters β_i versus $\sigma_{\varepsilon,i}$ does little to resolve the underlying source of the Low Vol Anomaly. Either both sources of risk are anomalous in terms of their associated return, or one source of risk is behind the anomaly, but positively correlated to the other source of risk. Indeed, a closer examination of the data shows that the cross-sectional correlation between historical observations of the security risk parameters β_i and $\sigma_{\varepsilon,i}$ is consistently positive and quite high, on the order 0.2 to 0.7 at the start of any given month. In other words, stocks with high market betas also tend to have high levels of idiosyncratic risk.

EXHIBIT 9.3   Beta Risk Quintile Portfolio Performance: (1967–2016)

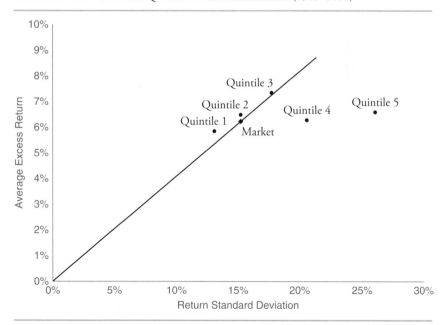

EXHIBIT 9.4   Idiosyncratic Risk Quintile Portfolio Performance (1967–2016)

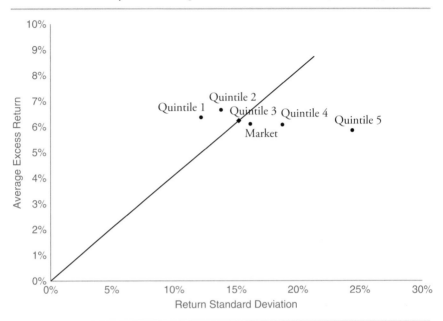

Multivariate regression analysis is a common tool for examining the interaction between a dependent variable and two or more independent variables. To investigate which security risk parameter is the most influential with respect to the Low Vol Anomaly, we converted both the historical market beta and idiosyncratic risk for each stock into capitalization-weighted z-scores each month. We then ran monthly capitalization-weighted Fama-Macbeth (1973) cross-sectional regressions of realized security returns, with both measures of security risk as the independent variables, as described in Clarke et al. (2017).

The slope coefficients of this monthly 1,000-observation cross-sectional regression equal the difference between the factor portfolio return to each source of risk and the market benchmark return, given by the intercept term. The sum of the intercept term and the specified slope coefficient is thus the total excess (of risk-free rate) return for the factor portfolios, as reported in Exhibit 9.5. Because both measures of security risk are included in the monthly regressions, each risk-factor portfolio controls for the influence of the other factor and are thus "pure" factor portfolios. Specifically, the pure Beta Factor Portfolio has security weights that exactly match the market-wide average idiosyncratic risk exposure, and the pure Idiosyncratic Risk Factor Portfolio has an ex ante estimated market-beta of exactly one.

The second and third columns of Exhibit 9.5 report the return performance from 1967 to 2016 (600 months) of the univariate or *primary* beta factor and idiosyncratic

EXHIBIT 9.5   Primary and Pure Risk Factor Portfolio Performance (1967–2016)

		Univariate		Multivariate	
	Market	Beta Factor	Idio Factor	Pure Beta	Pure Idio
Average Return	6.23%	6.34%	5.97%	6.78%	5.60%
Standard Deviation	15.21%	12.23%	12.87%	12.79%	14.12%
Sharpe Ratio	0.41	0.52	0.46	0.53	0.4
Market Beta	100.00%	74.00%	78.00%	79.00%	88.00%
Market Alpha	0.00%	1.75%	1.11%	1.85%	0.11%
Active Risk		4.90%	4.97%	4.32%	4.38%
Information Ratio		0.36	0.22	0.43	0.02

factor portfolios, from two different capitalization-weighted Fama-Macbeth regressions. In contrast, the performance of the *pure* risk factor portfolios from one multivariate capitalization-weighted Fama-Macbeth regression are shown in the fourth and fifth columns of Exhibit 9.5.

The second and third columns show that both the uncontrolled Beta Factor and the uncontrolled Idio Risk Factor portfolios have outperformed the market on a risk-adjusted basis over 50 years, with Sharpe ratios of 0.52 and 0.46, respectively, compared to the market portfolio Sharpe ratio of 0.41. To calculate an annualized alpha, a single time-series regression over the entire 50 years gives the active return performance numbers in the lower half of Exhibit 9.5. The 1.75% alpha of the Beta Factor portfolio, and the 1.11% alpha of the Idio Risk Factor portfolio, indicate that a substantial low-volatility anomaly exists in both, although the Information Ratio (alpha divided by active risk) of the Beta Factor portfolio is slightly higher at 0.36, compared to 0.22 for the Idio Risk Factor portfolio.

The fourth and fifth columns of Exhibit 9.5 show the performance results for the two *pure* factor portfolios, based on a monthly capitalization-weighted Fama-Macbeth regression that includes *both* independent variables. The performance results on these two pure factor portfolios makes the assignment of the Low Vol Anomaly to a beta rather than idiosyncratic risk property of individual securities quite clear. The Pure Beta Factor portfolio has an Information Ratio of 0.43, improved from the 0.36 Information Ratio from the univariate regression analysis. On the other hand, the 0.02 Information Ratio of the Pure Idio Risk Factor portfolio is substantially lower than the 0.22 Information Ratio of the uncontrolled univariate portfolio, and not statistically different from a zero. With respect to inferential statistics, the *t*-stat for the null hypothesis of a zero alpha is the Information Ratio (as given in Exhibit 9.5) times the square root of 50 (the number of years). The *t*-stat for the *pure* Beta Factor portfolio is thus 0.43*SQRT(50) = 3.0 (highly significant) while *t*-stat for the *pure* Idiosyncratic Risk Factor portfolio is 0.02*SQRT(50) = 0.1 (close to zero).

EXHIBIT 9.6   Primary and Pure Risk Factor Portfolio Performance (1967–2016)

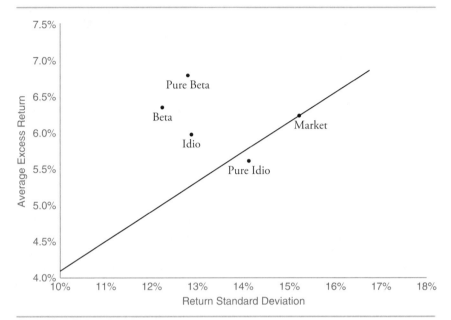

Exhibit 9.6 plots the portfolios in Exhibit 9.5, similar to the plot in Exhibit 9.1, except that the range of both axes has been adjusted to focus in the risk-return area where the portfolios are concentrated. Both primary risk factor portfolios plot above the market's 0.41 sloped Capital Allocation Line. But the pure Idio Risk portfolio actually lies below the line, with a Sharpe ratio of 0.40, while the pure Low-Beta portfolio plots well above the market's Capital Allocation Line, with a Sharpe ratio of 0.53. The conclusion from the multivariate Fama-Macbeth regression analysis is that the well-known Low Vol Anomaly is associated with low-beta stocks rather than low idiosyncratic risk stocks and is thus more correctly called the Low-Beta Anomaly. This empirical result (new to this book chapter) is ironic, given that the low-volatility anomaly received much of its academic credibility based on an examination of stock's *idiosyncratic* risk in Ang et al. (2006).

IV. SECONDARY FACTORS OF LOW-BETA PORTFOLIOS

In general, the returns to low-beta portfolios are not independent of the returns to other popular equity factors. To illustrate, we calculated the returns to several additional factors over the half-century from 1967 to 2016 for the largest 1,000 US stocks, similar to Clarke, de Silva, and Thorley (2016). Besides low-beta, the factor exposures are:

Value: Inverse P/E ratio or "earnings yield" using the beginning-of-month stock price (from CRSP) and earnings-per-share, with a one-quarter lag on the most recent annual Income Statement (from Compustat). Earnings yield is an alternative to the Book-to-Market ratio (annual Balance Sheet book equity over equity market-cap) originally identified as the Value factor in Fama and French (1996).

Momentum: The 11-month stock return, with dividends, lagged by one month, sometimes called Carhart (1997) momentum. The momentum factor in this study refers to the price momentum of the stock, first identified as a factor by Jegadeesh and Titman (1993), not the earnings momentum of the corporation.

Small Size: The log of 1 over beginning-of-month market capitalization (i.e. negative log market capitalization), as used in Fama and French (1996). This factor measures smallness within the investable set of the largest one thousand US common stocks (approximately the Russell 1000 Index), not the exposure to an even smaller capitalization index like the Russell 2000.

Profitability: Gross profit margin, defined as Revenues minus Cost of Goods Sold from the most recent annual Income Statement, divided by Total Assets from the most recent annual Balance Sheet. We use these accounting numbers with a one-quarter lag to ensure the data would have been available to investors historically. This factor is often called Novy-Marx (2013) Profitability but is also referred to as a Quality factor by some investors.

We convert the factor exposures to z-scores and calculate the relative returns to the factor portfolio using the capitalization-weighted Fama-Macbeth regression technique. Exhibit 9.7 reports the performance the single-variable factor portfolios, similar to the second and third columns of Exhibit 9.5. However, in Exhibit 9.7 we adjust the presentation to focus on market-relative returns. For example, the market-relative mean return to the Value portfolio is 1.05%, for a total return including the embedded market return, of 6.25% + 1.05% = 7.30%. Note that the return to the market portfolio of 6.25% in Exhibit 9.7 is slightly different than the 6.23% return in the

EXHIBIT 9.7   Return Performance of Primary Factor Portfolios (1967–2016)

		Market Relative				
	Market	Value	Momentum	Small Size	Low Beta	Profitability
Mean	6.25%	1.05%	2.32%	1.32%	0.06%	0.92%
Standard Deviation	15.22%	4.55%	6.12%	4.22%	6.33%	3.93%
Market Beta	1	−0.08	−0.01	0.08	−0.26	−0.02
Market Alpha	0.00%	1.54%	2.39%	0.84%	1.70%	1.02%
Active Risk		4.40%	6.13%	4.06%	4.93%	3.93%
Information Ratio		35.00%	39.00%	21.00%	34.00%	26.00%

prior sections, because the additional accounting data requirements for the Value and Profitability exposure calculations result in a slightly different set of the largest 1,000 stocks in the US market. The Value, Momentum, Small Size, and Profitability portfolios in Exhibit 9.7 all have positive long-term averages, although the market-relative return to the Low-Beta portfolio is quite low at just 6 basis points.

The lower rows in Exhibit 9.7 show that value-added of the Low-Beta portfolio comes in terms of the realized market beta of – 0.26, in contrast to realized market betas that are closer to zero for the other factor portfolios. Exhibit 9.7 reports on market-relative returns, so the Low-Beta portfolio's realized beta of – 0.26 equates to the more familiar total return beta of 1.00 – 0.26 = 0.74. As a result of this low realized beta, the Market Alpha and Information Ratio of the Low-Beta portfolio is competitive with the performance of the other equity market factors.

The univariate or "primary" factor portfolios reported in Exhibit 9.7 have substantial secondary exposures, and thus return correlations with each other. The realized market-relative return correlations over the entire 50-year period from 1967 to 2016 for the various factor portfolios are reported in Exhibit 9.8. The correlations are not stable, so point-in-time exposure correlations discussed later provide a better perspective on the inter-dependencies of the various factors. However, the single realized return correlation of – 0.41 between Value and Momentum is quite substantial, while the realized positive return correlation of 0.44 between Value and Low-Beta is substantial in the other direction. Note that the return correlation coefficients in Exhibit 9.8 are for market differential returns. All six-factor portfolio *total* returns (i.e. with the market return included) would have large positive correlations to each other.

For a visual perspective on the track record of the factor portfolios in Exhibit 9.7, Exhibit 9.9 plots the cumulative market-differential returns through the end of 2016, starting with zero at the beginning of 1967. For example, the outstanding market-relative performance of the Momentum portfolio appears to flatten out after the turn-of-the century tech-bubble, which was simultaneously marked by large drawdowns in the Value and Low-Beta portfolios, while the performance of the Profitability portfolio appears to be more slow and steady, at least since the 1980s. The Low-Beta portfolio's cumulative return ends in 2016 at about zero, consistent with a mean market-relative return of about zero, as reported in Exhibit 9.7. But again, the

EXHIBIT 9.8   Correlations of Market-Relative Primary Factor Portfolio Returns (1967–2016)

	Value	Momentum	Small Size	Low Beta	Profitability
Value	1	–0.42	0.2	0.44	–0.48
Momentum	–0.42	1	–0.14	0.02	0.25
Small Size	0.2	–0.14	1	–0.27	–0.32
Low Beta	0.44	0.02	–0.27	1	–0.04
Profitability	–0.48	0.25	–0.32	–0.04	1

EXHIBIT 9.9   Cumulative Market-relative Primary Factor Portfolio Returns (1967–2016)

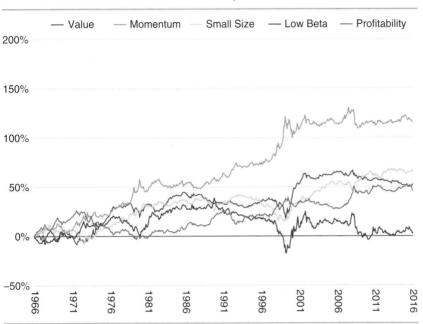

advantage of the Low-Beta portfolio is not measured by cumulative market-relative returns, but by the negative market-relative beta of those returns.

While the large positive correlation between the Low-Beta and Value portfolio returns in Exhibit 9.8 is indicative of a substantial correspondence between Low-Beta and Value exposures in the individual securities, the return correlation is not stable in that nature of the exposure correlation changes from month to month. Rather than depend on the realized correlation in factor portfolio returns over time, month-by-month factor exposures provide a better point-in-time perspective on the interdependencies between the factors. Specifically, Exhibit 9.10 plots the standardized exposures at the beginning of each month from 1967 to 2016 of the Low-Beta portfolio. Note that the low-beta factor exposure of the Low-Beta portfolio is exactly one by design in Exhibit 9.10, while the other exposures vary over time.

For example, the Value exposure of the Low-Beta portfolio is generally positive over time, ranging between 0.0 and 0.4, but with negative exposure episodes in the 1970s, and then again in more recent years. A negative Value exposure indicates that the Low-Beta portfolio is more "expensive" than the capitalization-weighted market benchmark portfolio, in that the earnings yield is lower (i.e. P/E ratio is higher) than the market. However, because this is not the typical state of affairs, in that the Low-Beta's value exposure tends to be positive over time, the 50-year correlation coefficient between the Low-Beta and Value portfolios is large and positive at 0.44, as reported in Exhibit 9.8. The only other Low-Beta portfolio exposure in Exhibit 9.10

EXHIBIT 9.10   Standardized Exposures of the Primary Low-Beta Factor
Portfolio (1967–2016)

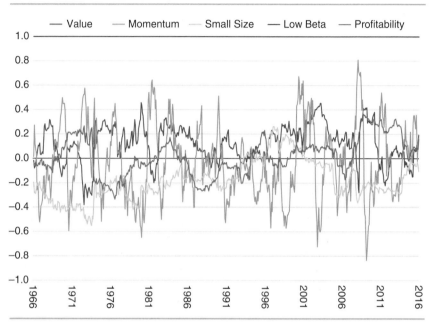

that is fairly consistent over time in terms of sign is the Small Size exposure, which generally ranges from – 0.4 to 0.0, although with a positive episode at the turn of the century. The exposure pattern means that Low-Beta stocks tend to be larger stocks within the market benchmark, except for the turn-of-the century technology bubble. The result is that the long-term 50-year correlation coefficient between the Low-Beta and Small Size portfolios is negative at – 0.27, as reported in Exhibit 9.8.

As is Clarke, de Silva, and Thorley (2017), we can employ the capitalization-weighted Fama-Macbeth regression methodology with several factor exposures on the right-hand side, to calculate the return performance of factor portfolios that are pure. The portfolios are pure because the standardized exposures to other non-market factors are set to zero at the beginning of each month. Exhibits 9.11 and 9.12 report on pure factor portfolios in the same format as Exhibits 9.7 and 9.8.

The mean return and alpha of the pure Low-Beta portfolio in Exhibit 9.11 of 0.58% and 1.96%, respectively, are slightly higher than the Low-Beta portfolio in Exhibit 9.7, which has nonconstant secondary exposures. Even more conceptually important, the Exhibit 9.11 active risk of 4.26% is lower than Exhibit 9.7 because the secondary exposures and risks have been neutralized. The result is that the Low-Beta portfolio's Information Ratio increases from 0.34 in Exhibit 9.7 to 0.46 in Exhibit 9.11, as it does for all of the other pure factor portfolios where the secondary

EXHIBIT 9.11   Return Performance of Pure Factor Portfolios (1967– 2016)

	Market	Market Relative				
		Value	Momentum	Small Size	Low Beta	Profitability
Mean	6.25%	1.91%	2.73%	1.16%	0.58%	1.44%
Standard Deviation	15.22%	3.17%	4.81%	3.67%	5.41%	3.25%
Market Beta	1	−0.04	−0.008	0.049	−0.219	−0.01
Market Alpha	0.00%	2.16%	2.78%	0.86%	1.96%	1.50%
Active Risk		3.11%	4.81%	3.60%	4.26%	3.25%
Information Ratio		0.69	0.58	0.24	0.46	0.46

risk exposures are removed. The result is lower although still nonzero return correlations over time between the factor portfolios, as shown in Exhibit 9.12. The Low Beta to Value factor portfolio return correlation drops by about half, from 0.44 in Exhibit 9.8 to 0.19 in Exhibit 9.12. The negative correlation of the Low-Beta and Small Size factor portfolio return, goes from – 0.27 in Exhibit 9.8 to – 0.15 in Exhibit 9.12.

The overall performance of the pure factor portfolios are shown visually in Exhibit 9.13, with cumulative return plots that can be compared with Exhibit 9.9. Notably, the simultaneous turn-of-the century drawdown in both the Low-Beta and Value portfolios in Exhibit 9.9, only appears in the Low-Beta portfolio in Exhibit 9.13, suggesting that a more correct characterization of the build-up to the technology bubble was high beta stocks, rather than growth stocks per se. In any event, the most important visual characterization of Exhibit 9.13 is that the cumulative return plots for the pure factor portfolios are much smoother than in Exhibit 9.9 for the primary factor portfolios, with all of their secondary risk exposures. Note that we do not provide a plot of secondary exposures for the *pure* Low-Beta portfolio, similar to Exhibit 9.10 for the *primary* Low-beta portfolio, because the market relative exposures would be exactly zero at each point in time (i.e. the lines would all plot on the *x*-axis) except for the Low-Beta exposure, which would continue to plot at one at each point in time by design.

EXHIBIT 9.12   Correlations of Market-Relative Pure Factor Portfolio Returns (1967–2016)

	Value	Momentum	Small Size	Low Beta	Profitability
Value	1	−0.15	0.04	0.19	−0.17
Momentum	−0.15	1	−0.06	0.02	0.03
Small Size	0.04	−0.06	1	−0.15	0.01
Low Beta	0.19	0.02	−0.15	1	−0.12
Profitability	−0.17	0.03	0.01	−0.12	1

EXHIBIT 9.13   Cumulative Market-Relative Pure Factor Portfolio Returns (1967–2016)

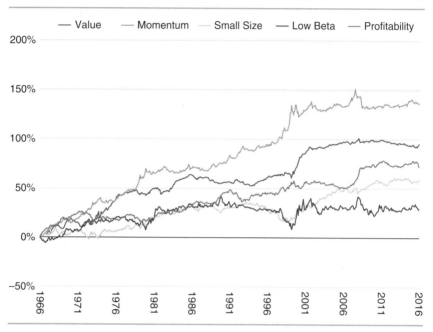

V.   BUILDING A LOW-VOLATILITY PORTFOLIO

A number of steps are involved in constructing any factor portfolio, like low volatility, and each step involves multiple decisions that affect the eventual performance of the portfolio. In general, these steps can be summarized as: selecting the universe of investable securities (e.g. country/region, capitalization size, liquidity, ESG considerations) including any filtering (e.g. data sufficiency requirements) that narrows the scope of acceptable stocks; choosing a portfolio construction technique (i.e. weighting scheme) for how to combine the selected securities; and specifying any constraints or limitations on the portfolio.

With respect to low-volatility portfolios, we mention three general approaches to portfolio construction that have been employed in practice: First, optimization with respect to various objective functions including minimum variance, maximum Sharpe ratio, target tracking error, maximum diversification, and security risk parity. Second, heuristic rules like sorting and taking the top ranked securities down to a cutoff point, together with equal-, risk-, or capitalization- weighting. Third, factor return replication using the portfolio weights from a Fama-MacBeth regression. This third category includes the primary beta and pure beta portfolios described in earlier sections. The second category includes the quintile sorts discussed briefly in the first section.

One of the first direct empirical observations of the low-volatility anomaly came in examining an optimization process, the first category above, which we discuss next. Clarke et al. (2006) examined minimum variance portfolios is the US equity market, where the objective function was simple portfolio risk minimization, irrespective of any particular forecast of security returns. The only input to the numerical optimizer is some reasonable estimation of the security covariance matrix. For example, using the investable universe of the largest 1,000 US stocks, a one-million element covariance matrix can be based on a matrix of prior 36 months of excess returns, transposed and multiplied by itself. This 1,000-by-1,000 "sample" matrix is combined with a "prior" matrix where all 1,000 securities each month have the same volatility (i.e. the sample average across all stocks), and each stock has the average correlation coefficient with all the other stocks.

The exact amount of "Bayesian shrinkage" toward the prior can be based on statistical methods that incorporate the number of securities (e.g. 1,000) and the number of historical return observations (e.g. 36), but here we use a simple Bayesian shrinkage parameter of 50%. With a long-only constraint added to the numerical optimizer (i.e. only positive security weights are allowed), the process yields a portfolio with an average of about 150 securities in solution, although this number varies slowly over time between about 50 and 250 positions. The performance of this long-only minimum variance portfolio over the last half-century is given in in the second column of Exhibit 9.14. Despite the fact that higher returns are not explicitly part of the objective function, the average return of the long-only minimum variance portfolio is 6.64%, slightly higher than the 6.24% market return, with a substantial reduction in risk. For example, the market beta of the minimum-variance portfolio (one number based on the entire 50-year time series) is 0.70, giving an annualized alpha 2.26%, and an Information Ratio of 0.37.

An important concept of Low Volatility investing is that portfolios are still sensitive to the overall market performance, so tend to underperform when the market is up. For example, using the long-term results in Exhibit 9.14, if the market is up 15% in a given year, the Minimum Variance portfolio would be on average up only 2.26% + 0.70 * 15.00% = 12.76%. On the other hand, if the market is down – 15% in a given year, the Minimum Variance portfolio on average would only be down 2.26% + 0.70(– 15.00)% = – 8.24%. Also note that the Active Risk number of 6.08% in Exhibit 9.14 is calculated based on benchmark of 0.70 (the realized beta) times the market return. Tracking error, defined as the simple difference between the Minimum Variance and Market portfolio returns, is 7.60% (not reported), compared to 6.08%. Such a high level of tracking error may be unacceptable to investors who are primarily concerned about returns relative to the market.

Notably, the third and fourth columns of Exhibit 9.14 report on the performance of the long-only minimum variance portfolio since the publication of Clarke et al. (2006), where the results ended in December 2005. Unlike some market anomalies, where performance seems to disappear after the initial publication of the anomaly (either because the factor was data-mined, or because general awareness of the anomaly leads to its elimination), the market-relative performance of the minimum variance portfolio has been similar ex-post (i.e. after publication). The average return from

EXHIBIT 9.14   Minimum Variance Portfolio Performance

	50 Years (1967–2016)		11 Years (2006–2016)	
	Market	Long-Only	Market	Long-Only
		Min Var		Min Var
Average Return	6.24%	6.64%	7.72%	7.57%
Standard Deviation	15.24%	12.28%	14.64%	12.51%
Sharpe Ratio	0.41	0.54	0.53	0.61
Market Beta	100.00%	70.00%	100.00%	77.00%
Market Alpha	0.00%	2.26%	0.00%	1.61%
Active Risk		6.08%		5.47%
Information Ratio		0.37		0.3

2006 to 2016 is not quite equal to the market-wide return, but the risk reduction from 14.64% down to 12.51% for the minimum variance portfolio, is substantial. The realized market beta (based on a single time-series over these 11 years) is 0.77, leading to an annualized alpha 1.61%, and an Information Ratio of 0.30, similar to the 0.37 Information Ratio over the entire 50-year history.

VI.   PUBLICLY AVAILABLE LOW-VOLATILITY ETFs

The interest in the low-volatility anomaly has led to a number of low-volatility Exchange-Traded Funds (ETFs), developed using a variety of choices in their construction. The ETFs cover both US and non-US equity universes, particular geographic regions, and developed and emerging markets. The ETFs vary by security capitalization ranges as well as hedged or unhedged currency exposure. The funds are also distinguished by how the portfolios are constructed. ETF providers may construct the portfolios by optimizing to minimize volatility, or by ranking securities by volatility or market beta and then choosing securities from the lowest ranks. Exhibit 9.15 reports on some of the larger ETFs by assets under management (AUM) as of March 21, 2017, as given in "ETDdb.com."

VII.   SUMMARY AND CONCLUSION

The historical performance of low-volatility securities has been well-documented in both the US and non-US equity markets. Counter to the traditional risk return trade-off of higher return for more risk, the long-term historical record suggest that there has been little if any return penalty relative to investing in riskier securities. Given the lower systematic risk of the low-volatility securities, the pattern of returns to low-volatility equities is dependent on the direction of the market. Low-volatility securities tend to underperform in up markets and outperform in down markets. This pattern of returns creates substantial tracking error relative to the broad market

EXHIBIT 9.15   Low-Volatility ETFs

Symbol	ETF Name	AUM ($ mil.)
USMV	iShares Edge MSCI Min Vol USA	12,292
SPLV	PowerShares S&P 500 Low Volatility	6,463
EFAV	iShares MSCI EAFE Min Vol	6,236
EEMV	iShares MSCI Emerging Markets Min Vol	3,727
ACWV	iShares MSCI All Country World Min Vol	2,968
XMLV	PowerShares S&P MidCap Low Volatility	957
XSLV	PowerShares S&P SmallCap Low Vol	934
IDLV	PowerShares S&P International Developed Low Volatility	446
ONEV	SPDR Russell Low Volatility Focus	422
EELV	PowerShares S&P Emerging Markets Low Volatility	248
SMLV	SPDR Russell 2000 Low Volatility	201
LGLV	SPDR Russell 1000 Low Volatility	89
JPMV	iShares MSCI Japan Min Vol	30
EUMV	iShares MSCI Europe Min Vol	24
AXJV	iShares Edge MSCI Min Vol Asia ex Japan	6

portfolio even though the average returns are about the same. From a long-run per-spective, low-volatility portfolios offer the hope of market returns at lower volatility, although with a different return pattern over time.

A variety of approaches can be used to build a portfolio that captures the low-volatility effect. Some portfolios use heuristics like sorting the securities based on either total volatility or on market beta and choosing the ones with the lowest volatility. Other portfolios are built by using the entire correlation structure to optimize a portfolio with minimum variance. In this chapter, we emphasize a portfolio generated from a Fama-MacBeth regression designed to capture the low-volatility effect. We also show that the Low Volatility anomaly should be called the Low-Beta anomaly, based on an empirical "horse race" between idiosyncratic and systematic risk. The various portfolio construction approaches can be tailored with different constraints and limitations, so will generally not give the same performance results because they result in slightly different portfolio positions. Focusing primarily on just the low-volatility factor usually leaves the portfolio exposed to secondary factors that may be correlated with low volatility, so care should be taken to control secondary exposures. Without this control, some of the performance, either positive or negative, may be due to factors other than low beta.

PART V

SMART BETA IMPLEMENTATION

CHAPTER 10

STRUCTURING BETTER EQUITY PORTFOLIOS: COMBINING SMART BETA WITH SMART ALPHA

In this chapter, we analyze various potential challenges that investors face in structuring multistrategy, multimanager portfolios. These challenges partially arise from current portfolio structuring practices, which, in our opinion, do not provide adequate guidance on how to implement efficient style and manager diversification. Therefore, we propose an alternative portfolio structuring framework that seeks to improve upon current practices by facilitating the building of potentially more efficient overall portfolio structures.

CHAPTER SUMMARY

- In principle, portfolio structures that incorporate uncorrelated strategies and active managers offer diversification benefits by reducing active risk and enhancing information ratios.
- In practice, however, in working with asset owners, we find that such diversification benefits may not be fully realized in many instances.
- We believe this is partially driven by current portfolio construction practices, which include alpha-beta portfolio structure, decomposition of policy benchmark into size (large/small) and style (value/growth) segments, and seeking risk model-based factor exposures through active management, as they do not provide adequate guidance on which strategies and active managers to include in a composite portfolio.
- We propose an alternative framework for structuring multistrategy, multimanager portfolios to potentially improve on current practices.

- This framework decomposes active return into two components: one emanating from static exposure to basic factors and one driven by sources unexplained by basic factors. This decomposition (1) recognizes the existence of certain factors or styles, (2) provides clarity on which active returns to pursue through active management, and (3) introduces a layer of diversification as the two active return components are largely uncorrelated.
- In our framework, basic factors refer to the five smart beta factors, namely, size, value, momentum, volatility, and quality. As shown in Chapter 8, when combined, these factors can offer significant diversification benefits and thus introduce an important layer of style diversification. Further gains from style diversification can be realized by adding active strategies that derive their active returns from sources other than a static exposure to smart beta factors. These active strategies may include advanced quant, focused fundamental, market timing, factor timing.
- We define "smart alpha" as smart beta factor-adjusted active return. Smart alpha is calculated relative to the smart beta implementation vehicles actually used in the active portfolio. This definition makes smart alpha an asset owner-specific measure, as it should be, in our opinion.
- Asset owners should focus on smart alpha in analyzing active managers and achieve manager diversification by selecting those with lowly correlated smart alphas.
- In determining the allocations between smart beta and smart alpha, asset owners may pursue various approaches, such as weighting by active risk contribution, weighting by active risk, or optimizing.

I. INTRODUCTION

The overall equity portfolio of asset owners typically consists of a passive component, which replicates the returns of a policy benchmark, and an active component, which seeks to outperform the policy benchmark through active management. In implementing the active component, very few, if any, asset owners use a single strategy or a single active manager. It is clearly the norm to employ multiple strategies and managers. Sharpe (1981) referred to the practice of using multiple managers as "decentralized investment management." He argued that by employing multiple managers, asset owners could potentially gain from "diversification of style" (such as value and growth) as well as "diversification of judgment" (managers holding different portfolios within a given style). From an investment perspective, by investing in strategies and active managers with uncorrelated active returns, asset owners, in principle, can achieve diversification benefits in the active portfolio in the form of lower active risk and higher information ratio (IR).

In our experience working with asset owners, however, it is not uncommon to find the active portfolio delivering limited diversification benefits. We believe this outcome is partially driven by current portfolio structuring practices, which we review in the next section.

II. CURRENT PORTFOLIO STRUCTURING PRACTICES

In this section, we discuss three portfolio structures that are commonly used by asset owners.

A. Alpha-Beta Portfolio Structure

Asset owners widely use the alpha-beta portfolio structure in implementing their equity allocations, as depicted in Figure 10.1. In this structure, "beta" represents the passive replication of the policy benchmark, and therefore delivers approximately the policy benchmark returns. "Alpha" refers to the active component of the equity portfolio and captures returns associated with active management. The objective of the active component is to outperform the policy benchmark. This objective is achieved by assuming some reasonable level of active risk consistent with the desired outperformance. In this traditional alpha-beta portfolio structure, any returns in excess of the benchmark are viewed as alpha by practitioners.

In our view, this simplistic definition of alpha is not very helpful in determining how the active component of the equity portfolio should be structured. It doesn't provide any guidance on what drives excess returns. It doesn't distinguish between excess returns driven by additional forms of beta (factors) and those emanating from true manager skill. It provides no guidance on which strategies or styles might enhance diversification benefits within the active portfolio and how these styles should be implemented. This definition of alpha tends to place too much emphasis on just excess returns and not enough on their source and ability to provide diversification benefits when multiple strategies and managers are combined.

FIGURE 10.1 Alpha-Beta Portfolio Structure

FIGURE 10.2   Size and Style Decomposition

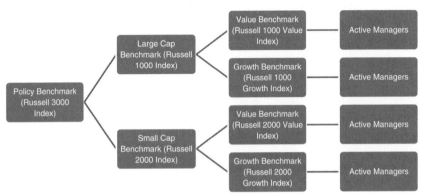

B. Size and Style Decomposition of Policy Benchmark

In order to incorporate some style diversification, and to recognize that active managers tend to specialize in certain segments of the market, some asset owners and index providers, especially in the US, further decompose the policy benchmark into size (large/small) and style (value/growth) categories, as shown in Figure 10.2. This decomposition does not provide adequate style diversification in our view. For instance, value and growth styles may be negatively correlated, but their active returns are not independent. The style benchmarks used, by construction, have offsetting active returns. If value outperforms, then growth underperforms, and vice versa. Momentum and/or quality styles are much better diversifiers of value, as they have independently positive active returns and negative correlation of active returns with value. Although the size and style structure seeks to account for manager specialization and selection, it is also relatively complex and offers very limited style diversification.

C. Gaining Risk Factor Exposures Through Active Management

Many other asset owners, especially outside the US, do not follow the conventional value-growth categorization of styles. Instead, they believe that there are other styles, such as momentum and quality, that deliver important diversification benefits in a multimanager portfolio. These asset owners seek explicit exposure to these styles primarily through active managers. The exposures are typically assessed using commercial risk models, such as Barra or Axioma. For example, an asset owner may combine value managers that depict high exposure to the Barra value factor with other managers that produce high exposure to momentum or quality risk factors. The objective is to achieve both style and manager diversification. In our experience, however, such portfolio structures typically lead to portfolio active risk being driven by the basic risk-model defined risk factors. This is, of course, by design, but it may be important to recognize that risk-model factors are designed to predict active risk, as opposed to alpha factors that predict active returns (more discussion on this topic appears in Typical Investor Question 10.6). Additionally, with the advent of smart beta investing, gaining exposures to risk-model factors through active management may no longer be an efficient implementation vehicle for capturing smart beta factors, both from an investment and cost perspective.

To summarize, the current portfolio construction practices described earlier have some limitations, which may lead to subpar portfolio structures. Next, we discuss an alternative portfolio structuring framework that seeks to address some of these limitations and, hence, potentially improve on current practices.

III.   PORTFOLIO STRUCTURING: A SUGGESTED FRAMEWORK

We believe that a given portfolio structuring method should, at a minimum, (1) clearly define the sources of active returns that an asset owner wishes to capture, and (2) provide guidance on which strategies and managers to consider for inclusion in a multistrategy, multimanager construct.

Our suggested framework seeks to achieve these objectives by answering four potential key questions, as outlined in Figure 10.3.

A. How to Decompose Active Return?

This question seeks to identify the sources of active return that the asset owner wishes to capture. In our framework, we propose decomposing the active return, at a minimum, into two main components; static exposure to basic factors and active return unexplained by basic factors, as shown in Figure 10.4.

In our opinion, this decomposition of active return is important for several reasons. First, it recognizes the existence of certain factors, which represent additional forms of beta or systematic returns. Second, it provides clarification on the type of active returns asset owners should seek from active managers. That is, active returns that go beyond those delivered by the basic factors. Third, by design, it introduces a first layer of diversification in the portfolio structure. If basic factor and manager active returns are driven by different return sources, then they are also largely uncorrelated.

Some asset owners may not agree with the sources of active return identified above, as they may not believe in the existence of any smart beta factors. They may seek to capture only active returns emanating from other sources. This is a perfectly reasonable approach, as long as these asset owners do not inadvertently end up mostly capturing smart beta factor pay-offs through active management.

B. How to Diversify Across Strategies?

The decomposition of the active return in Figure 10.4, however, raises the question of which factors and which active strategies an asset owner should pursue.

FIGURE 10.3 Potential Key Questions in Portfolio Structuring

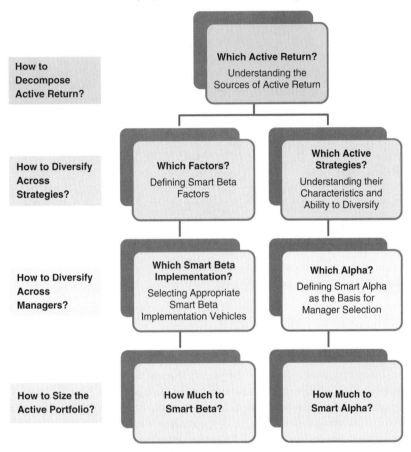

FIGURE 10.4 Decomposition of Active Return

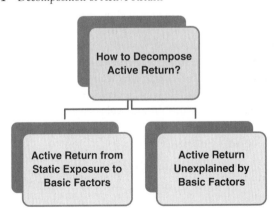

a. Which Factors?

One important challenge posed by the suggested active return decomposition is that it forces asset owners to identify which factors (styles) to pursue, whereas that decision in the conventional alpha-beta structure was left to active managers. The choice of basic factors may be difficult because it may be partly driven by philosophical beliefs. However, in our experience, there appears to be some degree of consensus in the industry that the basic factors may comprise of size, value, momentum, low volatility, and quality. These factors/styles have generated positive out-of-sample active returns and depicted low or negative active return correlations. Therefore, they offer the potential, when combined, to reduce active risk and enhance the IR of the active portfolio. Because smart beta offerings typically also focus on these basic factors, in previous chapters we have referred to these five factors as "smart beta factors."

b. Which Active Strategies?

As a next step, we need to identify which active strategies should be considered in the active portfolio. The choice of active strategies should be driven by a conceptual rationale and understanding of what drives their active returns and why such strategies can be expected to provide diversification benefits when combined with smart beta factors and other considered active strategies. As an illustration, the active strategies of interest may include quantitative strategies, fundamental stock-picking, and other investment processes, such as, market timing, factor timing, or covered call writing.

i. Quantitative Processes

Quantitative processes often fall within the broad category of "factor" investing. Broadly speaking, there are two types of quant processes; those that mainly deliver smart beta factor exposures and returns and those that create a value proposition relative to smart beta offerings. In our proposed structure, the former type of quant processes, which we refer to as "traditional quant," should not be of interest to asset owners, as they provide limited diversification benefits when combined with smart beta factors (in fact, many of their strategies *are* smart beta factors). Only the latter type, which we refer to as "advanced quant," should be considered. The primary focus of advanced quant processes is either to significantly improve upon the conventional smart beta factors and/or to research and implement new proprietary factors. Since advanced quant processes are designed to go beyond the conventional smart beta factors, their active return and risk will be largely driven by sources that are unexplained by smart beta factors. This provides the rationale, at a strategy level, of combining smart beta with advanced quant processes to realize additional diversification benefits.

ii. Fundamental Processes

There are various types of fundamental processes. At one extreme are managers who take relatively small active positions, run low tracking errors and active share, and hold a relatively large number of positions. These managers are typically called "closet indexers," as they don't deviate much from the benchmark. At the other extreme, are concentrated or "focused managers," who hold a very limited number of securities and have high active share and active risk compared to the benchmark as well as high conviction in their best ideas. In the middle are managers, who are modestly diversified and tend to have relatively high exposures to smart beta factors. These managers are sometimes called "factor replicators," as they explicitly or implicitly replicate factor payoffs through active management. The closet indexers are not an interesting group to consider, as they generally tend to deliver benchmark returns, but with active fees. Similarly, the factor replicators charge much higher fees than smart beta providers, and potentially introduce some degree of noise in the portfolio through higher stock-specific risk. As such, in our view, asset owners' primary interest should be on the concentrated/focused managers.

One important distinction between smart beta and quant processes and focused fundamental processes is the nature of active returns being generated. By investing in factors, smart beta and quant processes tend to harness risk premia as well as exploit behavioral biases and structural frictions. By investing in companies, and having an in-depth knowledge of their businesses, focused fundamental processes leverage their deep insights to generate superior assessments and forecasts relating to company management, growth prospects, development of new products and markets, and company financials. To the extent that these sources of active returns are uncorrelated, adding focused stock-picking to a mix of smart beta and quant strategies should be beneficial in a multistrategy structure.

iii. Other Investment Processes

Other equity investment processes, such as those focusing on market timing, factor timing, or lowering volatility through the use of derivative products, may also provide significant diversification benefits in a multistrategy context. Figure 10.5 provides a graphical summary of the strategy diversification discussion.

C. How to Diversify Across Managers?

a. Which Smart Beta Implementation?

Once the desired smart beta factors have been identified, the asset owner also needs to select the products and offerings that will be used to implement these factors. There are many considerations in choosing an appropriate smart beta product. In previous chapters, we have discussed some of the salient features of smart beta investment processes including product design, product structure, and implementation flexibility (Chapter 1), weighting schemes and construction efficiency (Chapter 4), signal specifications (Chapter 5), and approaches to factor diversification (Chapter 8).

Some asset owners implement the selected individual smart beta factors through different providers. For instance, they may select a provider for value, a different provider for momentum, etc. Others implement a multifactor diversification strategy through a single provider. In our view, single-factor implementation is more effective

FIGURE 10.5   Strategy Selection and Diversification Example

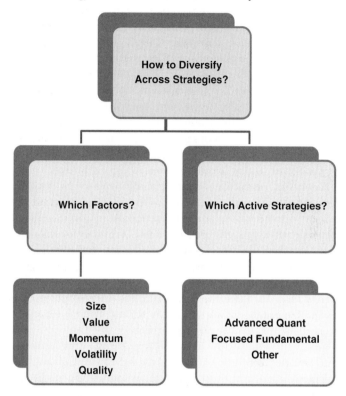

for asset owners who wish to time factors, trade and implement the selected products internally or who have existing licensing or other fee arrangements with providers that allow them to realize significant cost savings (please also refer to Application Example 8.2).

In our framework, the signal-tilted (ST) and Enhanced ST individual factor portfolios and multifactor portfolios (MFPs), discussed in Chapter 7 and Chapter 8, would represent examples of implementation options for capturing smart beta factor returns.

b. Which Alpha?

With the selection of the smart beta factors and implementation vehicles, we have a basis for properly defining alpha. In the context of the suggested active return decomposition, alpha is defined as "smart beta factor-adjusted active return." We refer to this active return as "smart alpha."

In the proposed framework, smart alpha is computed relative to the selected smart beta vehicles that are actually implemented in the active portfolio. This is quite different from the calculation of alpha using Fama-French factors or commercial risk model–based factors. The determination of factor exposures and alpha based on such risk models, though informative, is not very useful in portfolio structuring, as the risk factors incorporated in the risk models do not match the factors implemented by the asset owner. The diversification benefits achieved in a given portfolio are driven by the correlations between the implemented strategies. To the extent that asset owners implement different smart beta factors and prefer different implementations, smart alpha becomes an asset owner-specific measure, as it should be, in our opinion. In analyzing and selecting active strategies and managers, therefore, asset owners should focus on, not just any alpha, but smart alpha. To achieve manager diversification, asset owners should focus on active managers with lowly correlated smart alphas (please also refer to Typical Investor Question 10.6).

In our framework, we calculate smart alpha relative to the ST (or Enhanced ST) factor portfolios. Managers that deliver a positive ST factor-adjusted alpha, which is uncorrelated with the smart alpha of other selected managers, are candidates for inclusion in the portfolio. As an illustration, Table 10.1 presents a risk decomposition of a US large cap advanced quant manager's strategy against the five ST factor portfolios. Apart from modest exposures to quality and momentum, which were significant, the manager had no other meaningful factor exposures. In fact, 93% of the total active return of 4.06% and 85% of the total active risk was contributed by alpha. And the alpha of 3.76% per annum was statistically significant at the 1% level. This is the "quant smart alpha" that asset owners should seek.

Along similar lines, Table 10.2 shows an example of a risk decomposition of a fundamental manager benchmarked against the MSCI EAFE Index. This manager had no statistically significant smart beta factor exposures. The manager generated a highly impressive and statistically significant alpha of 4.67% per annum from sources other than smart beta factors. Once again, this is the "fundamental smart alpha" that asset owners should pursue.

Figure 10.6 provides a graphical summary of the manager selection and diversification discussion.

TABLE 10.1 Example of Smart Quant Alpha: Russell 1000 Benchmark

Advanced Quant Manager	ST Size	ST Value	ST Momentum	ST Volatility	ST Quality	Alpha	Total Active Risk
Exposure	0.26	0.12	**0.24**	−0.12	**0.11**		
Contribution to Active Return	0.03	0.13	0.02	−0.05	0.17	**3.76**	
Contribution to Active Risk	0.02	0.06	0.15	0.04	0.06	1.85	2.18

Note: Figures in bold are statistically insignificant at the 5% level.

TABLE 10.2 Example of Smart Fundamental Alpha: MSCI EAFE Benchmark

Fundamental Manager	ST Size	ST Value	ST Momentum	ST Volatility	ST Quality	Alpha	Total Active Risk
Exposure	0.06	0.06	0.10	0.22	0.21		
Contribution to Active Return	0.00	−0.04	0.07	0.24	0.28	**4.67**	
Contribution to Active Risk	0.00	−0.04	0.07	0.24	0.28	4.37	4.93

Note: Figures in bold are statistically insignificant at the 5% level.
Source: GSAM.

FIGURE 10.6 Manager Selection and Diversification Example

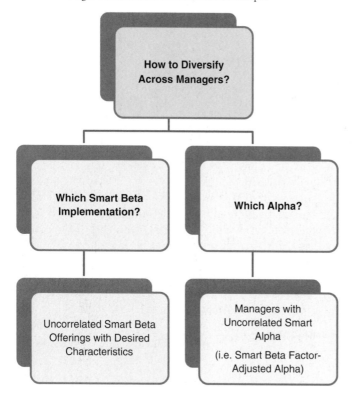

D. How to Size the Active Portfolio?

How should asset owners determine the allocations between smart beta and smart alpha? The answer to this question depends on the investment objectives of an asset owner. For instance, if the primary investment objective of the asset owner is to reduce the total volatility and drawdown of the portfolio, then a meaningful allocation to low-risk strategies would be required, whether such strategies are implemented through smart beta products or through active managers. In such instances, the sizing decision may well become a strategic allocation decision.

a. Weighting by Active Risk Contribution

When the focus is on active returns and IR, various approaches may be followed to allocate between smart beta and smart alpha. One approach might be to choose an allocation that achieves a specific active risk contribution from smart beta and smart alpha. Typically, asset owners seek to outperform a given policy benchmark, subject to an active risk budget (e.g. 2%). The allocations to smart beta and smart alpha may be determined by distributing the active risk budget across these two components. For instance, a 25% active risk contribution (or $0.25 \times 2\% = 0.5\%$ active risk) coming from smart beta and 75% (or $0.75 \times 2\% = 1.5\%$ active risk) from smart alpha.

Application Example 10.1

A pension plan has a total active risk budget of 1.5% relative to the MSCI World policy benchmark. In assessing the allocations between smart beta and smart alpha, the plan's objective was to remain within the total active risk budget and achieve a 50% active risk contribution from smart beta and 50% from smart alpha. On the basis of the selected smart beta vehicles and a composite of smart alpha active managers, an analysis was conducted to determine the allocations between smart beta and smart alpha. This analysis, summarized below, showed that when 25% of assets were allocated to smart beta, the active portfolio remained close to its overall active risk budget, but the contribution to active risk from smart beta was only 15%. When 75% of assets were invested in smart beta, the objectives relating to the active risk contribution from smart beta and overall active risk budgets were not achieved. In this case, the plan would achieve its desired objectives by allocating 50% to smart beta and 50% to smart alpha.

Smart Beta Allocation (%)	Smart Beta Active Risk Contribution (%)	Overall Active Risk of Active Portfolio (%)
25	15	1.58
50	50	1.59
75	80	1.87

Source: GSAM.

FIGURE 10.7   Weighting Strategy Buckets by Active Risk Example

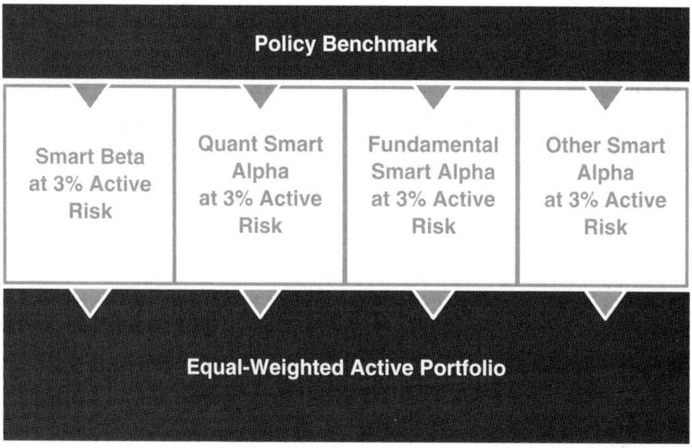

b. Weighting by Active Risk

Another approach might be to target active risk parity in allocating funds across the various strategy buckets, as shown in Figure 10.7. Suppose an asset owner has four strategy buckets, namely, smart beta, quant smart alpha, fundamental smart alpha, and other smart alpha. If the four strategy buckets were constructed, such that they had the same active risk to the policy benchmark (e.g. 3%), then equal weighting the strategy buckets would achieve active risk parity in the active portfolio. If equal active risk buckets cannot be constructed (e.g. focused managers tend to run high active risk), then the asset owner could weight the buckets by active risk. If correlations are reasonably stable over time across strategy buckets, then weighting by active risk may also result in similar active risk contribution over time.

c. Ability to Find Smart Alpha

Allocations between smart beta and smart alpha may also be driven by considerations relating to market efficiency and asset owners' ability to find skilled active managers. For example, it may be more difficult to find skilled active managers in the US large cap space than in global Emerging markets or global small cap. Therefore, an asset owner may decide to assign a much higher allocation to smart beta for US large cap (e.g. 75%) compared to global Emerging markets (e.g. 25%).

The allocation between smart beta and smart alpha can also be determined using a variety of other methods, such as risk model-based optimizing. Figure 10.8 provides a graphical summary of the sizing discussion.

FIGURE 10.8 Allocating between Smart Beta and Smart Alpha Examples

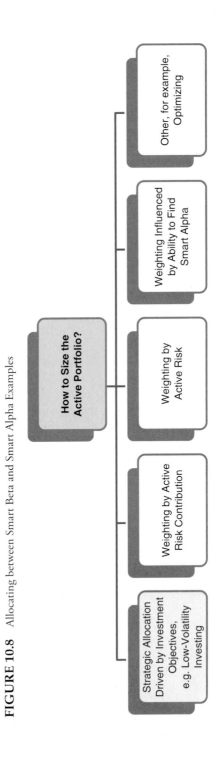

FIGURE 10.9   Summary of Proposed Structure

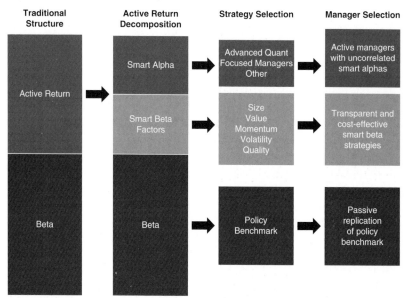

E. Summary

Our proposed framework, which is summarized in Figure 10.9, potentially generates more efficient overall portfolio structures because it introduces multiple layers of diversification in its design. Within the smart beta component, one layer of strategy diversification is offered by the choice of smart beta factors and their active return correlation attributes (please refer to Chapter 8). Another layer is offered by combining the selected smart beta factors with other strategies and investment processes that can be reasonably expected to offer additional diversification benefits in a multistrategy structure. Beyond strategy diversification, by focusing on lowly correlated smart alphas as well as the source of smart alpha (e.g. advanced quant and focused fundamental), asset owners will further ensure that additional layers of diversification are introduced in the active portfolio. For instance, the smart alpha of a focused fundamental manager should be uncorrelated or lowly correlated with the smart alpha of other focused managers, the smart alpha of advanced quant managers, and with the smart beta factors.

IV.   TYPICAL INVESTOR QUESTIONS

10.1 How Are Investors Funding an Allocation to Smart Beta?

Depending on the perspective investors take on smart beta, the allocations could come from the passive, active or both components of the overall portfolio.

The allocation from the capitalization-weighted passive component to smart beta may be driven by various considerations. For instance, investors who view capitalization weighting as being inefficient in some form allocate to smart beta from this component. Such investors tend to view smart beta as an "alternative to passive." However, in our experience, an alternative-to-passive perspective rarely leads asset owners to fully replace their capitalization-weighted policy benchmarks. Typically, for large asset owners, allocations to smart beta range between 5% and 25% of the passive allocation.

In other cases, some large plans have experienced considerable inflows over the last few years. These inflows have primarily been allocated to the passive component, as the asset owners have been unable to find additional skilled managers or increase the allocations of existing managers for fear of diseconomies of scale. As a result, the passive component has grown over time to undesirably high levels. These asset owners are also using smart beta to reduce their passive allocation to more normal levels. Although the allocation to smart beta is coming from passive, these asset owners generally view smart beta as a high-capacity alternative to active management.

Application Example 10.2

A pension plan was seeking to reduce the total volatility and drawdown of the overall equity portfolio by having a meaningful allocation to minimum-variance (low-volatility) strategies. Since such strategies are quite unattractive in a benchmark-relative implementation (they have high tracking errors and low information ratios (IR)), the investment staff internally recommended that minimum-variance investing should be approached from a strategic asset allocation perspective. They argued for a respecification of the policy benchmark from MSCI World Index to 50% MSCI World Index and 50% MSCI World Minimum Volatility Index. The respecification of the policy benchmark would make tracking error and IR considerations irrelevant by shifting the focus to total risk reduction and Sharpe ratio improvement for the overall portfolio. In terms of implementation, the minimum volatility index would be replicated passively and/or used as a performance benchmark for active managers who are hired to implement low-volatility approaches.

Application Example 10.3

An investment consultant recommends that clients consider changing their policy benchmark by allocating a portion of their capitalization-weighted passive allocation to diversifying smart beta strategies, such as those that introduce value or low-volatility tilts. The respecification of the policy benchmark would lead to more diversification at the strategic asset allocation level, potentially resulting in more efficient (i.e. higher risk-adjusted returns) overall portfolio structures.

Application Example 10.4

A Sovereign Wealth Fund (SWF) had most of its equity assets managed passively against their global equity benchmark. Recently, they decided to allocate to smart beta. They opted for a factor diversification strategy that targets a 0.75% tracking error to their benchmark. The SWF views the allocation to smart beta as an extension of their passive portfolio. The objective is to improve the performance of the extended passive portfolio by seeking to add 50 basis points of extra return, net of costs, while limiting the amount of tracking risk.

Application Example 10.5

A pension plan viewed US large cap as the most efficient segment of global equity markets with little or no opportunity to add value through active management. Therefore, the US large cap allocation historically was implemented entirely through passive investing. The plan's investment staff viewed smart beta as an opportunity to harvest additional systematic sources of long-term excess returns without deviating too much from the indexing (passive) philosophy toward US large cap. Given this perspective, they implemented a multifactor strategy through a transparent, rules-based index-like approach, targeting a 1% tracking error to their US large cap benchmark. The strategy was licensed in the form of a model portfolio and implemented in-house by the plan, similar to the internal replication of the US large cap benchmark.

Application Example 10.6

A few years ago, a large institutional plan had a 60% allocation to passive and a 40% allocation to active within the global public equity portfolio. As the plan grew in size, it was unable to find more active managers to allocate to. The plan also was unwilling to increase the allocations of most of their existing managers due either to concerns relating to diseconomies of scale or to unsatisfactory performance. Consequently, inflows were primarily "parked" in passive and the equity portfolio structure changed over time to almost 80% passive and 20% active. Smart beta presented an opportunity for the plan to reduce the passive allocation to more normal levels, while generating excess returns that were otherwise expected from active management.

Many asset owners also view smart beta as an "alternative to active." In this approach, smart beta is typically used to replace "closet indexers" and/or "factor replicators," that is, active managers who deliver either market-like returns and/or extra-market factor returns, while charging alpha fees. We reviewed several examples of such managers in Chapter 6 in our discussion of the risk decomposition of active strategies. With the development of simple, rules-based, and cost-effective approaches to capturing factor returns, we believe such managers can be easily replaced with smart beta. Other asset owners, who either have been disappointed with their active managers or who do not have confidence in their ability to select skilled active managers, also are allocating to smart beta from the active component of the equity portfolio.

Smart beta may also be used as an alternative to active in other applications, such as in the structuring of various types of investment vehicles.

Application Example 10.7

Four mutual funds of an investment company were subadvised by external active managers. These mutual funds invested in a range of developed and emerging markets stocks. Although the active managers had high and significant exposures to common factors, their performance was disappointing, as negative contributions from stock selection (alpha) more than offset the positive excess returns emanating from factors. The investment company, therefore, decided to replace the active managers with smart beta factor strategies. Since the objective is to harvest long-term excess returns of factors, the investment company selected a highly diversified (i.e. low stock specific risk) multifactor strategy at the desired level of tracking error. In the process, the investment company also reduced the management fee by about 50% compared to the replaced active managers, thus significantly improving the economics of the underlying mutual funds.

Application Example 10.8

An insurance company, offering subadvised international mutual funds in its product suite, views the median manager, not the underlying market index, as their primary performance benchmark. That is, for international equities, the primary objective is to beat the median manager in the Morningstar International Large Blend Category, and a secondary objective is to outperform the MSCI EAFE Index.

A risk decomposition analysis of the median manager active returns (e.g. please refer to Chapter 6) revealed that the median manager had no meaningful factor exposures and high and negative factor-adjusted alpha, which led to an overall underperformance relative to the MSCI EAFE Index. Given the historical evidence relating to smart beta factor performance, the insurance company viewed gaining efficient and diversified exposure to smart beta factors as a simple and cost-effective potential solution, compared to identifying active managers with above-average skill, for achieving its desired primary objective of outperforming the median manager.

Investors also use smart beta to complement their existing portfolios through exposure management and portfolio completion strategies. In this application, smart beta is used to mitigate undesirable factor exposures and/or gain exposures to additional factors. For instance, the composite active portfolio of an asset owner, which includes multiple active managers, may show that it has a positive exposure to value and quality and a negative exposure to momentum. The negative exposure to momentum may dilute overall portfolio returns, if momentum outperforms the market in the long run. Therefore, the asset owner could potentially improve portfolio performance by mitigating or offsetting the undesirable negative momentum exposure through a smart beta momentum overlay strategy, without excessive dilution of the value or quality exposure. Additionally, smart beta strategies may be considered when investors are unable to find an active manager to gain exposure to additional factors. For example, an investor may use a smart beta quality strategy to complement the existing value, momentum, and low-volatility active managers in order to enhance factor or style diversification within the portfolio. When investors use smart beta as a complement to the existing portfolio, the allocation to smart beta may come from the passive and/or the active component of the portfolio.

Application Example 10.9

An investment consultant offers a US large cap multimanager fund. At the time when the analysis was conducted, the fund consisted of seven active managers selected by the consultant on the basis of their stock selection skill and diversification potential within the fund. The fund had outperformed its benchmark by 1.24% per annum over the last five years. An active return and risk decomposition of the fund's performance revealed that, net of factor exposures, the fund realized an alpha of about 1% per year. This result suggested that the consultant successfully identified active managers with some level of stock selection skill. However, the risk decomposition analysis also revealed that the stock picking activities of the active managers led to negative exposures to value and (low) volatility. These negative exposures detracted 1.2% of return per year from the performance of the fund. In other words, if the negative exposures to value and volatility were neutralized, through a smart beta overlay strategy, the fund's outperformance would have been 2.44% per annum, which is a significant improvement over the realized outperformance of 1.24% per year. These findings led the consultant to consider incorporating exposure management strategies using smart beta within the structure of the multimanager fund.

Application Example 10.10

A pension plan employed several active managers in the US large cap segment of the global equity portfolio. A risk decomposition of manager active returns showed that, for more than 80% of the active managers, the primary contribution to active return and tracking error came from alpha. The plan's investment team had done a fantastic job at selecting skilled managers. At the composite level, the US large cap portfolio's active returns were also primarily driven by alpha. The portfolio had no meaningful exposures to smart beta factors, other than a modest exposure to quality. These results suggested that the plan could benefit by complementing the existing portfolio with additional smart beta factor tilts. The analysis conducted for the plan showed that even a modest allocation to a factor diversification strategy resulted in reasonable active risk reduction and IR improvement for the overall portfolio.

10.2 How Are Investors Structuring the Smart Beta Component of the Portfolio to Better Meet Its Various Applications?

In order to achieve various investment objectives, the allocation to smart beta is sometimes split between a core component and a satellite component, as shown in Figure 10.10. In the core component, a diversified static exposure to smart beta factors is sought. This component has a strategic perspective and its performance is assessed on a long-term basis. The satellite component is more tactical in nature. It may be used by the asset owner to implement short-term market views or exposure management and portfolio completion exercises. For instance, an asset owner may have short-term concerns about declines or higher volatility in the US

FIGURE 10.10   Core and Satellite Components of Smart Beta

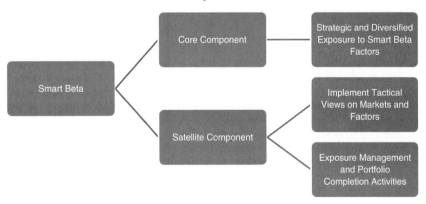

market. The asset owner may wish to put on a tactical low-volatility trade in the US. Also, the activities of the active managers may lead to negative or undesirable exposures to certain factors in the overall portfolio. The satellite component may be used to implement overlay strategies designed to mitigate these factor exposures.

10.3 In Many Instances, the Active Risk and Return of the Overall Active Portfolio Ends Up Being Driven by Basic Equity Factors. What Considerations May Be Driving This Result?

In some cases, this is by design, such as when the asset owner selects active managers based on their exposures to risk model-based risk factors. In other cases, it may potentially be because of the factor concentration problem identified by Kahn and Lemmon (2016) and Garvey et al. (2017). The way this problem manifests itself is as follows. The investment process of a typical active manager derives its active return and risk from exposures to basic factors as well as stock-specific risk. When individual managers, who largely assume stock-specific risk, but also have common exposures to basic factors, are combined, the contribution to active risk from basic factors in the multimanager portfolio increases because this risk is positively correlated across managers. As such, the multimanager portfolio proportionally delivers more factor risk than the individual managers. For instance, Garvey et al. (2017) documented that, for US large cap long-only funds, when 1,000 multimanager portfolios were generated, randomly combining five managers, the proportion of active risk explained by the factors (beta, size, value, and momentum) for the multimanager portfolios increased significantly compared to the proportion explained by the average of the five underlying funds. The increase in factor risk ranged from 1.2 times for value to 2.1 times for size. The authors argued that the much higher increase for size may be due to the fact that long-only funds tend to have higher exposure to small stocks, while value funds may be counter-balanced by growth funds.

10.4 In the Implementation of Smart Beta Investing, What Considerations May Lead Investors to Choose Either Smart Beta Public Indexes or Solutions Offered by Smart Beta Managers?

Smart beta public indexes are an important innovation for various reasons. First, they can be used to facilitate the policy-level passive implementation of smart beta investing. Second, they can serve as the performance benchmark for solutions offered by smart beta managers or for active style managers. And third, smart beta public indexes are better suited to serve as the basis for creating structured products. In general, smart beta index solutions typically appeal to asset owners for whom simplicity, transparency, and low cost are the driving considerations from a governance and implementation perspective.

Application Example 10.11

The investment staff of a pension plan reviewed a number of smart beta strategies offered by index providers as well as investment managers, while considering an allocation to smart beta. The staff decided to implement the smart beta allocation through a public index solution. The index provider was well known and respected by the staff and the Board of Trustees, as the plan already used the index provider's capitalization-weighted market indexes as the policy benchmark. The staff felt that using a simple and transparent index solution would be better received and understood by the Trustees. The index provider's data feeds were well integrated into the plan's investment activities, making in-house implementation relatively seamless. Licensing agreements with the index provider were also in place and would cover the considered smart beta index, thus saving time and resources that would otherwise be spent in contract negotiations. Finally, a certain level of licensing fees for index products was already included and approved in the current operating budget.

Application Example 10.12

An SWF was considering an allocation to low-volatility investing. The SWF invited submissions for a Request for Proposal (RFP) from investment managers for smart beta low-volatility strategies. The RFP specified that the performance of smart beta managers would be evaluated against an MSCI Minimum Volatility Index. The investment objectives were outlined as: achieve similar or better total risk reduction compared to the market as the minimum volatility index, while delivering outperformance of 0.5% per annum with a tracking error of no more than 3% relative to the minimum volatility index over rolling three-year periods.

Application Example 10.13

A pension plan uses a fundamentally weighted index as the benchmark for active value managers. The plan does not view fundamental indexation as a better alternative to a capitalization-weighted market portfolio, but does recognize it as a better value index compared to capitalization-weighted value indexes, such as the Russell or MSCI Value Index series. The investment staff at the plan is of the opinion that existing capitalization-weighted value indexes employ methodologies that result in a less efficient (capitalization weighting distorts the link between attractiveness based on value and security weights) and less diversified (indexes include only a subset of stocks from the parent universe) capture of value compared to fundamental weighting or value-weighted methodologies.

Smart beta public indexes also present some challenges for investors. One challenge relates to consistency of methodologies employed. Most public index strategies are based only on the standard market indexes of the index provider. This forces asset owners to use smart beta indexes with differing methodologies for various markets/regions, such as Russell methodologies for the US market and MSCI methodologies for international and Emerging Markets. These methodological differences are more pronounced than those relating to capitalization-weighted market indexes created by various index providers. Additionally, within an index family, some index providers do not use a consistent methodology for capturing factors. For example, an index provider may use multiple methodologies for capturing a single factor, such as value or low volatility. An index provider may also use different methodologies for capturing different factors, such as employing one methodology to capture value and a different methodology to capture momentum and quality. This results in asset owners having to understand and explain multiple methodologies and their differences to investment committees and boards. The differences can sometimes be quite subtle, which even the index providers have difficulty articulating in a clear and concise fashion.

Another challenge presented by smart beta public indexes is the lack of ability to implement factor exposures in a risk-controlled manner. In a benchmark-relative implementation, asset owners seek to gain exposure to common factors within the constraints of their tracking error budgets. Even though smart beta public indexes are typically conditioned on or derived from the underlying market benchmarks, the methodologies employed in most smart beta public index offerings do not allow for tracking error targeting. The tracking error of these indexes is simply a by-product of the methodologies used.

Finally, some index providers create multifactor strategies by combining individual factor indexes based on different methodologies (that lead to different portfolio characteristics), typically in equal proportions. This simple combination of factor indexes potentially does not take full advantage of the active risk-reduction and IR-enhancement benefits offered by factor diversification. Factor combination indexes created in this fashion may not take full advantage of turnover reduction opportunities provided by low cross-sectional correlation across factors.

Smart beta investment managers tend to provide more advanced, customizable, and benchmark-aware solutions in order to distinguish their offerings from the public indexes. These solutions allow asset owners to select the policy benchmarks relative to which common factor tilts are to be implemented. The policy benchmark could be a market index covering global equities, such as MSCI ACWI, or benchmarks covering segments of global equities, such as S&P 500 Index, Russell 2000 Index, or MSCI Emerging Markets Index, or a custom policy benchmark, such as US All Cap ex. Tobacco and Firearms. The factor tilts are implemented relative to the investor-specified policy benchmark using a single, consistent methodology.

Smart beta nonpublic solutions, however, also present some challenges. In our experience, one significant challenge for investors is to figure out if an offered approach is truly smart beta or just active management disguised as smart beta. With smart beta investing gaining in popularity and assets, it is not surprising that many active managers, and not only quant managers, want to ride the smart beta bandwagon. For instance, some nonpublic smart beta offerings are based on proprietary processes, which are not fully disclosed. Some are highly concentrated strategies with very high turnover levels. And some charge fees, that are similar or even higher than traditional active management. To avoid investing in active strategies claiming to be smart beta, investors may find it useful to specify up-front what characteristics or features they view as essential in a smart beta offering and to have the identified characteristics dictate the strategy screening and selection process.

In our experience, asset owners also tend to prefer investing with smart beta managers, as opposed to smart beta indexers, when they place a higher emphasis on more flexibility in implementing investment process enhancements. Additionally, large institutional asset owners, who are considering making a sizable allocation to smart beta, often are concerned about the potential for front-running and higher market impact costs associated with (more popular) public smart beta indexes. Such asset owners, therefore, also tend to prefer nonpublic, customizable smart beta solutions.

Application Example 10.14

After more than three years of careful and extensive due diligence and analysis, a large asset owner decided to implement a smart beta program using investment managers as opposed to smart beta public index solutions. The asset owner wanted nonpublic, customized solutions that were tailored to their choice of policy benchmark, tracking error, and factor combinations. Additionally, the asset owner expected the smart beta allocation to grow considerably over time, and potential sizable dollar investments raised concerns relating to front-running, execution delay, and market impact with regards to public index solutions. The asset owner, therefore, licensed the nonpublic smart beta strategies from investment managers and implemented them in-house. This structure provided the asset owner the high degree of flexibility and control over implementation that was sought.

10.5 What Challenges Do Investors Face in Adopting and/or Implementing a Smart Beta Program?

With regard to retail investors, the major challenge may be understanding smart beta investing. Indeed, for retail investors, smart beta can be more difficult to understand compared to a market index fund or an actively managed fund, which seeks to beat the market through stock picking. Education of clients, therefore, is perhaps the biggest hurdle in the widespread adoption and implementation of smart beta in the retail space.

For institutional investors, the challenges may revolve around various considerations. For instance, historically, asset owners have delegated the responsibility for factor selection and allocation to active managers. The consideration of smart beta investing brings the factor selection and factor allocation decisions back to the investment staff, boards, and consultants of asset owners. It forces asset owners to assume responsibility for identifying the "right" factors and allocating investment funds across the chosen factors. These decisions are often viewed as difficult and the reluctance of asset owners to assume responsibility for them may become a hurdle to implementing a smart beta program. In other instances, the education of the board, which may consist of many trustees with limited investment knowledge and experience, sometimes becomes a hurdle.

Application Example 10.15

The investment staff of a pension plan viewed capitalization weighting as inefficient. They requested the board, which included several noninvestment trustees, to consider complementing the existing capitalization-weighted policy benchmarks with fundamentally weighted indexes. This request led to deep philosophical and technical discussions at the board level regarding the drawbacks of capitalization weighting as well as the rationale for the proposed alternative solution. These discussions, which started more than two years ago, are still ongoing, as of this writing.

The implementation and monitoring of a smart beta program can also lead to serious and prolonged internal discussions. These discussions typically relate to which internal team, passive (index) or active, should assume responsibility for supervising a smart beta program. The active team may argue that they should have oversight of smart beta assets as smart beta is active. The index team may respond that smart beta is passive indexing and can be implemented in-house similarly to the replication of capitalization-weighted market indexes. As sizable allocations to smart beta are considered and discussed, the desire to retain or manage more assets invariably gives rise to heated debate and discussion. For some large asset owners, these internal sensitivities represent one of the major hurdles and can significantly delay the implementation of a smart beta program.

Application Example 10.16

After a prolonged period of internal discussion and debate between internal index and active teams, the investment committee of a large asset owner reached the view that (1) the selection and performance of smart beta strategies, relative to the policy benchmark, would be the responsibility of the committee and (2) the implementation would be the responsibility of the internal index team. To the extent that the performance of the active team is assessed based on the level of excess returns generated over short-term rolling periods, it was determined that their ability and willingness to stay the course when smart beta strategies undergo a prolonged period of market underperformance would be limited. The performance of the index team, on the other hand, is typically assessed on how closely they replicate or supervise the replication of a given smart beta strategy, and not on how it performs versus the policy benchmark. Therefore, the internal index team was deemed to be better suited to facilitate the long-term investment perspective, which the investment committee believes is needed to harvest factor premia.

10.6 In the Context of Portfolio Structuring, When Assessing Factor Exposures and Alpha, Why Is It Advisable to Conduct a Risk Decomposition Analysis Against the Implemented Smart Beta Solutions?

Asset owners typically use commercial risk models, such as Barra or Aximoa, to analyze the factor exposures of various active strategies and to construct portfolios with desired factor exposures. However, in portfolio structuring, since the basic objective is to choose strategies and managers that, when combined, deliver diversification benefits, in our opinion, this objective is more appropriately achieved by analyzing the factor exposures and correlation attributes using the smart beta strategies that are actually implemented, as opposed to risk model-based decompositions.

As discussed in Chapter 6 Typical Investor Questions 6.2 and 6.3, a risk decomposition analysis conducted using commercial risk models can sometimes show counterintuitive factor exposures. This typically happens because of mismatches between the active strategy and the risk model. The mismatches can arise from many sources. For instance, the factor set used may be different. That is, an active strategy may use a different factor set compared to the risk model, such as noninclusion of quality as a risk factor in a risk model, or inclusion of other risk factors, such as liquidity in a risk model. Factor definitions may vary. A risk model may define value as a cross-sectional book value-to-price ratio, while a smart beta manager may specify value as a industry-relative signal and/or as a composite of various valuation ratios. Different methods may be used to calculate factor scores. A risk model may use z-scores, whereas a manager may use ordinal ranks as the basis for calculating factor score. Some of these mismatches arise because the objective of a risk model is to identify and select factors that can predict ex-ante risk. That is, factors that can explain the cross-sectional variation in risk. In the design of smart beta and other active strategies, the emphasis is on factors and/or factor specifications that can predict expected returns and IRs. In other words, risk factors may be different from return factors, which can cause mismatches and counterintuitive exposures emanating from a risk decomposition analysis based on a risk model.

In addition, the inability of risk models to capture contextual relationships may sometimes lead to counterintuitive factor exposures. For example, an active strategy may be designed to take advantage of the finding that the low-volatility effect is stronger among small cap low-volatility stocks. Risk models generally do not capture such contextual returns. Finally, because of the reasons mentioned earlier, different risk models also often produce different exposures.

V. CONCLUSION

In our assessment, current portfolio structuring practices provide little guidance on what sources drive active returns, which strategies may offer diversification benefits, and, for managers within strategies, which manager alpha asset owners should seek. To address these challenges, we have proposed a framework for structuring better equity portfolios. This framework decomposes the traditional alpha into active returns emanating from factor selection and smart alpha that goes beyond factor selection. In this structure, smart alpha is defined relative to the smart beta strategies that are actually implemented. In our opinion, asset owners should focus their strategy and manager selection efforts on the identification of smart alpha, not just any active returns. Smart alpha can be found across strategies (e.g. quant and fundamental) and across managers within a given strategy. To the extent that smart alpha is uncorrelated with factor active returns and across strategies and managers, the proposed framework should deliver better overall diversification benefits compared to current practices, such as the traditional alpha-beta structure.

CHAPTER 11

INCORPORATING ESG WITH SMART BETA

Investors have an increasing desire to reflect environmental, social, and governance (ESG) values and perspectives in their overall equity portfolios. In this chapter, we propose a framework for incorporating as well as combining ESG factors with smart beta investing. The framework emphasizes customization and transparency in performance attribution, while maintaining some degree of benchmark-awareness.

CHAPTER SUMMARY

- Environmental, social, and governance (ESG) investing is one of the fastest growing areas within global equities.
- In implementing ESG factors, some investors apply industry or stock-level ESG screens and/or tilts. Others prefer the integration of ESG within the investment process.
- For investors who have yet to incorporate ESG considerations in their overall portfolios, understanding the risk-return implications of ESG factors and their impact on other portfolio characteristics, such as turnover and diversification, remain important challenges.
- We propose a framework that seeks to address these challenges for incorporating ESG factors.
- With respect to ESG data, quantity is not an issue, but quality and relevance are. According to one study, 62% of all data surveyed had disclosure rates below 20%. Furthermore, 84% of ESG factors consisted of "binary" (yes or no) answers relating to ESG-focused policies. In our view, such factors are less useful in conducting cross-sectional analysis of companies. Numeric metrics, which may be more useful for analysis purposes, are limited and 70% of such metrics had disclosure rates below 20%.
- Despite these constraints, ESG data has improved over time, and coverage and disclosure rates are adequately high for many ESG factors to conduct reasonable analysis. However, to the extent that ESG data is subject to a selection and a look-ahead

bias, we believe that historical simulations should be approached with caution. Investors' focus should perhaps not be on active returns, but rather on other portfolio characteristics, such as active risk, turnover, and diversification.

- The illustrated framework for incorporating ESG factors in the equity portfolio consists of two steps. In Step 1, two exclusionary screens are applied to a given universe: (1) Product Involvement screens, which exclude the stocks of companies engaged in the manufacture and distribution of certain products, such as controversial weapons, small arms, and tobacco, and (2) Controversies screens, which exclude companies involved in ESG-related controversies. In Step 2, ESG tilts are applied to the screened universe to reflect additional objectives. As an example, we study the impact of incorporating a low emissions tilt, which seeks to reduce emissions by 70% compared to the market.

- The ESG Portfolios derived from the application of the two screens and the low emissions tilt resulted in an active risk of only about 1% relative to the corresponding market benchmark in the US, World ex. USA, and Emerging Markets universes. The turnover of the ESG Portfolios was about 12% and these portfolios held at least 75% of the securities from the underlying universe.

- When ESG investing is combined with smart beta a similar process is followed. In Step 1, exclusionary screens are implemented. In Step 2, smart beta factor tilts are applied to the screened universe by creating a multifactor strategy. And in Step 3, the low emissions overlay is implemented to construct an ESG-focused multifactor portfolio.

- The historical performance of the analyzed ESG-focused multifactor portfolios shows that factor tilts, when applied to a screened universe with reduced breadth, still deliver attractive after-cost active returns and information ratios (IR). Additionally, the application of the low emissions tilt does not meaningfully alter the risk-return profile and other portfolio characteristics of the smart beta multifactor strategy.

I. INTRODUCTION

According to a recent Bank of America Merrill Lynch report (2018), ESG has been one of the fastest growing strategies within the equity asset class, with an estimated increase in assets of over 50% per annum from 2013 to 2017. ESG factors are also increasingly being combined with smart beta factors. In implementing ESG factors, some investors employ industry- or stock-level screens to align their investments with their values. For instance, an asset owner may employ a custom policy benchmark that excludes certain industries, such as firearms and tobacco. This custom benchmark is then used as the portfolio construction universe for active managers. Other asset owners may create a list of restricted securities for their managers, such as companies associated with serious controversies surrounding labor abuse or bribery and corruption. And some asset owners may not employ any exclusionary screens. Instead, they may have a strong preference for hiring active managers that integrate

ESG factors into their investment process. These asset owners may not approach ESG investing necessarily from a values-alignment perspective. They may simply regard ESG factors as being important drivers of growth and risk prospects and, hence, of future company performance. As an example, the Bank of America Merrill Lynch study documents that 17 companies filed for bankruptcy during the period under review. Five years prior to bankruptcy, if investors had focused only on companies with above-average ESG scores, they would have avoided 15 of the 17 companies.

While the ESG adoption rate has been high in recent years, many investors still remain on the sidelines. These investors may have a desire to create ESG-focused portfolios, but may struggle to understand not only the risk and return consequences of such decisions, but also their impact on other portfolio characteristics, such as turnover and diversification. We illustrate a framework that seeks to address some of these considerations in implementing an ESG strategy as well as combining ESG factors with smart beta factors. However, we start with issues surrounding ESG data.

II. ESG DATA

The quantity of ESG data is not an issue. Bingham et al. (2017) surveyed a number of third-party data providers and found a significant proliferation in ESG data over the past few years. One ESG database they surveyed expanded its data points between 2010 and 2017 from 1,200,000 to more than 6,000,000, a fivefold increase. Despite this proliferation in data, quality and relevance remain a concern. Bingham et al. (2017) report that for 300 total E&S metrics they evaluated, 62% had disclosure rates below 20%. Additionally, 84% of all data they surveyed consisted of "binary" (yes or no) answers to questions relating to certain ESG-focused policies, such as: Do you have a policy against the use of child labor? Such ESG data points offer limited information and are not useful in cross-sectional analysis of companies. Quantifiable, numeric metrics may be more useful. However, the disclosure rate for such metrics was found to be even lower than binary metrics by Bingham et al. (2017), as more than 70% of all numeric metrics had a disclosure rate below 20%. Of the top 25 most disclosed ESG metrics, only one was numeric. And only two numeric metrics, Total CO_2 Emissions and % Women Employees, had disclosure rates of more than 50%.

Despite ongoing concerns relating to the quality and relevance of available ESG data, in the past few years, progress, nonetheless, has been made. Coverage and disclosure rates have generally increased over time. For many ESG metrics, disclosure rates across different regions of global equites are adequately high to conduct reasonable analysis. According to Bingham et al. (2017), it is also interesting to note that, compared to the US, current disclosure rates are generally significantly higher for Europe and Australia/New Zealand and similar or higher for Japan and Emerging Markets. Further, we are also seeing a rapid increase in the availability of additional numeric metrics. Bingham et al. (2017) report that, between 2007 and 2015, numeric metrics expanded by 120% compared to 68% increase for binary data fields.

In our analysis, we use the Sustainalytics and Trucost databases. We study three universes, namely, US (Russell 1000 universe) and World ex. USA and Emerging Markets (MSCI universes). Reasonable-quality data, with adequate coverage and disclosure rates, starts in October 2009 for the US and World ex. USA universes, and from October 2011 for Emerging Markets. We highlight that, since data is voluntary and in some cases backfilled, the results we report are subject to a selection bias as well as a look-ahead bias. Therefore, in our opinion, the reported simulated historical performance should be interpreted with caution. In particular, the focus should perhaps not be active returns, but rather on other portfolio characteristics, such as active risk, turnover, and diversification.

III.   INCORPORATING ESG STRATEGIES

We illustrate a framework for incorporating ESG strategies within the equity portfolio. The strategies we discuss may be implemented within the active component of the equity portfolio or within the passive component. Indeed, for the vast majority of asset owners, the allocation to passive represents a significant portion of total funds invested in the equity asset class. Therefore, for ESG investing to make a serious impact from a capital allocation perspective, an ESG focus needs to be embedded in the passive component as well. However, many asset owners and their boards may be reluctant to incorporate ESG considerations in their passive allocations for concerns that they may lead to large deviations relative to the market indexes currently used as policy benchmarks. In our framework, we aim to show that many ESG-focused strategies, consisting of screens and/or tilts, may be incorporated in the passive component without assuming excessive tracking risk relative to market policy benchmarks. Additionally, the ESG strategies can be customized to suit a specific active risk budget.

Our framework, which is depicted in Figure 11.1, consists of two steps. Starting with an asset owner-specified universe, in Step 1, certain ESG Exclusions are implemented. The ESG Exclusions comprise of screens that exclude the stocks of companies involved in the manufacture and distribution of certain products and services as well as companies that are ranked "Severe" or "High" by Sustainalytics on controversies relating to ESG issues. As an illustration, the Product Involvement screens that are implemented relate to controversial weapons, small arms, and tobacco. The screens we employ relating to ESG Controversies cover many areas, some of which asset owners may find as excessively stringent or not in alignment with the specific values they wish to reflect in their portfolios. However, we use these exclusions to highlight the impact on portfolio performance of comprehensive screens based on Controversies. As of October 2017, examples of companies that are ranked Severe or High by Sustainalytics on various ESG Controversies included:

• Companies facing serious environmental controversies include Chevron for lawsuits relating to contamination of ground water as well as responsibility for pipeline spills, emissions incidents.

FIGURE 11.1   Process Overview: Constructing ESG Portfolios

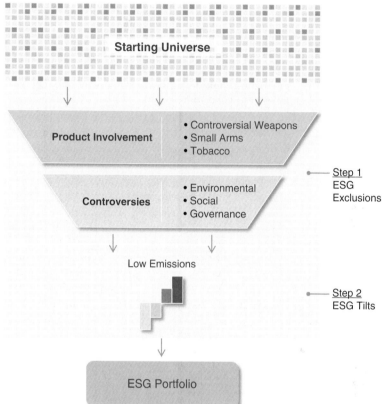

- Companies facing employee-related social controversies include Walmart for law-suits relating to violations of labor rights, discrimination, and wrongful termina-tions. Walmart is also linked to suppliers involved in labor abuses, such as forced labor, child labor, excessively long hours, and worker health and safety.
- Companies facing customer-related social controversies include Johnson & John-son for pharmaceuticals and medical devices safety incidents, Mastercard for regu-latory scrutiny over its interchange fee structure, Alphabet for multiple anticom-petitive investigations, and Merck for lawsuits regarding undisclosed side effects and safety of its products.
- Companies facing governance-related controversies include Wells Fargo for creating 3.5 million customer accounts without their permission, Apple for scrutiny over tax avoidance, JP Morgan Chase for recurring allegations of sig-nificant compliance breaches, and Walmart for numerous allegations of bribery and corruption.

In Step 2 of the process, various ESG Tilts are applied to the screened universe to reflect additional objectives. For illustration purposes, we implement a low emissions tilt, which may be a relevant objective for those asset owners who wish to mitigate the current impact their investments may have on climate risk. We calculate total emissions using two commonly used metrics: Scope 1 emissions occurring from sources owned or controlled by the company and Scope 2 emissions occurring from the generation of purchased electricity, steam, or heat consumed by the company. Total emissions are then scaled by market capitalization to create an emissions measure that facilitates comparisons across companies. The emissions measure, thus defined, becomes a signal, which is used to create an emissions-tilted portfolio using the signal-tilted (ST) methodology defined in Appendix 4.1 of Chapter 4. The use of this methodology makes the process of implementing an ESG-tilt consistent with how smart beta factor tilts are incorporated. Additionally, the methodology allows for the targeting of a specific tilting objective, such as a targeted reduction in emissions relative to the market, similar to how tracking errors are targeted in implementing smart beta factor tilts. The emissions tilt is reflected by overweighting (underweighting) companies with low (high) carbon footprint. In our case, we implement a low emissions tilt that targets a 70% reduction in emissions compared to the market universe.

A. Impact of ESG Exclusions

Table 11.1 shows the weight impact of ESG Exclusions across the three universes as of October 2017. In the US (Panel A), Total Product Involvement screens resulted in the exclusion of companies that accounted for 5% of the weight in Russell 1000 universe. Total Controversies screens constituted 17.2% by weight. The weight impact of implementing the Product Involvement and Controversies screens in MSCI World ex. USA and MSCI EM universes is shown in Panel B and Panel C, respectively.

Table 11.2 reports the impact of ESG Exclusions on historical performance. In assessing historical performance, we use the same implementation cost assumptions we derived in Chapter 5, that is, 0.50% round-trip for the US, 0.80% for World ex. USA, and 1.50% for Emerging Markets. The application of the ESG screens resulted in an active risk relative to the corresponding benchmark of 0.81% in the US (Panel A), 0.64% in World ex. USA (Panel B), and 0.76% in Emerging Markets (Panel C). Across the three universes, the ESG Exclusions produced a turnover of about 10% and eliminated about 5% of the names.

B. Impact of Low Emissions Tilt

In Table 11.3, a low emissions tilt, which targets a 70% reduction in emissions compared to the corresponding market benchmark, is applied. Tilting the benchmark universe by emissions resulted in an active risk of 0.62% in the US and World ex.

TABLE 11.1 Exclusion Impact by Weight: Various Universes, as of October 2017

	Weight (%)
PANEL A: Russell 1000 Universe	
Controversial Weapons	2.7
Small Arms	0.8
Tobacco	1.5
Total Product Involvement	**5.0**
Environmental Controversies	1.2
Social Controversies	8.9
Governance Controversies	7.7
Total Controversies	**17.2**
PANEL B: MSCI World ex USA Universe	
Controversial Weapons	1.1
Small Arms	0.4
Tobacco	2.9
Total Product Involvement	**4.4**
Environmental Controversies	2.4
Social Controversies	4.1
Governance Controversies	6.6
Total Controversies	**10.9**
PANEL C: MSCI EM Universe	
Controversial Weapons	0.3
Small Arms	0.0
Tobacco	1.2
Total Product Involvement	**1.5**
Environmental Controversies	1.1
Social Controversies	3.7
Governance Controversies	7.6
Total Controversies	**11.9**

Source: GSAM.

TABLE 11.2 Performance Impact of ESG Exclusions: Various Universes, Periods Ending March 2018

	Start Date	Total Gross Return (%)	Total Risk (%)	Sharpe Ratio	CAPM Beta	Active Return (%)	Active Risk (%)	Information Ratio	Worst 3-Year Underperformance Annualized (%)	Turnover (%)	% of Names Held
PANEL A: Russell 1000 Universe	Oct-2009										
Russell 1000 Index		**13.78**	**12.21**	**1.10**	**1.00**						
Total Product Involvement		13.56	12.29	1.08	1.01	-0.22	0.29	-0.77	-0.37	5	97
Total Controversies		13.99	12.26	1.11	1.00	0.21	0.74	0.29	-0.45	10	97
Total ESG Exclusions		**13.76**	**12.28**	**1.10**	**1.00**	**-0.02**	**0.81**	**-0.02**	**-0.61**	**10**	**95**
PANEL B: MSCI World ex U.S. Universe	Oct-2009										
MSCI World ex U.S. Index		**6.19**	**14.58**	**0.46**	**1.00**						
Total Product Involvement		6.02	14.63	0.45	1.00	-0.17	0.22	-0.77	-0.37	5	98
Total Controversies		6.58	14.47	0.49	0.99	0.39	0.61	0.63	0.13	8	96
Total ESG Exclusions		**6.42**	**14.53**	**0.47**	**1.00**	**0.23**	**0.64**	**0.36**	**-0.03**	**9**	**94**
PANEL C: MSCI EM Universe	Oct-2011										
MSCI EM Index		**7.33**	**16.25**	**0.49**	**1.00**						
Total Product Involvement		7.25	16.30	0.48	1.00	-0.08	0.15	-0.51	-0.20	8	98
Total Controversies		7.61	16.22	0.51	1.00	0.27	0.76	0.36	0.00	10	96
Total ESG Exclusions		**7.64**	**16.27**	**0.51**	**1.00**	**0.31**	**0.76**	**0.41**	**-0.02**	**10**	**95**

USA and 0.48% in Emerging Markets. The turnover created by the tilt was about 10% in the three universes and the tilted portfolios held around 80% to 90% of the names from the underlying universe.

C. Combined Impact of ESG Exclusions and Low Emissions Tilt

In Table 11.3, the low emissions tilt was applied to the underlying benchmark universe. We now apply the emissions tilt, which still targets a 70% reduction in emissions relative to the market benchmark, to the portfolios that incorporate the ESG Exclusions (Table 11.2). We refer to the resulting portfolios as ESG Portfolios. The backtested historical performance of the ESG Portfolios is reported in Table 11.4. We first note that the ESG Exclusions portfolios in the three universes had an emissions profile ranging from 88% relative to the market for Emerging Markets to 95% for the US. The application of the emissions tilt reduced the carbon footprint of the ESG Portfolios to 30% of market. In the US, it increased the active risk by only 0.24% (from 0.81% to 1.05%) and turnover by 3%, and reduced the number of names held by 14%. Similar changes in active risk, turnover, and percent of names held were recorded in the other two universes.

Some useful insights we gain from the characteristics of the ESG Portfolios are as follows. First, the application of ESG Exclusions, which screen out about 20% of the underlying universe, plus a low emissions tilt, that reduces carbon footprint by 70% relative to the market, result in a combined active risk of only about 1% in the three universes. This amount of active risk for the ESG Portfolios may be viewed as quite reasonable for the level of ESG constraints that are incorporated. Second, the implementation of a low emissions tilt to the ESG Exclusions portfolios increased the active risk of the ESG Portfolios by about 0.20% only, whereas the low emissions tilt relative to the market introduced an active risk of about 0.50% or higher across the three universes (Table 11.3). This result is driven by the fact that active risk is not additive (active risk squared is) and the ESG Exclusions and Tilted portfolios were not perfectly positively correlated. Third, the emissions tilt also resulted in only a small increase in turnover of 3% and the ESG Portfolios remained adequately diversified, holding 75% or higher of the securities from the underlying universe. Furthermore, the ESG Portfolios also can be customized to meet an asset owner's risk budget. For instance, an asset owner may wish to implement the discussed ESG characteristics in the passive component of the equity portfolio and subject to an active risk constraint of about 0.50%. In our illustration, this may be achieved by excluding companies that rank only Severe on Controversies, as opposed to Severe and High, and targeting a lower level of emissions reduction, such as 50%.

D. Performance Attribution

In our experience, many investors view the ability to attribute performance to the various ESG factors as an important and desirable feature of an ESG-focused pro-

TABLE 11.3 Performance Impact of ESG Low Emissions Tilt: Various Universes, Periods Ending March 2018

	Start Date	Total Gross Return (%)	Total Risk (%)	Sharpe Ratio	CAPM Beta	Active Return (%)	Active Risk (%)	Information Ratio	Worst 3-Year Underperformance Annualized (%)	Turnover (%)	% of Names Held	Emissions Relative to Market (%)
PANEL A: Russell 1000 Universe	Oct-2009											
Russell 1000 Index		**13.78**	**12.21**	**1.10**	**1.00**							
Low Emissions Tilt		14.02	12.29	1.11	1.01	0.24	0.62	0.39	-0.17	10	85	30
PANEL B: MSCI World ex USA Universe	Oct-2009											
MSCI World ex USA Index		**6.19**	**14.58**	**0.46**	**1.00**							
Low Emissions Tilt		6.40	14.55	0.47	1.00	0.21	0.62	0.33	-0.22	10	81	30
PANEL C: MSCI EM Universe	Oct-2011											
MSCI EM Index		**7.33**	**16.25**	**0.49**	**1.00**							
Low Emissions Tilt		7.47	16.09	0.50	0.99	0.14	0.48	0.30	-0.20	11	89	30

Source: GSAM.

TABLE 11.4 Combined Performance Impact of ESG Exclusions and Low Emissions Tilt: Various Universes, Periods Ending March 2018

	Start Date	Total Gross Return (%)	Total Risk (%)	Sharpe Ratio	CAPM Beta	Active Return (%)	Active Risk (%)	Information Ratio	Worst 3-Year Underperformance Annualized (%)	Turnover (%)	% of Names Held	Emissions Relative to Market (%)
PANEL A: Russell 1000 Universe	Oct-2009											
Russell 1000 Index		**13.78**	**12.21**	**1.10**	**1.00**							
ESG Exclusions		13.76	12.28	1.10	1.00	-0.02	0.81	-0.02	-0.61	10	95	95
+ Low Emissions Tilt = ESG Portfolio		**13.96**	**12.40**	**1.10**	**1.01**	**0.18**	**1.05**	**0.17**	**-0.67**	**13**	**81**	**30**
PANEL B: MSCI World ex USA Universe	Oct-2009											
MSCI World ex USA Index		**6.19**	**14.58**	**0.46**	**1.00**							
ESG Exclusions		6.42	14.53	0.47	1.00	0.23	0.64	0.36	-0.03	9	94	94
+ Low Emissions Tilt = ESG Portfolio		**6.56**	**14.55**	**0.48**	**1.00**	**0.37**	**0.90**	**0.41**	**-0.12**	**12**	**75**	**30**
PANEL C: MSCI EM Universe	Oct-2011											
MSCI EM Index		**7.33**	**16.25**	**0.49**	**1.00**							
ESG Exclusions		7.64	16.27	0.51	1.00	0.31	0.76	0.41	-0.02	10	95	88
+ Low Emissions Tilt = ESG Portfolio		**7.88**	**16.13**	**0.52**	**0.99**	**0.55**	**0.91**	**0.60**	**0.10**	**13**	**84**	**30**

Source: GSAM.

cess. Our building-block framework provides this ability by decomposing the contributions to active risk and return made by each step of the investment process. Table 11.5 shows the performance attribution of the ESG Portfolios in the three universes. This table highlights that the active risk of the ESG Portfolios was largely driven by the Controversies exclusions, as more than 55% of the active risk was explained by these screens. The low emissions tilt was the next largest contributor to active risk. The Product Involvement screens did not contribute much to active risk in the three regions.

TABLE 11.5 Performance Attribution of ESG Exclusions and Low Emissions Tilt: Various Universes, Periods Ending March 2018

	Start Date	Active Return Contribution(%)	Active Risk Contribution (%)	Percent of Active Risk Explained
PANEL A: Russell 1000 Universe	Oct-2009			
Product Involvement		-0.22	0.12	11.6
Controversies		0.21	0.62	58.6
Low Emissions Tilt		0.19	0.31	29.8
ESG Portfolio		**0.18**	**1.05**	**100**
PANEL B: MSCI World ex USA Universe	Oct-2009			
Product Involvement		-0.16	0.04	4.1
Controversies		0.39	0.50	55.3
Low Emissions Tilt		0.14	0.37	40.7
ESG Portfolio		**0.37**	**0.90**	**100**
PANEL C: MSCI EM Universe	Oct-2011			
Product Involvement		-0.02	-0.02	-2.1
Controversies		0.33	0.72	78.3
Low Emissions Tilt		0.24	0.22	23.8
ESG Portfolio		**0.55**	**0.91**	**100**

Source: GSAM.

IV.   INCORPORATING ESG WITH SMART BETA

Our proposed process for incorporating ESG with smart beta is depicted in Figure 11.2. As previously, in Step 1 of the process, ESG Product Involvement and Controversies Exclusions are implemented. In Step 2, desired smart beta factor tilts are applied to the screened universe. In our case, we apply value, momentum, volatility, and quality tilts through the construction of the signal-tilted (ST) Multi-Factor Portfolio (MFP) we discussed in Chapter 8. Finally, in Step 3, a low emissions tilt is applied to the ST MFP to derive the ESG-Focused MFP.

FIGURE 11.2   Process Overview: Incorporating ESG with Smart Beta

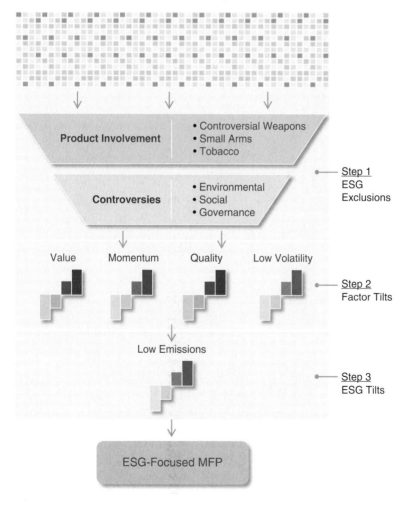

A. Historical Performance of MFP Based on Market Index

Before we look at the historical performance of the ESG-Focused MDP, which incorporates the ESG screens and tilts, let's briefly review the performance of smart beta factor tilts, for the time period under review, when applied directly to the underlying parent universe. This is shown in Table 11.6, which reports the simulated historical performance of the "MDPs Based on Market Index" in the various universes. Across the three universes, the MDPs generated IRs ranging from 0.64 in the US to 1.19 in World ex. USA. The annual turnover varied from 12% in the US to 26% in Emerging Markets. The MFPs held about 80% of the names from the underlying parent universe in the US and World ex. USA, while this number was considerably lower in Emerging Markets at 47%. This is because in the construction of the MFP for the Emerging Markets universe we applied liquidity and other trading screens to improve the investability and capacity of the portfolio. Finally, we note that the emissions profile of the MFP was higher than the market in the US (120%), while it was lower than the market in World ex. USA and Emerging Markets (91% and 83%, respectively).

B. Historical Performance of ESG-Focused MFP

For the US, as reported in Table 11.7, when the factor tilts were implemented on the screened universe, the "MFP Based on ESG Exclusions" generated an after-cost active return of 0.85% and an information ratio (IR) of 0.52 for the period under review. The MFP generated a turnover of 14%, held 79% of the names, and realized an emissions profile of 112% relative to the Russell 1000 Index. The application of a low emissions tilt to derive the ESG-Focused MFP increased active risk by 0.09% and turnover by 2%, and reduced names held by 5% and emissions to 30% of the market.

For World ex. USA, the MFP Based on ESG Exclusions realized an IR of 1.12 with a turnover of 18% and an emissions profile averaging 90% of market. The ESG-Focused MFP, which incorporates the low emissions tilt, reduced the carbon footprint to 30% of market, while adding 0.19% to active risk and 2% to turnover and reducing names held by 10%.

In Emerging Markets, the MFP Based on ESG Exclusions also realized an IR in excess of one with a turnover of 25% and an emissions profile of 72% of market. Similar to other universes, the application of a low emissions tilt resulted in marginal increases in active risk and turnover.

In comparing Table 11.6 and Table 11.7, we note the following. First, the creation of the MFP from the screened universe (MFP Based on ESG Exclusions in Table 11.7) resulted in slight increases in active risk across the three universes, when compared to the MFPs Based on Market Index (Table 11.6). This is to be expected, as ESG screens, which reduce the breadth of the underlying universe, introduce a higher level of tracking risk relative to the market index. Second, the MFPs Based on ESG Exclusions still generated respectable IRs that were similar to those of the MFPs Based on Market Index. Finally, a low emissions overlay, which targets a 70%

TABLE 11.6 Historical Performance of MFP: Various Universes, Periods Ending March 2018

	Start Date	Total Gross Return (%)	Total Risk (%)	Sharpe Ratio	CAPM Beta	Active Return (%)	Active Risk (%)	Information Ratio	Worst 3-Year Underperformance Annualized (%)	Turnover (%)	% of Names Held	Emissions Relative to Market (%)
PANEL A: Russell 1000 Universe	Oct-2009											
Russell 1000 Index		**13.78**	**12.21**	**1.10**	**1.00**							
MFP Based on Market Index		14.64	11.93	1.18	0.97	0.86	1.34	0.64	-0.34	12	81	120
PANEL B: MSCI World ex USA Universe	Oct-2009											
MSCI World ex USA Index		**6.19**	**14.58**	**0.46**	**1.00**							
MFP Based on Market Index		8.17	13.87	0.61	0.95	1.98	1.66	1.19	1.03	16	79	91
PANEL C: MSCI EM Universe	Oct-2011											
MSCI EM Index		**7.33**	**16.25**	**0.49**	**1.00**							
MFP Based on Market Index		8.91	15.35	0.60	0.94	1.58	1.72	0.92	0.47	26	47	83

Source: GSAM

TABLE 11.7 Historical Performance of ESG-Focused MFP: Various Universes, Periods Ending March 2018

	Start Date	Total Gross Return (%)	Total Risk (%)	Sharpe Ratio	CAPM Beta	Active Return (%)	Active Risk (%)	Information Ratio	Worst 3-Year Underperformance Annualized (%)	Turnover (%)	% of Names Held	Emissions Relative to Market (%)
PANEL A: Russell 1000 Universe	Oct-2009											
Russell 1000 Index		**13.78**	**12.21**	**1.10**	**1.00**							
ESG Exclusions		13.76	12.28	1.10	1.00	−0.02	0.81	−0.02	−0.61	10	95	95
MFP Based on ESG Exclusions		14.63	12.10	1.17	0.98	0.85	1.66	0.52	−0.50	14	79	112
+ Low Emissions Tilt = ESG-Focused MFP		**14.86**	**12.22**	**1.18**	**0.99**	**1.08**	**1.75**	**0.61**	**−0.05**	**16**	**72**	**30**
PANEL B: MSCI World ex USA Universe	Oct-2009											
MSCI World ex USA Index		**6.19**	**14.58**	**0.46**	**1.00**							
ESG Exclusions		6.42	14.53	0.47	1.00	0.23	0.64	0.36	−0.03	9	94	94
MFP Based on ESG Exclusions		8.26	13.82	0.62	0.94	2.06	1.84	1.12	0.90	18	77	90
+ Low Emissions Tilt = ESG-Focused MFP		**8.38**	**13.79**	**0.62**	**0.94**	**2.19**	**2.03**	**1.08**	**1.20**	**20**	**67**	**30**
PANEL C: MSCI EM Universe	Oct-2011											
MSCI EM Index		**7.33**	**16.25**	**0.49**	**1.00**							
ESG Exclusions		7.64	16.27	0.51	1.00	0.31	0.76	0.41	−0.02	10	95	88
MFP Based on ESG Exclusions		9.26	15.46	0.62	0.95	1.93	1.77	1.09	0.70	25	47	72
+ Low Emissions Tilt = ESG-Focused MFP		**9.36**	**15.38**	**0.63**	**0.94**	**2.03**	**1.88**	**1.08**	**0.70**	**26**	**44**	**30**

Source: GSAM.

reduction in carbon footprint compared to the market, did not fundamentally alter the risk-return profile and other portfolio characteristics of the MFPs Based ESG Exclusions.

B. Performance Attribution of ESG-Focused MFPs

The impact of incorporating ESG factors alongside smart beta factors is shown in Table 11.8. Across the three universes, smart beta factor tilts contributed at least 80% to the active return. The active risk contributions for smart beta factors ranged from 56% in the US to 75% in Emerging Markets.

V.   TYPICAL INVESTOR QUESTIONS

11.1 What Considerations Should Investors Keep in Mind in the Design and Implementation of ESG Strategies?

A good discussion of potential considerations for investors exploring ESG strategies appears in Alford (2018). In this article, Alford (2018) focuses on three main areas: ESG perspectives, implementation, and monitoring.

With regard to the perspectives that investors adopt in implementing ESG strategies, Alford (2018) argues that investors could benefit from a better understanding of the various potential trade-offs involved. For example, the choice between two ESG implementation approaches—one that integrates ESG factors in the investment process and one that uses screens and/or tilts—may have different implications with regard to the interaction between ESG and non-ESG factors. In the case of an integrated approach, ESG factors constitute one of the inputs, and not the only input, in the security selection process. Therefore, it is possible that a stock with a weak ESG profile may be included, or even overweighted, in the portfolio because it appears attractive on other non-ESG inputs. In the case of screens and/or tilts, it is also possible that an undervalued stock, which represents an attractive investment opportunity, is excluded from consideration in the portfolio. Investors, therefore, would need to understand, and feel comfortable with, how ESG and non-ESG factors interact in a given implementation perspective.

In the implementation of an ESG strategy, Alford (2018) also discusses various considerations relating to the design of the investment process. For example, should the process focus on current performance, measured by the level of the ESG factor, or on the rate of improvement, as measured by the change in the ESG factor? Should the process evaluate companies relative to its industry peers or relative to a broader universe? How should ESG metrics be scaled to facilitate meaningful cross-sectional comparisons? Should the process be benchmark-aware and, if so, what active risk budget should be assigned to the ESG strategy? These are some of the considerations that investors will have to form specific views on in considering an ESG investment process.

TABLE 11.8 Performance Attribution of ESG-Focused MFPs: Various Universes, Periods Ending March 2018

	Start Date	Active Return Contribution(%)	Active Risk Contribution (%)	Percent of Active Risk Explained
PANEL A: Russell 1000 Universe	Oct-2009			
Product Involvement		-0.22	0.04	2.4
Controversies		0.21	0.57	32.8
MFP Based on ESG Exclusions		0.87	0.99	56.7
Low Emissions Tilt		0.22	0.14	8.0
ESG-Focused MFP		**1.08**	**1.75**	**100**
PANEL B: MSCI World ex USA Universe	Oct-2009			
Product Involvement		−0.16	−0.06	−3.1
Controversies		0.40	0.40	19.6
MFP Based on ESG Exclusions		1.84	1.47	72.4
Low Emissions Tilt		0.12	0.23	11.1
ESG-Focused MFP		**2.19**	**2.03**	**100**
PANEL C: MSCI EM Universe	Oct-2011			
Product Involvement		−0.02	−0.04	−2.0
Controversies		0.33	0.37	19.8
MFP Based on ESG Exclusions		1.62	1.42	75.5
Low Emissions Tilt		0.10	0.13	6.7
ESG-Focused MFP		**2.03**	**1.88**	**100**

Source: GSAM.

Finally, with regard to monitoring an ESG strategy, Alford (2018) outlines many challenges that investors potentially face. For instance, one possible challenge is the long and uncertain investment horizon required for evaluating ESG risks and performance. Indeed, the performance impact of many ESG factors, such as climate risk, may not be fully visible for many years to come. Investors with a short-term performance evaluation horizon may find it difficult to maintain confidence in an ESG strategy when it underperforms, even if such investors have a long-term philosophical belief in the strategy. Another potential challenge relates to performance attribution, which involves gaining a clear understanding of the risk and return contributions of various ESG factors. Investors typically use commercial risk models for evaluating portfolio risk and performance. However, such risk models currently do not include ESG factors. As such, they are often not useful in assessing the risk and performance impact of ESG factors. One solution to this problem entails building a custom risk model, which includes the relevant ESG factors. This solution is, of course, not feasible for most investors. A much simpler alternative solution, suggested by Alford (2018), is to construct paper or hypothetical portfolios designed to isolate the impact of various ESG components in a given investment process. These paper portfolios could then be used to attribute active risk and return contributions coming from the ESG factors. The building-block framework we have suggested and outlined in this chapter follows the spirit of the solution proposed by Alford (2018). It is designed to facilitate an understanding and attribution of the performance impact of various ESG constraints in the overall portfolio.

11.2 Do Smart Beta Factors Have Varying ESG Characteristics, Such as Emissions Intensity?

In general, smart beta factors do have different exposures to various ESG factors. To the extent that individual smart beta factors may depict industry biases, they may also depict varying exposures to ESG factors. For instance, the construction industry may show higher employee injury rates than the banking industry. The retailing industry may be more exposed to certain controversies, such as child labor and labor abuse through its supply chain, than the insurance industry. Specifically with regard to greenhouse gas emissions, smart beta factors, such as value, that favor industries, such as utilities and energy, may depict a much higher emissions profile than the market. This is shown in Table 11.9. This table reports the average emissions relative to the market experienced by individual smart beta factor portfolios used to construct the MFPs Based on Market Index in Table 11.6. Across the three universes, we note that the value portfolios had a considerably higher carbon footprint than the market. On the other hand, the quality portfolios had a much lower carbon footprint of around 30% of market.

These results have important implications for how investors should assess the ESG profile of their overall equity portfolios. Consider the following situation. A US public plan implemented a low-emissions strategy, which sought to reduce emissions

TABLE 11.9 Emissions Profile of Individual Smart Beta Factors: Various Universes, Periods Ending March 2018

	Start Date	Average Emissions Relative to Market (%)
PANEL A: Russell 1000 Universe	Oct-2009	
Value		241
Momentum		96
Low Volatility		127
Quality		31
MFP Based on Market Index		**120**
PANEL B: MSCI World ex USA Universe	Oct-2009	
Value		179
Momentum		71
Low Volatility		91
Quality		33
MFP Based on Market Index		**91**
PANEL C: MSCI EM Universe	Oct-2011	
Value		161
Momentum		79
Low Volatility		116
Quality		24
MFP Based on Market Index		**83**

Source: GSAM.

relative to the market by around 60%. The plan then proceeded to allocate an amount equivalent to that invested in the low-emissions strategy in a specific low-volatility strategy. The chosen low-volatility strategy had an emissions profile 40% higher than the market, thereby undoing most of the emissions reduction targeted by the low-emissions strategy. Similarly, in our experience, it is not uncommon to find that one strategy or component of the overall portfolio often negates the ESG benefits sought by another strategy or component of the portfolio. For instance, it may be that investors seeking to reduce their carbon footprint through the implementation of an ESG strategy may have a strong value-bias in the rest of their portfolio. These situations highlight that investors should ascertain the ESG factor exposures of various implemented strategies in order to gain a better understanding of the ESG profile of the overall portfolio.

11.3 When ESG Is Combined with Smart Beta, Isn't There Potential for ESG Factors to Dilute the Smart Beta Factor Tilts?

Yes. However, we believe this should not be viewed as a problem if the primary objective of a combined strategy is to reflect certain ESG characteristics in the final portfolio. For instance, the ESG-Focused MFPs illustrated in Table 11.7 incorporate the desired ESG exclusions as well as emissions reduction. This is why in our proposed process we start with the ESG screens (Step 1 in Figure 11.2) and end with the emissions overlay (Step 3 in Figure 11.2) in order to ensure that both constraints are reflected in the final portfolio. The cost of incorporating various ESG constraints may well be some level of dilution of certain smart beta factor tilts. However, from Table 11.8, we also note that, when ESG factors were included, the active return and risk of ESG-Focused MFPs was still primarily driven by the smart beta factor tilts.

VI. CONCLUSION

In this chapter, we have used a simple framework to show that many ESG-focused strategies, comprising of screens and/or tilts, may be incorporated in the passive component of the equity portfolio without assuming excessive tracking risk relative to a given market policy benchmark. Additionally, ESG investing can also be combined with smart beta investing. Indeed, investors can incorporate ESG considerations in a smart beta multistrategy without fundamentally altering its risk-return profile. Finally, an ESG focus also can be incorporated in a customized fashion to suit a specific active risk budget.

CHAPTER 12

AN ALTERNATIVE TO HEDGE FUND INVESTING: A RISK-BASED APPROACH

Oliver Bunn[1]

Vice President, Goldman Sachs Asset Management

I.   INTRODUCTION

By virtue of their lack of investment constraints relative to traditional equity and fixed income managers, hedge funds have produced positive, diversifying returns for more than 20 years.[2] Investors have therefore used hedge funds to complement core equity and fixed income allocations with the expectation that this will result in an increase in overall portfolio efficiency. However, investing in hedge funds presents a distinct set of challenges for investors, notably liquidity restrictions, potential lack of transparency into the investment strategy, extensive due-diligence requirements as well as their fee structures. In the context of public equity market mutual funds, one response to some of those challenges has been to passively track a representative market benchmark. Unfortunately, the concept of the market portfolio as a representative benchmark,

---

[1] Mr. Stephan Kessler contributed to this chapter while employed at Goldman Sachs Asset Management.

[2] Hedge fund returns—as measured by the HFRI Fund Weighted Composite Index—returned a Sharpe ratio of 0.61 and an information ratio versus equities of 0.51 from September 1997 until September 2017, illustrating their ability to deliver strong returns in excess of the equity risk premium.

founded in the Capital Asset Pricing Model (CAPM) and Efficient Market Hypothesis (EMH), does not exist with hedge funds. Against this background, this article discusses an alternative to hedge fund investing. Informed by techniques from other asset classes, it outlines a factor-based approach to identifying the systematic risk exposures taken by hedge funds. These economically intuitive factors based on academic research are well-defined, liquid and can be implemented at relatively low cost. A portfolio of these systematic factors can provide investors with access to a hedge-fund-like return profile.

There are several reasons why a representative market benchmark does not exist for hedge funds. Leaving aside the fact that there is hardly a consensus definition of what a hedge fund is, it is impossible to passively track a benchmark representative of the entire hedge fund universe because of, among other issues, coverage restrictions of hedge fund data sources and investment frictions. On the one hand, hedge funds may report information to one or more of multiple hedge fund databases at their sole discretion, with the result that each database, and all databases collectively, provides only a partial representation of the hedge fund universe. On the other hand, the investment frictions associated with hedge funds (e.g. lockups, minimum investment amounts) and extensive due-diligence requirements represent significant barriers to initiate and maintain coverage of any sizeable and diverse portfolio of hedge funds, therefore posing further challenges to a passive investment approach.

Given the lack of a viable hedge fund benchmark for investors to track passively, the question arises—is there a case to be made for a select portfolio of hedge funds instead. Investors may naturally strive to select those hedge funds that consistently and persistently produce diversifying and positive returns. In practice, the lack of transparency not only in the investment strategy but also in the reporting of hedge fund performance, positions, and attribution (which is often voluntary with no clearly defined standards in existence), can make it difficult to distinguish luck from skill. Additionally, this article quantifies the lack of performance persistence among hedge funds on a year-on-year basis. As outlined in Section II.B, out of the top 20% funds in terms of past-year performance, only 29% of funds are found to be able to repeat this placement in the next year. This is in line with the academic literature on hedge fund manager performance persistence, as summarized for example by Agarwal et al. (2015) and Eling (2009). While there may be a degree of persistence over a shorter-term horizon, that is, periods of six months or less, this literature finds that the evidence for persistence becomes much more challenged over intermediate- to long-term horizons. This in turn implies that even if a hedge fund investor can continuously identify successful individual hedge funds ex ante they would be required to turn over their portfolio quite frequently. Additionally, subscription/redemption cycles as well as manager relationship constraints present material implementation challenges, leaving only potentially the most sophisticated investors with sufficient expertise and resources to dynamically adjust these types of portfolios.

The alternative investment approach proposed in this article acknowledges both the lack of a representative market benchmark as well as the challenges around maintaining a well-performing select portfolio of hedge funds. In order for investors to manage the dispersion in the performance of individual hedge funds, it argues in favor of a sufficiently diversified universe of hedge funds. While individual hedge funds may be highly idiosyncratic in their investment styles and resulting return profiles, such broadly diversified portfolios of hedge funds exhibit a higher degree of stability when it comes to the drivers of their return evolution over time. The discussed portfolio construction approach argues in favor of inferring such return drivers using systematic factor exposures of hedge funds, instead of the creation of large portfolios of direct hedge fund holdings. This study is grounded in the work of Fama and French (1992) on cross-sectional equity pricing and of Sharpe (1992) on asset-class factor models, Fung and Hsieh (1997, 2001, 2004), and Agarwal and Naik (2000a, 2000b, 2004), among others, that have pioneered this type of analysis of systematic return drivers for hedge funds.

The well-defined, liquid and relatively low-cost factor exposures we employ fall into two categories, traditional and alternative risk premia. Traditional risk premia are individual "long only" market factors (betas), such as equities or fixed income. Alternative risk premia are defined as collections of investment rules and strategies that are often employed by hedge funds that can be implemented using liquid financial instruments and therefore have similar liquidity as traditional market factors. Particularly through its emphasis on alternative risk premia, the suggested methodology accomplishes enhanced tracking of the performance of a broad portfolio of hedge funds in comparison to, for example, Hasanhodzic and Lo (2007) or Hill et al. (2004). Liquid access to these two categories of risk premia in an investment vehicle provides advantages over portfolios of individual hedge funds, and potentially even over investments in fund-of-hedge funds, such as liquidity, affordability, transparency, and clear return attribution. A portfolio of these two categories of risk premia could be the solution for investors concerned about the challenge of performance consistency of portions of their hedge fund universe. Another advantage of such an investment approach is that it leaves open the possibility of investors to complement their portfolios with investments in specifically selected individual high-conviction hedge funds.

Individual high-conviction hedge funds might indeed be delivering attractive returns over and above the performance of traditional or alternative risk premia. This raises an important caveat about the investment approach to make the traditional and alternative risk premia exposures of hedge funds available to investors, as it does not provide access to the "unexplained" portion that may be present in the hedge fund universe beyond these systematic factor exposures. However, as outlined in Section IV.A, only 16% of the return of the hedge fund universe constructed for our analysis can be attributed to this unexplained portion. In turn, 84% of the return of the universe can be provided to investors by means of traditional and alternative risk premia. This percentage is not only due to static exposures to these risk premia but also captures time variation of hedge fund exposures to such risk premia, as the discussed methodology updates at regular intervals. Overall, the high degree of hedge fund performance capture translates into a correlation of 93.5% to the return time series of the underlying hedge fund universe.

While the proposed investment approach might represent a remedy for investors to the noninvestability of a hedge fund benchmark, it is important to note that it behaves very differently from a passively tracking benchmark portfolio in the realm of, for example, public equity markets. Notwithstanding the very nonpassive nature of the risk premia, particularly the alternative risk premia, the difference between the well-defined and liquid nature of the factors and the opaqueness and illiquidity of some hedge fund investment strategies will necessarily lead to a degree of tracking error. In the specific case of the proposed alternative to hedge fund investing, the tracking error amounts to approximately one third of the volatility of the hedge fund universe benchmark, per backtested analysis.

This document is structured as follows: Section II presents a more detailed introduction into the universe on which we base this analysis. We then analyze hedge fund performance persistence and elaborate on the similarities of portfolios of hedge funds of different sizes compared to the overall hedge fund universe. In Section III, we present the set of traditional and alternative risk premia that allow us to identify the systematic drivers of hedge fund performance and discuss the weight estimation framework to allocate to those premia to emulate the risk-return characteristics of hedge funds in liquid form. Section IV discusses the efficacy of the discussed weight estimation procedure. It further presents an explicit return and risk decomposition of overall hedge fund returns into traditional risk premia, alternative risk premia as well as an unexplained component. Section V complements the analysis with a cross-sectional analysis of the evolution of fees and liquidity of hedge funds. It also presents an outlook on the role that liquid tracking might be able to play against the background of recent developments in the hedge fund universe. Finally, Section VI concludes with a perspective on the broader universe of liquid alternative investment vehicles that has emerged in recent years.

II.   BENEFITS OF A DIVERSIFIED PORTFOLIO OF HEDGE FUNDS

In this section, we focus on the hedge fund dataset that is at the core of the subsequent analysis of systematic performance drivers. We first describe the construction of the proprietary aggregate hedge fund data set and review its current and historic properties such as number of funds and assets under management.

We then focus on an analysis of performance persistence and highlight the lack thereof on a year-on-year basis. This lack of persistence suggests that hedge fund investors aiming at selecting top performing hedge funds would have to rebalance hedge fund portfolios more frequently and to a larger extent than is practically feasible, a concern that hedge fund investors may address by increasing their hedge fund portfolio's diversification.

However, another finding in this section is the degree of convergence between hedge fund portfolios and the overall studied hedge fund universe, even for hedge fund portfolios with a limited number of individual funds. Paired with the persistence result, this finding is the fundamental justification for the use of a broad and diverse set of hedge funds and their corresponding investment strategies to draw inferences about systematic hedge fund return drivers.

A. Hedge Fund Universe

We source hedge fund information directly from hedge fund database providers. Hedge funds or their management companies[3] typically provide information about hedge-fund-level monthly returns as well as assets under management (AUM) on a monthly basis, paired with a host of more qualitative information such as classification or their fee structure.

The universe of hedge funds this study is based on is constructed from data provided by two hedge fund database providers, Hedge Fund Research, Inc. and BarclayHedge, LLC. As of December 2017, these two databases provide us with access to close to 14,000 hedge fund time series.[4] As found in Joenvaara et al. (2016), these two databases exhibit a high degree of complementarity. In order to ensure comparability of the hedge fund return time series, we restrict attention to US$-denominated return time series and require all return information to be reported net of all fees. Using a proprietary merging algorithm,[5] we then construct a point-in-time representation of the hedge fund universe from the filtered raw information available from the hedge fund data providers.[6] Using this merging algorithm allows the analysis to be driven by a more comprehensive universe of hedge fund strategies while reducing

---

[3] Disclosure to hedge fund databases is voluntary and one might express concerns about the selection bias inherent in hedge funds or their management companies deciding to be included in a hedge fund database or not. Reasons for reporting hedge fund returns to a database are manifold and include, amongst others, increased publicity, requests by investors or a perceived higher institutional quality. Implementing the methodology on as broad a hedge fund universe as possible makes the results robust to individual hedge fund managers stopping to report their returns and abates some concerns about the data's comprehensiveness.

[4] Note that the approximately 14,000 time series include the overlap of funds reporting to both databases as well as, for example, multiple share classes being reported for individual funds.

[5] The algorithm groups time series that exhibit a high degree of commonality to limit duplication. This way, we ensure that specific hedge fund's returns are not disproportionately represented in the universe by virtue of their reporting style or their reporting to both databases simultaneously.

[6] As we have access to point-in-time files from the database providers, we can rely on their information about hedge funds as being available at historic points in time to construct our aggregate database, which addresses concerns about survivorship biases. Prior to 2009, we rely on so-called graveyard files, which contain information about funds that no longer report to a database, to derive approximations of point-in-time available information to counteract survivorship bias. We further address concerns about backfill bias by using hedge fund database inclusion dates to accurately reflect when a specific fund's information became available through either of the two database providers.

EXHIBIT 12.1   Number of Funds and Total AUM of Hedge Fund Studied Universe

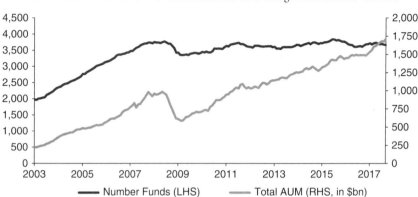

Source: Data from HFR, BarclayHedge, GSAM, as of December 2017.

noise in the analysis due to double-counting entries, which appear multiple times across both databases.

Exhibit 12.1 shows the number of funds as well as the total AUM of this universe. For the past 10 years, its coverage in terms of the number of funds has remained fairly steady at around 3,500 funds, which, according to the Hedge Fund Research Inc. (HFR) Global Hedge Fund Industry Report from the third quarter of 2017, represents slightly less than half of the number of funds commonly considered to be in the hedge fund universe. In terms of AUM, the universe has declined in the aftermath of the Global Financial Crisis, but has been steadily increasing since then. It now stands at around $1.7trn, which, as with the number of funds, is approximately half of the overall AUM managed within the hedge fund industry.[7]

In line with the results from Exhibit 12.1, the average AUM across hedge funds dipped by around $100mn during the Global Financial Crisis in 2008, but has subsequently increased and now sits at two and a half times the level of the average AUM post-Global Financial Crisis (Exhibit 12.2). While the median AUM generally co-moves with the average AUM, it is worth pointing out that it is noticeably less than $100mn. When contrasting the median and the average, it becomes apparent that the average is skewed by the presence of a few high-AUM funds, which overpowers the presence of a substantial number of smaller AUM funds.

When constructing aggregate hedge fund return time series from individual hedge fund information, there are typically two main weighting approaches, AUM-weighting and equal weighting. In contrast to AUM-weighting, equal weighting has the benefit that the composition of the overall hedge fund universe is not dominated

---

[7] This representation of AUM coverage considers the AUM coverage of the hedge fund universe captured by our database in relation to estimates about the overall size of the hedge fund universe from the 3Q 2017 HFR Global Hedge Fund Industry Report.

EXHIBIT 12.2   Median and Average AUM of Hedge Fund Studied Universe

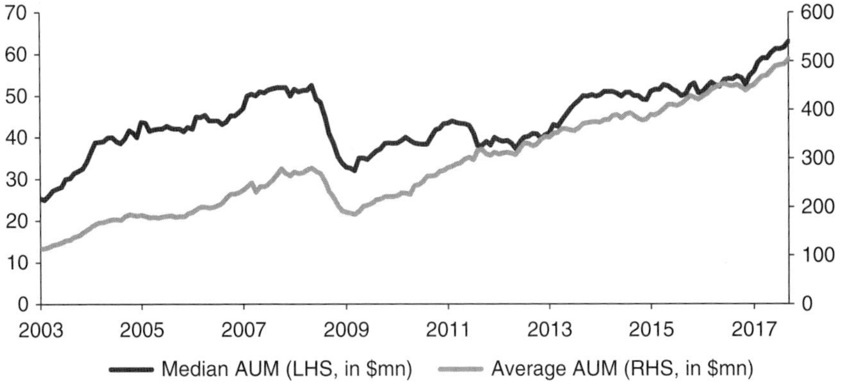

Source: Data from HFR, BarclayHedge, GSAM, as of December 2017.

by a few very large hedge funds, which is an imminent concern provided the evidence from Exhibit 12.2.[8] Relatedly, equal weighting implies that our return representations capture all size segments of the hedge fund universe comprehensively. This is particularly relevant in the context of the complexities for hedge fund investors to perform hedge fund due diligence on a large set of hedge funds. Equal weighting has the advantage of providing access to a diverse set of smaller-capitalization funds that investors might otherwise find difficult to subject to a thorough and comprehensive due diligence procedure.

Another key component of the hedge fund universe construction in addition to equal weighting is a "bottom-up" process of grouping hedge funds. Instead of considering the universe of hedge funds as a single abstract average of all available return time series, we break the universe down according to common hedge fund investment styles. These styles represent selections of hedge funds from the overall universe that generally are still broad and diversified, but are more homogeneous than the overall universe in that they share certain investment characteristics. These styles then enable us to develop an understanding of the systematic drivers of their returns, which we subsequently aggregate back to the overall hedge fund universe.

---

[8] Despite concerns about differences in concentration between an AUM-weighted and an equally weighted aggregate hedge fund return time series, it should be noted that these two construction approaches result in fairly highly correlated aggregated return time series. Comparing the HFRI Asset Weighted Index (AUM weighted) to the HFRI Fund Weighted Composite Index (equally weighted) over the maximum available overlapping time period from December 2007 until November 2017, it becomes apparent the two time series are 92.7% correlated with a Root Mean Square Error (RMSE) of 2.3%. For more information about the two hedge fund indices, please refer to the Hedge Fund Research Inc. website, www.hedgefundresearch.com.

Commonly considered aggregations of hedge fund styles are Equity Long Short, Macro, Relative Value, and Event Driven. Hedge Fund Research Inc. generally characterizes these four aggregations, which we will refer to as categories, as follows:[9]

1. Equity Long Short:
This category contains hedge funds, whose exposure—both long and short—is primarily in equities. These funds employ a variety of investment styles, ranging from quantitatively to fundamentally driven approaches.

2. Macro:
The Macro category represents funds, whose investment process and resultant exposures to a broad set of different asset classes is predicated on movements in underlying economic variables. Investment theses are based on a variety of discretionary or systematic techniques.

3. Relative Value:
Hedge funds in this category take positions across different asset classes in order to exploit valuation discrepancies in the relationship between multiple securities.

4. Event Driven:
Hedge funds in this category establish exposures to companies currently or prospectively involved in corporate transactions. The types of such exposures cover the whole spectrum of the corporate capital structure.

Exhibit 12.3 shows the relative proportions of these categories in December 2017. Equity Long Short hedge funds make up almost 50% of the universe, while Macro hedge funds make up between a quarter and a third. The remainder is split approximately two thirds to one third between Relative Value and Event Driven hedge funds, respectively. This relative composition of the overall universe does not change much over time. In fact, the average month-on-month change across the weights to all four categories amounts to only slightly below 0.8%.

B. Persistence of Hedge Fund Performance

Having established the hedge fund dataset, we now turn to the analysis of performance persistence. In order to gain a high-level insight into potential performance persistence, we consider return aggregates for the four main categories of the hedge fund universe. Exhibit 12.4 shows the annual performance of each of these four categories and ranks their performance from 2003 through 2017. While there may have been a certain degree of stability in the very first years of the sample, the ranking of the categories subsequently changes dramatically year over year. The Macro category, for example, jumps from the bottom performer in 2009 and 2010 and again in 2012 and 2013 (0% in each year) to being the second

---

[9] Hedge Fund Research, Inc. provides information about hedge fund indices and descriptions of common hedge fund investment styles on their website, www.hedgefundresearch.com. The summaries for the four hedge fund categories source information from these descriptions.

EXHIBIT 12.3   Weighting of Individual Hedge Fund Categories in Studied Universe

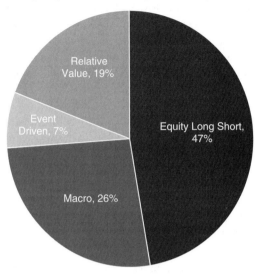

Source: Data from HFR, BarclayHedge, GSAM, as of December 2017.

EXHIBIT 12.4   Annual Hedge Fund Category Performance

2003	2004	2005	2006	2007	2008	2009	2010	2011	2012	2013	2014	2015	2016	2017
ED 23%	ED 15%	ELS 12%	ED 14%	ELS 13%	MA 8%	RV 27%	RV 12%	RV 1%	RV 10%	ELS 15%	MA 6%	RV 0%	ED 10%	ELS 14%
ELS 22%	ELS 9%	ED 9%	ELS 14%	MA 11%	RV −20%	ELS 27%	ED 12%	MA −3%	ELS 9%	ED 13%	RV 4%	MA −1%	RV 9%	ED 6%
RV 14%	RV 8%	RV 7%	RV 12%	RV 8%	ED −20%	ED 26%	ELS 11%	ED −4%	ED 8%	RV 8%	ELS 2%	ELS −1%	ELS 5%	RV 5%
MA 11%	MA 2%	MA 5%	MA 7%	ED 7%	ELS −26%	MA 5%	MA 9%	ELS −9%	MA 1%	MA 0%	ED 1%	ED −4%	MA 2%	MA 3%

Legend

ELS – Equity Long Short   MA – Macro   RV – Relative Value   ED – Event Driven

Source: Data from HFR, BarclayHedge, GSAM, as of December 2017.

best performer in 2011 (–3%) and even the top performer in 2014 (+6%) before dropping again in 2015 and 2016. Equity Long Short is never the worst performer after 2011 but it alternates year by year between top and third strongest performer. Overall, there is little evidence of performance persistence on this fairly high aggregation level of the four hedge fund categories.

In order to more accurately reflect the challenges in assembling a hedge fund portfolio, we complement this high-level analysis with a fund-level analysis of persistence. Corresponding results in the academic literature are mixed. Agarwal and Naik (2000a, 2000b), and Amenc et al. (2003), as well as Bares et al. (2003), for example, have established evidence in favor of performance persistence for shorter periods up to a quarter. Ter Horst and Verbeek (2007), Boyson (2008), and Eling (2009) provide a more nuanced perspective that is supportive of performance persistence for shorter-term periods up to six months but regard the evidence for intermediate- to longer-term horizons as more challenged. These intermediate- to longer-term results are in line with Brown and Goetzmann (2003), Capocci and Huebner (2004), Capocci et al. (2005), and Malkiel and Saha (2005).

Acknowledging the practical complexities in adjusting hedge fund portfolios dynamically, this analysis focuses on an annual period to evaluate performance persistence in single hedge funds. For each year from 2003 until 2015, we sort all hedge funds that have reported returns throughout the entire year into performance quintiles. We subsequently measure the performance over the following year and apply another quintile sort. For the following year's performance, we however need to be mindful that hedge funds may no longer report returns to the hedge fund database providers. This may be driven by, for example, fund restructurings or liquidations. For this reason, the ranking in the subsequent year also contains a column termed "NR," which stands for "Not Reporting." This column reflects those funds that have stopped reporting returns at some point throughout the subsequent year.

Exhibit 12.5 contains 55,727 observations from 2003 until 2016. For each row, the different columns show how likely a fund is to end up in the respective performance quintiles in the following year.[10] For example, for a fund that is initially ranked in the third quintile, there is a 13% likelihood that it will be in the first quintile in the subsequent year and an 18% likelihood that it will be in the second quintile. High performance persistence would be demonstrated by the diagonal elements of this matrix being an order of magnitude larger than the off-diagonal elements. While we

EXHIBIT 12.5 Transition Matrix for Performance Quintiles of Individual Hedge Funds

		Subsequent Year Ranking					
		1	2	3	4	5	NR
	1	29%	18%	13%	12%	20%	8%
	2	17%	21%	19%	15%	15%	12%
Initial Year Ranking	3	13%	18%	19%	18%	14%	18%
	4	12%	16%	15%	17%	15%	25%
	5	18%	11%	10%	12%	22%	27%

Source: HFR, BarclayHedge, GSAM, as of December 2017.

---

[10] Each element in this matrix is the average over the transition likelihoods for all initial sorts from 2003 to 2015.

find some very limited evidence for this effect for the very best and worst performing hedge funds in the initial year ranking, instability abounds and one even observes evidence of mean reversal of returns in the extreme quintiles.

As a matter of fact, the probability of starting off in quintile 1 and ending in the worst performing quintile is the second highest probability after staying in quintile 1. The same holds true for the worst performer where moving from quintile 5 to quintile 1 in the following year has the second highest probability after remaining at the bottom. Generally, in contrast to the required pattern to establish performance persistence, each row in Exhibit 12.5 actually displays a much more pronounced tendency towards a uniform distribution of likelihoods across the different quintiles. Overall, Exhibit 12.5 confirms the lack of unified evidence in the academic literature of performance persistence in single hedge funds once one imposes a minimum evaluation time period.

Another point to note about Exhibit 12.5, which is problematic for the selection of portfolios consisting of only a few individual funds, is the high likelihood of a fund not reporting 12 months of returns in the subsequent year. While there is already an approximately 1 in 13 likelihood that funds in the top quintile do not report returns in the following year, this probability increases monotonically for worse-performing quintiles and exceeds a one in four likelihood for the worst-performing quintile. It is noteworthy that these likelihoods only represent one-year quantities and imply an even higher fraction of hedge funds that may potentially stop reporting over a multiyear period.[11]

This type of inevitable hedge fund turnover may lead to potentially costly searches for replacement funds and may involve periods where certain fractions of a hedge fund portfolio are left unallocated and therefore cannot deliver the return characteristics that investors seek. This is a challenge to which the proposed alternative approach to hedge fund investing will not be subject.

C. Convergence of Hedge Fund Portfolios to the Overall Hedge Fund Universe

While the lack of performance persistence warrants caution when it comes to the construction of select hedge fund portfolios, the question arises whether selections of hedge funds could provide sufficient diversification to deliver alternative returns without the risk of exposing a portfolio to the idiosyncrasies of individual hedge funds while still offering the potential to generate superior risk-adjusted returns.

Exhibit 12.6 provides answers to this question by comparing portfolios of differing number of hedge funds to a broad universe of hedge funds as well as to the average performance of funds in that universe. In this analysis we randomly form hedge

---

[11] For example, if a hedge fund starts off in quintile 1, there is approximately a 36% likelihood that this fund will stop reporting at some point in the subsequent three years.

EXHIBIT 12.6   Sharpe Ratio and Correlation for Simulated Hedge Fund Portfolios
(October 2012 to September 2017)[13]

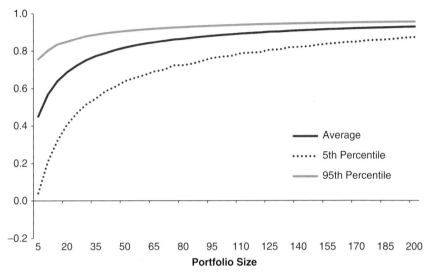

Source: Data from HFR, BarclayHedge, GSAM, as of December 2017.

fund portfolios of various sizes and hold these portfolios for a period of five years
using data covering a time period from October 2012 to September 2017.[12]

The portfolio sizes we consider range between 5 and 200 funds. We then run a
bootstrapping analysis of 10,000 selections per portfolio size and calculate the Sharpe
ratio as well as the correlation to the average return of all hedge funds in our database
for the analyzed time period, for each random selection.

Exhibit 12.6 displays the Sharpe ratio and correlation characteristics for the distribution associated with each specific hedge fund portfolio size in the simulation.
The most striking feature of this analysis is the high correlation of the simulated
portfolios with the average returns across all hedge funds in our universe. For a
portfolio with only five-member hedge funds the correlation is at 0.45 and increases
to 0.69 for a portfolio of 20 hedge funds. This illustrates how even portfolios with
a relatively small number of hedge funds behave very similar to the average return
across all hedge funds. The average Sharpe ratios of the simulated portfolios are

---

[12] If a hedge fund ceases to publish returns during the time frame considered for this analysis,
we reallocate its weight to the remaining hedge funds in the respective sampled portfolios of
hedge funds. If all hedge funds from an initial selection cease to publish returns, we there are
no more hedge funds in an initial selection from the universe.

[13] A five-year time period is used for the simulation in order to ensure the inclusion of an
appropriate number of Funds with overlapping time periods without inducing excessive
survivorship bias in the analysis.

EXHIBIT 12.7   Historical Risk/Return Distribution

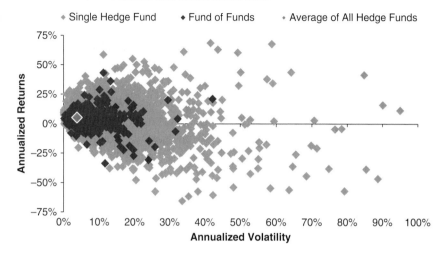

Source: Data from HFR, BarclayHedge, GSAM, as of December 2017.

below the ones from the hedge fund average returns but converge for larger portfolios. This is partially driven by the diversification effect of larger portfolios given
that the applied selection mechanism does not model any skill in selecting hedge
funds. However, the dispersion between the 5th and 95th percentile illustrates the
variability in terms of Sharpe ratio that the simulation is still subject to across different portfolio sizes.

While the simulation study relies on indiscriminate selections of hedge funds, the
following paragraphs complement this analysis by analyzing portfolios of fund-of-
funds, which deliberately select specific funds from the hedge fund universe that they
cover. Exhibit 12.7 highlights the risk-return characteristics of our overall representation of the universe of individual hedge funds in conjunction with the characteristics
for a universe of fund-of-funds. It considers single hedge fund as well as fund-of-fund
data[14] over the past five years up until the fourth quarter of 2017 and also includes
the performance of the equally weighted average return across all hedge funds over
the same time period.

It becomes apparent that fund-of-funds generally accomplish diversification, as
their distribution is located within the distribution of the overall universe of hedge
funds. The average volatility across all fund-of-funds is approximately 6.1%, while
the average for all individual hedge funds amounts to close to 11.4%. It is, however,
not necessarily the case that the additional diversification translates into superior risk-
adjusted returns, particularly when compared to a diversified aggregate of individual

---

[14] We construct a universe of fund of funds analogous to the construction of the universe of
single hedge funds as outlined in Section II.A.

hedge funds. The average time series constructed from the universe of all hedge funds delivers a return of 5.2%; more than 1% higher than the 4.1% return of the fund-of-fund universe at a risk level of around 3.7%, which is 2.4% lower than the average volatility of the fund of funds at 6.1%. This translates into a Sharpe ratio of 1.3 for the average time series constructed from the universe of all hedge funds, which is 0.4 higher than the average Sharpe ratio of the fund-of-funds (0.9).

In summary, the lack of performance persistence and its implications for the necessary turnover of investors' hedge fund portfolios may provide an argument against hedge fund portfolios with very few individual funds. If a hedge fund investor deviates from a very select portfolio by increasing the number of funds, the resulting performance may already exhibit a high degree of resemblance, on average, with a broad and diversified set of hedge funds. However, there is still substantial risk to deviate from the broader universe, as evident from the deviation in Sharpe ratios in the top chart of Exhibit 12.6.[15] Seeking exposures of a broadly diversified portfolio of hedge funds instead is an effective means for a hedge fund investor to navigate this risk. Such portfolio furthermore proves to exhibit attractive risk-adjusted return characteristics, even compared to the average fund-of-funds, as highlighted in Exhibit 12.7.

III.   SYSTEMATIC DRIVERS OF HEDGE FUND PERFORMANCE

Building on a broadly diversified portfolio of hedge funds, our approach to identifying the systematic risk exposures delivered by hedge funds consists of three steps: The first step is the identification of our universe of hedge fund returns together with a hedge fund categorization scheme. As discussed in Section II.A, we break the universe down into four main categories. Within each category, we then identify individual hedge fund styles, for which we aim to characterize the systematic return drivers. The second step is the identification of a selection of factors, which can be classified as either traditional or alternative risk premia associated with each of the different hedge fund styles within a hedge fund category. Finally, these two steps are tied together by a weight estimation methodology, which is applied for each hedge fund style and determines exposures to traditional and alternative risk premia in order to best emulate a given hedge fund style's returns.

---

[15] In unreported results we repeat the simulation analysis using the information ratio versus the MSCI World index rather than the Sharpe ratio as performance metric. The results are similar in as much as the random portfolios converge to the information ratio of the average returns across all hedge funds as the portfolio size grows. The one noteworthy difference is that the information ratio decays as the portfolio size increases (for example, from an average of 0 for a portfolio of 10 holdings to an average of –0.03 for 200 holdings).

A. Characteristics of Systematic Factors in Hedge Funds

The approach used to identify systematic factors delivered by hedge funds is based on insights from the academic literature on common risk premia for mutual funds. The advent of factor analysis of mutual fund returns can be traced back to the Capital Asset Pricing Model (CAPM) by Sharpe (1964), Lintner (1965), and Mossin (1966) who link return expectations back to exposures to the equity market factor. Fama and French (1992, 1993) extend this factor set by a value and a size factor and apply the resulting 3-factor model to equity returns. Carhart (1997), based on Jegadeesh and Titman (1993), extends the Fama and French (1992, 1993) factors by a momentum factor and finds that there is a significant loading on this factor in the cross-section of mutual funds.

Based on this work on factor analysis for mutual funds, Fung and Hsieh (1997) pioneer the analysis of the systematic return drivers for hedge fund styles. Research by Schneeweis and Spurgin (1998), Liang (1999), Edwards and Caglayan (2001), Capocci and Huebner (2004) as well as Hill et al. (2004) refines the factor set used to determine the drivers of the returns of hedge fund styles by focusing on more easily interpretable factors as well as by considerations around tradability. Fung and Hsieh (2001, 2004) as well as Agarwal and Naik (2000a,b, 2004) further expand the set of return drivers beyond the inclusion of basic representations of asset classes or parts thereof by introducing implementable trading strategies to improve the explanatory power of their approximation of hedge fund returns. Their factor sets can already be decomposed into traditional and alternative risk premia, with both types of factors playing a key role in understanding and emulating the risk-return characteristics of hedge funds.

As defined in the introduction, traditional risk premia are individual "long only" market factors (betas), such as equities or fixed income. Alternative risk premia instead are systematic, multiasset, long/short investment strategies, backed by academic research and employed by market practitioners. Roughly, alternative risk premia fall into four categories:

1. Value strategies, which take advantage of the tendency for cheap assets to outperform expensive assets on a relative basis;
2. Carry strategies, which capitalize on the tendency for higher yielding assets to outperform lower yielding assets;
3. Momentum strategies, which exploit the tendency for recent relative price movements to continue in the near future; and
4. Structural strategies, which capture returns from market anomalies arising from structural constraints rather than economic fundamentals.

Attractive risk-adjusted returns, return persistence, economic intuition, and their highly liquid and cost-efficient profile have led an increasing number of investors to adopt alternative risk premia strategies in their portfolios. Many such strategies have historically realized low correlation to the price movements of traditional asset classes, and have proven effective in explaining sizeable portions of the returns of particular hedge fund styles.

B. Mapping Systematic Factors to Hedge Fund Categories

As outlined in Section II.A, we do not just consider a single representation of the hedge fund universe as a whole, but we rather aim to develop a precise and tailored understanding of the traditional and alternative risk premia factors that play a role for each hedge fund category. The applied approach to factor identification even goes a level deeper to not only look at individual hedge fund categories but to consider aggregates of hedge funds within a category, so-called styles, that share commonalities in terms of the investment approach as well as investment exposures.

When identifying the appropriate factor set for specific styles within an individual hedge fund category, we rely on fundamental insights verified by a quantitatively driven weight estimation methodology. Fundamental insights allow us to cross-validate factors using a range of qualitative sources from hedge fund database information to prime brokerage reports, hedge fund consultant reports or hedge fund holdings from 13F filings.[16] This approach puts us in a position to not only identify correlation between hedge funds and risk premia, but also to address causation, which is beneficial for the out-of-sample properties that the estimated weights will exhibit to the returns of the hedge fund style under consideration.

The following overview outlines general characteristics for the identification and selection of traditional and alternative risk premia. For ease of presentation, the overview aggregates these characteristics to the level of the four main hedge fund categories identified in Section II.A:

1. Equity Long Short:
A core exposure of funds within the Equity Long Short category is global equity market exposure. This can be complemented by additional traditional risk premia providing exposure to equity sectors actively held by Equity Long Short funds, such as energy, technology, or health care. Alternative risk premia such as Value strategies further complete the set of exposures. Finally, systematic stock selection aspects can be captured with a factor based on 13F filings.

2. Macro:
The core exposures for this hedge fund category are alternative risk premia—specifically Momentum strategies across a diverse set of asset classes. From the perspective of alternative risk premia, Carry strategies in foreign exchange also contribute to understanding the drivers of Macro hedge fund returns. Traditional risk premia representing exposures to, for example, commodities or emerging market equities exhibit a suitable degree of complementarity to the aforementioned alternative risk premia.

---

[16] 13F filings refer to Form 13F by the US Securities and Exchange Commission (SEC). Institutional investment managers satisfying certain criteria such as holding more than $100mn in qualifying assets need to submit this form on a quarterly basis. The form contains information about the holdings of those investment managers. Filings are made publicly available with a 45-day delay after the end of each calendar quarter. See the SEC website, www.sec.gov/divisions/investment/13ffaq.htm for more information.

3. Relative Value:

Risk exposures for the Relative Value category consist of a diverse set of traditional risk premia paired with alternative risk premia falling into the category of Structural strategies. The set of traditional risk premia is fairly diverse in this hedge fund category, consisting of not only exposures at various seniority points of the corporate balance sheet, but also of government debt instruments, Master Limited Partnerships (MLPs) as well as Real Estate Investment Trusts (REITs). With respect to alternative risk premia, factors with return profiles similar to those of illiquid strategies[17] arise from index option strategies as well as from the optionality component in convertible bonds.

4. Event Driven:

Similar to the Relative Value category, alternative risk premia exposures capture illiquidity-type return profiles and fall into the Structural strategies block. The set of traditional risk premia provides exposure to different levels of market capitalization for equities as well as to different seniority points of the corporate balance sheet.

C. Principles of the Weight Estimation Methodology

The weight estimation builds on original insights from Sharpe (1992), who uses factors to decompose and understand the returns of mutual funds and suggests a framework, which actually invests in the respective factors in order to mimic mutual fund returns. More explicitly, we lean on subsequently developed approaches proposed, for example, by Hasanhodzic and Lo (2007), Hill et al. (2004), and Jaeger (2008), which take Sharpe's (1992) methodology and extend it further to mimic the returns of hedge funds.

For a hedge fund style s, the methodology focuses on error terms of the form

$$e^S(t) = HFS^S(t) - \left[\alpha + \sum_{f \in TRP^S} \beta_f \cdot RF_f(t) + \sum_{f \in ARP^S} \beta_f \cdot RF_f(t) \right],$$

where α denotes a constant and β_f denotes the weight estimate for a risk premium from either the set of "Traditional Risk Premia" TRP^S or the set of "Alternative Risk Premia" ARP^S for hedge fund style S. We further denote the excess return of the average return of hedge fund style S by HFS^S and the excess return of risk premium f (traditional or alternative) by RF_f. As outlined in Section II.A, HFS^S represents an equally weighted average of the returns of a subset of hedge funds from the hedge fund dataset that we construct from single hedge fund time series originally provided by the two data providers. For t

---

[17] These can be broadly understood as patterns of smooth accumulation of performance with intermittent periods of sharp drawdowns.

spanning a time period of 24 months, we then determine α and the vectors $\{\beta_f\}_{f \in TRP^S}$ and $\{\beta_f\}_{f \in ARP^S}$ that minimize a quadratic transformation of the error terms $e^S(t)$.[18]

In line with the philosophy of the academic literature that originated from Sharpe (1992), we aim to translate the outcome of the in-sample weight estimation methodology into an out-of-sample portfolio allocation, which is the core of our construction of liquid representations of the factor exposures that hedge funds exhibit. As outlined in the introduction, we generally distinguish between traditional and alternative risk premia exposures for hedge funds and acknowledge the existence of an unexplained portion. The first two are incorporated in the factor sets TRP^S and ARP^S specified for each hedge fund style s, and what we refer to as the unexplained portion is captured by the constant term α. This portion, for example, reflects the fact that, by construction, the well-defined and liquid risk premia may naturally exhibit a degree of divergence to the opaqueness and illiquidity of some hedge fund investment strategies. It is then crucial for the determination of the overall success of the weight estimation procedures to verify the relative proportions of unexplained returns and returns driven by the two classes of risk premia, which we will further elaborate on in the subsequent section.

For the out-of-sample implementation of the methodology, this implies in turn that only the components from the factor sets TRP^S and ARP^S can be made available to an investor, as

$$\sum_{f \in TRP^S} \beta_f \cdot RF_f(u) + \sum_{f \in ARP^S} \beta_f \cdot RF_f(u),$$

where u denotes an out-of-sample time period that occurs after any of the periods t used for the in-sample weight estimation. As this process relies on collated hedge fund data, there is an inevitable gap between u and any of the respective periods t in order to account for the publication lag inherent in any hedge fund database. Once this delay has passed, weights to sets of traditional and alternative risk premia factors are re-estimated on a monthly basis based on the most recently available hedge fund database information by both data providers. This monthly re-estimation of weights is targeted toward capturing the dynamic nature of hedge fund positioning. It complements the other source of dynamism present in this portfolio construction, which arises from shifts in investment exposures within each of the alternative risk premia.

The next crucial step is the aggregation to the level of the overall hedge fund universe. Even though we identify sets of traditional and alternative risk premia for individual styles within hedge fund categories, the objective remains to provide access

---

[18] The discussed transformation creates a convex objective function that ensures that the minimization problem is well-defined. It overweights more recent observation and also controls for illiquidity-induced autocorrelation using an adaptation of the methodology proposed by Scholes and Williams (1977). Note that the objective function is dynamic in the sense that it will change each month based on updated data points, albeit that the actual transformation function is static.

to the return profile of the overall hedge fund universe. We accomplish this aggregation by weighting sets of estimates for traditional and risk premia by the relative number of funds captured within a specific style, in line with the equal weighting approach outlined in Section II.A.

The out-of-sample implementation can be further adjusted to make the performance more realistic from the point of view of an investor. First, this entails certain assumptions about the trading costs that the implementation of the portfolio of traditional and alternative risk premia might incur in the marketplace. Second, we will also assume a hypothetical management fee of 75bps that an investor might face. The final net performance of the portfolio of traditional and alternative risk premia is what we refer to as "Liquid Tracking Portfolio." It can then be compared to the performance of the average of returns across the broad and diversified universe of hedge funds, as described in Section II.A, referred to as "Hedge Fund Index." It is important to note that, while the Liquid Tracking portfolio is explicitly tradable, the Hedge Fund Index is merely a representation of average hedge fund performance that is not actually investable and therefore directly accessible to investors. This nontradability mainly arises because of the sheer scope of the universe covered as well as liquidity and turnover restrictions that investors face in emulating the composition of the aggregate hedge fund universe.

A final noteworthy aspect of the applied weight estimation methodology is its linearity. This paradigm is, for example, challenged by Kat and Palaro (2005) as well as Amenc et al. (2008, 2010), who suggest nonlinear regression approaches as well as distribution-based considerations. Hasanhodzic and Lo (2007) and Bollen and Fisher (2014), however, counter their suggested enhancements in favor of a linear relationship. Besides the case for simplicity in the identification mechanism as well as in the translation of the in-sample estimation to the out-of-sample portfolio of factors, their argument rests on the preferable out-of-sample performance of linear approaches compared to nonlinear approaches that tend to be prone to overfitting. Furthermore, distribution-based approaches only match the distribution characteristics in the longer term, which could lead to substantial return mismatches over shorter periods of time.

IV.   LIQUID TRACKING PORTFOLIO SIMULATED PERFORMANCE

A. Performance Comparison

This section reviews the simulated performance of the Liquid Tracking Portfolio whose construction we described in the previous section. We initially discuss the simulated performance of the Liquid Tracking portfolio relative to the Hedge Fund Index before switching the focus to an attribution analysis of the overall hedge fund universe. Both in terms of return contribution as well as marginal contribution to risk, this enables us to explicitly assess the fraction of hedge fund performance that is due to traditional and alternative risk premia and compare it to the fraction that is left unexplained.

EXHIBIT 12.8   Aggregate Performance Comparison of Hedge Fund Index and Liquid
Tracking Portfolio

April 2003–September 2017	Hedge Fund Index	Liquid Tracking Portfolio (Simulated)
Total Return (Annualized)	6.20%	5.20%
Volatility (Annualized)	5.80%	4.90%
Sharpe	0.83	0.77
Maximum Drawdown	−18.10%	−14.00%
Correlation	-	93.50%
RMSE (Annualized)	-	2.10%

Source: Data from HFR, BarclayHedge, GSAM as of December 2017. As outlined in Section
III.C, the Liquid Tracking Portfolio is net of assumed transaction costs and 75bps management fee.

Exhibit 12.8 compares the performance of the Hedge Fund Index to the simulated
performance of the Liquid Tracking Portfolio for a period of almost 15 years.[19] The
Liquid Tracking Portfolio delivers an annualized simulated return that only falls 1%
short of that of the hedge fund index, which translates into a Sharpe ratio difference
of less than 0.1.[20] As the Liquid Tracking Portfolio is constrained by construction,
as outlined in Section III.C, to exclude the unexplained part of the returns of the
hedge fund universe, we expect the volatility of the Liquid Tracking Portfolio to be
below that of the hedge fund index, as the unexplained return component will, by
definition, be uncorrelated with the liquid and alternative risk premia but has itself
nonnegligible volatility. This is confirmed by Exhibit 12.8.

In terms of co-movement between the two time series, the Liquid Tracking Portfolio exhibits a monthly return correlation of 93.5% to the Hedge Fund Index, i.e.
the return observations of the liquid tracking align well with those of the Hedge Fund
Index. The close co-movement not only in direction but also in quantity is further
substantiated by an annualized Root Mean Square Error (RMSE)[21] of 2.1%.

The high degree of co-movement is driven by a high in-sample quality of fit
of the weight estimation procedure, which carries over to the out-of-sample performance displayed in Exhibit 12.8 and 12.9. This provides evidence for the appropriateness of the concept of relying on historic weight estimates to determine
forward-looking risk exposures that we posit for the hedge fund index in the out-of-
sample performance analysis. An approach like this necessitates that the turnover of

---

[19] The time window for this analysis is curtailed by the availability of the time series for some
of the alternative risk premia.
[20] Note that, according to the single hedge fund assessment of unexplained returns from
Section III.C, only less than half of the hedge funds actually drive the outperformance of the
overall hedge fund universe.
[21] The Root Mean Square Error represents the square root of the average squared difference
between predicted values (here: Liquid Tracking Portfolio) and observed values (here: Hedge
Fund Index).

EXHIBIT: 12.9   Time Series Performance Comparison of Hedge Fund Index and Liquid Tracking Portfolio

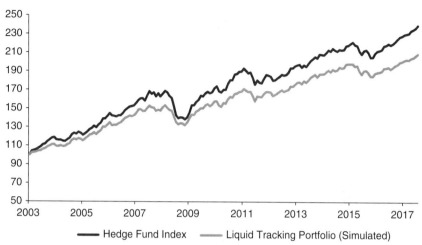

Source: Data from HFR, BarclayHedge, GSAM, as of December 2017. As outlined in Section III.C, the Liquid Tracking Portfolio is net of assumed transaction costs and 75bps management fee.

the weight estimates is limited, which is confirmed by an average monthly turnover of the weight estimates of 7.3% (with a standard deviation of 3.7%) for the Liquid Tracking Portfolio.

At the same time, the turnover figures provide evidence for a certain degree of adaptability in the weight estimation methodology. Necessarily, the process needs to be able to detect and react to shifts in the role of certain risk premia (traditional or alternative) over time. For example, Cai and Liang (2012) and Patton and Ramadorai (2013) confirm this notion and emphasize the varying nature of exposures hedge funds take and the need to have the ability to react to such changes. Our methodology accomplishes this objective through turnover in the weights estimated for individual risk premia as well as through allocation changes in the investment strategies inside individual alternative risk premia strategies. For example, in the portion of the Liquid Tracking Portfolio capturing Macro hedge funds, the month-on-month turnover of the risk premia weights is around 5%, while the turnover within the alternative risk premia used for Macro hedge fund tracking can be much higher, as illustrated by a month-on-month turnover of 290%[22] for the Momentum strategies employed in this category.

---

[22] In order to put the turnover figures in context, over the time frame in question, the Macro Liquid Tracking portfolio and the Momentum Alternative Risk Premium realized annualized volatilities of 4.5% and 9.4%, respectively.

While Exhibit 12.8 presents aggregate statistics for the Hedge Fund Index and the Liquid Tracking Portfolio, Exhibit 12.9 shows the evolution of both time series. It is apparent that the degree of co-movement between the two time series is very consistent over time and that there are no periods of significant divergence.

While the co-movement is very consistent in the time series representation of Exhibit 12.9, it turns out that there is a sizeable degree of cross-sectional variation in how the 1% annualized performance difference of the Hedge Fund Index to the Liquid Tracking Portfolio is distributed among hedge funds. Based on the style-by-style portfolio construction of selected traditional and alternative risk premia outlined in Section III.A and III.B, one can construct performance comparables for individual hedge funds according to the hedge fund style that each hedge fund is categorized in.[23] This way, although the general focus lies on the aggregate hedge fund universe, it is possible to make inferences about the cross-sectional distribution of the unexplained returns in the overall universe of hedge funds.

For the hedge fund sample outlined in Section II.A, which covers a period of almost 15 years with initially around 2,000 funds that later grows to close to 4,000 funds, it turns out that only 45.8% of the funds actually manage to have positive unexplained returns when measured against their liquid performance comparable. At the same time, however, there is a considerable degree of variation in the unexplained returns. According to our analysis, while the 75th percentile of hedge funds manages to realize 47bps of monthly positive unexplained performance, the 25th percentile falls short by 75bps per month. Keeping in mind the 1% overall performance difference between the Hedge Fund Index and the simulated Liquid Tracking Portfolio, this points to a fairly high degree of concentration of positive unexplained returns within the universe of hedge funds. This consideration reiterates difficulties hedge fund investors may face in their allocation to individual funds.

B. Decomposition of Hedge Fund Performance

On the aggregate hedge fund universe level, the previous section demonstrates the co-movement between the Hedge Fund Index and the out-of-sample performance represented by the simulated Liquid Tracking Portfolio. Below, we will quantify the return and risk contributions of the unexplained returns of the Hedge Fund Index relative to the proposed Liquid Tracking Portfolio and

---

[23] We compare the cumulative performance of each hedge fund captured by the analysis over all months that this fund has a return observation in our database to the performance of the liquid portfolio of traditional and alternative risk premia constructed for the hedge fund style, under which the specific hedge fund falls, over the same months.

EXHIBIT 12.10   Factor Attribution of Hedge Fund Index Performance

April 2003–September 2017	Relative Return Contribution	Relative Marginal Volatility Contribution
Unexplained	15.90%	20.30%
Alternative Risk Premia	37.50%	13.60%
Traditional Risk Premia	46.50%	66.10%
Aggregate	100.00%	100.00%

Source: Data from HFR, BarclayHedge, GSAM, as of December 2017.

put them into comparison with the impact of the traditional and alternative risk premia.[24]

Exhibit 12.10 presents the return contribution[25] as well as the marginal contribution to risk of the returns of the Hedge Fund Index coming from unexplained returns and traditional and alternative risk premia. In line with Exhibits 12.8 and 12.9, the fraction of returns attributed to unexplained returns is only 16% of the overall returns of the Hedge Fund Index, with the remaining portion of 84% attributable to traditional and alternative risk premia. Further breaking down the return contribution of the two classes of risk premia, the return split between traditional and alternative risk premia comes out at approximately 55/45, which is a clear indication of the important and sizeable contribution that alternative risk premia make toward capturing hedge fund returns.

In terms of marginal contribution to risk, the breakdown between traditional and alternative risk premia shifts toward traditional risk premia, which explain about 66% of the overall volatility. This is driven by the directional nature of the traditional risk premia, which tends to imply higher volatility for these factors, in comparison to the more diversified and long/short types of exposures typically embodied by alternative risk premia. For the unexplained return component, the contribution to the overall volatility remains at a level (~20%) that is similar in magnitude to the proportional contribution to returns.

---

[24] In an out-of-sample context, unexplained returns can essentially be decomposed into two parts: (1) Unexplained returns from the in-sample weight estimation procedure and (2) prediction error arising from the process of inferring out-of-sample weights from in-sample estimates. The prediction error in (2) can further be decomposed into a portion that arises as exposures to traditional and alternative risk premia change during the out-of-sample period compared to the window used for estimation as well as a portion attributable to the relative proportions of the different hedge fund investment styles changing over time. While the effect of changing weights has already been addressed in the context of the discussion about turnover in the previous section, it also turns out that the relative weight shifts of individual styles are minor, in line with the evidence presented in Exhibit 12.3 in Section II.A for the four main hedge fund categories.

[25] While Exhibit 12.8 presents annualized total returns, the return decomposition in Exhibit 12.10 uses nonannualized return quantities; 136.9% total return over the time period considered translates to 6.2% annualized total return.

EXHIBIT 12.11   Correlation of Hedge Fund Attribution Factors

April 2003–September 2017	Unexplained	Alternative Risk Premia	Traditional Risk Premia
Unexplained	100%	−0.30%	25.40%
Alternative Risk Premia		100%	17.70%
Traditional Risk Premia			100%

Source: Data from HFR, BarclayHedge, GSAM, as of December 2017.

An important determinant of the stability of the out-of-sample contribution analysis in Exhibit 12.10 is the complementarity of the individual components of the return and risk contribution breakdown. For this reason, Exhibit 12.11 displays the pairwise correlations of the three hedge fund return components. Since the unexplained portion of the returns is orthogonal to traditional and alternative risk premia, we expect the correlation of unexplained returns to the other factors to be close to zero, which is confirmed for alternative risk premia and to a lesser degree for the traditional risk premia. We attribute the residual correlation between unexplained returns and traditional risk premia to short-term market timing by some hedge fund styles, which only gets picked up in an incomplete manner by the monthly weight estimation process.

A final point to highlight about Exhibit 12.11 is the low correlation between traditional and alternative risk premia. This bodes well not only for the stability of the contribution analysis, but also highlights the complementarity of the role that alternative risk premia play in explaining hedge fund returns out-of-sample in the applied methodology over and above the attribution that can already be inferred from traditional risk premia.[26]

Exhibit 12.12 elaborates further on the return decomposition from Exhibit 12.10 by breaking down the contribution into three subperiods of approximately five years each. At first, it is noteworthy that hedge fund performance has actually undergone quite a high degree of time variation, as evidenced by the aggregate of the three columns displayed for each time period. A period of exceptionally strong returns in the run-up to the Global Financial Crisis is followed by a period of more challenged performance thereafter, which has then given way to a slight performance improvement in the latest part of the sample. Assessing the impact of the individual components, the exhibit proves the consistency of the return contribution of the alternative risk premia, as the impact of alternative risk premia has a higher contribution than that of unexplained returns in each of three subperiods.

In terms of the relative contribution of traditional and alternative risk premia, it becomes apparent that the 55/45 overall split is similar in the early part of the sample, while during the 2008–2013 period of market distress and subsequent recovery the

---

[26] The low residual correlation is predominantly driven by the Momentum strategies present in the Macro category that can take directional exposures based on sustained price moves in assets that also reflect traditional risk premia.

EXHIBIT 12.12   Factor Attribution of Hedge Fund Index Performance over Time

Period	Unexplained	Alternative Risk Premia	Traditional Risk Premia
May 2003–Apr 2008	11.53%	27.04%	27.15%
May 2008–Apr 2013	1.35%	9.52%	7.90%
May 2013–Sep 2017	4.10%	4.37%	11.89%

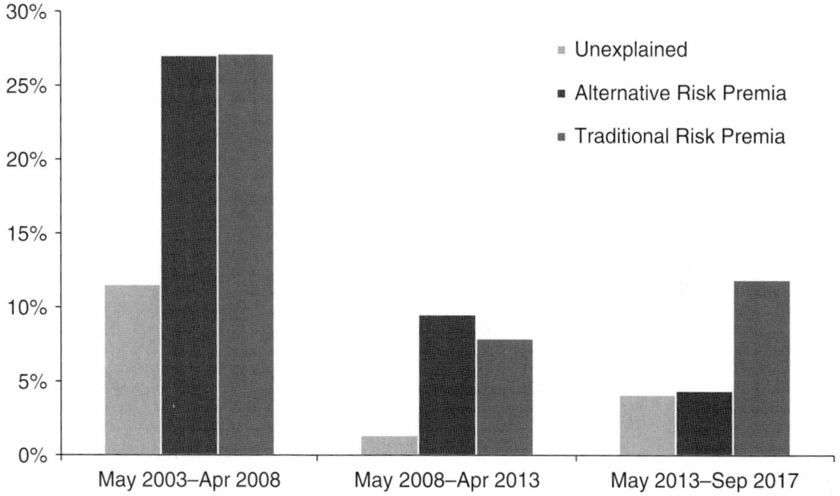

Source: Data from HFR, BarclayHedge, GSAM, as of December 2017.

contribution of alternative risk premia actually exceeded that of traditional risk premia. This further highlights the crucial role that these strategies play in understanding and emulating the returns of hedge funds. In the later part of the sample, traditional risk premia outrank alternative risk premia in their contribution to hedge fund returns because of their higher degree of directionality in this long-trending market environment.

The final part of the analysis of returns and risk of the Hedge Fund Index applies this contribution analysis to the four main hedge fund categories over the full sample period. Focusing on the contribution of unexplained returns, Exhibit 12.13 indicates that the overall return impact of unexplained returns on the hedge fund index is predominantly concentrated in the Equity Long Short and Relative Value categories. Furthermore, the exhibit points to clear disparities in terms of the contribution of traditional risk premia relative to alternative risk premia across the four hedge fund categories. Whereas Equity Long Short is the most extreme case with an approximately 85/15 split of the proportional contribution in favor of traditional risk premia, the Macro category is at the other extreme with a 95/5 split of the proportional contribution in favor of alternative risk premia relative to traditional risk premia. Compared to these extremes, Relative Value's return contribution comes out very evenly between the three components.

EXHIBIT 12.13 Factor Attribution of Hedge Fund Index Performance for Individual Hedge Fund Categories (April 2003–September 2017)

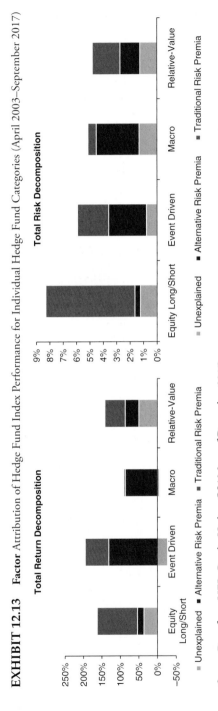

Source: Data from HFR, BarclayHedge, GSAM, as of December 2017.

The marginal contribution to risk by hedge fund category confirms the effect from the overall risk contribution analysis. Across all four categories, the relative role played by traditional risk premia to explain risk increases relative to the role played by alternative risk premia because of their higher inherent volatility. An additional noteworthy point relates to the relative proportion of volatility related to unexplained returns. Among the four categories, Relative Value turns out to have the highest proportional contribution, which hints at the complexities of identifying appropriately liquid vehicles to represent the complex and illiquid risk exposures hedge funds in this category tend to take.

V. DEVELOPMENTS IN THE HEDGE FUND INDUSTRY

We conclude with some perspectives on the hedge fund industry, in particular their fee structure and overall liquidity. We also provide a forward-looking perspective on some near-term developments for the hedge fund industry.

A. The Evolution of Hedge Fund Characteristics

Fees are at the forefront of every investor's allocation decision, particularly in relation to the performance that the corresponding investment vehicle may offer and has historically realized. The question arises to what degree fee pressures may have also found their way into the hedge fund industry.

Exhibit 12.14 focuses on the fees that hedge funds charge. Their fee structure is typically composed of an incentive fee as well as a management fee. The incentive fee is charged on the profits[27] that a hedge fund generates while the management fee is charged on the total assets under management regardless of performance.

Within the overall cross-section of hedge funds, Exhibit 12.14 takes an average over the observed fees across all hedge funds in our sample in a given year. It is therefore not necessarily a statement about the fee evolution of individual funds, but rather an assessment of the fee evolution of the overall hedge fund universe. As far back as 2009,[28] both the incentive fee and the management fee are below the popularly quoted fee structure of "2+20," referring to a management fee of 2% paired with an incentive fee of 20%. Moreover, fees have actually turned out to be on a generally downward sloping trajectory. Incentive fees have shrunk from slightly below 19% to less than 16% over the span of eight years. Management fees initially proved more

---

[27] It tends to be the case that incentive fees are associated with certain threshold conditions, so-called watermarks, and incentive fees only apply to profits that exceed these watermarks. The fee overview in Exhibit 12.14 ignores any considerations around watermarks, as the bespoke and idiosyncratic nature of watermarks presents impediments to the cross-sectional aggregation across hedge funds.

[28] The time frame is determined by our availability of point-in-time data for the fee structure of hedge funds.

EXHIBIT 12.14 Cross-Sectional Averages of Incentive and Management Fees across Hedge Funds

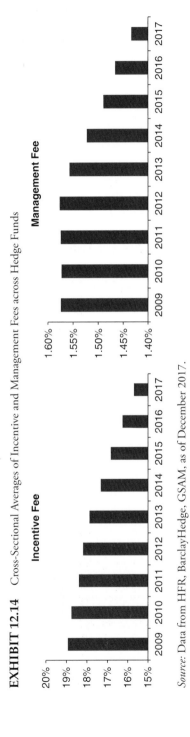

Source: Data from HFR, BarclayHedge, GSAM, as of December 2017.

resilient at levels between 155 and 160bps but have since also succumbed to fee pressure to fall below 145bps.

Overall, Exhibit 12.14 points to the existence of fee pressure for hedge funds and the end of the commonly quoted "2+20" fee structure. That said, it is worth noting that fees are still noticeably higher than the typical fees charged for, say, exchange-traded products (ETPs) that provide passive exposure to a general equity market index or even ETPs that provide investors with access to specialized portions of the fixed income market, such as convertible bonds or bank loans.

Another investor concern, among others, is the liquidity of their investment portfolio. In the context of hedge funds, we use the existence of a lock-up period as a proxy for liquidity. A lock-up period is typically imposed in order to enable hedge fund managers to make investments in illiquid assets and puts restrictions on the ability of hedge fund investors to redeem or sell their investments in hedge funds.

As is the case for Exhibit 12.14, Exhibit 12.15 also focuses on the overall cross-section of hedge funds and provides an assessment of the composition of the overall hedge fund universe instead of individual hedge funds. It displays the fraction of hedge funds that impose a lock-up period compared to all hedge funds in the universe that report in a given year. Over the span of eight years, the prevalence of lock-up periods has fallen continuously and now stands at 25%— almost 10% below the level in 2009, suggesting that there has been pressure on hedge funds overall to make adaptations to their liquidity restrictions.

EXHIBIT 12.15   Percentage of Hedge Funds with a Lock-Up Period

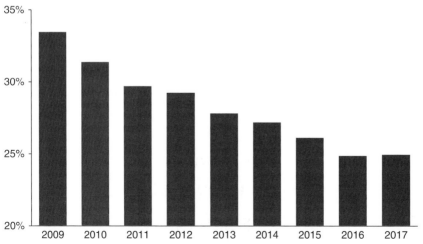

Source: Data from HFR, BarclayHedge, GSAM, as of December 2017.

B. Considerations Around the Implementation of Liquid Hedge Fund Tracking Strategies

Whereas Section V.A has focused on historic, backward-looking trends in the hedge fund industry, we now aim to provide a near-term forward-looking outlook on the hedge fund universe, both in terms of performance as well as in terms of their impact in hedge fund investors' portfolios.

In terms of performance, we actually argue to move away from a narrow focus on absolute return but advocate for a measure of risk-adjusted outperformance. Particularly given heightened fee sensitivity, hedge fund investors should at least be looking for outperformance over a fairly simplistic passive benchmark, such as a global equity market index. Because of their differing volatility levels, it is however not appropriate to compare hedge fund returns with outright returns of an equity index. Thus, we consider hedge fund returns only to the extent they outperform a beta-adjusted equity benchmark and normalize this adjusted return by the volatility of their idiosyncratic return to construct an information ratio.[29] In this sense, Exhibit 12.16 presents the risk-adjusted performance of the overall hedge fund universe compared to the global equity market, as represented by the MSCI World Net Total Return Index.

EXHIBIT 12.16   Beta-Adjusted IR of Overall Hedge Fund Studied Universe to MSCI World Index

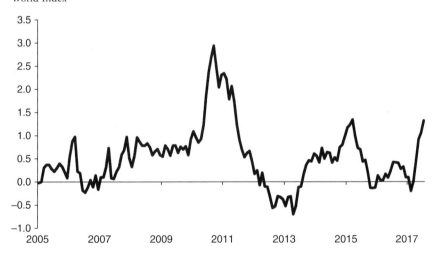

Source: Data from MSCI, HFR, BarclayHedge, GSAM, as of December 2017.

---

[29] Technically, we define the beta-adjusted IR as the annualized ratio of the intercept of a regression of the overall hedge fund index on the equity index and the standard deviation of the error term from this regression. Exhibit 12.16 displays this information ratio calculated based on a rolling 24-month window.

In line with the growth of the AUM in the overall hedge fund universe presented in Sections I and II.A, hedge funds have—after adjusting for their equity beta-generated positive value over the general global equity market over the past 10-plus years. However, it is also apparent that this outperformance has been far from uniform. In particular during late 2012 and 2013 and also intermittently in more recent years, hedge fund performance has been challenged, which may have led some to call into question the attractiveness of hedge funds as sources of alternative returns and has certainly had an impact on the fees that investors proved to be willing to pay and the liquidity restrictions they were willing to accept. However, the second half of 2017 has seen a sharp increase in the information ratio to levels above one. Historically, that puts current performance into the 10th percentile of the best performing time periods going back to 2005. If this continues, questions about the attractiveness of hedge funds should decline. Given the close co-movement between the Liquid Tracking and the Hedge Fund Index, such developments also look to be potentially beneficial for the risk-adjusted returns of access vehicles to the common systematic factor exposures of the broad universe of hedge funds.

Another noteworthy development in the hedge fund universe relates to diversification. Particularly toward the end of the studied sample period, diversification among hedge funds has increased dramatically to a level previously not seen in our sample that extends back to early 2003 (see what we refer to as "Diversification Ratio" in Exhibit 12.17). This diversification effect implies that active managers of hedge fund portfolios express more diverse views in their positions. While this effect may increase the benefits to hedge fund selection it can also increase the risks of selecting the "wrong" fund, as discussed in Section II.B. An investor that is concerned about these

EXHIBIT 12.17   Hedge Fund Volatility and Diversification

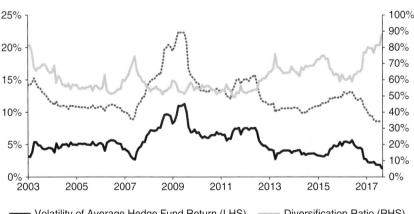

Source: Data from HFR, BarclayHedge, GSAM, as of December 2017.

types of risks might find it beneficial then to rather rely on liquid investment vehicles designed to track the returns of the hedge fund universe as a whole.

Our measure of hedge fund diversification, as displayed in Exhibit 12.17, is based on volatility comparisons. The volatility of the Hedge Fund Index is driven by the overall level of volatility of the hedge funds making up the universe as well as the degree to which these hedge funds are correlated to each other. It is apparent from the chart that hedge funds have generally become less volatile, as evidenced by the decline in the Average of Hedge Fund Volatilities. However, a comparison of the volatility of the Hedge Fund Index (referred to as "Volatility of Average Hedge Fund Return") to the Average of Hedge Fund Volatilities provides us with an indication of diversification between individual hedge fund returns. The more Volatility of Average Hedge Fund Return diverges from Average of Hedge Fund Volatilities, the greater the impact of diversification or lack of correlation. In this case, the Volatility of Average Hedge Fund Return has fallen more sharply than the Average of Hedge Fund Volatilities providing evidence for increased diversification.[30] The capability of the simulated Liquid Tracking Portfolio to approximate the returns of the hedge fund universe has however proven to be resilient to this increase in diversification, as evidenced by the 24-month correlation being with 96.1% in the 97th percentile when compared to history.

VI. CONCLUSION

This chapter discusses an alternative to hedge fund investing based on a risk-based approach that dynamically infers the exposures to traditional and alternative risk premia present in a broad and diversified universe of hedge funds. The difference between the well-defined and liquid nature of the factors and the opaqueness and illiquidity of some hedge fund investment strategies leads to a tracking error of 2.1% between the simulated Liquid Tracking Portfolio and the aggregate performance of the hedge fund universe. However, a correlation of 93.5% between the two and the fact that 84% of hedge fund returns can be captured to an almost equal degree by exposures to traditional and alternative risk premia make this methodology a viable alternative. A potential challenge to this high degree of hedge fund return attribution in the future rests on the ongoing impact of, for example, illiquidity or nonpublic aspects of stock picking. Sources of hedge fund returns like these will limit the efficacy of the proposed alternative because of the reliance on liquidity and publicly available information of this approach, although historically the impact over the past 15 years has proven to be limited.

---

[30] Technically, the "Diversification Ratio" is defined as 1 minus the ratio of the difference of the volatility of the return average and a volatility measure that assumes uncorrelated hedge fund returns to the difference of a measure that assumes perfectly correlated hedge fund returns (average of individual hedge fund volatilities) and the uncorrelated measure.

This article emphasizes the time varying nature of hedge fund positioning, as evident not only from the shifting attribution of hedge fund returns to traditional and alternative risk premia but also from the inherent dynamism of the allocations inside the alternative risk premia as well as the allocation to all risk premia. Any dynamic allocation and hedge fund positioning in particular hinges on the quality of the data to be able to monitor and assess it, which is why it is of eminent importance to have ongoing access to many and diverse sources of hedge fund information. Moreover, it is crucial to continuously enhance and refine the understanding of hedge fund investment strategies, especially through usage of alternative risk premia.

While the investment philosophy based on the identification of traditional and alternative risk premia from a broad universe of hedge fund returns is fairly unique, it generally fits into the classification of so-called "Liquid Alternative Funds" that has been created in recent years by investment research firms, such as Morningstar, Inc. As of the end of 2017, there were 640 funds with aggregate AUM of $316.8bn in this category according to an analysis based on data by Morningstar, Inc.,[31] illustrating the increased appeal of this concept to the marketplace. Over the years to come, it will be interesting to see how the interplay between hedge funds and liquid alternative funds plays out. Particularly interesting will be developments around fees, liquidity hurdles and more generally if hedge funds will be fast enough to innovate in order to generate attractive unexplained returns while an increasing amount of hedge fund know-how becomes common knowledge and finds its way into liquid alternatives funds.

* * *

Please see the Additional Disclaimers section at the end of this book.

---

[31] The aggregate of 640 funds is decomposed of 551 funds across 17 different categories that Morningstar, Inc. categorizes as liquid alternatives as well as 89 funds in the Nontraditional Bond category, which contains many funds that qualify as alternative strategies. See the Goldman Sachs Asset Management publication Liquid Alternative Investments MAPS Year End 2017.

PART VI

ASSET OWNER
PERSPECTIVES

CHAPTER **13**

IMPLEMENTING SMART BETA AT CALPERS, A CONVERSATION WITH

Steve Carden
Investment Director, Global
Equities, California Public
Employees Retirement System

Thank you, Steve, for speaking with us today. To start, tell us what was the motivation at CalPERS for considering smart beta investing?
You know, at the outset we were not thinking in terms of smart beta or factor investing. Initially, we were mostly interested in addressing what we perceived to be potential inefficiencies of capitalization-weighting. In particular, we believe that, although markets are generally efficient, mispricings do occur and that capitalization-weighting is a trend-following strategy, which may lead to a systematic overweighting of overvalued stocks and underweighting of undervalued stocks. We also believe that mispricings ultimately correct, which causes medium- to long-term mean reversion in prices and valuations. We were looking for ways to exploit that mean reversion. So, when fundamental indexation was introduced, we viewed it as a reasonable way of implementing a mean reversion strategy. Therefore, we invested in a customized version of that index in 2006. That really was the beginning of our smart beta investing endeavors, although I am not sure that the term smart beta was coined at that time. We probably were thinking more in terms of an alternative beta strategy, focusing on mean reversion.

How did you move from an alternative beta perspective to more of a focus toward factor investing?
So, we implemented the fundamental indexation concept for about four or five years before we did anything else in this space. During this implementation phase, we also

gained a better understanding of the sources that drive the excess returns of this strategy. We realized that fundamental indexation gave us a high exposure to the value factor, which in turn largely explained its performance relative to the market. To the extent that we did not seek an explicit exposure to value, the question for us was whether we were comfortable with the implicit value exposure. I think it would be fair to say that, in general, we all believe in the value factor premium. Also, value investing is consistent with our core investment beliefs and the long-term investment horizon we generally adopt. As such, we accepted the value exposure we got through fundamental indexation. But, at the same time, we experienced the cyclicality of value returns and started asking ourselves whether we can do better. That is, diversify the value exposure, while retaining the best aspects of it. And then that's really the time when factor investing became at the forefront of our minds. For example, we started thinking about momentum as historically a good way to diversify the value exposure.

As kind of a parallel to that we were also thinking about low-volatility investing at the plan level. Specifically, how can we use the low-volatility anomaly, however you want to describe it, as a source of alpha for our global equity portfolio? Can we improve the information ratio of our overall portfolio using that type of strategy? Knowing that it's not going to get a lot of drawdown protection, but within a certain level of risk such a strategy may serve as a diversifier to what we already have and improve portfolio performance.

But as we worked through these various factors, low volatility, momentum, and then ultimately quality, it really kind of came together organically without a final goal of having a diversified factor portfolio, initially. But, over time, it led in that direction. So, in terms of the evolution of our portfolio, we started with fundamental indexation in 2006, then we implemented a volatility reduction strategy in 2013, momentum in 2014, and finally quality in 2016. And now we are at point where we have all these different factors or the ability to get exposure to them, and our focus has shifted toward how to efficiently blend them. That is, how do we use these factor portfolios and the smart beta lever to improve the overall holistic portfolio?

Over time, it seems that CalPERS has moved from a strong philosophical belief in value to more of a factor diversification approach. Did you become more philosophically comfortable with the other factors, or was it just to manage risk through factor diversification?

Maybe a little bit of both. At the outset, as I mentioned, we had this value exposure through fundamental indexation. And we wanted to diversify that exposure. That's where momentum and quality came in. But, we also had to feel comfortable with the alpha-generating capability of these factors. That is, believe in the existence and persistence of their excess returns.

But from a broader risk management perspective, and as a background, I should also mention that we were going through an evolution within the Global Equity

Team in identifying unintended risks that existed in our legacy portfolio. And as we identified those, we started to see some of the more prominent exposures kind of flesh out, such as, the factors, which are easier to see. We then started asking ourselves is this an avenue we want to go down where we do focus on the factors in order to reduce noise within the overall portfolio. Is factor investing the next evolution of beta where this is a better way of harvesting that equity risk premium than the cap-weighted approach? And so, I think as we started to think about it more, we probably gained more conviction in pursuing factor investing.

The various factor strategies are implemented internally at CalPERS. Could you explain what drove the decision to develop significant internal implementation capabilities?
Maybe it was luck on the part of CalPERS and maybe a gift from BGI. When BGI closed its Sacramento office, there was a lot of local talent that suddenly became available to CalPERS. Specifically, investment professionals who had managed lots of index fund accounts for BGI mostly on the international side. At that time, CalPERS had internal domestic capabilities only. When Dan Bienvenue, our Head of Global Equities, joined CalPERS, it was partly with the mandate to bring in the international passive management. So, the BGI situation created an opportunity to hire a lot of very talented people with considerable experience in international equities and building very strong internal execution capabilities. From that point forward, we have adopted a structure, in which systematic strategies offered by asset managers are delivered in the form of a model portfolio to our index calculation agent, who then delivers a custom index to CalPERS, which is replicated internally much like replicating a market index. This gives us a hybrid implementation model, which combines active and index management, for implementing external strategies.

So now we're at a point where whatever it is we want to do, whatever type of strategy, we ask ourselves the following.

- Is it something that we want to build soup to nuts and implement internally?
- Is it something where we're better off sourcing a model portfolio from an external manager and then implementing internally?
- Or is it something where really the source of alpha and how it's linked to the trading function is something where you can't really break those links?

So, the implementation decision becomes flexible, and we can focus on the investment process and other characteristics of considered strategies.

All the Smart Beta strategies you currently invest in are sourced in the form of a model portfolio/custom index and implemented in house. Is that correct?
Correct.

You trade them at the same time?
Yes.

So, you have a lot of crossing and netting of trades going on.
True.

How much turnover reduction do you typically achieve through this process?
The turnover reduction hasn't changed because we implement them as individual portfolios. But the cost of that turnover, if that's what you are asking, is significantly lower. At the time of our rebalances, trade netting takes place across the smart beta portfolios, but a lot of it is also netting or crossing with the Index Fund. Generally speaking, it is not unusual to see 50% cross at any given rebalance. However, a lot of it also depends on the money flows. If funds are not going into a smart beta product or coming out of a smart beta product, then the cross is lower, typically in the 30% to 40% range.

What other cost savings do you realize in this hybrid implementation structure?
Generally, it is, of course, much cheaper for us to implement the model portfolios in-house compared to paying an external manager for implementation in a typical separate mandate. Also, internal implementation is highly scalable. We have been able to grow this function considerably without having to increase headcount in any meaningful way.

Also, when we source the model portfolios from external managers, we pay them licensing fees. These fees tend to be a lot closer to index management fees than they are to even low-fee active management.

How do you go about selecting a smart beta product? What guidance can you provide to the readers of this book in this regard?
This is an important question. As you know, the large number of product offerings in the smart beta space can be overwhelming for most investors, including us. In my opinion, one useful approach is to gain clarity upfront on the motivation for considering smart beta or factor investing and identifying upfront what manager and strategy characteristics are important or even critical. And to have that motivation and characteristics drive product screening and selection.

At CalPERS, we view institutional robustness, ability to deliver on the hybrid implementation model, and transparency of the investment process as key features that drive manager and product selection. Given the large account sizes we typically allocate, the requirement of institutional robustness is obvious.

From an implementation perspective, if a firm really hasn't been in the business of producing model portfolios, whether they've been licensing them or not, then it gives me pause. In addition to that, they have to be willing to work with index providers where they can deliver the model portfolio in a robust, timely manner so that we actually get a decent transfer coefficient out of whatever research they've done. So that's more on the business side. I should also mention that early on when we first started talking about doing the model licensing, there were a number of asset managers that weren't comfortable with that business model. Some expressed legal concerns about front running and fairness and that sort of thing. And some of the managers just flat out said, "We're not ready for that" or "We're not interested." Fast-forward a few years, they're calling us back saying, "We're ready now." So, I would say that, in terms of partnering with CalPERS, there's been a first mover advantage to firms that really embraced the new implementation model early on. This implementation model probably doesn't work for a lot of asset owners. But because CalPERS is the size it is and has developed significant internal capabilities over the years, it's made sense for us. And we've been able to get others in the market to join us in that kind of partnership.

In terms of the investment process and the strategy itself, transparency is key. We have to be able to fully understand the investment process and be able to communicate it to senior management. Ultimately, we also have to be able to get our consultants on board with understanding it. Not that we need them to sign off in order to do it but at some point, it's going to be reported to the board. And if the consultants don't have good transparency and it's hard for the board to understand, then there's probably not going to be enough credibility to pursue the strategy.

So, we generally consider highly reputable firms, with good histories, deep benches of talent on the research side, and who send people out who can explain in a clear way what it is that they're trying to accomplish. This helps to reinforce the message that staff is sending upward. That kind of a strategic partner is important to us. And we've had that with many firms, such as, Research Affiliates and Goldman Sachs.

CalPERS has developed some smart beta strategies in-house, and some other large asset owners are also developing strategies or at least thinking of developing strategies in-house. Where does this trend go in the long run? Is the objective that all smart beta strategies be internally developed and managed? And is that something that offers an advantage, in your opinion?
I don't think it offers an advantage. In fact, we have never expressed it as a goal that all smart beta strategies be internally developed.

In some areas, such as implementation, execution, and trading, we feel relatively comfortable. These areas allow us to benefit from scale and result in other cost savings. But in other areas, such as the frontend research function, we are not going to be able to compete as effectively with some other firms. As you well know, CalPERS' ability to create positions, hire and retain talent is challenged by being a state agency, a government institution. And even if we could compete in this area, it still would only represent the equivalent of one firm. Why would we limit ourselves to that? Why not take advantage of the talent that's available from multiple firms? So, I believe it's in our best interest to continue to outsource a lot of the work we do, and not pretend that we can efficiently do everything ourselves.

For example, when we were considering momentum, we evaluated many external strategies as well as internal capabilities. And we determined that the best path was to partner with an external manager that offered an insightful product to capture the momentum factor. With regard to quality, we determined that an internal product was better suited to our specific needs. And right now we're evaluating how to complement fundamental indexation with a more pure value portfolio. We're lining up multiple providers as well as an internal strategy. In this case, it is likely that we will consider investing in a combination of internal and external strategies. But, in terms of manager selection, as I mentioned previously, we are also likely to work with larger firms that have considerable research and product development capabilities and that can serve as a strategic partner to CalPERS. These firms must also have robust operations, because one or two mistakes in this space and we'd probably lose the credibility to do the entire smart beta program.

In terms of research and product development, what is the current focus of your smart beta program?

In our evolution, we are at a stage where we are saying, okay, regardless of where we source the smart beta strategies from, what is the best way to bring them together? What is the best way to mix factors? We realize that there's a required skill there, too. And we ought to be looking at how we do that versus how other organizations do it. Some firms, such as GSAM, EDHEC and others, have acquired considerable expertise in this area and have a robust platform of multifactor strategies and a good way of bringing them together. Those should be our peers for what we do internally. And if we can't show that we're competitive in doing that, then we should also perhaps outsource those decisions. For example, maybe we identify external managers that each do a good job in the allocation decision amongst factors and also have a good lineup of factor portfolios, and then we diversify that effort among two or three managers.

What is the sizing of the Smart Beta Program right now?

As of December 2017, we have in the region of US$23 billion invested across the various smart beta strategies, which represents roughly 15% of our global equity portfolio.

Is that the strategic allocation to smart beta in the long run?

You know, we don't have a strategic allocation. It's just been the case where we've grown a lot in this space. I believe our smart beta allocation has almost doubled in the last four to five years. And we've also at the same time culled our external active manager lineup. So, we have fewer accounts but each one is more meaningful. These are generally higher conviction managers. And that's a set of managers and strategies that we're comfortable with.

At this point, we're comfortable with where we are with Smart Beta. For us now the question is: Should we start taking more risk or tracking error in our smart beta strategies, perhaps at the expense of the index exposure or passive management, which represents about two-thirds of the portfolio? There are a lot of other initiatives and efforts happening at CalPERS that aren't necessarily distracting us from answering that question but maybe are bigger questions, more important things to answer right now. For instance, how we look at allocating across asset classes. There are a lot of resources going into that, and that's a big question.

So, I think smart beta at CalPERS is in a stabilization and monitoring phase. We've rolled out the factor portfolios over the years, each one in and of itself had to look like a good standalone strategy, had to not degrade the IR of the Global Equity portfolio, had some requirements in that way. But now that we have each of the pieces and we can blend them, I think each one individually can take more risk, can look more like pure value, more like pure quality, and so forth, because now we can offset them. We can be more explicit about what exposures we want as long as we understand how those exposures work together. In this regard, one of the concerns also is the situation where the low correlation across factors breaks down. Perhaps such episodes or events aren't being seen and aren't fully understood with respect to factor investing. So, I take a little pause in terms of putting more money into smart beta until we better understand factor interactions under stress conditions and their impact on performance.

Was the doubling of the allocation to smart beta partly driven by disappointment with active management?

Not disappointment, but I think better understanding of what we're getting from active management. And also the evolution of the industry, where we went from just the market beta plus error term forty years ago to something like Fama French factors breaking out expected returns, to today where we look at all the smart beta factors, strip that out of the return stream, and then what is left over is true alpha. We get that alpha from active management. We don't need to get factor returns from active management. And we don't want to pay for static factor exposure; we don't want to pay active fees for that.

You know, true alpha is not common. But, there are managers who have shown skill to identify it and deliver it efficiently through activities, such as stock picking or factor timing. Those are the kind of processes we can't implement passively. So, we outsource and pay active fees. But, we don't want to outsource factor exposures to active management. We can strip those out and go the smart beta route for all the identifiable exposures that we want to maintain strategically and structurally over time.

In assessing true alpha, what factor portfolios do you use to conduct a return and risk decomposition?

For now we use Barra. I am not sure if that is the ideal way of doing this, but we view the Barra risk factors as generic factors. And so, we risk decompose contributions from the various Barra factors to each of the strategies. And we do that on the attribution side, too, to determine where the contributions are coming from. Is it stock-specific? Is it styles? Is it countries or industries, etc.?

But, I'll tell you my prior is that most of that is not going to matter and we'll probably end up with directionally a desire to get strategic exposure to certain factors that we think carry a premium. What the factor premiums will be in the long term is unknown, though we believe they'll persist.

What is your view on factor timing?
In the conventional factor timing sense, I think it detracts from those long-term premiums. But, it's something I want to better understand. However, medium-term mean reversion in factor premiums may offer an opportunity, such as, when we've captured a premium well above what we would expect. For instance, value at the end of 2016 was at a point historically where I hadn't seen our since inception performance on the value strategies ever being that strong. And so, you ask yourself, well, have we captured the majority of the value premium that this cycle was going to pay? And if so, do we want to maybe bring down our exposure? That kind of opportunistic rebalancing might be within reach for us, but maybe not true factor timing.

You've been implementing smart beta for over a decade. How do you evaluate the smart beta program? Relative to the objective set out at the start, how has it done?
There are so many moving parts in our overall portfolio that it's really hard to answer that question. Also, recall that our initial objective in 2006 was just to implement a mean reversion strategy. We haven't had what I would consider a comprehensive and fully fleshed smart beta program until we launched quality a year and a half ago.

So, we haven't looked at it as an isolated program where we can measure the performance and efficacy of the smart beta book. There hasn't been a smart beta book. However, what I've asked the team to do is to look at the performance of the products we implemented throughout the entire period of time since 2006, assuming we don't have a view on whether value works better in the US versus EM or DM. So, we built some composites, region-neutral theoretical composites of our actual strategies. We then combined them using the weighting scheme that we currently consider, and if we had done that over this full period of time, what would it look like?

So, we have three regional composites: US, Developed ex-US, and Emerging Markets, that have each of the four factor strategies we pursue and weighted over time using our current weighting scheme. The historical performance of these composites provides support for value added from our smart beta strategies. It improved the information ratio, both in terms of the alpha and the risk reduction. So, it's been a better way to harvest the equity risk premium. Better than index, of course, and also better than our legacy active book. This exercise gives us confidence that we are on the right path.

What kind of challenges did you face along the way with the board, the internal committees, and so on?
Well, I think we've been really lucky in terms of our ability to do this. Under the delegated authority that the staff has, we haven't needed board approval to do this work.

But, if we screw it up then we'll lose that ability. Back in 2006, when we did the RAFI strategy, that was a time when we did go to the board for approval of this type of initiative. However, presenting it as a mean reversion strategy for the purposes of capturing any inefficiency in the cap-weighted index wasn't met with resistance. We ran that for four or five years before we did anything else in this space. Then we slowly went into the other factors. And now that's not something for which we need board approval. It's something that we were able to do simply with approval from the Head of Equities.

In terms of governance, who has responsibility for the smart beta program?
Well, at CalPERS, it's not really a program per se; it's not independent like that. It's a piece of the holistic portfolio view. But in terms of governance, the way we decide how much to put into smart beta, or any other strategy, that decision is made by our Capital Allocation Committee. This committee meets once a month. It makes decisions about all the different products and strategies. And then, of course, we have an oversight team that monitors month-to-month all of the strategies, whether they're actual segregated mandates or the smart beta hybrid implementation model or even the index funds. So that's just part of our normal governance.

You have acquired significant experience in designing and implementing smart beta. What guidance would you provide to investors who are now considering smart beta investing?
First, I would say keep it simple and make sure you fully understand what you are doing. This is the reason why we place so much emphasis on the transparency of the investment process. We hesitate to work with firms that are unwilling to provide that required level of transparency. In addition to transparency, it is also the ability to take something that could be very complex and distilling it down into something that's easier to understand and, almost more importantly, easier to communicate, because there are constituencies that are going to need to know this. This is one of the reasons why we value our strategic partnership with certain firms. They provide access to talented people who have this ability to communicate complex ideas in simple, easy-to-understand terms. Unlike CalPERS, I'm sure a lot of the asset owners do need to go to their boards for permission to do this sort of thing. If they can't even explain it to their peers among staff, how are they going to be able to get buy in from the board? I think that would be very challenging. So, I would say that, in working with our strategic partners, it has been highly beneficial for me to be able to fully understand the approach and communicate that to my manager to get sign off. Simplicity, transparency, and ability to communicate are very critical, in my opinion.

The next thing I would say in terms of guidance is for folks not to expect too much from smart beta. In my mind, it's not a broad replacement for active management. I haven't come to a conclusion whether it's a replacement for a piece of the beta or a piece of the alpha; it's probably some combination of both. But, I think asset owners have to be honest about their ability to identify skilled managers, on an ex ante basis. If somebody thinks that they can't identify skilled active managers, then yes, wipe that out and just do smart beta. But if they think or they still like the challenge of trying to identify skilled active managers, then don't expect smart beta to take the place of that. Don't assume that active management doesn't have something to offer above and beyond the factor exposures.

Then, beware of crowding. I don't have a real good feel for exactly when something's too crowded, but I do have an intuition around it. If I'm hearing about something becoming very popular, I get nervous. It is not clear to me how to quantify crowding. People look at the valuation levels of smart beta strategies, for example. But, crowding to me means it gets more and more expensive to get the trade done. It means when things start to unravel, there are a lot of people heading for the exits at the same time. We want to be trying to get out a different door. For us, all this means that we should be trying to gain the same general exposure to a factor but do it in a different way. Smart beta has gotten very popular. And as a market competitor, I would like other investors to pile into the off-the-shelf products. And we will try to do something different. To further elaborate on this point, we do measure valuations of various public indexes published by the index providers. And then, using the same measurement technique, we also measure the valuations of what we've built or what we've sourced from our model providers. And it's oftentimes fairly different. For instance, when we launched quality, every source we could find said quality is very expensive. And we said, okay, we'd better take a look for our own product. And for our own product we were actually moderately cheap relative to its history. That gives us confidence that yes, we're chasing the same general exposure but we're coming at it form an angle that's different enough that we're not going to be impacted by crowding as much. So, again, in terms of potential guidance, I would suggest to investors that they should consider unique, customized smart beta solutions as much as possible. The idea is to be different, while achieving the same general goal. Then, regardless of whether or not we can measure crowding, we can perhaps mitigate it to some extent.

Finally, I would say choose your managers/partners carefully. I have talked a lot about our desire and ability to work with strategic partners, whether they're managers or model providers. Partners that give us the transparency we seek, but also have conservative expectations and conservative assumptions in the work they're doing. I want the model providers to be telling us to be realistic about what can be achieved from smart beta. And not just sell us high backtested IRs. We like working with folks who are humble, legitimately. We think we talk to enough folks on the outside, such as managers, researchers, and so forth that we can usually see whether or not somebody thinks they have the next best thing or that they're still asking themselves all the right questions. Folks that have enough integrity to accept if the value proposition behind their smart beta approach starts to diminish, if it's arbitraged away, whatever it is, that they would come to us and say, "Hey, we don't think this is going to pay off for you in the future." And those types of shops, I think, will also come to us with maybe some forward-looking solutions that could replace it, but have the willingness and also maybe the breadth to do that, as opposed to being a one-trick pony where it's like they couldn't come to us and say maybe you shouldn't do this because it's all their business. We value integrity and choose our partners carefully.

Steve, thank you again for taking the time to speak with us today.

On behalf of Ho Ho and Sin Sai Vang, my former and current colleagues who helped build our smart beta platform, thank you for giving us the opportunity to share our perspectives and our story with your readers.

CHAPTER 14

A PENSION FUND'S JOURNEY TO FACTOR INVESTING: A CASE STUDY

Hans de Ruiter

Chief Investment Officer,
Stichting Pensioenfonds TNO
Associate Professor,
Vrije Universiteit Amsterdam

I. INTRODUCTION

It was in 2014 that pension fund TNO (corporate pension plan for the TNO company, a Dutch organization for applied scientific research) started its smart beta equity project. Up till that point, the equity investments were passively managed through traditional index funds. This project was an interesting journey, which provided us with new insights and that finally led to the appointment of two smart beta managers in 2015. Along the way we had to find answers to various questions relating to smart beta strategies, but also relating to the way we used to invest. We did this journey together with the board. At the start of the journey we asked ourselves why we invest the way we do (passively through traditional index funds), and what new insights would lead us to question this approach. This is discussed in Section II. We also asked ourselves the question whether smart beta strategies would be superior relative to our current way of investing, and if so, under what circumstances would that be the case? This is dealt with in Section III. Finally, there were various practical challenges we had to deal with, which are discussed in Section IV. We end this chapter in Section V with the main conclusions.

II.   THE CASE FOR PASSIVE MARKET CAP–WEIGHTED STRATEGIES

Both academics and practitioners have spent a lot of time and effort in understanding the drivers of stock returns. The oldest and most well-known model for describing stock returns is the Capital Asset Pricing Model (CAPM), developed in the 1960s by Sharpe, Lintner, and Mossin. The model is built on the mean-variance portfolio theory of Markowitz. Assuming investors are rational mean-variance optimizers, they will allocate their money between two assets: the risk-free asset and the market port-folio. If we would limit ourselves to the stock market, the market portfolio represents the market cap–weighted composite of the total equity market. The implication of the insight that investors will hold perfectly diversified portfolios of risky assets is that investors will only be compensated for bearing systematic risk. The systematic risk is measured by the stock's beta (β), which measures a stock's sensitivity to the market. The relationship between a stock's realized return and its beta can be written as:

$$R_i = R_f + \beta_i \left(R_m - R_f \right) + e_i \qquad (14.1)$$

with R_i, R_f, and R_m being the return of respectively stock i, the risk-free asset and the market. The last term, e_i is a residual with $E(e_i) = 0$. Along the same lines the risk of stock i can be decomposed into a systematic component and an idiosyncratic component.

$$\sigma_i = \beta_i \sigma_m + \sigma \left(e_i \right) \qquad (14.2)$$

According to the CAPM theory the last term in Equation (14.2) will vanish to zero if the number of securities in the portfolio becomes sufficiently large.

Based on the insights of the CAPM theory, passive index investing gained a lot of popularity in the 1970s. If investors are not expected to be compensated for bearing idiosyncratic risk, the best recipe is to hold the market cap–weighted index portfolio (popular examples include the MSCI indices and the S&P 500 index).

Even though early studies on the empirical validity of the CAPM provided only weak support for the beta as being the sole relevant risk factor, it did not prevent investors from adopting the market cap–weighted index as the prime benchmark for their equity investments.

Apart from academic considerations, there are good practical considerations for doing so. First, the market cap–weighted index is the most cost-efficient passive benchmark. This is the result of the fact that it is skewed toward large cap stocks for which trading costs are low, and also because the market cap–weighted index entails a buy-and-hold strategy. Alternative passive strategies contain an element of rebalancing, and therefore incur trading costs.

Second, for most market cap–weighted indices a liquid derivatives market is available which facilitates efficient portfolio management. From a practical point of view that is a relevant consideration.

Third, in practice it is hard to find active managers that are able to outperform the market cap–weighted indices on a persistent basis, which makes market cap–weighted indices a logical starting point and benchmark for equity investors.

And fourth, the market cap–weighted index is the only macroconsistent investment, meaning that it is the only portfolio that all investors can hold (Bender et al. 2013).

In spite of its practical appeal, market cap–weighted buy-and-hold indices have been attacked by a new strand of strategies, which are labeled smart beta strategies. As the name suggests, proponents of smart beta strategies hold the view that market cap–weighted indices are inefficient strategies. They may be inefficient for a number of reasons:

1. market cap–weighted indices are trend-following strategies, which means that over time they will overweight overvalued stocks and underweight undervalued stocks, making them more vulnerable to market shocks;

2. market cap–weighted indices tend to be less diversified and skewed toward the stocks with the largest market capitalization;

3. market cap–weighted indices do not explicitly account for all the risk factors that have been found to explain the cross-section variation in stock returns, for example, value, size, and momentum.

The next section discusses the view we have developed at pension fund TNO with regard to smart beta strategies.

III.   ARE SMART BETA STRATEGIES THE BETTER ALTERNATIVE?

In the well-known study by Ang et al. (2009) for the Norwegian Reserve Fund, it was found that most of the added value of the active equity managers could be explained by implicit exposures to systematic factors. Their recommendation was to adopt factor investing in the investment process: allocate risk capital to proven factors in a top-down fashion. Other studies showed that multiple factors were able to explain cross-sectional differences in returns over time, next to the market factor. Based on the available academic research there were good reasons to take a closer look at the added value of smart beta strategies. When we started looking at smart beta strategies we established a list of three critical questions that needed to be answered. These three questions were the following:

1. Which factors qualify for inclusion in a smart beta strategy? What are the relevant criteria?

2. Do smart beta strategies perform better than market cap–weighted buy-and-hold index strategies, and if so do they outperform both on a short-term and long-term basis?

3. If smart beta strategies outperform market cap–weighted buy-and-hold index strategies, what are the sources of their excess returns?

In the next three sections these three questions will be addressed.

A. Factors That Qualify for Inclusion in a Smart Beta Strategy

With regard to the first questions we have, based on the existing literature, we developed four criteria for determining which factors are eligible for inclusion in a smart beta strategy. These criteria are:

1. Factors need to be economically sensible (there must be a good reason why the factor should offer a persistent premium);
2. Factor returns must be persistent and pervasive (the factor return does exist for a long time period, and the factor return has not disappeared after it was documented in the academic literature);
3. Factor returns must be robust (the factor return has been documented for different regions and countries; if the factor return does also hold for other asset classes this would also contribute to the factor's robustness; the factor return should not significantly change with small changes in the factor definitions); and
4. It must be possible to capture the factor return in a cost-efficient way.

Using these four criteria the number of eligible factors comes down significantly. Harvey et al. (2016) examined 315 factors from top journal articles and working papers. They found that most of the 315 factors that have been discovered in the academic literature do not pass the test when using the four criteria mentioned earlier. Their results corroborate the findings of Van Gelderen and Huij (2014) who found that the most successful equity managers in the US for the period 1990–2010 are those who have adopted factor investing strategies with exposure to factors that fulfill the earlier mentioned four criteria.

Based on our own analysis the factors that are most notable in the academic literature and that fit the four criteria are the following:

1. The Market factor, represented by the CAPM beta;
2. The Value factor, represented by the price-to-earnings ratio (Basu, 1977), the price-to-book ratio (Fama and French, 1992); in general, low valuation stocks outperform high valuation stocks;
3. The Size factor, represented by the market capitalization of a stock (Banz, 1981; Fama and French, 1992); in general, small cap stocks outperform large cap stocks;
4. The Momentum factor, represented by the total return of a stock over the past twelve months (Jegadeesh and Titman, 1993; Carhart, 1997); in general stocks with a high return over the past 12 months outperform stocks with a low total return over the past 12 months;
5. The Volatility factor, represented by the volatility of the stock's return over the past period (Haugen and Baker, 1991; Clarke et al., 2006); in general stocks with a low return volatility outperform stocks with a high return volatility; and

6. The Quality factor, for example, represented by the firm's profitability (Novy-Marx, 2013); in the academic literature there is a vast amount of characteristics that fit the Quality factor description; in general high-quality stocks outperform low-quality stocks.

The six factors have been tested extensively in the academic literature and their existence has proven to be persistent and robust. Even if we control for the other factors, these factors show a significant added value.

B. The Performance of Smart Beta Strategies

Chow et al. (2011) have analyzed the performance of different smart beta strategies for both the US stock market and the Global stock market. For the US they have studied the period 1964–2012 and for the Global stock market they have used the period 1991–2012.

The first conclusion that follows from their study is that all their smart beta strategies outperform the market cap–weighted buy-and-hold index (MSCI World Index). The largest outperformance is realized by the Fundamental Weighting (Fundamental Indexing) strategy; the performance of the Diversity Weighting strategy and the Maximum Diversification strategy is only slightly better than the MSCI World Index. Except for the Diversity Weighting strategy, all smart beta strategies have higher Sharpe ratios than the MSCI World. If we would perceive smart beta strategies as active strategies, the information ratio would be a valid measure. Based on the information ratio, the heuristic-based weighting strategies seem to do a better job as an active strategy than the optimization-based weighting strategies. This is caused by the relatively high tracking errors for the minimum variance and maximum diversification strategies.

The results for the US are in line with the results for the Global strategies. Like the Global strategies, all US smart beta strategies outperform the market cap–weighted buy-and-hold index (S&P 500). However, the outperformance for the US strategies is more significant.

Arnott et al. (2005) have studied the risk-return characteristics of a set of fundamental factors (Book Value, Income, Revenue, Sales, Dividends, and Employment) and a composite (similar to what Fundamental Index strategies do). Their study was confined to the US stock market (Russell 1000 Index constituents), covering the period 1962–2004. Their study shows that all fundamental index strategies outperform the S&P 500 and the Russell 1000. The smart beta strategies also report better Sharpe ratios. The same is true for the information ratio; all information ratios are statistically significant. In Arnott et al. (2013) the analyses are expanded to 2012 and to the Global stock market. The results in this paper confirm the results of earlier studies.

To check the robustness of their results, Arnott, Hsu, and Moore split their sample in five 10-year periods. Their results appear to be rather stable, with the exception of the 1990s. That period was dominated by the mega-cap companies; in addition to that the second half of the 1990s was dominated by the so-called TMT (Technology-Media-Telecom) stocks that had high valuations based on high expectations regarding future growth. However, this was not yet visible in the current fundamentals. In times like the 1990s one would expect smart beta strategies to underperform market-cap weighted indices.

Koedijk et al. (2013) have analyzed the size of a set of factor premiums for both the US and Europe. The factors they have looked at were Market (beta), Size, Value, Momentum, and Low Volatility. Their findings corroborate the results of earlier studies: all fundamental factor premiums in their study are higher than the return of the market cap–weighted index.

Although the previous studies are just a snapshot of all available empirical studies with regard to smart beta strategies, they provide a fair representation of the vast body of empirical research. What these studies show is that various forms of smart beta strategies outperform their market cap–weighted buy-and-hold counterparts over the long run. What is not clear yet is the behavior of smart beta strategies over the short run. If smart beta strategies may underperform market cap–weighted indices with a large margin over a three- to five-year period, this may be regarded an unacceptable risk for a pension fund. Therefore, it is important to have some insight into the behavior of smart beta strategies over shorter time periods.

Several studies have shown that factor returns are cyclical and can underperform the passive buy-and-hold cap-weighted index for three- to five-year periods (e.g. Bender et al. 2013). That may be a challenge for pension funds since for the average pension fund board three to five years is a long time. There are at least two things a pension fund can do to deal with the short-term risk of factor strategies. Most importantly, instead of focusing on one or two factors, it is better to build a portfolio with a diversified exposure to multiple factors. Given that factor returns are not perfectly correlated, this may lead to a more stable return and a smaller risk of a longer-term underperformance relative to a cap-weighted benchmark. This was the choice we made at pension fund TNO. In addition to that it is important to embed the smart beta concept within the investment beliefs of the pension fund. This is discussed in Section III.C.

C. Explanations for the Factor Returns and Their Practical Relevance

Although all smart beta strategies contradict the validity of the CAPM, they do not necessarily agree on the sources of the excess returns relative to the market cap–weighted indices. Essentially there are two schools of thought in explaining the excess returns.

The first school assumes that markets are informationally efficient and investors are rational. Therefore, the excess returns that can be gained by having different risk exposures than the market cap–weighted index are simply a compensation for risk.

The other school claims that markets are informationally inefficient and investors are subject to behavioral biases. To the extent that these behavioral biases are persistent, this leads to mispricing of stocks from which one may profit by having a strategy that tilts toward stocks with specific characteristics.

To some extent this seems an academic debate, however, it can also have practical relevance. In case the excess returns reflect a compensation for risk, the probability that it will sustain in the future is high. However, when excess returns reflect a mispricing it could evaporate in the future once discovered by "smart investors." This does not necessarily need to happen. From behavioral finance studies we know that people in general are rather consistent in their inconsistencies and biases. If people are confronted with their mistakes, it does not automatically mean that people will change their behavior accordingly. To (mis)quote John Legend, it is sometimes hard for human beings to withstand their "perfect imperfections." Against this backdrop one could expect excess returns to sustain in the future, even if they are rooted in mispricing of stocks.

At pension fund TNO we are agnostic with regard to the explanation of the factor returns. There is enough academic research available to support either view. We do not think that we have the final answer in this debate. We also think that it does not make a lot of difference for the efficacy of smart beta strategies. Even if the behavioral explanation would be correct, we hold the view that human behavior is rather persistent, also in its behavioral imperfections.

What is important, though, is that the belief that a long-term exposure to factors pays off in the form of a positive return is sufficiently embedded in the investment belief of the pension fund. We have spent a lot of time with the board to discuss the characteristics of smart beta strategies and also the reasons why these strategies are expected to contribute to a better return. A good understanding of these strategies is of critical importance, especially at times when performance is lacking, which may happen now and then. When equities underperform bonds for a few years, nobody would propose to move out of equities and invest the money in bonds. That is because everybody—at least the pension funds in The Netherlands—understands that having a long-term exposure to equities contributes to the return of the fund and is necessary for realizing the long-term pension ambition. The same belief is needed for smart beta strategies, and that requires a good fundamental understanding of these strategies by the board. If that is not in place, the fund runs the risk that it may not reap the long-term fruits of this strategy.

IV.   PRACTICAL CONSIDERATIONS

After the discussions with the board and the embedding of our views regarding the long-term factor returns in our investment beliefs, we had to solve a number of practical issues. The first issue was portfolio construction, in particular the factor allocation of the portfolio and the risk constraints imposed. This is discussed in Section IV.A. A second issue is the choice of a proper benchmark. Although there are various factor benchmarks available in the market, there is still not a *communis opinio* about what constitutes a proper factor benchmark. This topic is dealt with in Section IV.B. A last point we had to address was the impact of costs on the strategy and portfolio construction. Relative to the passive buy-and-hold cap-weighted index approach there are incremental transaction costs and fees that need to be taken into account. This is addressed in Section IV.C.

A. Portfolio Construction

A proper portfolio construction methodology requires at least a clear definition of the objective function of the investor. With regard to smart beta strategies an investor can, *grosso modo*, choose between two approaches. In the first approach, the absolute risk-return approach, smart beta strategies are considered as an enhanced passive equity strategy and therefore the objective function can be formulated in terms of absolute risk and absolute return (Sharpe ratio). In the second approach, the relative risk-return approach, smart beta strategies are seen as active equity strategies, and therefore the objective function should be formulated in terms of relative risk and relative return (Information ratio). At pension fund TNO we approach smart beta strategies as enhanced passive equity strategies, since we look for a consistent long-term exposure to a set of factors for which we expect a positive factor premium. Basically, we see the transition to a smart beta equity portfolio as a shift from a passive single-beta inefficient strategy to a passive multibeta efficient strategy.

In case smart beta strategies are seen as enhanced passive equity strategies, the equity benchmark should in principle be a factor-based index. The reason for replacing the cap-weighted index with a factor-based index is because adopting a factor-based investment strategy as an enhanced passive strategy implies that the cap-weighted index is seen as an inefficient benchmark. There is no logical reason to use a benchmark that is seen as *a priori* inefficient. In terms of portfolio construction and factor strategy evaluation, it is important to recognize that the smart beta strategy is basically the new default for equities. Therefore, the factor allocation is a multiple-beta problem instead of an alpha problem. Consequently, the strategy should be evaluated in terms of Sharpe ratio.

Evaluation of smart beta strategies can yield different outcomes depending on the approach that is used. For example, several studies (e.g. Bender et al. 2013) have shown that low-volatility strategies tend to have high Sharpe ratios but relatively low Information ratios. This makes sense since low-volatility strategies tend to have long-term returns that are similar or slightly higher than the return of the market cap–weighted index but with lower risk. However, their tracking error can be significant (e.g. Hsu and Li 2013). As a result, low-volatility strategies are more preferred by investors that adopt the absolute approach than by investors that adopt the relative approach. Since we approach smart beta strategies from an absolute risk-return perspective we appreciate the risk-return characteristics of low-volatility strategies. We interpret the high tracking error of low-volatility strategies as a risk absorber in the portfolio, since the tracking error is particularly high in strong down markets. It is also in these markets that low-volatility strategies show strong relative performance due to their defensive nature.

In Section III it was mentioned that pension fund TNO has identified six factors—including the market factor—that are eligible for inclusion in its smart beta strategy. Combining these factors does not only offer the possibility to take advantage of the return potential of the individual factors but also of the diversification benefits resulting from the imperfect correlations between the factors. However, there are different ways of combining factors into a multifactor strategy. So, we had to find out what approaches could be used and their relative attractiveness for our pension fund.

In principle there are two ways to construct multifactor portfolios, the top-down approach (also known as factor mixing or portfolio blending) and the bottom-up approach (also known as factor integration or signal blending). The top-down approach is essentially a two-step portfolio construction process. In the first step individual factor portfolios are constructed, and in the next step these stand-alone factor sleeves are combined into a blended portfolio. For this final step the investor has to choose a weighting procedure (e.g. equal weighting or an optimization process). The bottom-up procedure combines the individual factor signals into a combined or integrated factor signal, which forms the basis for constructing the portfolio.

A potential drawback of the top-down approach is that it comes with undesired factor exposures. This is especially relevant when factors are negatively correlated. For example, if Value and Momentum are negatively correlated one automatically selects stocks with negative momentum signals in the Value sleeve and stocks with negative value characteristics in the Momentum sleeve. The bottom-up approach takes into account these correlations when integrating the factor signals. One way to solve this problem is to "decorrelate" the factor sleeves and transform them into pure factor portfolios. Combining pure factor portfolios into a multifactor portfolio should significantly reduce the problem of undesired risk exposures.

The top-down approach also comes with advantages that are particularly relevant from a practical point of view. The top-down approach is transparent and therefore it facilitates performance attribution.

Looking at the academic literature, Clarke, de Silva, and Thorley (2016), Bender and Wang (2016), and Fitzgibbons, Friedman, Pomorski, and Serban (2016) conclude that the bottom-up approach is preferred as it yields higher absolute and risk-adjusted returns. Amenc, Goltz, and Sivasubramanian (2018) and Leippold and Rüegg (2017) on the other hand come to the conclusion that the superiority of the bottom-up approach disappears once methodological weaknesses of the former studies are taken into account. For example, Chow, Li, and Shim (2018) conclude that the superiority of the bottom-up approach vanishes once portfolio concentration and turnover is taken into account.

Comparing the different studies is difficult as most of the studies compare portfolios given a certain risk metric (volatility or tracking error). However, this leaves the possibility that portfolios differ significantly in terms of factor exposure. Ghayur,

Heaney, and Platt (2018) show in their study that for low to moderate levels of factor exposures the top-down and bottom-up approach yield similar results. Only for high levels of factor exposure the two approaches show diverging outcomes. Therefore, the relative attractiveness of both approaches is dependent on the investor's objective function and preferences.

Pension fund TNO does not prefer high factor risk exposures as it usually comes with more concentrated portfolios. Therefore, from a risk-return perspective, we do not have a strong preference for either the top-down or bottom-up approach. However, since the top-down approach is more transparent and makes performance attribution easier we tend to have a preference for the top-down approach.

A last portfolio construction issue we had to decide on was the risk limits we want to impose.

At pension fund TNO we have chosen to define the smart beta mandate at the level of the global developed markets. That means that country risk and FX-risk are important contributors to the overall risk level. If we would only care about the overall risk level relative to the benchmark we could set a constraint at the tracking error level. However, if we would care about the overall risk profile of the smart beta strategy we should also set limits to specific risk exposures. With regard to FX-risk, we apply a currency overlay program, so FX-risk is hedged on a total portfolio level. Two other major risk factors that need to be addressed is country risk and sector risk. An interesting question here is to what extent country and sector risk limitations impact the performance of smart beta strategies. It could be that a preference for certain factor exposures steers the portfolio in the direction of specific countries and sectors. With one of the smart beta managers we had on our short list we did some extensive analysis into the impact of country and sector constraints. As it turned out, tight country and sector constraints have a negative impact on the risk-return trade-off of smart beta strategies (having no constraints at all is not optimal either, as it leads to extreme underweights and overweights). The return-risk ratio of the strategy using tight constraints (±0,5% relative to the benchmark) was 0,76; for the strategy with loose constraints (±10%) it was 1,0; the sample consisted of all stocks in the MSCI World and the sample period was 1985–2015. As a result, we decided to use loose constraints with regard to countries and sectors.

B. Defining the Right Benchmark

The next challenge is finding the right benchmark. There are various well-accepted benchmarks for capturing market risk (e.g. the S&P 500, the MSCI indices), but not yet for smart beta equity strategies. Although a few index providers have developed factor indices (e.g. MSCI, Russell, FTSE), these indices may differ in their portfolio construction and factor definition from the actual strategies they should represent. Also, these factor indices are not necessarily a good default, which can be realized in a cost-efficient way. Given these limitations, at pension fund TNO we have chosen to retain the cap-weighted indices as the benchmark for the smart beta strategies. If factors do indeed provide an additional return in addition to the market return, we should see an outperformance over a longer time period. The board is aware that the performance of the smart beta strategies should be evaluated over a longer time span, say three to five years.

C. The Impact of Costs

The final issue that had to be addressed is costs, in particular transaction costs and fees. If not properly addressed and managed, costs can have a big impact on the returns of smart beta strategies. In the end we want to optimize the trade-off between net returns and risk.

There is a big difference in transaction costs between a passive buy-and-hold cap-weighted index fund and a smart beta strategy. The latter is clearly more expensive since it requires more rebalancing, and relatively more trading in the small cap segment where transaction costs are higher. Since pension fund TNO used to invest its equity portfolio in a passive cap-weighted index fund we knew that transaction costs would be higher in the new situation. It is important to realize when looking at the vast amount of academic studies, that most of these studies are based on paper portfolios (simulated portfolios) without accounting for transaction costs. Therefore, these studies tend to overestimate the added value of smart beta strategies. An exception is the study of Beck et al. (2016). They show that the attractiveness of certain factor strategies vanishes once transaction costs are taken into account.

In the same study it is shown that the impact of transaction costs on performance can differ a great deal among factors. For example, value and minimum volatility strategies tend to have low turnover and therefore have low transaction costs. However, turnover for momentum strategies can be quite high. Especially when most of the turnover takes place with the small caps, transaction cost can have a major impact on performance.

In analyzing the performance of smart beta strategies, we have explicitly accounted for the effects of turnover on the smart beta strategies.

Another cost that is typically ignored in academic studies is fees. Typically, fees for smart beta strategies are higher than for passive buy-and-hold cap weighted index funds (though typically lower than for active equity funds). Just like the incremental transaction cost, the additional costs of fees should be taken into account before making a decision with regard to smart beta strategies and portfolio construction. We have made these analyses, and that led us to conclude that smart beta strategies provide added value over traditional buy-and-hold cap-weighted index funds; therefore, it is in the interest of the pension fund to add smart beta strategies to the portfolio.

V.   CONCLUSION

This chapter describes the journey of pension fund TNO from a traditional passive buy-and-hold cap-weighted index strategy to a smart beta strategy. What was clear from the outset was that for a successful transition it is essential to involve the board in the process. Although smart beta strategies have been shown to provide a better risk-return trade-off over the longer term, there could be periods of underperformance relative to the traditional approach. In that situation it is important that the underlying reasons for investing in smart beta strategies are embedded in the fund's investment beliefs and are fully understood.

A large part of the analyses that we did is based on academic studies. These studies have been extremely helpful in pointing us to the right factors, and to improve our understanding of the risk-return characteristics of smart beta strategies and the explanations for their existence. *Grosso modo*, the academic literature makes a compelling case for smart beta strategies. Relative to passive cap-weighted indices they have shown a better performance. Nevertheless, before making any decisions with regard to smart beta strategies, both in terms of allocation and portfolio construction, it is critically important to take into account the practical issues an investor has to deal with. In this respect, the importance of knowing the investor's objective function and preferences, portfolio construction (factor mix and risk constraints), benchmark definition and costs is stressed.

CHAPTER 15

USING SMART BETA FOR EFFICIENT PORTFOLIO MANAGEMENT

Ilian Dimitrov
Head of Growth Assets,
Oak Pension Asset Management Limited
Vice President, Investments,
Barclays Bank UK Retirement Fund

I. INTRODUCTION

The basic concept of smart beta and factor investing is not new. Indeed, historically, fundamental, and quant active managers have used exposures to certain smart beta factors, in combination with stock selection, to generate excess returns. With regard to smart beta, what is new, however, is the ability to isolate the capture of persistent long-term factors through transparent, low-cost offerings. This decoupling of excess returns coming from factor exposures and excess returns attributable to stock selection skill is an important development for asset owners because it allows for the construction of more efficient overall equity portfolios. At Barclays Bank UK Retirement Fund (BUKRF), we have been one of the early adopters of smart beta factor investing. And since inception, smart beta has contributed meaningfully to enhancing the risk-return profile of the overall equity allocation. In this chapter, smart beta implementation experience is discussed.

II. MOTIVATION AND STRATEGY SELECTION

In recent years, increased and enhanced data availability, improved risk models, and more focus on quantitative investment management techniques have allowed institutional investors to better decompose overall portfolio performance and to gain a deeper understanding of the drivers of performance. In our case, such activities, over time, have led to a clearer identification of the factor exposures embedded in our passive and active portfolios. This, in turn, led to internal discussions regarding which factors we want to gain exposure to, which factors were actually represented in the portfolio, and how do we balance the risk exposures to factors. The advent of factor-based smart beta strategies provided an efficient vehicle for implementing underrepresented factor exposures. Therefore, initially we used certain smart beta product offerings for portfolio completion purposes. For instance, we recognized that our overall portfolio lacked adequate exposure to defensive strategies. As such, our smart beta strategy selection efforts initially focused on defensive or low-risk strategies.

As our overall equity strategy evolved, the mix of smart beta strategies also broadened to facilitate efficient portfolio management. For instance, large cap value strategies were introduced to balance the small cap growth exposures from the active equity portfolio. In some highly efficient market segments, smart beta factor strategies have also been identified as a more efficient, transparent, and cost-effective alternative to actively managed strategies. In such instances, we have favored a multifactor allocation that has the potential to improve risk-adjusted returns by combining factors with low correlation, along with cost-efficient implementation.

Over time, therefore, smart beta factor investing, in our case, has evolved from a portfolio completion application to strategies that allow us to capture a particular risk premium for a low cost as well as to serve as an alternative to active management, where appropriate. In the end, the main objective of smart beta for us is to aid in portfolio construction and improve investment efficiency relative to pure passive, through higher Sharpe ratios, and active portfolios, through higher IRs.

III. CHALLENGES

As is the case with most investors, we faced several challenges as we sought to implement a smart beta program. First, we had to decide on the motivation behind the factors. This decision is difficult because it involves a discussion of why factors work and, more importantly, why we can expect them to keep working. On this topic, the academic literature provides limited guidance because it is divided between an efficient markets-based risk premium explanation and a behavioral finance-based anomalous returns explanation. At a practical level, we feel that factor returns may be driven by a combination of risk and mispricing or that different factors may be driven by different considerations. That is, some may represent more of a risk premium, while others may be better explained through behavioral biases. Also, at a practical level, persistence in factor premiums is an important consideration. In our view, a premium for additional risk and limits to arbitrage relating to behavioral mispricing are reasonable arguments for the persistence of factor returns.

Second, we had to decide on which specific factor premiums we should seek to capture. Again, although in the academic literature hundreds of factors have been identified, our view is that the focus of smart beta strategies should be on the well-accepted basic factors, such as value, momentum, low volatility, and quality. At a very minimum, asset owners should aim to capture these basic factors through transparent and cost-effective smart beta solutions. Other potentially more advanced and sophisticated factors, we believe, are best captured through active management.

Third, we had to decide on how to use our existing risk management systems in the new smart beta framework. Historically, we have made use of commercial risk models to assess the risk exposures of our portfolios. The advent of smart beta strategies potentially challenges the use of commercial risk models to assess risk exposures. For instance, if we decide to invest in a certain smart beta value strategy, it is because we believe that strategy represents a good capture of value. It may be that when assessed against a commercial risk model, that smart beta value strategy may not show a meaningful exposure to value, because the commercial risk model defines and captures value factor differently. Such results are actually quite common and highlight the need for asset owners to carefully analyze counterintuitive exposures emanating from commercial risk models. It may also be a good idea for asset owners to complement risk model-based exposure analysis with a risk decomposition of active strategies against the smart beta strategies that they are considering and implementing.

Finally, another challenge was determining what steps to take to mitigate the potential impact of factor crowding on future performance. As smart beta continues to gain in popularity and adoption, crowding and its impact on the valuation of factors becomes a reasonable concern. Additionally, crowded trades in individual stocks may imply that in the event of a factor crash, exit can potentially entail high market impact and implementation expense. We believe asset owners can mitigate the potential negative impacts of crowded trades by keeping a long-term perspective and by focusing on customized smart beta solutions with differentiated features, as we discuss next.

IV. PRODUCT SELECTION

In selecting smart beta products, we tend to focus on the following considerations.

A. Factor Mix

The factor mix decision involves determining which specific factors to invest in. When smart beta is used in a portfolio completion application, this decision is straightforward as a specific factor or risk premium is targeted. When smart beta is used as an alternative to active management, we prefer multifactor solutions. In a multifactor strategy, we also prefer the inclusion of all the smart beta factors mentioned earlier, that is, value, momentum, low volatility, and quality. Some smart beta managers do not include momentum in their multifactor strategy. Their argument is that momentum has very high turnover, which increases implementation costs and negatively impacts the overall capacity of the strategy. Other smart beta managers do not include low volatility, as it tends to lower the IR of the overall strategy. Although these potential shortcomings of momentum and low volatility are generally valid, we also find smart beta managers that have designed good methodologies to address them. They employ innovative techniques to control the turnover of momentum and improve the active return and IR associated with low-volatility investing. In the end, the point is that asset owners do not necessarily have to forgo the diversification potential of certain factors, as many smart beta offerings exist that aim to strike an appropriate balance in the various potential trade-offs involved. Therefore, at the start of the process, we use a complete factor mix, which delivers adequate factor diversification, as a screen to narrow the universe of strategies that we wish to analyze further.

B. Factor Signal Definitions

With regard to signal definitions, our focus is on two main areas; the trade-off between simplicity and complexity and individual factor versus multifactor application.

Although we are advocates of simplicity and transparency, we also recognize that some level of complexity may be needed to adequately define a particular factor or style. For instance, price-to-book value may be too simple and narrow of a definition to define value. We would prefer appropriately designed value composites that adopt a broader perspective of value investing. On the other hand, some smart beta managers use 10 or even 20 different metrics to define quality. We find such composites are overly complex, as they do not facilitate a clear understanding of risk exposures and performance attribution of the strategy.

In a multifactor application, we believe that the various factor definitions used should be relatively independent of each other. Otherwise, the expected benefits of factor diversification may be compromised. As such, we pay particular attention to potential unintended or ancillary exposures of specific factor definitions. In this regard, we may ask a smart beta manager to establish the orthogonality of various factor definitions used. This typically entails conducting an exposure decomposition analysis of one factor relative to the other factors used in the strategy.

C. Weighting Scheme and Portfolio Construction

The basic objective of portfolio construction is to deliver an "efficient" capture of targeted factors. However, different smart beta managers may approach the objective of efficiency from different perspectives. Therefore, we ask the managers to clearly specify how they define the efficiency objective function and how their portfolio construction helps them achieve that objective.

In our view, it is also important to fully understand the potential exposure and risk concentrations introduced by a given weighting scheme and other portfolio construction parameters. In our experience, the size exposure represents one important concern. Certain portfolio construction techniques lead to a dominant exposure to size relative to the other factors in the strategy. Although we understand that some exposure to size will invariably be embedded in strategies that deviate from cap weighting, having size be the dominant factor exposure represents a problem in our view. In certain other cases, the constraints specified in an optimized solution may lead to implicit factor timing. In general, a reasonable argument could be made in favor of factor timing. However, the benefits of implicit factor timing remain questionable. In our view, factor timing is better implemented in an explicit fashion through talented active managers, as opposed to smart beta offerings, as it requires a higher degree of skill.

In creating a multifactor strategy, some smart beta managers combine factor signals to construct a single multifactor portfolio, while others combine individually constructed factor portfolios. From an investment efficiency perspective, we believe that both approaches are reasonable ways of constructing multifactor strategies. In the implementation and monitoring of smart beta multifactor strategies, we view the ability to understand and explain performance as an important advantage.

Finally, we value clear and transparent investment processes that are specifically designed to improve diversification and mitigate overall implementation costs. Diversification is an important consideration in the capture of factor returns, as highlighted by academic studies. Ideally, a factor capture should be implemented with high diversification and low stock-specific risk, such that factor risk is the main driver of the total active risk assumed. The objective of mitigating overall implementation costs leads us to prefer strategies that have a reasonable annualized turnover and are offered at a reasonable price.

V. SMART BETA ALLOCATION

Our process for determining the allocation to smart beta involves two steps. In the first step, the Equity Investment Team works with the internal Portfolio Construction Group to develop recommendations regarding the strategic weights for smart beta strategies in the context of the overall investment strategy. In the second step, the recommendations are reviewed and approved by the Investment Committee. As the initial aim of our smart beta allocation was to act as a completion portfolio to the active and passive equity allocations, the sizing was a result of overall equity and factor exposures across the fund. In the long run, while still being conscious of overall factor exposures, some smart beta strategies are likely to be part of the core Equity allocation for the fund.

VI. GOVERNANCE, MONITORING, AND PERFORMANCE BENCHMARKING

In terms of governance, the Investment Committee has ultimate responsibility for oversight of the smart beta program. On a daily basis, the Equity Team oversees and manages the implementation of the smart beta allocation. Most of the smart beta strategies we employ are externally developed and can be implemented in a separate mandate, ETF, mutual fund, or a total return swap on an index. In some cases, the internal Equity Team is more involved in the factor strategy development in order to ensure that specific plan-level strategic considerations and guidelines are taken into account.

In terms of monitoring, we pay particular attention to realized factor exposures, active risk contributions, large country, sector and industry active positions, and realized turnover and overall implementation costs. These aspects help us determine if a given investment process is working as it's intended to. On a periodic basis, we also ask managers to conduct a capacity analysis for their strategies.

Performance benchmarking of smart beta strategies can be a challenging task. Ideally, we would want to use standard or public factor indices to assess the performance of implemented customized strategies. However, in practice this is difficult to do, as it may be hard to determine what a "standard" index might be for certain factors or strategies, such as, quality or a multifactor strategy. As such, our primary performance benchmark continues to be the same as the strategic cap-weighted benchmark for the overall equity allocation. Nonetheless, where appropriate, we do use secondary benchmarks, in the form of standard factor indices, to analyze and measure the performance of individual smart beta strategies.

VII. CONCLUSION

So far, our experience with smart beta has been a positive one. The smart beta allocation has provided diversification, reduced risk, and improved long-term performance. In addition, the introduction of smart beta strategies has put more emphasis on factor exposures across the overall fund and has led to a more granular performance and risk contribution analysis. In our experience, smart beta and factor strategies have proven to be excellent tools for efficient portfolio management. However, they do require careful and bespoke consideration and should not be seen as "one size fits all" investment strategy.

PART VII

CONSULTANT
PERSPECTIVES

CHAPTER 16

SMART BETA FROM AN ASSET OWNER'S PERSPECTIVE

James Price
Director,
Willis Towers Watson

Phil Tindall
Senior Director,
Willis Towers Watson

In our contribution to the smart beta debate, we focus mainly on the often-overlooked perspective of the asset owner. We set the broad scene in which asset owners (e.g. pension funds and endowments) should operate, articulate the issues they face, and highlight some new challenges when using smart beta concepts and products.

We also explore how smart beta is currently evolving and will likely evolve in the future.

First though, we begin with some scene-setting.

I.   THE SMART BETA REVOLUTION OR EVOLUTION?

A. Introducing Our View of "Smart Beta"

The story of smart beta goes back nearly 30 years, with origins very different to the today's product-filled world. This journey reflects changes in an investment industry that has (in places) "industrialized" over time. We also see increased recognition from asset owners that play to their strengths[1] has the potential (if well executed) to confer a competitive advantage.

In the early 2000s Willis Towers Watson's Thinking Ahead research team wrote about how asset owners could gain a competitive edge by using some of the ideas found in many of today's smart beta products. However, we did not anticipate that the topic would be so high on investors' agenda nor that it would elicit such strong opinions.

We see the heated debate around smart beta as a positive—innovation that doesn't provoke a response from incumbents is unlikely to have a long-lasting impact. But the debate can descend into hyperbole and misunderstanding, and many valuable nuances lost. Stepping back, we find that, despite the back and forth between different members of the industry, there is actually wide agreement about many of the concepts behind smart beta, albeit with a vibrant debate about definitions, labels and the implications for markets and investors.

B. The Origin of Smart Beta

The investment industry generates more than its fair share of jargon, and smart beta is no exception. Beta, smart beta, factors, alpha, alt beta, signals, strategies are terms that, unfortunately, everyone seems to use differently. We attempt to be consistent in our nomenclature, explaining as we go.

a. Market Beta and Alpha

Before modern finance theory, equity returns were attributed only to stock picking—returns, positive or negative, were down to the portfolio manager and nothing else. However, a seismic shift occurred with the development of the efficient market hypothesis and Capital Asset Pricing Model (CAPM). With this more scientific approach, as well as the consequent invention of passive management, the idea of separating returns into a market component and a residual took hold. CAPM assumes that nonmarket residual returns are zero on average and uncorrelated to the market—essentially noise. In a linear regression model, the Greek letter beta is used for the market coefficient, with the residual labelled as alpha.

These labels stuck, and today investment professions often refer to "beta" meaning market or asset class exposure, and "alpha" as the additional positive or negative return generated relative to the market.[2] The framework has been informally extended to incorporate the idea that some asset managers are "skillful" (they can deliver positive alpha over time) while others are not. Needless to say, if an investor does not just want to own the market (best described for practical purposes as a broad

---

[1] For example, asset owners with a long-term investment horizon are able to exploit opportunities that short-term investors cannot.

[2] Unhelpfully, alpha is sometimes used to mean the extra return relative to the market, and other times it is the extra returns adjusted to reflect the market exposure (as per a linear regression).

market capitalization–weighted portfolio), then he/she should employ an asset manager with the expectation of delivering positive alpha. With no belief in positive alpha, it would be logical for asset owners to invest in beta (the market portfolio), which is low cost because little unique investment insight is involved.

b. A New Model: Factors Beyond Market Beta and Alpha

Having identified the first order market beta effect, which explains a lot of individual stock price movement, the search naturally moved to what else mattered. Over the years a number of factors have been identified and tested,[3] including momentum, low volatility (and similarly low beta), value, and size.[4] The additional factors more fully describe stock price movements, but also historically show positive alphas in the old CAPM beta-alpha model. In other words, some "old alpha" can be captured with new beta.

The smart beta term was originally coined to refer to long-only equity strategies that captured returns from new factors (as well as market beta). As we discuss in Section IV, the idea can also be applied to other markets and strategies; for example, merger arbitrage and trend-following are well-recognized hedge fund strategies that can be captured with factors (typically implemented as a long-short portfolio) and now often referred to as alternative beta.[5]

c. What Do We Mean by "Alpha"?: A Broader Principle

From the previous section, we have a model that explains returns in terms of three things: market exposure, factors, and a residual. However, to define investment skill *purely* in terms of the residual of a model is, to us at least, incomplete or possibly misleading. We view a "skilled" asset manager (with positive alpha) as having a competitive edge over other market participants, and that edge is both sustainable (unlikely to be competed away) and scarce (it cannot be copied by other asset managers or be incorporated into the market's collective pricing of securities). We also add assessable. Asset owners (or their representatives) must be able to form a robust view about the presence of investment skill before allocating capital.[6] In our view scarcity, as a

---

[3] Factors are best thought of as investment strategies to group and weight securities with common characteristics and/or to capture some overall market "effect." To be useful, the factor strategy should generate a positive risk adjusted return.

[4] Initially value, size, and momentum were "discovered" in the early 1990s. Low volatility did not become "mainstream," and in many factor models remains absent, until after around 2008, despite being discovered as a CAPM anomaly in the late 1960s.

[5] This is not to say that asset managers can't add value in a strategy, such as merger arbitrage, but that any added value should be set against the incremental fees over the cost of an alternative beta product.

[6] We believe that the cost of false positives (assigning investment skill inappropriately) is high, whereas false negatives (missing a great investor) is low. This is because false positives affect portfolios, but false negatives result in regrets. This asymmetry in the cost of errors leads us to put significant emphasis on assessability in our manager research.

defining feature of alpha, does not depend on how complicated a strategy is, nor the results of a factor model.

C. Implications for Active Managers

a. Raising the Bar

We think that smart beta represents a significant challenge for some asset managers and an opportunity for others. For example, an asset manager investing in small cap or low price/book companies should have a lower alpha under the "new model" than under the old one. Is the manager less skilled because some "old" alpha is in fact size or value factor exposure? Smart beta strategies, which capture returns previously labeled as alpha at low cost, are a disruptive technology in the same way that the Internet has disrupted markets in goods and services.

In many respects the increasing awareness of smart beta is refining the expectations of asset managers. Asset owners are prepared to pay reasonable fees that deliver something genuinely different, but if a strategy is widely available, then naturally cost and other observable attributes become important in the manager selection process.

b. The Need to Innovate

We believe an overlooked aspect of smart beta is that it is not a static set of strategies. "Alpha strategies" can evolve into smart beta over time as the strategy is defined, tested, rationalized and becomes well understood.

As a result, asset managers must keep innovating to continue to deliver genuine alpha or accept that over time they will become smart beta providers. In our opinion, this is a difficult mind-set shift for some to accept, but ultimately they may have no choice.

c. The Rise of the Index: Unbundling the Asset Management Product

We could think of any investment product as combining two functions. The first is strategy design, that is, security selection and allocation. The second is implementation—executing the trades required to invest in the target security weights in the most effective manner.

At its heart, an index is a technology that joins these two functions. The design of the strategy is carried out by a set of specialists,[7] which can then be delivered via an index to implementation specialists. In traditional asset management these two functions are part of the same company, and may even be the same person or team, but with the right technology (i.e. an index) this need not be the case.

---

[7] In principle an "index" could be delivered in real time based on the discretionary view of a fundamental stock picker. The current incarnation of indices as quantitative strategies (of varying complexity) is only one version of the technology.

Over recent years indices have evolved to include those based on company fundamentals (e.g. value, quality) and market prices (e.g. momentum, low volatility), with securities selected and/or weighted on these characteristics. Indices now cover both single factor strategies and combinations of factors. They can be constructed using simple weighting rules or optimization procedures. Some of these indices look very similar to asset manager quantitative strategies and in some areas, such as ESG investing, we would argue that indices are ahead of many asset manager offerings.

We expect that indices will continue to evolve and offer strategies that overlap with, and potentially surpass, those offered by asset manages. Likewise, we observe a trend where asset managers are creating indices based on their strategies to provide asset owners with additional implementation options.

d. Take Care with Indices and Benchmarking

i. Indices Do Not Define Smart Beta (or Passive) Management

Often it is claimed that smart beta strategies are either passive or need to track an index—the implication being that anything else qualifies as active management. This is not the case.

First, in a broad economic sense, all strategies that allocate away from market capitalization weights are active. This is because *in aggregate* all securities are owned at market capitalization weights (the market price, and therefore weight, for each security representing the balance of supply and demand). A portfolio that does not hold market cap weights is taking active bets against all other investors.

Second, an index is not needed for the definition of passive management. As a simple thought experiment consider a 100 stock portfolio with securities weighted either in line with market cap or at 1% each (i.e. equally weighted). Now suppose that there are three pooled funds to choose from:[8] (1) one that tracks a market-capitalization-weighted index, (2) one that tracks an equally weighted index, and (3) one that does not track any index but invests 1% in each stock.

- If we choose to invest in the fund that tracks the market cap–weighted index, then we are a passive investor.
- If we choose to invest in the fund that tracks the equally weighted index or the non-index fund, then should we view ourselves differently? Are we a passive investor in one and an active investor in the other? Should there be any differential in fund terms between these funds? We believe that these two implementation options are the same.

The simple example highlights that the presence of an index per se does not determine a strategy to be passive, let alone smart beta. Likewise, the absence of an index does mean something isn't a smart beta product. It's the underlying strategy that matters.

---

[8] For convenience we are ignoring the further pool of capital that represents the offsetting positions to our choice, as it is not important in this example.

ii. Is There a "Correct" Smart Beta Index?

The index is a fairly good, and well accepted, way to assess a broad long-only strategy relative to its opportunity set. However, in the smart beta space does the same level of consensus exist?

Using value as an example, it is not obvious that there is a correct "value index" to use as a benchmark, just as there is no correct "value asset manager." Indeed, even the design choices of the strategies used in the original studies of factor investing should not be thought of as "correct" or idealized version of the strategies. This means that selecting a smart beta index is very similar to selecting any active investment strategy. This has implications for benchmarking that we highlight in Section II.A.

II. SMART BETA FROM THE ASSET OWNER PERSPECTIVE

A. A Meaningful Change in the Investment Landscape

Asset owners previously had the choice of investing in (market cap) passive products (implying a belief in efficient markets) or in actively managed products (implying that persistently skilled asset managers exist and can be identified in advance). Now asset owners have a third choice—allocate capital to smart beta strategies with the belief that successful strategies can be pre-identified. Asset owners can now:

- Make top-down allocations to smart beta strategies, which add diversifying factors to a portfolio (i.e. low correlation to equity and credit markets); and
- Consider factor exposures more generally across the portfolio, and the appropriateness of fees that they are paying for these exposures versus those available from active management.

For the asset owner this change of emphasis—shifting the sources of return from manager selection (idiosyncratic sources of alpha) to investment strategy (systematic sources of mispricing)—requires a different set of skills. Allocating top-down to strategies requires time and expertise. For example, some of these strategies are, in part, based on behavioral/structural phenomena and therefore require investor beliefs about the rationale and sustainability of returns.

For asset owners the governance emphasis is shifted toward understanding, constructing, and managing strategy allocations rather than manager monitoring and evaluation. We would argue that this broader framework entails more up-front governance, but less ongoing governance than traditional alpha management. Investors can, of course, have both market exposure, smart beta, and alpha in their portfolios, where governance allows.

FIGURE 16.1   Traditional Investment Review Process

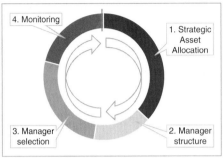

Comments

1. Selection of traditional asset classes. Typically use long-term Asset Liabillty Modelling (ALM) analysis. Assess risk reward trade off for various combinations and set risk and / or return targets
2. Choice of active vs passive (market cap) security selection, some variation between asset classes. Asset allocation rebalanced to fixed weights, occasionally with a tactical asset allocation overlay.
3. Selection of a short-list of managers, with selection via a 'beauty parade'
4. Focused on active manager monitoring. Market cap benchmarks used to measure success.

(Cycle labels: 1. Strategic Asset Allocation; 2. Manager structure; 3. Manager selection; 4. Monitoring)

B. Portfolio Construction Perspective: New Building Blocks

In a traditional top-down process, investors first decide between asset classes (equities, bonds, etc.) to form a "strategic" allocation. For each asset class, the subsequent "implementation" decision is normally a choice between active and (market cap) passive management. This process is illustrated in Figure 16.1.

Smart/alternative beta challenges the traditional approach by bringing;

- A new top-down set of "building blocks" in the form of factors and strategies.
- Low-cost implementation options in long-only (factor tilts or similar) and long-short formats (alternative beta).
- Increased portfolio efficiency since these factors typically have better diversification than traditional asset classes.[9]

Figure 16.2 illustrates a broader way of thinking about portfolio construction, and with it an expanded set of building blocks. Traditional asset allocation is shown vertically, and examples of factors/strategies horizontally. When considered from an implementation point of view, note that we see smart beta as a bridge between the options of investing in a passive market cap portfolio and active management based on unique investment insights, as shown in the second and right-hand columns. For completeness, we extend asset classes from equities and bonds into more diversifying markets (where, as an aside, market cap makes less sense or can't be defined). We can also neatly bring active stock selection and other ideas such as sustainability/thematic strategies into the framework.

---

[9] To exaggerate the point a little, the correlation between US and European equities or between equities and high yield bonds is around 0.5 to 0.9, whereas the correlation between the value and momentum factor is typically around –0.2 to –0.4. The lower the correlation between building blocks, the greater the portfolio efficiency. Note that portfolio construction is best considered between the most independent building blocks.

358

FIGURE 16.2   New Portfolio Building Blocks

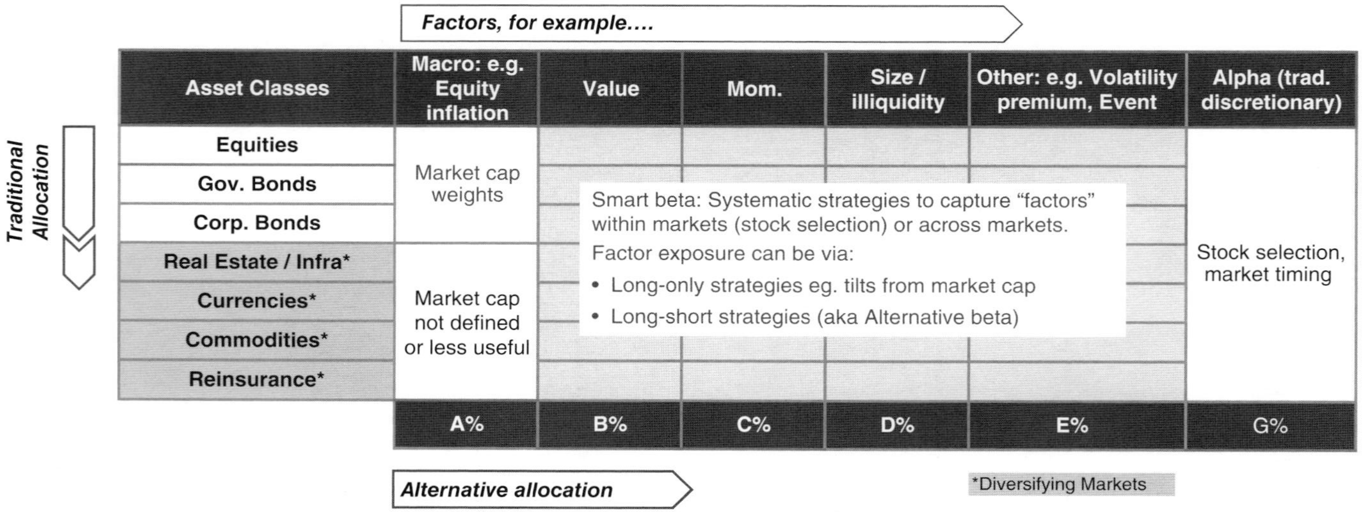

Asset Classes	Macro: e.g. Equity inflation	Value	Mom.	Size / illiquidity	Other: e.g. Volatility premium, Event	Alpha (trad. discretionary)
Equities	Market cap weights				Smart beta: Systematic strategies to capture "factors" within markets (stock selection) or across markets. Factor exposure can be via: • Long-only strategies eg. tilts from market cap • Long-short strategies (aka Alternative beta)	Stock selection, market timing
Gov. Bonds						
Corp. Bonds						
Real Estate / Infra*	Market cap not defined or less useful					
Currencies*						
Commodities*						
Reinsurance*						
	A%	B%	C%	D%	E%	G%

Factors, for example....

Traditional Allocation

Alternative allocation

*Diversifying Markets

Perhaps not surprisingly, we believe that this more sophisticated approach entails higher governance, as well as a change in mind-set for asset owners. While a full discussion is beyond the scope of this chapter, we believe that the additional effort leads to a significant improvement in portfolio efficiency through more robust portfolio construction and improved implementation.

C. Asset Owners Need Beliefs for Smart Beta (as Well as Market Cap and Alpha)

Regardless of whether asset owners consider smart beta to be a new investment management approach, or as a mechanism to enhance portfolio construction, they need to believe that portfolio outcomes will be improved in order to justify the cost and effort.

Because smart beta strategies entail *somewhat* higher costs than market cap,[10] and that costs are certain and outcomes are not, it is important for investors to consider the beliefs needed for their investment choices. And the higher the cost, the higher the burden of proof. Often investors express beliefs implicitly, for example in their use of active or passive management, but we think that an explicit articulation of beliefs is a valuable exercise in its own right.

Table 16.1 shows some illustrative beliefs that lead to differing uses of market cap, smart beta and alpha investment approaches, with varying strength.

TABLE 16.1 Asset Owners Should Align Beliefs to Investment Strategies

Example Beliefs	Views/Understanding	Action
Markets are efficient and hard to beat	Efficient market hypothesis, CAPM	Predominantly market cap passive
No strong view on market efficiency, but wide range of outcomes for any weighting method	No specific view	Mix simple non-market-cap approaches with market cap to diversify outcomes over medium term
Size weighting leads to too much concentration risk	Risk management beyond just volatility	Specific strategies to reduce concentration at stock or country/sector level
There are specific effects, or factors, that can produce better outcomes	Specific reasons for effect, e.g., risk premium or behavioral.	Strategies targeted at specific factors/effects
Markets are strongly inefficient, skilful active managers can be identified in advance	Reasons for inefficiency	Use active management and some smart beta, depending on costs

[10] Market cap has the benefit that security weights move with market prices and so is "self-rebalancing," leading to lower transaction costs.

As far as possible, beliefs should be supported with a solid rationale and evidence. Typical questions for asset owners are:

- What is the underlying rationale—risk premium, behavioral, or structural effect?
- What evidence is there? How well tested is it, for example, how much out-of-sample testing?
- In what environments does the strategy do well or poorly? How does this relate to the current or likely future environment?
- What are the risks (e.g. volatility, tail risks, cyclicality, and liquidity)? What is a reasonable time horizon for success?
- How different is the strategy from others in the portfolio?

Note that we believe that investors should also ask the same questions about traditional asset classes. However, it is fair to say that there is a higher degree of uncertainty about smart beta strategies than traditional market betas, for example:

- No universally agreed rationale. Many arguments are behavioral or structural, rather than as risk compensation.
- Less data in some cases.
- Zero sum game arguments: Who is losing if smart beta is winning? Will returns be competed away?

D. Not a Free Lunch: Smart Beta Requires Governance

a. Up-Front, Top-Down

From the earlier examples, we think that asset owners need to consider the investment rationale for smart beta strategies carefully. Because smart beta strategies are highly process driven (but need not be expressed as an index), subsequent performance follows more mechanically. The material decision is therefore up-front, rather than ongoing, and has similarities to asset allocation decisions, such as the equity and bond split. This contrasts to traditional active management, where more effort is required in monitoring the people, process and organization for changes in unique investment skill.[11]

b. Absolute and Relative Return Worlds

Another big question for investors is whether tracking error or absolute risk is more relevant. At face value, absolute risk would seem more important since it directly relates to underlying investment goals.[12] As noted earlier, the centrality of strategic

---

[11] Some up-front governance is also required for active management, for example the beliefs in alpha itself as well as the philosophy and process of each manager selected.

[12] For simplicity, assuming that investors have a "cash+" or "inflation+" investment goals, or that other liability risks are dealt with separately. Few, if any, asset owners have "bottom line" goals of "Equities+" or similar. Put another way, equity goals are a means to an end, not an end in themselves.

asset allocation and market cap benchmarking leads most investors to consider tracking error. In turn this puts a high weight on the "correctness" of these processes/concepts, with tracking error as a measure of implementation risk or "delivery failure" on the investment strategy. This is open to challenge, however. For example, the problem of assumption dependency in asset allocation analysis is well known. Certainly, a focus on tracking error would seem inconsistent for investors with strong beliefs in nonmarket cap approaches.

To illustrate the dilemma, consider a low-volatility equity strategy. From an absolute perspective a low-volatility strategy has less risk than market cap—often by some margin. But its tracking error would put it into the aggressive camp for an active strategy! Which is correct?

c. Time Horizon and Monitoring

Longer time horizons allow tolerance for deviation from market cap performance. While certain types of asset owners naturally have longer time horizons,[13] this needs to be embedded in a decision-making framework as well. For example, quarterly monitoring can lead to an inappropriate bias to action. In part this is due to a natural tendency to confuse luck and skill (by ascribing meaning to random outcomes). Short-termism is not unique to smart beta, however.

Taking into account all of the above, and depending on mind-set, asset owners typically find that higher tracking error strategies are more difficult to handle—higher governance—than low tracking error strategies.

Setting appropriate benchmarks and management objectives is very important and helps to mitigate the problems discussed earlier. Equally, inappropriate benchmarks can make matters worse. Depending on strategy, here are some ways that we think asset owners should consider to mitigate pitfalls:

- Put achieved returns in a wider context. For example, consider the returns achieved by a wide range of smart beta and active strategies (e.g. upper and lower quartile). This approach is most aligned for absolute return investors where market cap is one of many possible alternative strategies.
- Consider absolute risk and return, even for tracking-error oriented investors. Absolute returns are more aligned to underlying investment goals.
- Ensure that the equity beta is appropriate. For example, a benchmark of 2/3 * equity market cap index +1/3 * cash is more appropriate for a low-volatility strategy, to align with its absolute risk and equity sensitivity.
- Use smart beta/factor indices. For example, a fundamentally weighted strategy has a value exposure. Some of its performance can be explained by whether value

---

[13] For example, institutions with long-term liabilities, that are well-funded, with some "flexibility" over commitments/liabilities (e.g. charities, sovereign wealth funds), or not subject to regulatory funding rules, such as Solvency II.

securities are in or out of favor. Many factor indices are now available from index providers. Note that an index of the strategy itself is not independent by definition, but again may be more suitable for investors who see market cap as one of many possible alternative strategies.[14]

- Whatever benchmark is chosen, understand the range of relative returns up front. This helps guide a reasonable range for disappointing outcomes, as well as upside ones.
- Evaluate performance over a long time period—at least five years, ideally longer.

However, performance is measured, there is a question of interpretation and action. Again, an up-front understanding of smart beta characteristics, and environments for good and poor performance, helps. For example, the following are reasonable explanations for poor performance:

- Value strategies: falling interest rates boosts (longer duration) growth companies at the expense of value companies
- Momentum strategies: a sudden change in sector leadership, for example, at the boundary between phases of an economic cycle or due to monetary or fiscal policy changes.
- Small cap strategies: a phase of favoritism for large global corporations or a period of credit expansion what allows larger/mid-sized companies with access to debt to expand their business faster than smaller companies.

While all of this means that smart beta is a higher governance endeavor, many similar questions could be raised for a market capitalization strategy. The acceptance of market capitalization strategy performance is a testament to its near universal acceptance as the definition of the equity (or other) market—"it is what it is." This is in line with the old adage that it is better to fail conventionally than succeed unconventionally—asset owners take more regret risk with smart beta.

d. Simple Versus Complicated

The degree of complexity varies considerably between smart beta strategies, which we see in two broad areas:

1. Underlying idea or effect: For example, rebalancing/mean reversion is arguably easier to understand and agree to than momentum or low volatility.
2. Implementation: For example, simple portfolio construction rules versus optimization.

---

[14] Some smart betas are available as pubic indices, or investors can have private indices constructed. We do not think it necessary for smart beta to be codified in an index, but it can be helpful.

Consistent with the idea of favoring robust strategy implementations, we think smart beta strategies should be "As simple as possible, as complicated as necessary." There are some pitfalls with complicated strategies, for example:

- Lack of understanding by an asset owner may lead to inappropriate action, that is, quitting of a strategy at the wrong time.
- Confusion over whether the factor or implementation is responsible for performance.
- Reliance on models for portfolio construction, particularly correlation and volatility—model risk.

Note that there is no link between "complicated" and high tracking error. For example, a simple strategy such as fundamental weighting may have a tracking error of around 4% to 6%, and can out- or underperform market cap significantly over extended periods—certainly not enhanced indexation.

e. Governance as a Source of Competitive Advantage: Buy or Build?

The discussion earlier makes the case that asset owners need to raise their governance levels to invest in smart beta effectively. But asset owners have a choice to develop governance in-house or to outsource, depending on priorities and the level of internal resources. Where governance has been outsourced, it has traditionally been in the area of security selection rather than asset allocation, that is, in bottom-up implementation rather than top-down strategy.

The increasing use of fiduciary management (outsourced CIO) models has allowed asset owners to take advantage of new innovations, such as liability hedging, increased asset diversity and smart beta, that have increased portfolio efficiency, but also complexity. It also frees asset owners to focus on the important high-level issues, such as investment goals, risk tolerance, and funding.

Assuming asset owners largely retain in-house governance, there are some "implementation" aspects of smart beta management that can be outsourced to fund managers, in the same way as for other asset classes. See Table 16.2.

TABLE 16.2 Various Levels of Outsourcing for Smart Beta Beliefs

Decision Area	Outsource to Asset Manager?
Factor/smart beta strategy selection	No
Factor/strategy allocation (initial and ongoing)	Perhaps
Factor/strategy development*	Yes, for most asset owners

*Because smart beta is a developing area, there is scope to refine and improve strategies over time. For example, the securities or markets included, portfolio construction method.

TABLE 16.3 Practical Considerations for Smart Beta Strategies

Example Beliefs	Market cap "Orientation"	Governance	Approach/ Strategies	Benchmark/ Monitoring	Time Horizon
Some flaws in market cap[1]	Absolute risk / return	Lower	Alternatively weighted[3], focus on absolute risk	Index proxy for strategy. Multiple references[4]	Longer
Factor effects	Absolute	Highest	Factor targeting, security weights are absolute	As above, plus factor indices.	Longer
Some flaws in market cap	Relative risk and return[2]	Lowest	Alternatively weighted, focus on tracking error	As above plus market cap index	Shorter
Factor effects	Relative	Higher	Factor targeting, security weights relative to market cap	Market cap, factor tilted indices	Shorter

(1) Weaker to stronger versions, but no specific views on alternative factors/effects.
(2) "Market cap is not perfect, but is still the lowest cost approach, issues such as peer group comparisons or internal governance means a relative return world is at least partly relevant."
(3) Sophistication varies somewhat, which has an impact on governance, e.g. equal weight, volatility weighted. Can result in strategies with lower risk than market cap, but high tracking error.
(4) For example, inter-quartile range of actively managed and smart beta funds/indices.

We attempt to bring the various strands together in Table 16.3 accepting that there are some variations around the broad categorizations. Overall, there are many ways in which asset owners can access smart beta ideas, depending on beliefs, governance, and time horizon.

III. ASSET OWNERS FACE NEW CHALLENGES WHEN USING SMART BETA STRATEGIES

A. Introduction

From Section II we can see that there is a lot for asset owners to consider when investing in smart beta strategies. Some of the considerations will be familiar because they are important when constructing any portfolio. But there are a number of challenges that investors have previously not had to consider because management was outsourced.

These new challenges arise because of a shift in decision making between asset owners and asset managers. As discussed in Section II.B, in a traditional portfolio construction process, asset managers are appointed to implement asset allocation decisions—to outperform market cap benchmarks in the case of active management.

The asset manager can choose the best approach, including in many cases conscious and pronounced smart beta (factor) exposures.[15] Because asset managers are expected to outperform the broad market, we believe that they should actively manage factor exposures. For example, if value opportunities are scarce, then asset managers should address this by adapting to new conditions, potentially taking less risk.[16] A smart beta mandate is different because asset owners want to target specific factor exposures (e.g. value), which the asset manager should deliver. In this case we see that the decision to allocate (or remove) capital, or change the strategy, belongs to the asset owner.

B. The Risks of "Crowding" in Smart Beta Strategies

Crowding is an example of an issue that was previously handled by asset managers. With a top-down allocation to smart beta strategies, this is now an issue that asset owners must grapple with as well.

Crowding is a risk that smart beta strategies face (it exists in alpha strategies as well, but for genuine alpha this risk should be lower) because by their nature they are well-known and likely to be used by many investors. Essentially, crowding issues/risks can be thought of as those that arise from an increasing amount of capital adopting the same strategy and therefore taking similar positions in securities.

Unfortunately, concerns about crowding are not always well defined, which presents a problem when trying to manage potential risks. It is our view that issues related to crowding can be separated into two different concerns.

a. Too Many Sellers

The first is a fear that crowding may cause a sudden and sharp loss—with the impact of price movements in August 2007 on quantitative strategies as the posterchild. This type of crowding is less related to the amount of assets in a strategy (although a contributing factor), but more dependent on a synchronized asset manager's or investor's decision making. With too much commonality between strategies, decisions are more likely to be synchronized. And the more that strategies have in common (e.g. the use of common metrics/signals and calculation techniques) the more synchronized trading decisions can potentially be. For this risk to manifest itself the level of synchronized assets does not need to be large relative to market size, but relative to available liquidity. With the benefit of hindsight trigger events such as August 2007 or October 1987 can be rationalized (but not proved), although this is not always the case.

---

[15] A skilled value manager will have exposure to the value factor via its investment process but is able to use its unique insights to deliver additional returns beyond the smart beta.

[16] Many asset managers with a pronounced smart beta exposure (factor or "style" bias) are prepared to wait though periods of poor performance and expect their returns to be cyclical. There is nothing wrong with this approach either, but the asset manager is expected to justify this to the asset owner.

Unfortunately, this risk is very hard to identify in advance, and is not typically captured by risk models. In part this is because the problem arises from the emergent behavior of the system as a whole rather than current portfolio positioning.

The risk is therefore very hard to manage. Given the well-known nature of smart beta strategies this type of crowding from time to time may well be unavoidable. To us this suggests that strategies must be implemented using robust approaches that are likely to fail in predictable and understood ways rather than complicated strategies where failure is harder to predict or understand. Similarly, investors should avoid being in a position of a forced seller, either due to excessive leverage or to knee-jerk decision making.

The positive aspect of this type of risk is that not all asset owners are willing to accept it, and therefore it may be priced, that is, some element of return is compensation for short-term loss. This can help mitigate the second form of crowding discussed in the next section.

b. Too Much Capital

The second type of crowding is due to excessive flow of assets into a strategy/factor. As capital is allocated to a constrained set of securities (those selected and/or highly weighted by the strategy) the price of those securities rises. This attracts further capital and reinforces (past) returns, while in fact future prospects are diminishing. Eventually, as return expectations are lowered, concerns emerge about the strategy being "broken." We do not think that this effect is surprising[17] and is a natural part of how markets behave.

The impact on a popular strategy is likely to be lower future returns and potentially a more periodic return profile. In this case we think that expectations need to adjust to reflect this change in reality.

As with the previous crowding example, a strategy that does not work all the time is not acceptable to some investors. This selling low and buying high behavior is well documented and contributes to the periodic nature of performance. This behavior is one reason why, although the performance may become more cyclical, it can remain positive over time.

c. The Good Side of Crowding

Although often viewed as a negative, crowding does have a positive as it creates a first mover advantage. Asset owners that can invest in strategies before they become popular have the potential to benefit from buying low and selling high. Of course, this is not without risk, and begins to stray into the realms of strategy timing,[18] but suggests that looking for and allocating capital to new smart betas is a worthwhile undertaking for a long-term asset owner.

---

[17] While academic studies of smart beta strategies show positive returns over long backtest periods, they very rarely show a strategy that never has a multiyear period of poor performance.

[18] We believe that strategy timing is harder than asset class or market timing, and so find it puzzling when investors that think timing asset classes is "too hard" but are interested in timing smart beta strategies.

C. Timing Allocations to Strategies

If the returns of these strategies vary over time, then it's natural to ask if they can be timed. This is often expressed by considering if strategies (or factors) are cheap or expensive and therefore should be over- or underweighted. In some ways the idea of factor timing seems odd given that:

• Most institutions are skeptical about timing traditional asset classes;
• Timing smart beta is arguably harder than for traditional markets for similar reasons to those mentioned in Section II.C.

Of course, regret risk is natural when investing in a new area, so investors are concerned over valuations, whether strategies are temporarily expensive or have run their course and been competed away—"don't buy the backtest." At the time of writing, there is a heated debate on the merits and difficulties of timing factors. Where investors do consider factor valuations, a common measure is valuation spread, that is, the cheapness of securities on measure, such as price to book or price to earnings for securities with positive versus negative factor characteristics. For example, low price-to-book ratios for small companies relative to large companies indicates cheapness for the size factor and vice versa. There are several pitfalls in successfully converting these simple measures into tradable strategies, however.

Two other structural thoughts are also relevant in our view:

1. Factors have low correlations to each other, in other words, are highly diverse. Therefore, there is a high "concentration penalty" in focusing on just one or two factors on perceived attractiveness grounds.
2. With a limited number of factors to trade, the opportunity set is small. Random outcomes are much more influential on short- and medium-term outcomes compared to underlying returns—the high noise-to-signal problem.

Both suggest that investors need a high degree of skill to make factor timing successful. Overall, therefore, we think that investors should think carefully about how much of their risk budget to spend on factor timing, or perhaps first consider traditional markets before taking on this more difficult area, perhaps including factors to increase the opportunity set.

IV. FUTURE DEVELOPMENTS

A. Introduction: Where Have We Come From?

The ideas behind smart beta have their origins in equity research, in particular tests of whether factors other than broad market exposure can explain the performance of individual stocks. While concepts such as value or quality go back much further (think Benjamin Graham), a more quantitative approach developed from the 1960s.

Without wishing to go through this history in detail, we highlight some key developments from a practitioners' point of view:

- **Origins:** Testing of the CAPM lead to the idea of "factors" in the early 1990s, value and small cap initially, but quickly followed by momentum. The main use of these findings by asset owners was to refine performance measurement for active management. Active managers were put into style boxes to align investment processes (and natural stock habitats) to benchmarks. At the portfolio level, asset owners remained factor neutral, for example, balancing a growth (nonvalue) and value manager.
- **Development of nonmarket cap strategies:** Early rules-based strategies focus on specific alternatives to market cap, in particular wealth weighted and low correlation strategies. We originally referred to this as "beta prime."
- **Not all alpha is alpha:** Research into hedge fund strategies shows that a reasonable proportion of returns can be explained with rules-based approaches. The idea of hedge fund beta lead to early products that aimed to replicate hedge fund returns.
- **Early adopters:** Fundamental indexation provided an additional catalyst for investors to explicitly consider nonmarket cap approaches, in part due to its simplicity. Arguably the global financial crisis, following shortly after the TMT boom/bust, also caused investors to doubt the theory of market efficiency, and therefore the centrality of market cap weighting. Heated debate followed as to whether fundamental indexation was a form of value investing in disguise.
- **Wider take off:** Increasing proliferation of equity products, particularly low volatility. Interestingly, low volatility did not become "mainstream," and in many factor models remains absent, until after around 2008, despite testing from the late 1960s.
- **Branching out:** More recently and looking forward, we see smart beta moving in a number of directions: (1) single factor to multifactor equities; (2) smart beta/nonmarket cap ideas outside of equities; (3) alternative beta as a strategy in its own right; (4) asset owners adopting a broader approach to portfolio construction—covered earlier.

We comment on these developments in the following sections.

B. Moving from Single Factor to Multifactor Equities

In our view, getting exposure to several factors in one product is appealing to asset owners. In addition to the diversification benefits of combining several lowly correlated factors together, it requires lower governance—holding a single product rather than managing several. Governance is further reduced as combination products effectively outsource the selection and allocation of underlying factors to an asset manager. However, we believe that asset owners still need to have an understanding of the underlying strategies and how the combined portfolio will behave so as to have reasonable expectations for performance, and, importantly, in what future scenarios the performance may be poor.

Multifactor strategies are often more complicated as they can (but do not always) use optimization in portfolio construction. All else being equal we favor simpler approaches where possible, but there are advantages in more sophisticated methods to control risks in higher tracking error/factor exposure products.

Some industry participants do not consider multifactor strategies as smart beta because the approaches are more complicated or do not utilize an index. As discussed earlier, we do not see the need for an index for a strategy to qualify as smart beta.

Naturally, we expect that the evolution of smart beta strategies will continue and that strategies that today are considered alpha will eventually be thought of as smart beta strategies.

C. Smart Beta Outside of Equities

Many of the ideas behind the development of equity smart beta can be applied in other markets, albeit with different practical considerations. For example:

- **Using nonmarket cap weights in credit**. This seems intuitive to asset owners since market cap is proportionate to the size of debt, and therefore the most indebted companies get larger weights. However, it still requires beliefs that markets are not perfectly efficient in to some way.
- **Factor thinking in bonds**. There are direct analogs of equity factors to bonds, particularly credit. For example, value (spread vs. fair value spread), carry (higher yield/spread), momentum, low volatility/quality, size.
- **Commodity futures**. Smart beta strategies can allow for different (1) commodity weighting methods, (2) term of futures, (3) roll process. The thinking behind many of the variations again relates to factors such as carry, liquidity, and momentum.
- **Listed property and infrastructure**. Using nonmarket cap weights, and screens or tilts for low-volatility/quality factors.

This list was intended to be brief and illustrative. However, it demonstrates that investors can adopt smart beta techniques in most asset classes.

D. The Rise of Alternative Beta: The Long and Short of It

The typical smart beta product is a long-only strategy that invests in securities with attractive/target characteristics (value, small cap, etc.). Either implicitly or explicitly (depending on the underlying process) this portfolio can be thought of as a market cap portfolio plus a portfolio of relative over/underweights. This naturally shows a direct extension of the smart beta strategy into long-short investing: overweights become long positions and underweights become short positions. A long-short implementation can therefore be thought of as a way to construct a "pure" factor portfolio[19] and is relatively easy to implement because stocks can be shorted (borrowed and sold, with the aim of buying back at a lower price). Because long and short positions can be balanced, equity market exposure can be close to zero, and the factor portfolio therefore has strong diversification properties compared to traditional asset classes. We think that there are some other pros and cons of investing long-short compared to long-only:

+ Capital efficiency: more factor exposure per unit of capital. This is particularly useful for asset owners with high return targets or those that want to make larger allocations to nontraditional strategies/factors.

+ Easier to use in portfolio construction as factor buildings blocks are separate from traditional market exposure.

- Likely higher cost, in part due to costs of shorting stocks. However, a fair comparison should be made to long-only by considering costs per unit exposure, not capital allocation.

- There are some additional risks due to leverage and shorting, for example, short squeezes. For modest levels of leverage, this tends not to be an issue.

- Some capital is "wasted" as physical assets are held in cash and other collateral.

The example earlier extends long-only equity smart beta into the long-short "world." But factors such as momentum and value can be applied across markets as well—futures and forwards are typically used to take long and short positions. As mentioned earlier, strategies like these are now being referred to as alternative beta. We don't see alternative beta as new, but more as a recognition that well-known strategies employed by many hedge funds are in fact long/short implementations of smart beta strategies. Of course, recognizing these strategies explicitly is an interesting and innovative step in itself.

While the example makes a link to long-only smart beta, testing of hedge fund returns was also instrumental in the path to alternative beta. There are now numerous studies showing that hedge fund returns can be (partly) explained by beta factors, that is, some alpha is beta. Table 16.4 shows analysis we conducted a few years ago to illustrate this point. Over the period studied, some 84% of the variation in returns can be explained by the combination of beta strategies, both traditional and alternative. We discussed the asset owner perspective in Section II in the context of long-only equities. But we think that the points made are more general, and largely apply to the alternative beta/hedge fund world as well.

As a final point, there are strategies that are harder to define as factors but are nevertheless becoming available as alternative beta. Examples are merger arbitrage and volatility selling.

---

[19] This is true in a broad sense, although there is no precise definition of a pure factor as there (almost) is for market cap.

TABLE 16.4 Hedge Fund Returns Explained by Beta (December 1996–December 2013)

Hedge Fund Category	Percentage of Hedge Fund Returns Explained by Beta
Relative Value	64
Equity Long-short	84
Event Driven	67
Macro	48
Aggregate Hedge Fund Index	**84**

Source: Towers Watson, "Into a New Dimension: An Alternative View of Smart Beta" (October 2014). See paper for further details on data and methods.

We have seen a lot of asset owner interest in smart/alternative beta over the past few years, a key reason being that these strategies have high diversification compared to traditional asset classes. They also may have the following advantages relative to hedge funds:

- Lower fees
- Greater transparency
- More liquidity

V. CONCLUDING THOUGHTS

Smart beta has come a long way since its origins, particularly over the past 5 to 10 years. We have been surprised by the level of interest and (heated) debate on the subject, which we see as a good thing. Smart beta has shaken the investment industry. It has introduced new options for portfolio allocation and management for asset owners and challenged existing business models for asset managers. We see many positive aspects to smart and alternative beta, but do not claim it as a "free lunch," particularly in governance terms. Asset owners also need to carefully consider their beliefs before venturing forward.

Overall, we would say smart/alternative beta is moving out of the early adoption phase of the innovation cycle. We see potential for further development of new strategies, as well as further opportunities for asset owners and asset managers.

*   *   *

Please see the Additional Disclaimers section at the end of this book.

CHAPTER 17

SMART BETA: THE SPACE BETWEEN ALPHA AND BETA

Andrew Junkin
President, Wilshire Consulting

Steven Foresti
Chief Investment Officer,
Wilshire Consulting

Michael Rush
Vice President,
Wilshire Consulting

CHAPTER SUMMARY

Wilshire Consulting suggests that clients consider adopting smart beta approaches in equity portfolios as a replacement for or complement to active strategies. Smart beta strategies capture many of the systematic returns that active managers frequently implement, but do so in a systematic, consistent, and less expensive manner. Smart beta strategies may also be appropriate as a replacement for traditional passive strategies for investors who are looking to improve the risk-adjusted returns of their equity portfolios without using higher cost-active strategies. Wilshire Consulting believes that smart beta strategies, particularly when implemented in a multifactor approach, can be an efficient, cost-effective solution for asset owners wrestling with today's low return environment.

In this chapter, we discuss what is meant by smart beta and which factors are typically targeted. We outline implementation options for investors considering smart beta integration within their portfolios and present an implementation case study. Finally, although the factors are targeted based on their historical ability to improve risk-adjusted returns, we highlight potential risks.

We begin, however, by noting our mild protest against the clever marketing implied within the smart beta label. Academic and industry attention to smart beta strategies has led to a proliferation of various labels that broadly encompass a differentiated approach to index investing (i.e. Factor Based Investing, Alternative Beta, Strategic Beta, Advanced Beta, Active Beta). We are not fans of the smart beta label, as we find it to be somewhat misleading and unnecessarily disparaging to traditional beta. Despite our effort to espouse a more appropriate name, we use smart beta within this note for convenience and because it has been widely adopted by many in the industry.

Several catalysts have contributed to the rise in the popularity of smart beta strategies, including increased market demand for index-based investing, regulatory pressures to provide transparency and investor frustration with the high fees and disappointing returns of actively managed strategies. Additionally, technological advances have allowed index providers to deliver these strategies at reasonable (and declining) cost. Index investing has undergone significant evolution during the past century with many of the recent products and jargon flooding the industry focused on a departure from traditional, market capitalization–weighted indexing. Exhibit 17.1 presents a timeline of the major changes regarding passive and rules-based investing.

EXHIBIT 17.1   Modifications of Index Investing

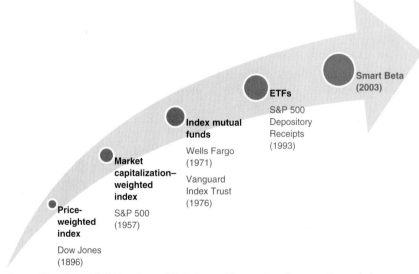

Source: Data from S&P Dow Jones, Wells Fargo, Vanguard, spdrs.com, Guggenheim.

I.   FACTORS: THE BUILDING BLOCKS OF PORTFOLIOS

Research by Eugene Fama and Kenneth French noted the explanatory power of characteristics other than market beta when examining a stock's return (Fama and French 1992). Fama and French found that small stocks tended to outperform large stocks and that stocks with low price multiples (e.g. value stocks) tended to outperform high-multiple stocks (e.g. growth stocks). These two "factors" are now generally referred to as size and style. One way to conceptualize factors is to think of them as unifying security characteristics beyond just size and style. Smart beta strategies attempt to capture the performance patterns of those factors that demonstrate the potential to serve as broad and persistent drivers of return.

Continued research in this area has led to additional equity factors that may be targeted. The number of identifiable factors with positive relative historical performance started in the single digits with several original strategies[1] but has grown to a few hundred in recent years (Arnott et al. 2016). While the menu of options is overwhelming, Wilshire Consulting's examination points to five key factors:

1. **Size.** Smaller stocks tend to outperform larger stocks. Size is typically measured by market capitalization.
2. **Value.** Less expensive stocks, based on price multiples, tend to outperform more expensive stocks. Value can be measured many ways: price to earnings, price to book, price to sales, etc.
3. **Quality.** Higher quality stocks tend to outperform lower quality stocks. Quality is typically measured by fundamentals, such as earnings stability, low debt ratios, and/or high return-on-equity.
4. **Momentum.** Positive momentum stocks tend to outperform negative momentum stocks. Momentum is normally expressed as price momentum. A momentum strategy could be expressed as "buy winners and sell losers."
5. **Volatility.** Lower volatility stocks tend to outperform higher volatility stocks. Volatility may be measured or estimated as standard deviation or beta.

II.   ALPHA OR BETA?

To fully appreciate smart beta, it is important to understand what is meant by beta investing and why one might be tempted to classify a particular approach as being "smart." In a traditional sense, beta is referred to as the nondiversifiable risk and return inherent in a broad asset class. An equity market beta typically represents the risk and return that can be accessed through a broad array of equity securities. Market capitalization weighting is the standard in this application for its ability to collect the aggregate return of all investors participating in the asset class. Market

---

[1] Among the first Smart Beta ETFs are PowerShares Dynamic Market Portfolio (2003) and PowerShares FTSE RAFI US 1000 Portfolio (2005).

capitalization weighted indexes were created to capture the statistical characteristics of a market beta and accommodate investor needs. This is passive investing in its traditional sense.

In contrast to passive investing, active managers attempt to add an incremental return—or "alpha"—to the market's beta return. In the pursuit of alpha, active managers must deviate from a market cap–weighted index. Investment managers offer a wide variety of active strategies that can encompass quantitative and qualitative disciplines to derive such deviations. In analyzing characteristics of actively managed portfolios, we note that active managers frequently have a consistent bias toward certain factor characteristics, such as value, size, momentum. For example, an active manager may say "we buy good companies at reasonable prices," implying both a quality and value bias. Smart beta investing uses similar factor-tilt investment concepts that are common elements of many active strategies. Therefore, while the concept of tilting toward these long-measured factors is not new, smart beta strategies provide systematic and consistent exposure to these and other factors through higher capacity, transparent vehicles with lower costs. These products typically reweight traditional cap-weighted indexes through a transparent rules-based manner to target exposure to specific factors.

To the extent that common smart beta factors are embedded in the historical alpha delivered by active strategies, many of these excess return streams cannot be viewed as part of a truly unique active management process. As such, we would suggest thinking of smart beta as falling between traditional beta and "true" alpha. We depict this concept visually in Exhibit 17.2, whereby the right panel of the schematic describes smart beta returns cutting into earlier definitions of alpha.

EXHIBIT 17.2 Rethinking Passive and Active Management

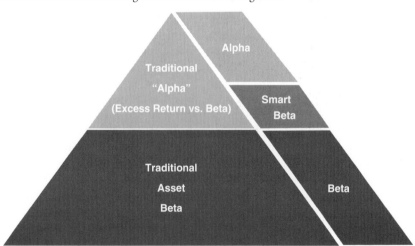

Source: Data from Wilshire Consulting.

As the chart illustrates, alpha is better understood through a more refined lens that removes the impacts of persistent systematic factor tilts. As a result, what can be called true alpha (i.e. the idiosyncratic returns derived from security selection or opportunistic market timing) can then only be achieved after accounting for persistent factor tilts.

III.   EQUITY FACTOR INVESTING: AN EXAMPLE

Focusing on the value factor, which is one of the most commonly utilized fundamental equity factors, we provide a simplified example to highlight how a smart beta portfolio might be built. An investor could tilt toward value by overweighting the "cheapest" 30% of stocks in the value-to-growth spectrum, for example, as measured by low Price/Book (or Price/Earnings, Price/Sales, etc.) ratio, while simultaneously underweighting the most "expensive" 30% of stocks using the same measure. Such a portfolio could be constructed through a long-only or long-short approach, depending on the desired level of factor exposure. More sophisticated portfolio construction techniques could be (and often are) utilized to harness the desired factor tilt while attempting to maintain neutrality to other undesired factor exposures and to avoid excessive security specific risk. Using similar construction techniques with different variables, strategies can be built to extract other significant equity factors.

IV.   PERFORMANCE OF KEY EQUITY FACTORS

Although there are many active smart beta products in the marketplace, we favor an initial assessment of equity factor investing by considering historical index performance. MSCI, well known for their global equity indexes, offers a suite of factor indexes that serve as a reasonable representation of the broad factors available within the smart beta marketplace. Exhibit 17.3 charts the historical risk and return of the five equity factors identified earlier,[2] along with a multifactor index[3] and a capitalization-weighted index, for the entire index history.

During this time period, the Quality and Volatility factor indexes have performed well in a relative sense in that they have delivered both lower risk and higher return versus the capitalization-weighted index. While the other indexes have outperformed as well, they have done so at higher risk levels. However, it is not uncommon for higher risk investments to deliver higher returns as compensation for bearing incremental risk. Exhibit 17.4 contains the underlying return and risk numbers along with additional performance metrics.

---

[2] The MSCI ACWI indexes that are utilized throughout the historical analysis are: Equal Weighted for Size, Enhanced Value for Value, Sector Neutral Quality for Quality, Momentum for Momentum and Minimum Volatility for Volatility.

[3] The MSCI "Diversified" index is comprised of four factors; value, momentum, quality, and size.

EXHIBIT 17.3 MSCI All-Country World Factor Indexes: 1999–June 2018

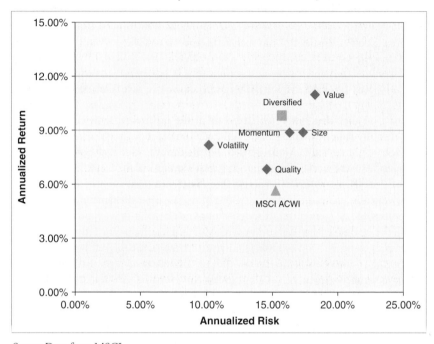

Source: Data from MSCI.

EXHIBIT 17.4 MSCI All-Country World Factor Indexes: 1999–June 2018

	Size	Value	Quality	Momentum	Volatility	Diversified	MSCI ACWI
Total Return	8.88%	10.98%	6.84%	8.87%	8.17%	9.82%	5.66%
Total Risk	17.33%	18.24%	14.55%	16.30%	10.16%	15.70%	15.23%
Return/Risk Ratio	0.51	0.60	0.47	0.54	0.80	0.63	0.37
Beta to MSCI ACWI	1.07	1.11	0.94	0.93	0.59	0.99	
Corr: Ex. Ret. v. ACWI	0.22	0.26	−0.35	−0.14	−0.81	0.00	
Maximum Drawdown	−57%	−58%	−51%	−57%	−39%	−55%	−55%
Upside Capture	114%	126%	96%	108%	68%	112%	
Downside Capture	99%	102%	90%	92%	49%	92%	
Correlation Excess Return versus Cap Weighting	0.22	0.26	−0.35	−0.14	−0.81	0.00	

Source: Data from MSCI.

Exhibit 17.5 suggests that, with the exception of low volatility, the factor indexes are "market-like." For example, their beta statistics, which capture their general sensitivity to moves in the capitalization weighted index, are clustered around 1.0; ranging from 0.93 for Momentum and 1.11 for Value. Note that, when combined into a multifactor construct, the diversified approach reflects a beta of 0.99. Additionally, the correlation between the excess return of the Diversified index versus the total return of the cap-weighted index is zero, an indication that general market returns have no bearing on the relative return of the Diversified smart beta index. These statistics generally confirm that smart beta strategies can be utilized to deliver capitalization-weighted beta plus the incremental returns from desired factor tilts. It should be noted that, although accommodations can be made to include Low Volatility, specifically, within traditional investment structure analysis, the statistics above also support Wilshire's previous research that advocates for the consideration of such strategies during the asset allocation process.[4]

V.   IMPLEMENTATION OF SMART BETA

For those investors choosing to pursue an allocation to smart beta, Wilshire Consulting favors a diversified, multifactor approach that would include a variety of factors identified earlier. One of the main benefits of following a multifactor approach is that individual factors have historically produced low correlations with one another and, therefore, should lower the risk of a single smart beta factor allocation and dampen the effects of individual factor drawdowns. We show the differentiation between these relative return relationships in two ways; first, through a "heat map" that demonstrates the changing leadership among smart beta factors from year to year.

Exhibit 17.6 contains the historical correlations among the five MSCI factor indexes, along with each factor's tracking error measured against a cap-weighted index. Correlations were calculated by first measuring the excess return of each index versus a cap-weighted index to isolate the incremental factor performance impact.

As the correlation numbers suggest, the return experience of the various factors during any given time period can be quite different. Exhibit 17.7 contains the three-year rolling excess returns (again vs. the cap-weighted index) for the five factor indexes plus a line showing the simple average of those same excess returns.

The minimum three-year excess return for each of the five single-factor indexes is noted within Exhibit 17.7 to highlight the fact that each of the factors experienced at least one lengthy period of underperformance. The average line exhibits negative three-year returns as well (with a minimum return of –0.8%), but is typically less volatile than the single-factor returns. The excess risk (tracking error) of the average return is 3.2% for the period of 1999 through June 2018. Looking back to

---

[4] While it is beyond the scope of this research piece, it should be noted that Wilshire advocates consideration of low-volatility strategies during the asset allocation process. For more information, see Foresti (2012).

EXHIBIT 17.5 MSCI All-Country World Factor Indexes Excess Annual Returns versus Cap-Weighted Index

2006	2007	2008	2009	2010	2011	2012	2013	2014	2015	2016	2017
Value 7.7%	Momentum 11.2%	Volatility 28.9%	Size 16.0%	Size 5.8%	Volatility 13.8%	Size 1.5%	Momentum 3.2%	Volatility 6.6%	Volatility 5.3%	Value 1.9%	Momentum 7.5%
Size 3.6%	Quality 5.4%	Quality 5.7%	Value 8.4%	Momentum 2.7%	Momentum 10.0%	Momentum 1.1%	Value 1.3%	Quality 2.3%	Momentum 4.3%	Size 0.7%	Size 1.4%
Volatility 3.4%	Size 3.7%			Volatility 1.6%	Quality 5.5%	Quality 0.9%		Momentum 1.6%	Quality 1.4%		Value 1.4%
Momentum 1.5%	Value 2.6%			Quality 1.4%							Quality 1.1%
Quality 0.8%											
0% Excess Return	Volatility −4.1%	Value −2.4%	Quality −0.5%	Value −1.8%	Value −5.9%	Value −0.2%	Quality −2.5%	Size −2.2%	Value −2.7%	Volatility −0.3%	Volatility −4.8%
		Momentum −5.3%	Momentum −11.5%		Size −7.3%	Volatility −5.1%	Volatility −4.7%	Value −4.4%	Size −4.3%	Quality −2.4%	
		Size −5.7%	Volatility −12.8%				Size −6.0%			Momentum −3.4%	

Source: Data from MSCI.

EXHIBIT 17.6 MSCI All-Country World Factor Indexes Excess Return Analysis: 1999–June 2018

	Size	Value	Quality	Momentum	Volatility
Size	1.00				
Value	0.73	1.00			
Quality	−0.24	−0.42	1.00		
Momentum	−0.08	−0.09	0.08	1.00	
Volatility	−0.06	−0.17	0.40	0.19	1.00
Tracking Error	5.6%	6.7%	2.7%	8.1%	7.9%

Source: Data from MSCI.

EXHIBIT 17.7 MSCI All-Country World Factor Indexes Excess Return

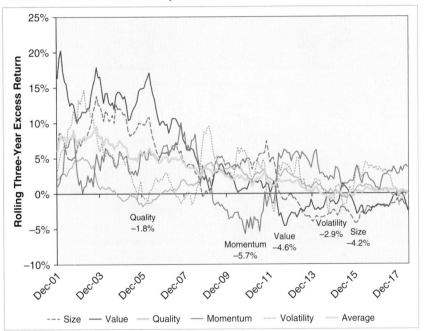

Source: Data from MSCI.

Exhibit 17.6, we see that only the Quality index exhibits a lower standard deviation of excess returns at 2.7%. This is further evidence of the benefits of diversifying across multiple factors.

Another benefit from multifactor investing is that the diversification can also help mitigate concerns over the relative valuation levels of individual factors. Valuation shifts can have a large impact on the performance of any market segment (or asset class) and are notoriously difficult to predict. Spreading the unpredictability

EXHIBIT 17.8 US Large-Cap Value versus Large-Cap Growth

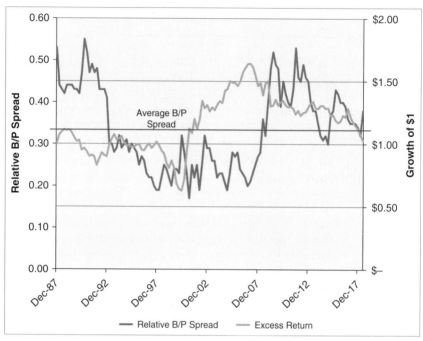

Source: Data from Wilshire Atlas, Wilshire Compass.

of that risk across multiple factors is an ideal way to dampen short-term impacts. Exhibit 17.8 contains a comparison of US large-cap value and large-cap growth stocks since 1987, including a relative valuation metric (B/P) and a measure of excess returns. For perspective, when relative B/P (the blue line) is trending downward on the chart, it is an indication that value may be getting more "expensive" versus its history; the opposite being true for an upward movement in relative B/P.

While the relationship between relative B/P and future factor returns is far from perfect, we can see that although the relative valuation signal was below its historical average (i.e. "expensive") for some time, large-cap value enjoyed subsequent outperformance versus large-cap growth (early 2000s). Following 2007, the market reversed from a value factor return perspective (the excess return line trended downward) and the valuation signal flipped as well. As an example of valuation levels across other factors, the Appendix provides a sample of several smart beta valuation metrics utilized by Wilshire in monitoring relative pricing shifts. In the next section, we highlight how an investor may implement smart beta within a diversified portfolio through a case study that focuses on the approach identified earlier, as part of an investment structure analysis.

VI.   SMART BETA CASE STUDY: A POTENTIAL COMPLEMENT TO TRADITIONAL ACTIVE MANAGEMENT

Wilshire suggests the consideration of smart beta within an investment structure analysis. Including these products during the investment structure process forces them to compete for capital versus traditional passive and active strategies. The investment structure case study below begins with a "traditional" US equity portfolio consisting of a cap-weighted index fund and then allows for active management in each of the four size/style market segments (i.e. large growth, large value, small growth, small value). In the second step, we expand the opportunity set to allow for an allocation to a multifactor smart beta product. This construct forces passive management, active management and smart beta to all "compete" for assets based on their expected return, risk and correlation profiles.

Exhibit 17.9 is the starting point of our investment structure analysis and contains assumptions for each segment within a US equity portfolio. All risk and return assumptions are expressed in excess terms versus the broad US equity market (i.e. the Wilshire 5000 Index), thus the nonzero risk and correlation estimates for the passive S&P 500 index fund. Additionally, the multifactor beta product was assumed to have a gross-of-fees information ratio (IR) similar to that of traditional active strategies, with relevant strategy/product fees deducted from each to arrive at the net-of-fees excess return assumptions.[5] The IR assumptions are well supported by the historical record of smart beta discussed earlier and as delivered through successful active management.

Focusing on the large-cap managers, Product 1 exhibits a relatively high correlation to the smart beta product while Product 2 reveals almost no correlation. This

EXHIBIT 17.9 Investment Structure Assumptions

	S&P 500	Multi-Factor Smart Beta	Small Cap Manager 1	Small Cap Manager 2	Large Cap Manager 1	Large Cap Manager 2
Expected Return	0.00	0.57	0.35	0.55	0.15	0.39
Expected Risk	1.19	2.51	8.28	8.13	2.74	3.64
Information Ratio	0.00	0.23	0.04	0.07	0.05	0.11
Correlation						
S&P 500	1.00					
Multi-Factor Smart Beta	−0.08	1.00				
Small Cap Manager 1	−0.80	0.21	1.00			
Small Cap Manager 2	−0.76	0.16	0.87	1.00		
Large Cap Manager 1	−0.70	0.28	0.85	0.82	1.00	
Large Cap Manager 2	0.16	0.03	−0.23	−0.12	−0.23	1.00

Source: Data from Wilshire Consulting.

---

[5] Live manager data from the Wilshire Compass database was used as a guide for establishing reasonable active management assumptions.

EXHIBIT 17.10 Optimization Outcome

	Optimal Without Smart Beta	Optimal With Smart Beta
S&P 500	28.48	3.96
Multi-Factor Smart Beta	0.00	68.78
Small Cap Manager 1	0.00	0.00
Small Cap Manager 2	16.02	4.86
Large Cap Manager 1	8.18	0.00
Large Cap Manager 2	47.31	22.40
Expected Return	0.28	0.51
Expected Risk	2.00	2.00
Return/Risk	0.14	0.25

Source: Data from Wilshire Consulting.

suggests that Large-Cap Manager 1 may have relatively high exposure to some of the factors that are common to smart beta investing. Both small-cap managers exhibit some correlation as well, likely due to the small-cap tilts that smart beta strategies typically employ. It is important to note that these risk statistics are product specific; suggesting that active managers with little embedded systematic exposures would likely reveal lower correlations to the excess returns of smart beta strategies. Additionally, large differences in these important inputs would likely lead to investment structure results that are quite different from this example case study. Exhibit 17.10 contains the optimized case study results both with and without allocation allowances to the multifactor smart beta strategy.

While an investor might not implement either structure shown above, instead choosing a smart beta allocation that falls somewhere between these two sample portfolios, the results are instructive. First, the large-cap active manager with a relatively high correlation to the multifactor product was completely removed. The other active large-cap manager experienced a meaningful decrease in allocation while some "optimized rebalancing" was done among the other products. Finally, the overall information ratio of the optimized smart beta–inclusive portfolio increased rather meaningfully, benefiting in part from the improved efficiencies of introducing another portfolio candidate, but primarily from smart beta's lower fees. To the extent that a smart beta strategy can replace some of the common risks found in some higher-fee active strategies, it can play a valuable role in a diversified investment program. As such, the above was meant to highlight what is possible for a portfolio with relatively high factor exposures embedded within active management products.

As a final step, we created efficient frontiers[6] using the above assumptions with and without the multifactor product to show the affect that this strategy can have

---

[6] An active efficient frontier plots the highest expected alpha portfolio at each level of expected tracking error (i.e. active risk).

EXHIBIT 17.11 Efficient Frontiers With and Without Smart Beta

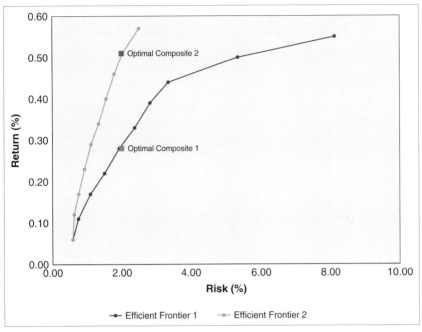

Source: Data from Wilshire Compass.

on a portfolio's expected risk and return. In Exhibit 17.11, the different lines are the efficient frontiers with and without smart beta, respectively.

The upward shift in the frontier once smart beta is introduced as a possible investment choice highlights the fact that a multifactor product can have a meaningful and positive effect on a balanced portfolio where factor exposures are present within traditional active management products. The shift is more extreme at the higher expected risk portfolios due, in part, to the fee savings that are available by moving from a traditional active product with embedded factor exposures to a diversified smart beta allocation.

VII.   THE PROS AND CONS OF SMART BETA

In the final section of this paper we review other potential benefits and risks of smart beta, in addition to the return history and valuation level caveats noted earlier. Exhibit 17.12 summarizes these pros and cons, which we discuss below.

A main advantage available through the successful use of smart beta strategies is the ability for an investor to access elements of the "alpha" that some active managers capture but at a lower cost. While active managers sometimes employ complex and broad investment philosophies and processes, smart beta portfolio construction

EXHIBIT 17.12 Smart Beta: Advantages and Disadvantages

Potential Pros	Potential Cons
• Transparent, liquid portfolios	• Integrity of the model drives strategy performance
• Systematic implementation	• Backward looking
• Lower costs versus active management	• Potential for high tracking error versus traditional index
• Focused exposure to risk factors	• Unknown capacity limits

Source: Data from Wilshire Consulting.

rules are typically transparent and implemented in a systematic way. Some smart beta managers may be thought of as index managers who manage to an alternatively constructed index rather than to cap-weighting. This sort of "rules-based" investing allows them to offer lower costs versus active management, much like what is delivered through traditional index investing.

The first two potential cons of smart beta listed in Exhibit 17.12—model integrity and backward looking results—have already been discussed to some extent. Any strategy or investment model must target persistent generators of excess returns for smart beta to be effective. Regardless of a factor's efficacy, if an investment manager or product does not effectively isolate and capture the factor return, future performance could disappoint. While the factors that are being promoted as worthwhile exhibit successful historical track-records, that history is no guarantee of future results. Therefore, before adopting a smart beta product, its history and investment model should be scrutinized. Absent a reasonable economic rationale underpinning why one should expect to be compensated with a positive systematic return for tilting on a given factor, investors should proceed with caution.

Another possible risk of smart beta is its potential for high tracking error versus traditional, cap-weighted indexes. The MSCI factor indexes highlighted earlier exhibit historical tracking error in the 3%–8% range, including the MSCI All-Country Diversified Multiple-Factor Index at 4%. Extended underperformance versus a traditional index is another event that could prompt decision makers to abandon smart beta perhaps at the worst time, highlighting Behavioral Risk, one of Wilshire Consulting's six Risk Lenses. In order to properly manage Behavioral Risk, the potential for tracking error is something that must be well understood and accepted before pursuing factor investing. Finally, capacity limits and the performance impact from an expanding asset-base are difficult to assess. Highlighting these potential capacity-related risks, Exhibit 17.13 provides an estimate of the growth in smart beta assets during the past 17 years.

EXHIBIT 17.13 US Strategic-Beta Exchange Traded Products Asset Growth

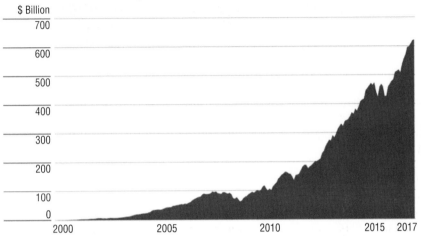

Source: Data from Morningstar Direct, Morningstar Research.

Assets under management in smart beta have increased 10-fold since the early 2000s, reaching more than a half-trillion US dollars currently. While the capacity for investing in value stocks, for example, is certainly large, the natural question is, "will these tilts stop working if too many investors are targeting the same factor?" It is worth noting that, even as smart beta becomes more widely accepted as a potentially valuable investment approach, its specific appropriateness is highly dependent on each institution's particular objectives and risk tolerances.

VIII.   CONCLUSION

While Wilshire Consulting believes that smart beta strategies, particularly when implemented in a multifactor approach, can be an efficient, cost-effective solution for asset owners, we recognize there are no "one size fits all" solutions in the world of investing and smart beta is no exception. An investor's goals and portfolio positioning, including the deployment of active management, should all play a role in deciding whether smart beta is a worthwhile pursuit. While potential incremental returns may be achieved, these exposures should be taken in a risk-controlled manner designed to deliver modest improvements over a long-term investment horizon. Whether smart beta is utilized, high-level asset allocation decisions will still dominate portfolio results. With some minor caveats noted earlier, Wilshire generally advocates the consideration of smart beta during the investment structure step of the investment process. We also favor a multifactor approach rather than single-factor implementation, as the diversification properties can be quite beneficial in managing the unpredictable nature of short-term factor risks.

Due to investor interest and technological advancements, the smart beta market is evolving at a rapid pace. It is difficult to predict with any degree of certainty where its adoption levels will be in the coming years. One thing that is clear within factor investing is the compelling fee savings when compared to capturing a systematic risk premium through traditional active strategies. The case study earlier highlights how the use of smart beta strategies might improve upon the risk-return profiles of certain portfolios. Investors who have either shifted away from or become frustrated with more traditional forms of active management as the result of inconsistent or disappointing results might appreciate the potential value of smart beta as a complement to purely passive investing.

APPENDIX: VALUATION EXHIBITS[7]

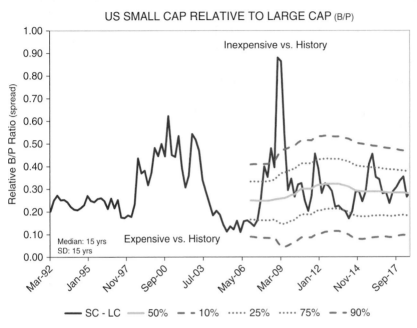

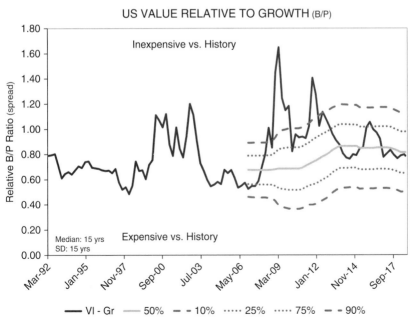

[7]Source: Wilshire Consulting.

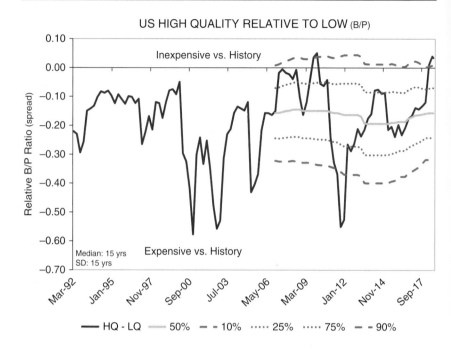

US HIGH QUALITY RELATIVE TO LOW (B/P)

Inexpensive vs. History

Expensive vs. History

Median: 15 yrs
SD: 15 yrs

Relative B/P Ratio (spread)

—— HQ - LQ ······ 50% – – 10% ······ 25% ······ 75% – – 90%

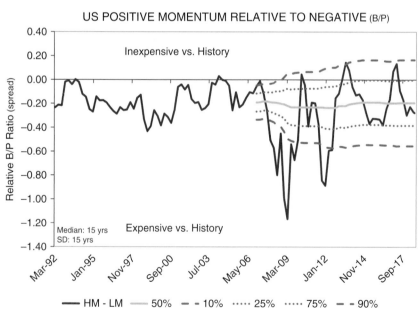

US POSITIVE MOMENTUM RELATIVE TO NEGATIVE (B/P)

Inexpensive vs. History

Expensive vs. History

Median: 15 yrs
SD: 15 yrs

Relative B/P Ratio (spread)

—— HM - LM ······ 50% – – 10% ······ 25% ······ 75% – – 90%

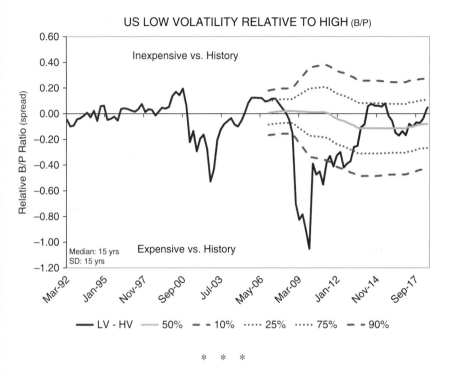

US LOW VOLATILITY RELATIVE TO HIGH (B/P)

* * *

Please see the Additional Disclaimers section at the end of this book.

PART VIII

RETAIL PERSPECTIVES

CHAPTER 18

SMART BETA INVESTING FOR THE MASSES: THE CASE FOR A RETAIL OFFERING

Lisa L. Huang[1]
Head of Artificial Intelligence
Investment Management and Planning,
Fidelity Investments

Petter N. Kolm
Director of the Mathematics in Finance
Master's Program and Clinical Professor,
Courant Institute of Mathematical Sciences,
New York University

The majority of investment professionals will agree that retail investing is a smaller and more limited area of work than institutional investing. For years, the well-trodden path in investment management is that innovative ideas and strategies are tested in institutional contexts, and then—often much later—they gradually traverse the divide into consumer-focused and retail investing. Such has been the case with smart beta investing. Now, in the second decade of the 20th century, smart beta ETFs are more broadly available, but there are surprisingly few smart beta portfolio offerings available in the retail market.

---

[1] Lisa L. Huang drafted this chapter while employed at Betterment and would like to thank Jamie Cartwright for editing the first version of this chapter.

This chapter details the case for why a retail advisor would—and should—offer a complete smart beta portfolio solution. In the institutional smart beta space, smart beta ETFs have seen continued investment due to improved technology, a precipitous reduction in the cost of trading (which in turn have decreased ETF expenses), and an ever-improving body of empirical evidence on what drives underlying risk premia. Because of this evolution, the retail advice market today has a strong foundation to build on when implementing smart beta portfolios on behalf of individual clients. However, advisors have been slow to offer complete smart beta strategies to the masses, even though the evidence for smart beta's efficacy and the costs of implementing a smart beta solution seem to be ripe for a retail audience.

When computers were first invented, they were big and expensive. While technology advanced and miniaturized in the 1960s and 1970s, computers were almost exclusively used in business contexts. To make the leap into the retail market, PC innovators like Apple and IBM had to change how people thought about the technology. In a broad sense, smart beta strategies today are like computers at the advent of the PC. From the quant alpha of the 1980s and 1990s to the introduction of smart beta ETFs over the past 20 years, we have seen smart beta advancing among institutional investors and clients. However, to increase the adoption and understanding among retail investors, the smart beta space will likely require further innovation and development from advisors in the retail space in the near future.

In this chapter is structured as follows. In Section I, we provide an introduction to so-called factor investing and smart beta. We explain how factors can be implemented and made available to retail investors as ETFs, often referred to as *smart beta ETFs*. We address the question of why to offer a smart beta product in the retail space in Section II. Thereafter, in Sections III and IV, we discuss challenges for offering a smart beta portfolio for retail. As this is a very active and rapidly evolving area, in Section V we highlight some of the key themes for the future of smart beta investing in the retail space. Section VI concludes.

Throughout this chapter, we keep the technical discussion to a minimum. We prioritize simplicity and brevity, at the risk of leaving out some details or being complete. We want to make this chapter accessible to a wide audience. It is also not our goal to provide a survey of the smart beta retail space. Needless to say, there are many interesting areas and aspects of smart beta investing that we do not cover herein.

I. INTRODUCTION TO FACTOR INVESTING AND SMART BETA

Rooted in the academic literature on the capital asset pricing model (CAPM) and arbitrage pricing theory (APT), factors can be thought of as atomic units that describe the return of a stock (see Sharpe 1964; Ross 1976; and Cochrane 1999). For instance, a certain company's stock return might be broken down into: (1) 50% of the *market factor*, (2) 30% of the *value factor*, and (3) 20% of the *company specific factor*. The company specific factor is often also referred to as the unexplained or idiosyncratic return. How much of each factor (the earlier percentages) contributes to the total stock return is called the *factor exposure* or *beta*.

The betas are determined statistically, and therefore the stock's return breakdown holds "on average." The market portfolio is perfectly correlated with and has the same volatility as the market factor. Therefore, the market's beta to the market factor is one. A stock with a market beta greater (less) than one implies that it more (less) volatile than the market.

By decomposing the return of individual stocks into factors we obtain a better understanding of their behavior or, what is commonly referred to as their *return characteristics*. Research spanning decades of academic and practitioner literature have identified a number of factors that are good atomic units of stocks.

We now turn to briefly describe the value, momentum and size factors below. Figure 18.1 shows the market, value, size, and momentum factors over the period January 1927 to May 2018.

A. Value

Value investing involves buying undervalued ("cheap") stocks and selling them again when they have gained in value (Graham and Dodd 2009). Academic studies have shown that cheap stocks tend to outperform "expensive" stocks in the long run. Cheap stocks can be defined in many different ways. One way is to look at the so-called price-to-book ratio (P/B for short) of the market price of the stock (P) and its

FIGURE 18.1   Growth of One Dollar Invested in Value, Size, and Momentum Factors over the Period January 1927 through May 2018

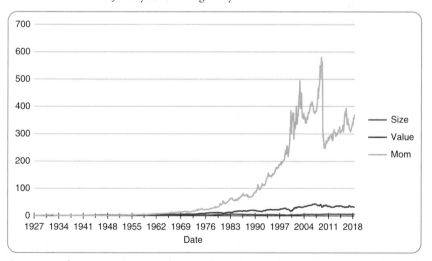

Source: Data from Kenneth R. French Data Library, http://mba.tuck.dartmouth.edu/pages/faculty/ken.french/data_library.html.

TABLE 18.1 Summary Statistics for Momentum, Value, and Size

Annualized	Mom	Value	Size
Return	7.99	4.52	2.65
Standard Deviation	16.29	12.11	11.09
Regression Beta	-0.3	0.16	0.19

Return is calculated as the arithmetic return over the period 1926–2018. Regression beta is the slope coefficient of the factor returns regressed on the market returns for the same period.

Data source: Kenneth R. French Data Library, http://mba.tuck.dartmouth.edu/pages/faculty/ken.french/data_library.html.

book value (B). For instance, if the price-to-book of the stock is low, then the stock is considered cheap. Conversely, if P/B is high, then the stock is considered expensive.

The so-called value factor provides an atomic unit in which value can be measured (Fama and French 1996). For a company stock, one can use the value factor to analyze how much of its return is attributed to the value effect.

B. Size

The *size factor* is based on the observation that small cap stocks tend to "on average" deliver higher returns than large-cap companies (Banz 1981). Generally, small capitalization stocks (called "small cap" for short) means stocks with a total market capitalization less than $2 billion. Mid-cap is between $2 billion and $10 billion. Large-cap stocks are companies with $10 billion or more in market capitalization.

C. Momentum

In physics, the momentum of an object is a function of its velocity. Therefore, momentum has both direction and speed. In investing, momentum is the observation that stocks that have performed well (poorly) on average continue to perform well (poorly). Academic research has shown that (1) stocks exhibit momentum on the time frame of 6 to 12 months (Jegadeesh and Titman 1993), and (2) the momentum factor can help explain stock returns beyond that of the market, size and value factors (Carhart 1997).

D. From Factors to Smart Beta ETFs

Named after the original authors, the three-factor model consisting of the market, size, and value factors is referred to as the Fama-French model. If also the momentum factor is added, the resulting four-factor model is often called the Fama-French-Carhart model. In extensive studies, Fama and French tested their three-factor model and found it can explain as much as 95% of the return in a diversified stock portfolio.

The unexplained return (about 5% of a diversified portfolio) is referred to as idiosyncratic or unsystematic risk.

While the technical details of how the factors are computed go beyond the scope of this chapter, there a few important results that follow from these well-established findings.

First, a factor decomposition allows the investor to measure and customize the return and risk characteristics of each stock and their portfolios as a whole. By controlling a portfolio's sensitivity to the factors, the investor can choose an appropriate level of risk. Closely related to that of managing portfolio risk is that of diversification, one of the pillars of sensible investing. Colloquially, the principle of diversification is expressed as "do not put all your eggs in one basket." When trying to improve on the diversification of a portfolio, how do we know that we do not have all our eggs in one basket? Factors provide great help here. Specifically, by decomposing our portfolio into their factor exposures, we can quantify the exposure to each of the factors. Therefore, if we think we are too exposed to a particular factor, we can decrease its exposure by rebalancing the portfolio. Take, for example, a portfolio of Google and Facebook stocks. A naive investor might think that they are diversifying holding two stocks. However, if we decompose these stocks into their factor components, we discover that they have very similar return and risk characteristics. From the factor perspective, they are therefore very similar stocks and together do not offer much diversification. Simplistically, it is like having a basket of McIntosh and Gala apples and thinking that we have got a lot of different types of fruit.

Second, today many factors are investable as *exchange-traded funds* (ETFs). Just like a stock, an investor can buy and sell ETFs on stock exchanges that mimic the behavior of the factors described earlier. ETFs can be attractive investments for individuals because of their stock-like features, low cost, and tax-efficiency. Factor-specific ETFs are often called *smart beta ETFs*. Smart beta ETFs employ rule-based methodologies for selecting stocks to invest in, such that the resulting portfolio behaves like one or several of the factors we discussed earlier. Investing in smart beta ETFs is one way to engage in what is commonly called *factor investing*, without having to deal with the complexities of managing and trading large amounts of individual stocks. Smart beta ETFs simplify the customization of investor portfolios.[2]

II. WHY PROVIDE A SMART BETA STRATEGY IN TODAY'S RETAIL MARKET?

Investment advisors are responsible for staying up-to-date on advancements and developments of new investment products. This includes careful evaluation of when a new product may be better suited for clients across dimensions, such

---

[2] See Hsu, Kalesnik, and Li (2012) for a good introduction to smart beta for the individual investor.

as transparency, performance, risks, expenses, and tax efficiency. Transparency means that investors need access to the decision-making process on how their money is being invested.

The idea of offering a smart beta strategy to a retail client is akin to a doctor's choice to prescribe a new drug. There may be important reasons to prescribe a drug to a patient, but there are also risks and side effects that could outweigh its potential benefits. A patient needs to understand the various aspects of the new drug, including its risks.

The main reason for advisors to implement smart beta strategies in client portfolios is the value they can add in terms of improved risk-adjusted performance. Needless to say, investment professionals know that evidence of smart beta's performance comes with risks and other "wrinkles" that could diminish an investors' appreciation of any value added as compared to traditional strategies.

The decision to implement a smart beta strategy for retail investors should be based on several considerations.

First, smart beta investing is well-understood and has an established track record. In particular, institutional investors have been using factor-based strategies (which provide the building blocks to smart beta strategies) for several decades. Just as Jack Bogle educated a generation of retail investors about passive index investing, today's retail investors are learning about other persistent drivers of returns aside from the market factor alone. This represents a natural evolution beyond the traditional CAPM model from the 1950s. The barrier to factor investing was high when Eugene Fama and Ken French published their seminal work on the cross-section of stock returns (Fama and French 1996). In fact, the factor portfolios in their original paper are not investable for the typical retail investor. Over the past decade, factor-based replication has become commonplace and suddenly it was possible to get exposure to the underlying factors that drive returns in a transparent, systematics, and rule-based way for a fraction of the cost of active management.

Second, there is demand in the retail space for portfolio strategies that mitigate market risk. This is because of the current high valuation of the market and the lingering efforts of the global financial crisis being fresh in the minds of this generation of investors. Many factor-based strategies offer greater flexibility in controlling and customizing portfolio risk to outperform traditional market benchmarks by making factor "tilts."

Third, smart beta strategies represent a form of investing that falls somewhere between active and passive strategies. They are active in the sense that they rely on allocating to factors that have a track record of enhancing returns. It is well documented in the academic literature that many high fee active managers have outperformed the market simply by taking implicit exposures to factors such as value, size, and momentum (Carhart 1997). Smart beta strategies represent a low-cost alternative to higher-cost traditional active management. Just like institutional clients, retail customers should be paying beta prices for beta risk. Similar to passive indexing, smart beta strategies are transparent, rule-based, and tend to have lower fees than active strategies.

III.   CHALLENGES IN DEVELOPING A SMART BETA PORTFOLIO STRATEGY FOR RETAIL INVESTORS

A.   What Smart Beta ETFs to Choose?

The academic and practitioner literature has identified a "zoo" of hundreds of factors (Hou, Xue, and Zhan 2017). To add to the complexity, there are factors that explain risk but are not associated with a risk premium. It can be a daunting task for the retail investor to navigate this factor zoo and make a selection from all the different offerings.

We make the following recommendations for retail investors when investing in smart beta ETFs:

- Only consider smart beta ETFs whose factors are associated with risk premia that have withstood the test of time (i.e. the factors show persistent performance).
- Emphasize smart beta ETFs whose factors have been shown to work across multiple asset classes and/or geographies (i.e. the factors are pervasive) (Asness, Moskowitz, and Pedersen 2013).
- Prioritize smart beta ETFs with high liquidity (i.e. smaller bid/ask spreads and higher trading volumes) and low costs (i.e. low fees and high tax efficiency).

These criteria should result in choosing smart ETFs that are built from true-and-tried factors with robust performance through time. Despite the hundreds of factors described in the literature, only a select few truly satisfy these criteria. These include value, size, momentum, quality, and low-volatility/low beta.[3]

B.   Long-Only or Long-Short

While there are as many approaches to implementing factors and smart beta ETFs, such details are beyond the scope of this writing. Naturally, each approach has its own merits.

One important choice, that we briefly elaborate on here, is whether to use a long-only or long-short implementation. In a long-only approach, the factor portfolio consists of long positions (i.e. the stocks in the portfolio were bought). In contrast, in a long-short approach the factor portfolio has both long and short positions (i.e. stocks were bought as well as sold short). In theory a long-short approach provides more flexibility over a long-only approach. However, it comes at additional risks and costs of having to short stocks.

We note that as the majority of retail investors measure their portfolio performance relative to the market benchmark, the benefits of a full long-short approach are small. In most situations, the benefits are nonexistent. For most retail investors, we favor a long-only approach for its simplicity and parsimony, while at the same

---

[3] See, for example, Berkin and Swedroe (2016).

time delivering (close to) the same performance as more sophisticated[4] long-short approaches.

C. Multifactor Strategies Are Optimal

How should an investment manager build a portfolio for a chosen set of factors? Of course, the answer depends on an investor's objective, investment horizon, and financial goals. If the objective is to have a lower risk portfolio, then a factor strategy comprised of the low-vol/low-beta factor makes sense. If the objective is to outperform the market cap benchmark, then combinations of factors may be more appropriate and also add some diversification. If the investment horizon is sufficiently long and outperformance is the main objective, then momentum factor strategies have (in the past) had the highest risk-adjusted return among the factors that satisfy our selection criteria mentioned earlier.

For the typical retail investor, we think a multifactor strategy is adequate.[5] It is well-known that individual factor performance is cyclical. Some factors, such as momentum and value, are negatively correlated long-term. Therefore, a combination of factors is expected to provide better diversification and higher risk-adjusted returns as compared to a one-factor strategy. In Figure 18.2, we rank the annual portfolio performance of the market, value, momentum, and size factors; and an equally weighted portfolio of all four factors. Notice that the equally weighted portfolio more often outperforms the other factors.[6] In other words, a multifactor approach as simple as the equally weighted portfolio does better on average than individual factors.

IV.   IMPLEMENTING A SMART BETA PORTFOLIO STRATEGY AS A FIDUCIARY ADVISOR

Investment principles that should guide any portfolio strategy choice for retail investors often include:

- Seek broad diversification.
- Weight investment cost and value.
- Account for taxes.

---

[4] For example, an investor can deploy a beta overlay to a long-short factor to satisfy market benchmark tracking restrictions. The resulting portfolio will be equivalent (or at least, close to equivalent) to a long-only approach.

[5] There is a body of research that demonstrate better risk-adjusted returns for multi-factor strategies. A good starting point is the following article and the references therein: "A Smoother Path to Outperformance with Multi-Factor Smart Beta Investing." https://www.researchaffiliates.com/en_us/publications/articles/594-a-smoother-path-to-outperformance-with-multifactor-smart-beta-investing.html (accessed June 28, 2018).

[6] To keep things simple, we have not risk-adjusted the returns. However, when adjusting for risk the qualitative result stays the same.

FIGURE 18.2 Hypothetical Performance Computed from the Fama-French-Carhart Factors

Sorted	2000	2001	2002	2003	2004	2005	2006	2007	2008	2009	2010	2011	2012	2013	2014	2015	2016	2017	Legend
1	40%	19%	26%	31%	11%	15%	14%	22%	13%	28%	17%	7%	16%	35%	12%	21%	23%	22%	MarketBeta
2	18%	18%	13%	26%	8%	8%	11%	1%	6%	9%	14%	0%	10%	8%	2%	2%	13%	5%	Mom
3	15%	14%	7%	5%	5%	7%	2%	0%	3%	-9%	6%	-2%	3%	7%	-2%	0%	7%	-5%	equalWeight
4	-2%	4%	5%	2%	4%	3%	0%	-7%	1%	-27%	5%	-6%	1%	6%	-3%	-4%	3%	-5%	Size
5	-18%	-15%	-23%	-25%	0%	-2%	-8%	-15%	-38%	-82%	-5%	-8%	-1%	2%	-8%	-10%	-20%	-14%	Value

Sorted	2000	2001	2002	2003	2004	2005	2006	2007	2008	2009	2010	2011	2012	2013	2014	2015	2016	2017
1	Value	Mom	Mom	MarketBeta	MarketBeta	Mom	Value	Mom	Mom	MarketBeta	MarketBeta	Mom	MarketBeta	MarketBeta	MarketBeta	Mom	Value	MarketBeta
2	equalWeight	Size	equalWeight	Size	Value	Value	MarketBeta	MarketBeta	equalWeight	Size	Size	MarketBeta	Value	Mom	Mom	equalWeight	MarketBeta	Mom
3	Mom	equalWeight	Value	Value	Size	equalWeight	equalWeight	equalWeight	Size	Mom	Mom	equalWeight	equalWeight	Value	Value	MarketBeta	Size	equalWeight
4	Size	Value	Size	equalWeight	equalWeight	MarketBeta	Size	Size	Value	equalWeight	equalWeight	Size	Mom	equalWeight	equalWeight	Size	equalWeight	Size
5	MarketBeta	MarketBeta	MarketBeta	Mom	Mom	Size	Mom	Value	MarketBeta	Value	Value	Value	Size	Value	Size	Value	Mom	Value
	19	18	17	16	15	14	13	12	11	10	9	8	7	6	5	4	3	2

Data source: from Kenneth R. French Data Library, http://mba.tuck.dartmouth.edu/pages/faculty/ken.french/data_library.html.

403

Decades of research has shown the benefits of diversification to mitigate portfolio risk. This should be the starting point of any retail investment strategy. We believe that in the absence of views about asset returns, the most diversified portfolio is the "market portfolio."

Any portfolio construction should weigh the cost of exposure to the asset with its added value. The cost of smart beta funds has declined in recent years, making their value to retail customers attractive. Indeed, we think the balance between cost and value has tipped in favor of their inclusion in a retail portfolio.

Finally, in the retail space, tax considerations and optimization are very important. We address this topic more in a subsequent section.

A. Implementation in Mutual Funds, ETFs, and Advanced Indexing

Just as the market cap index is a way for a retail investor to get exposure to the market factor, factor indexes provide a tool for them to obtain factor exposures in a transparent and cost-effective way. After the decision to invest in a factor, there are many ways in which such a decision can be implemented in the portfolio. This includes products such as mutual funds, ETFs, and newer types of "advanced indexing" products. The retail investor must do due diligence to distinguish the nuances in the implementation of each product to understand the impact on returns, such as liquidity, turnover, and rebalancing rules. Advanced indexing represents a new type of smart beta strategy at the security level that could be multifactor, and that often adds an overlay of tax strategies. These strategies may be appropriate for the taxable investor although their limited historical track record may be a barrier to entry. We advocate for evaluating factor investment vehicles on a number of characteristics, including (but not limited to) the following:

- Implementation: Factor methodology and portfolio construction
- Efficiency of the factor capture (i.e. tracking error to the underlying factor)
- Transparency of the implementation process
- Turnover (i.e. how often and how much of the securities are traded)
- Capacity (i.e. is the product scalable without the risk of degrading performance)
- Trading costs and fees
- Manager track record and experience

B. The Behavioral Cost of Factors

Aside from the expense ratio and bid-ask spreads for smart beta ETFs, a large "cost" of factor exposure and portfolio strategy is tracking error regret (Clarke, Krase, and Statman 1994). This is particularly challenging in the retail space because of individuals' low financial literacy (Elan 2011).

Most retail investors will benchmark themselves to the S&P 500 even though their portfolio is global. When the gap of their portfolio performance from the

FIGURE 18.3   The Number of Years That a Given Factor Has Underperformed the Market in This Histogram

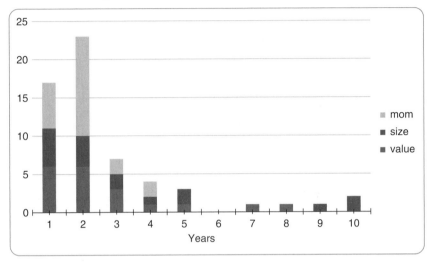

Data source: Kenneth R. French Data Library, http://mba.tuck.dartmouth.edu/pages/faculty/ken.french/data_library.html.

benchmark is positive, most of them will not think about it. However, experiencing a negative gap can lead them to question their investment plan and intervene with it by changing their allocations. Even worse, they might give up on their investment plan altogether. The result is that many retail investors end up selling low and buying high.

In Figure 18.3, we see how often a factor strategy underperformed the market since 1927. On horizons such as three- to five years, we observe that the number of years factors have underperformed is large. For instance, the figure suggests that momentum alone is not a good factor to hold on that horizon. Naturally, as the horizon gets longer, the performance of all the factors improves. However, notice that there have historically been long periods of underperformance in several factor strategies. For example, the value factor has historically have periods extending out to eight years of underperformance relative to the market. Investors need to understand that factors—just like any other investments—involve risk. Unless investors can accept risk and stick to their investment plan, a global allocation may not have much value. The largest cost of factor and smart beta investing in the retail space is behavioral.

C. Tax Overlay Algorithms

A key principle of retail investing in taxable accounts is that any portfolio strategy should be tax optimal. There are a number of ways to address taxes, some simpler and others more complex. One approach is to take the strategic asset allocation as a given and overlay "tax algorithms" either at the account level or the trading level to generate tax alpha. The two ideas that we describe here are tax loss harvesting and asset location.

a. What Is Tax Loss Harvesting?

Tax loss harvesting (TLH) is a strategy where assets that are held in a portfolio at a loss are sold opportunistically. When realizing the losses, they can offset capital gains and income from dividends. This is typically done at some predetermined frequency, such as quarterly or annually. Using computer algorithms, TLH can be done daily.

The complexity of TLH comes from navigating the *wash-sale rule*. The rule states that a wash-sale occurs when you sell an asset at a loss and then purchase that same asset or "substantially identical" securities within 30 days (before or after the sale date). The wash-sale rule was designed to discourage investors from selling an asset at a loss to claim a tax benefit. The cost of incurring a wash-sale must be outweighed by the benefit of harvesting a loss.

There are several ways to navigate the wash-sale rule. The basic idea is to sell a ticker at a loss and buy a "dual" ticker to replicate the exposure of the original ticker. For example, you might sell your holdings in an ETF tracking the S&P 500 index and buy back an ETF tracking the Russell 1000.

In the development of retail smart beta offerings, we advocate to execute TLH at the trading level. This will require the retail investor to identify dual tickers for each one of the factors.

ETFs are good vehicles for TLH for several reasons. Commonly, ETFs require authorized participants to create and redeem shares in kind, thereby enabling the ETF to avoid selling securities and realizing capital gains taxes to meet redemptions. Furthermore, the ETF manager can reduce the ETF's tax liability by providing the so-called authorized participant with the tax lots that have the lowest cost basis. With the rapid development of smart beta ETF offerings, it is becoming easier to identify dual (and multiple) tickers for many factors.

Based on the various investment alternatives available to retail investors to date, we believe that a carefully selected group of smart beta ETFs provides the best way to implement an efficient after-tax smart beta portfolio. Arguably, a bottoms-up approach to smart-beta investing, leveraging the trading of individual stocks, can offer some advantages for large retail accounts.

b. What Is Asset Location?

While often unknown or misunderstood by retail investors, another important tax overlay strategy is *asset location*. Assets have different after-tax profiles in taxable versus tax-advantaged accounts. Therefore, the after-tax return of an asset could look very different if it was sitting in a tax-deferred or tax-exempt account or a taxable account. Let us consider a coupon bond held in a taxable account. The coupon will be taxed as ordinary income. Therefore, an investor is better off allocating the bond to a tax-exempt account, if possible. Given that retail investors typically have a number of taxable, tax-deferred, and tax-exempt accounts, it is possible to optimally allocate assets preferentially to specific accounts such that the after-tax return is maximized while the overall strategic allocation is maintained. The static version of the problem is similar to the so-called knapsack problem, which has a well-known solution (Kellerer, Pfersky, and Pisinger 2004). Once there is cash flow, the optimal static solution is no longer dynamically optimal as cash flow typically goes into one specific account. Managing the dynamic problem with inflow and outflow is more complex and can be solved as a linear programming problem.

There is no barrier in implementing asset location for a smart beta strategy, provided that one can estimate the after-tax return of each asset used in the strategy.

V.   A LOOK INTO THE FUTURE

In the final section we highlight a few key themes that we think will be (or continue to be) important for the future of smart beta investing in the retail space.

A. Increased Customization and Goals-Based Investing

A recent survey by FTSE Russell suggests that smart beta products are increasingly popular among financial advisors across Canada, the UK, and the US as a way of diversifying client portfolios as well as to express strategic views. As more smart beta ETFs are becoming available, we expect an increased level of customization to become feasible to better fit investment objectives and financial goals of individuals.

What kinds of customization are retail investors looking for? First, we believe that one of the key components is to offer individuals a broadly diversified investment portfolio commensurate with their personalized risk profiles and financial goals. There is no "one size fits all." It is important to gather accurate information about an individual's financial situation and goals before building their portfolio.

Financial theory suggests that we should consider an individual's total assets and liabilities when building their investment portfolio. In other words, also less liquid assets, such as that of homeownership, should be included in the asset allocation decision. In the case of homeownership, we would expect that the resulting "optimal" portfolio will contain investments with low correlations to the housing market.

Based on the concept of *mental accounting* it is well-known that people do not treat all money the same.[7] Specifically, it has been shown that individuals will attach different "chunks" of money to different risk-return preferences, depending on their perceived use of that money. An individual may therefore see their homeownership very differently from that of their investment portfolio. In other words, an individual may have different financial goals when it comes to that of their home and their investment portfolio.

---

[7] See, for example, Thaler (1985, 1999).

Goals-based wealth management is an investment and portfolio management process that focuses on helping investors realize their different financial goals. Shefrin and Statman developed behavioral portfolio theory (BPT) in the late 1990s and suggested that investors behave as if they have multiple mental accounts. Each mental account has varying levels of aspiration, depending on its goals (Shefrin and Statman 2000). This form of behavioral thinking suggests a portfolio management framework where investors are goal-seeking (aspirational), while remaining concerned about downside risk in the light of their goals. In particular, rather than trading off risk versus return, investors trade off goals versus safety. Naturally, BPT leads to normatively different statements of the portfolio problem than those from classical portfolio theory. Das et al. propose a novel framework for goals-based wealth management (GBWM) where risk is understood as the probability of investors not attaining their goals (Das et al. 2018).

Based on its intuitive appeal and ability to model individual investor's financial goals in a flexible and highly customizable way, we conjecture that goals-based wealth management will emerge as an approach to investment management in the retail space.

B. SRI/ESG

When making investment choices, individuals are increasingly concerned about *socially responsible investment* (SRI) and *environmental, social, and governance* (ESG) impact. Different individuals assign different relative importance between SRI/ESG and investment performance. Which SRI/ESG issues should a portfolio incorporate and address? One investor may primarily be concerned with equality- and diversity-related issues, while another may care about environmental policy. Currently, there are only a limited number of SRI/ESG ETFs. As SRI/ESG preferences are often personal and specific, they may best be customized at the stock level rather than through ETFs.

C. The Importance of Investor Education

As we are looking to the future, it is clear that more investor education is needed in order to increase individuals' financial literacy. At the core of financial planning and advisory is communication. The financial industry is rich of highly technical and financial jargon in its communication, often making such communication ineffective or even impenetrable for individuals.[8]

There are costs to society for a financially illiterate population as governments and taxpayers may end up paying for the mistakes of others. In addition, there are benefits to society for having a population that has better financial habits and planning. Who should provide such education? These are important considerations for policy.

---

[8] See, for example, Lusardi (2015).

First, school could integrate course content designed to enhance financial literacy of the general population before they reach an age when they need to make important personal finance decisions. Second, financial advisors and other fiduciaries have a responsibility to educate their clients in "sound" financial practices in general, and investment and retirement decisions specifically. This also includes providing tools that are more intuitive and easier to use. Third, employers could play a role in providing employees with updated information and continued education about financial matters.

VI.   CONCLUSION

In this chapter we have made the case for smart beta offerings in the retail space. We highlighted a number of challenges and important considerations, including factor selection and implementation, portfolio construction and tax overlays. We also offered some suggestions of where the future of this space may lie.

The holy grail of retail investing is personalization. Smart beta strategies offer one aspect of personalization but is certainly not the end goal. Asset allocation—whether it is smart beta, risk parity, or market capitalization—is an important component for retail investors. Beyond asset allocation, a retail investor has to consider fund selection (i.e. mutual funds versus ETF), tax considerations, and appropriate risk taking (that depends on their investment goal and horizon). Of course, the entire financial picture of a retail investor is not defined by a single portfolio. An investor may have multiple goals, with different horizons and therefore varying risk profiles. Optimizing across all these goals and determining which portfolio strategy is best suited for what goal is an unsolved problem and remains an active area of research.

CHAPTER 19

POSITIONING SMART BETA WITH RETAIL INVESTORS, A CONVERSATION WITH

Jerry Chafkin
Chief Investment Officer,
AssetMark

Thank you so much for your time today, Jerry.
My pleasure.

How do you approach smart beta or factor investing?
I tend to think of smart beta or factor investing as a disciplined and systematic approach to alpha generation or phrased differently as a repeatable and transparent approach to active equity management.

So, you don't really distinguish smart beta from active management.
To the extent that the objective is alpha generation, and that the alpha comes from similar sources, or factors, it is not different from active. But, to the extent that the alpha is generated through a disciplined and systematic approach, it is somewhat differentiated in its implementation from traditional active management. Some of my colleagues refer to smart beta as actively passive, that is, active style strategies implemented in an index-like fashion.

We could go one level deeper and characterize smart beta as taking the highest value-added filter used by many active managers in a particular style, for example, value, and applying it in a disciplined and systematic fashion across a large universe of stocks. But frankly, for most conversations that I have with financial advisors, the conversation is not about filters or factors, it's about how to achieve the objective of active management with greater reliability and transparency.

So, how do you suggest advisors talk about smart beta with retail clients so that it becomes easier to understand?

Retail investors understand passive. They understand that it is the easiest and cheapest way to earn the market return. They also understand active. Most retail investors believe that through knowledgeable security selection it should be possible to earn higher returns than the market. They are also cognizant of the fact that earning a 1% or 2% higher annual return than the market in the long run results in significantly higher terminal wealth levels compared to a purely passive approach to investing. So, given these beliefs, it is reasonable for investors to pursue active returns, subject to their risk tolerance, of course.

But retail investors also understand the potential challenges associated with active managers. First, they may charge high fees, causing investors to only get a small fraction of any potential outperformance. Second, their process may be complicated or even opaque making it difficult to set investor expectations properly. Mismanaged expectations may lead to investors bailing out when disappointment strikes and as a result not realizing the full potential of the strategy in the long run. Third, active managers themselves, due to business considerations, sometimes fail to maintain discipline and abandon their own investment philosophy and process, such as when underperformance is significant or lasts for a few consecutive years. Fourth, active managers tend to hold somewhat concentrated portfolios that do not have deep capacity and may depict significant idiosyncratic risk. Therefore, even for talented active managers, performance may be erratic and growth in assets may challenge future returns.

From an investment process point of view, one might ask: what do active managers, as a group, deliver? I would argue that where outperformance exists, it is driven by two main sources. One source is "common insights" into what kinds of securities are likely to perform best over time. These are high-level stock or company characteristics that are broadly known and accepted in the investing world. For example, value and quality investing date back to the 1930s and Benjamin Graham. The second source of outperformance I'll call "manager-specific insights," derived from in-depth research of companies and industries conducted by the manager. Research and experience tell us that quite a large proportion of active manager outperformance is actually driven by common insights. These insights are what investment professionals call factors.

The bottom line is that retail investors appreciate the advantages of passive: low-cost, disciplined, repeatable, and transparent. But they also like the outperformance potential of active. What if we could create a solution that retains the advantages of passive investing and the outperformance potential of active investing? Enter smart beta. Viewed through this lens, smart beta becomes a compelling investment proposition. It becomes a good value compared to the more traditional active approaches. None of this is too complicated for the typical retail investor to understand and appreciate.

An argument is often made that smart beta requires a higher level of education for retail investors, which represents a challenge to its widespread adoption. Would you agree?

Yes and no. If you approach the conversation using terms like "beta" or "factors," then yes it can become a challenge. If you have to explain what factors are, why they work, why they persist, then yes, the conversation can quickly become complicated and therefore challenging. But, as I said previously, smart beta can be communicated in terms that investors understand. Smart beta is not differentiated from active by the characteristics it uses to select stocks, but rather by the systematic process used to identify and rank stocks with these characteristics.

Generally, I feel that any investment solution that requires significant client education is challenged from the get-go. I'm an advocate of simplicity. But, at the same time, I'm committed to making new investment approaches accessible to investors if those approaches can help investors achieve their financial goals. Smart beta is one such approach. The trick lies in communicating these ideas in a way so that clients can actually understand them.

You don't like the term beta in smart beta, you don't like the term factor in factor investing, so maybe you should just call it "smart investing."

That's exactly right. The way I like to think about factor investing is that it's "smart risk investing." I say that because you know exactly what characteristic it is that you're betting the market will reward, and you're taking active positions in a disciplined fashion, minimizing risks other than the key stock characteristics that you believe in.

I think anybody who's been doing diligence on active equity managers for any length of time knows that your typical equity manager has five great stock picks around which they have high confidence. They then add 100 other stocks to the portfolio, which they usually don't deeply believe in and have not been as thoroughly researched. Rather, adding these stocks is their attempt to control risk around a handful of companies that they have researched deeply and that they do believe in.

What this often boils down to, though, is that there are certain qualities or characteristics of that handful of stocks that makes managers passionate about the wisdom of their selection, and everything else is what I'll call "hamburger helper" purchased in order to fill out the portfolio and to some extent, mitigate risk relative to a capitalization-weighted index. In other words, managers are reluctant to accept the idiosyncratic risk of holding only a handful of individual stocks. With factor investing, or smart beta investing, it's a much more systematic approach, both to risk management and to security selection, allowing the investment manager to focus on the qualities of those companies, or more accurately the stocks that they believe in.

From the perspective of retail investors, what might be the motivation to consider smart beta or factor investing?
In the end, I think the motivation for retail investors is simple. It's primarily the combination of lower cost and better return over time. With regards to smart beta, there are a lot of investment reasons that one could argue make sense. But, in terms of what's on the mind of a typical retail investor, I think the reasons that resonate are cost and return.

"Inexpensive" relative to what? Active management?
Yes, relative to active management.

And "higher return" relative to what? The market?
Yes. The market.
Look, let me take a step back here. When I talk to financial advisors about how they position passive solutions with retail investors, they tell me they generally focus on the aspects that matter most to the end-investor. They talk about it being the easiest and cheapest way of realizing the market rate of return. They talk about it containing no surprises. Most advisors don't talk about the CAPM, or about why a cap-weighted portfolio is the market, or about efficient frontiers. Similarly, in the case of smart beta, advisors need to focus on why it is an interesting investment proposition for retail investors. And I think it mostly boils down to lower cost and higher expected return.

What do you say to the argument that if it is cheap it can't be that good?
(*Laughs*) Gosh, I can honestly say I've never had a retail adviser try to make that argument to me. But look, I think the response would be that price is a function of added value and capacity. And in a systematic approach like smart beta or factor investing, I think the explanation for its pricing is really that the approach is designed to have deep capacity and low implementation costs, and that's why it has a lower price point than traditional approaches to active equity management.

Are you seeing retail investors becoming more excited or motivated to consider factor investing in their portfolio?
So, at the risk of disqualifying myself for this interview, no is the answer. But that doesn't mean that we're not seeing greater adoption of factor investing. It doesn't mean that we're not seeing increased popularity of factor investing. What it means is that again, for the end investor, they don't think in terms of factors; they think in terms of discipline or style, and alpha. And so, the characterization of an investment solution as smart beta or factor investing, is not self-explanatory and instead leaves the investor with sense that, "I can't understand this."

Unlike you and me, who would be developing investment strategies for fun if we weren't doing it for a living, the typical person does not find investing fun and just wants to understand that their portfolio is being invested for them with a discipline and a philosophy that makes sense to them. That's one of the beautiful things about smart beta. It really is an active management style story but implemented in an easily explained and disciplined fashion.

From an advisor's perspective, could we say that factor investing should actually be interesting because it may well be easier to implement than manager selection? After all, there are only a handful of factors that matter and they're well-demonstrated, well-documented in the literature. Would an advisor view it to be an easier path to market outperformance?

As somebody who currently makes their living, at least in part, by selecting active managers, it's a challenging question for me. But regardless of whether I'm picking an individual manager or whether I'm picking a smart beta approach, for me it's about the process, the discipline or repeatability and the risk management. So, what I will say about smart beta is that the risk management and the discipline is built-in and, in many offerings, incredibly robust. And arguably, the security selection criteria are in many ways the same as what you would find with a good active manager.

But, look, smart beta may also present challenges.

One challenge for any investment strategy is managing investor expectations. It sounds simple, but it's incredibly hard. Part of the reason for that is that whether we as individuals recognize it or not, newspapers, television, and radio inundate us with cap-weighted index performance, and that becomes our mental benchmark. Behaviorists would say that we "anchor" to it for understanding how our investments should have performed. And in fact, what we're talking about with factor investing or smart beta is really an alternative approach to indexing. Whether it adds value relative to a cap-weighted approach can only reliably be judged over time. The outperformance will not be earned smoothly year after year after year. It will be a bumpy road. There are environments where certain factors might help you to outperform the broad market, and in other periods where the factors may cause performance to actually lag. Of course, this is a challenge with any type of investing other than cap-weighted indexing. From our experience, setting expectations is critical because it has the most to do with client discipline and client satisfaction.

The other challenge that I alluded to earlier was the idea that few, if any, retail investors are going to immerse themselves in the academic support for why different investment styles make sense. Rather, they rely on the fact that somebody else such as an advisor has been screening managers for them and has found a manager with an approach that they have confidence in and that they can explain at a high level. And so again, a key to success for smart beta products is making them easier for the end investor to consume; making explanations as intuitive as possible.

How exactly do you set expectations?

One easy example perhaps might be to just talk about the classic divisions of value and growth or momentum. I think your typical investor understands that there are times when the market is rewarding stocks that have to date been undervalued, however you want to define that. And that makes total and perfect sense to them. It also makes sense that there are other times when it's all about momentum. Stocks that have been growing quickly because some phenomenon, either in their industry or going on in the world, has benefited them, and it makes sense that for some period of time it's going to continue to benefit them. People understand that doesn't happen in each and every year. But, that there are periods of time when it's very helpful. And if you can combine these filters together, as part of a handful of characteristics that are going to be driving equity prices, then that can inspire investor confidence and lay a foundation for explaining performance going forward.

One of the points that I wanted to make earlier is about why it's so important to be able to explain performance. With regard to equity research and stock selection, there is a perception that it's very hard to add value. And in fact, it is very hard to add value. Yet there is no shortage of filters or signals or ideas that historically have added value over the long term. Given this it is understandable that the typical investor might ask how can it be so hard for people to beat the market when there are so many screens, so many signals that could help you to beat the market over the long term? Of course, the answer is the fact that people are emotional creatures; we tend not to stay disciplined. We tend to act on our disappointment or our fear. And generally, that happens at exactly the wrong moment, when that strategy would have paid off. That goes back to why it's so important to appropriately set and manage expectations, because the way investors hurt themselves, is by not understanding what to expect, getting disappointed or afraid, and abandoning discipline.

Is that one of the attractions of smart beta and factor investing, that it is disciplined and may help investors to maintain discipline?
I think that's exactly right. It's disciplined, and it helps investors stay disciplined. Part of how it helps investors to stay disciplined is that the stock positions you are taking are not a function of your trust in an omniscient market guru, who has picked a magic set of stocks. But rather, you are taking positions based on some pretty commonsense and intuitive ideas about how to invest. You're able to understand that those may be recognized by the market over time, but not necessarily recognized in each and every period in time. And so, it helps the investor to stay disciplined. Its transparency is a tool that helps to reassure investors and keep them invested.

Is there anything else that you would view as an important advantage of factor investing?
Sure. We've talked about a number of aspects that make the strategy of factor investing appealing. But the vehicle is also important. A good example would be momentum investing. The reason why there are more value investors than momentum investors is in part due to the fact that you're able to hold onto value positions for a longer period of time, and therefore on an after-tax basis, it's more attractive. If you have a smart beta strategy, where the strategy is actually delivered via an ETF, where the tax benefits of the turnover that would normally be associated with that strategy can be realized without the tax hit, it's a uniquely efficient way of accessing that factor or that style of investing, because you don't have to pay the taxes normally associated with the higher turnover of momentum relative to value.

I guess that brings us to strategy selection. Any thoughts on what kind of smart beta strategies resonate well with retail investors?

Kal, like you, I've been in this business for an embarrassing number of years, and one of the things that you see is that at any moment in time there will be factors that are particularly popular. There are other factors that fall out of favor and come close to being forgotten. But then, they reemerge and become popular again because they work for that environment. So, what are some of the factors that have attracted attention recently?

There was a period of time where a low beta or minimum variance approach was very popular, right after the 2008 financial crisis. Then, partly due to quantitative easing, investors became desperate for income. And so, dividend yield became a popular filter or screen. Whenever there's a bull market, momentum tends to be very popular, and during more typical times, people will fall back on the wisdom of value investing. So, the factor that resonates well with retail investors is whatever has been rewarded recently. My own view on this is that I try not to fall in love with any one factor. Because you only know what factors were helpful to you in the past. It's like driving by looking in your rearview mirror. What lies ahead could be very different from the past. So, factor diversification makes sense to me.

Another thing to highlight, however, is that while there may or may not be new factors, there will likely be new, and potentially more effective ways of specifying and capturing the factors that researchers are trying to measure. And again, because it's technical, or as some of my colleagues like to say, it's talking "inside baseball," this is not a conversation that you tend to have with the end investor. Yet it's quite important, particularly as a practitioner. When trying to select from multiple providers, we pay particular attention to how factors are specified, because they're not all the same. They're all related, but they're not all the same. Beyond how the factor is specified, smart beta strategies may also differ in terms of how the factor is integrated into the larger portfolio of stocks. So, that's how I think about it.

What are some of the other features that you look at in selecting a smart beta strategy or manager?

Gosh, everything from price to risk controls to brand to their ability to support advisors with retail clients. But, very high on the list is an assessment of the investment team. I'm a big believer in teams. So, one of the things I look at when evaluating any type of manager, including those using factors or smart beta is how long the team has worked together. Portfolio management is not a solo activity. There is value created when researchers, portfolio managers, traders understand how to help each other get the most out of their investment strategy. The familiarity that people have working together, having encountered problems in the past together, being able to challenge each other in a comfortable way, knowing what's worked and what hasn't. That kind of common history and succinct communication is a big plus in terms of refining their process, deepening their research, and continued stability of staff. Also, I care a lot about the active research agenda of the manager. Because, in my view, process innovations and enhancements are important to continued strong performance. With regard to implementation, on the list of things I look at, is liquidity or average daily trading volume for the instruments, especially in an ETF.

And then finally, as a function of having been in this industry for a long time, I try not to pigeonhole anybody. I say that because sometimes people say: well I want a boutique rather than a big institution, because I think they're going to be more nimble and they're going to be more focused. Yet, I know of big shops that have created a number of teams with exactly that concept, where each team has that focus and is nimble. And they have access to resources that a small boutique might not. Similarly, I've seen small boutiques with high degrees of risk control and automation that defies the stereotype of a small company. Therefore, I think it's important to look at each provider on its own merits, whether it be large or small.

Moving on to the topic of sizing, do you have any views on how much should be allocated to different strategy buckets; passive, active, smart beta?
The short answer is that I don't. The reason is that I don't think this is an optimization challenge, where there is a precisely right mix of passive, factor, and traditional active. Rather, I think it is a function of a retail investor's profile. How much tolerance do they have for deviating from what they hear reported on the news as the return of the market? You know, when individuals hear the market return number reported again and again and again, their assumption is that's what all of their neighbors are earning. And so, when they lag, they feel that they're actually falling behind their friends and family. And there's a bit of shame. On the flip side, when they're doing really well, they feel proud and they stand up. When in fact, there is nobody who is solely or entirely invested in these cap-weighted indexes. I guess the basic question is: if I've got a better approach to indexing, why would I use cap-weighted passive at all? Well, there's really only one answer to that, which is that the flavor of the smart beta or factor index that was available to you had more tracking error than you were comfortable with. And so, you choose to dilute it with some passive in order to sync up with your risk appetite. If you are not sensitive to fear or greed or regret, then you may not want to have any cap-weighted passive exposure. You may want to have exclusively active or smart beta exposure. By the same token, it may very well be that you don't want, for example, to have a value approach to investing; you want to have a deep value approach to investing. You might have a much higher tolerance for how much you can deviate from an index in any given year. And that can govern what you want to do with active. Therefore, it really depends on an individual investor's profile and customizing investment solutions to match that profile. The one exception I will make to that is the distinction between liquid and illiquid markets. With regard to smart beta, I have been talking about highly liquid public securities. That's where I believe it makes sense to have these smart beta approaches, these disciplines and systematic approaches to generating alpha. There are other sources of alpha, or what I'll call "risk premia," that you can't get from liquid public markets. An example of that might be an illiquidity risk premium or a credit risk premium.

For those, you may feel that an active approach is superior to any kind of index or factor-based approach.

Any other thoughts that you would like to share on smart beta or factor investing?
Yes. I think it might also be useful to think of smart beta or factor investing as "deep capacity" alpha strategies, which makes them quite attractive relative to traditional active management, where capacity often becomes a concern. Why do smart beta strategies have deep capacity? It's because many smart beta managers employ methodologies that are designed to keep turnover low and diversification high. Of course, not all smart beta offerings have deep capacity. For example, there are quant products that seek to offer a narrower, more concentrated exposure to a factor, such as "deep" value. I think such products may not be fully in line with the spirit of smart beta investing as I see it.

Smart beta strategies make use of the greater and greater computing power that has become available. We can now slice and dice thousands of securities much more quickly and efficiently than it takes an analyst to do a thorough evaluation of a single company. And change is driven by new financial technologies, not just systems, that may have tax benefits and/or liquidity benefits. Therefore, the impact of technology on investing should not be underestimated, because it basically enables smarter and perhaps more complex investment approaches to be implemented in a passive manner. A good example is smart beta index-type approaches where there is an explicit way to consider and manage tracking error relative to market indices. That is a highly useful feature in a smart beta offering.

The customization that smart beta investing can offer is also attractive. As an example, I generally deemphasize low beta or low volatility as a factor. Not that I don't think it's important, not that I don't think that I want to control for it, but I'd rather control for it dynamically, through tactical decisions. Since roughly 80% of the time the market has a positive return, I've tended to give greater weight to the other factors, which don't perform as well in bear markets, but which don't drag down performance during bull markets. But it is a luxury for someone constructing portfolios to be able to customize in this fashion. It's an advantage associated with smart beta technology, to be able to pick and choose from these different factor tools.

Another thought I have relates to cost. How important is cost? I think the answer depends on the context. Common wisdom would suggest that your cheapest strategies, your cheapest vehicles are going to be your best performers. The argument is that since it's quite hard to outperform the market, you might as well increase your odds by investing with the lowest cost vehicles. While that may be true if you're evaluating a fund that charges 150 basis points versus a fund that charges 15 basis points, it tends to be a bit unreasonable when evaluating funds that charge 30 basis points versus funds that charge 15 basis points. From my perspective, when you're comparing funds with fees that are low versus even lower, the decision really needs to be informed by the alpha that you associate with each of the different strategies. The assessment needs to be whether the strategy is likely to more than offset the 3, 10, or 15 extra basis points that you might be paying. So, I think it's just important for retail investors and their advisors to keep some perspective. Given that not all indexes are the same, not all factor approaches are the same, fees are important, but are only half of the equation.

Finally, you've caught me having just returned from an industry conference where one speaker after another was talking about the outflows from actively managed funds, and even greater inflows to passively managed funds. Extrapolating this into the future suggests to them that active management is going to struggle, though there will always be some portion of the industry in active strategies. However, as price becomes increasingly important, more and more advisors and do-it-yourself investors are going to be using passively managed funds instead of actively managed funds. In my opinion, that may very well be a false choice. I say that because I think that factor investing, or smart beta, arguably, does provide advisors and do-it-yourself investors with the best of both worlds. That is, the opportunity to have an approach to security selection that is smarter than basically cap-weighted indexes, but with the costs, risk control, and discipline of indexing. So, I think that smart beta is an incredibly valuable tool that advisors need to give consideration to, if for no other reason than it provides a way out of the false choice between expensive active management and low-cost cap-weighted indexing.

How would you summarize the smart beta value proposition for advisors and retail investors?

I'd summarize it as a repeatable and lower-cost approach to generating above-market returns over time.

Now, let's dig deeper.

First, smart beta relies on the highest value-added filters employed by active managers. As a source of potential alpha, these filters or factors are arguably more reliable than alpha generated through a more concentrated set of stocks selected with manager-specific insights.

Second, I think to some extent retail investors understand stock selection styles, or what you and I call factors, better than the one-off stories spun by a gifted stock picker. For example, they can understand that value investing can go in and out of favor. They can understand that small companies struggle during economic recessions but tend to perform well during expansionary periods. With this understanding, their ability to stay the course may be improved. As such, it may be that investor expectations are better-managed and more reasonable with smart beta and factor investing, which may facilitate discipline and the achievement of financial goals in the long run.

Third, smart beta also provides discipline for managers. To the extent that smart beta is a well-defined systematic approach, the risk of a manager abandoning that approach at the wrong time is significantly reduced.

Finally, the lower cost of smart beta due to its systematic implementation, large capacity, and low turnover should represent a significant benefit for retail investors.

Before ending our conversation, I want to be careful not to draw too fine a distinction between smart beta and active management. While smart beta is an attractive alternative relative to the average active manager, so are the best active managers, if you can identify them. In the end, I'm an advocate of disciplined and reasonably priced active investment processes, including smart beta.

*   *   *

The views expressed are those of Mr. Chafkin and do not necessarily represent the views of AssetMark.

PART IX

CONCLUDING REMARKS

CHAPTER 20

ADDRESSING POTENTIAL SKEPTICISM REGARDING SMART BETA

Arguments that are typically made against smart beta investing tend to focus on factor existence (factors are data-mined, factors are inconsistent with theory), factor implementation (capturing factors requires skill, smart beta is active management repackaged, smart beta is based on backtested results), and factor persistence (smart beta excess returns will be arbitraged away by smart investors, smart beta is becoming a crowded trade). In this chapter, we address such skepticisms.

I.   SKEPTICISM REGARDING FACTOR EXISTENCE

A. Factors Are Data Mined

- **Argument:** Hundreds of factors have been documented in the academic literature over the last few decades, and the list keeps growing every year. The vast majority of documented factors are simply a result of data-mining. Such factors do not deliver persistent out-of-sample outperformance.
- **Our Perspective:** It is fair to say that the vast majority of documented factors may show in-sample statistical significance in individual tests, but not in testing environments that account for problems associated with data mining. Such factors also often do not perform well on an out-of-sample basis. However, in studies that attempt to correct for multiple testing in order to distinguish between true and spurious factors, a handful of well-known factors still retain statistical significance. Smart beta offerings generally tend to focus only on these validated and rewarded factors, which include size, value, momentum, quality, and low volatility (refer to Chapter 2).

B. Some Factors Are Inconsistent with Theory

- **Argument:** Some factors, such as low volatility, defy the fundamental principles relating to the relationship between risk and return in well-functioning capital markets. Other factors, such as momentum, challenge even the weak form of market efficiency, in which past prices cannot be used to predict future prices. As such, these factors cannot be reasonably rationalized, if markets are viewed as highly efficient.
- **Our Perspective:** Investors should certainly follow their philosophical beliefs and should not invest in factors that violate those beliefs. However, it is not reasonable to deny the existence of certain factors simply because they cannot be rationalized according to a given school of thought. Low volatility and momentum may not be consistent with a rational risk pricing argument, but we find it hard to argue that these factors are not real. Clearly, these factors exist and have persisted at least historically. They may not be fully explainable based on risk-based arguments but appear to be well-supported by behavioral mispricing arguments (refer to Chapter 3).

II. SKEPTICISM REGARDING IMPLEMENTATION

A. Factor Implementation Requires Skill and Smart Beta Is Just Dumb Alpha

- **Argument:** In the academic literature, as well as in many smart beta offerings, factors are typically defined in terms of single-dimension specifications. For example, value is defined as book value-to-price and quality/profitability as gross profits scaled by total assets. Such specifications may not fully capture the various dimensions of value and quality investing. An efficient capture of such factors requires a certain level of skill and sophistication. Active managers possess these required skills. For example, active managers may be able to capture the value premium better by defining value in smart ways, such as using different valuation ratios for different industries rather than just using a simple book value-to-price ratio across all industries. Or using various metrics to define quality rather than using a simple gross profitability measure. Similarly, other factors, such as momentum, depict very high turnover and require a high level of implementation skill to deliver an efficient after-cost capture. Trying to capture these factors through simplistically designed smart beta offerings does not realize the full potential of these sources of excess returns. As such, smart beta offerings simply deliver a "dumb" alpha, not the "smart" alpha that talented active managers can deliver in exploiting these same factors.
- **Our Perspective:** It is fair to argue that simplistic definitions of factors may not be as efficient as more advanced and well-thought-out specifications. For instance, book value-to-price may no longer be as effective a specification of value in today's economy, which is dominated by technology and other "growthy" sectors, as it was two decades ago. However, many smart beta managers do define factors through carefully designed composite signals to address such concerns (please also refer to

Chapter 5). Similarly, smart beta managers have developed innovative methodologies to address the high turnover of certain factors and to significantly lower implementation costs (refer to Chapter 7). So, for investors, it becomes a matter of due diligence relating to smart beta strategy selection. Additionally, the argument that smart beta delivers a dumb alpha perhaps misses the basic philosophy behind smart beta. One of the primary motivations of smart beta is to deliver the basic sources of excess returns (factors) in simple, transparent and cost-effective offerings. Such offerings seek to deliver reasonably attractive risk-adjusted returns (Sharpe ratios and IRs) compared to traditional passive and active strategies (refer to Chapters 7 and 8). Active managers can certainly claim that they can provide a more efficient capture of the same sources of excess returns, but, in our opinion, they have to validate that claim relative to the smart beta offerings (refer to Chapter 6).

B. Smart Beta Is Active Not Passive

- **Argument:** Capitalization-weighted market indexes represent a true passive solution. In the construction of such indexes, very few active decisions are involved. Market capitalization as a scaling metric is well defined, the weighting scheme is transparent, and the index is largely self-rebalancing. The creation of smart beta indexes, on the other hand, typically involves many active decisions. Which factors should be included? How should factors be defined? Which weighting scheme and portfolio construction methodology should be employed? Which rebalancing frequency should be adopted? Given the degree of activeness generally embedded in smart beta offerings, it is misleading to label smart beta indexes as passive solutions.
- **Our Perspective:** We agree that in the design of smart beta offerings, many active decisions are involved. In that sense, smart beta is closer to active than to passive indexing. On the other hand, many smart beta products employ transparent and well-defined methodologies, which results in systematic, disciplined, and cost-effective solutions, and in that sense, makes such products much closer to indexing than to active management. That is why it is most commonly argued that smart beta is neither truly active or passive, but more a hybrid solution (refer to Chapter 1).

C. Multifactor Strategies Are Not What They Seem

- **Argument:** Multifactor strategies claim to deliver higher risk-adjusted returns compared to individual factors through factor diversification. However, that may not be necessarily true. This is because factors have offsetting exposures. They are contra-bets and can cancel each other out. For instance, value stocks have negative exposure to momentum, and vice versa. Quality stocks have essentially growth characteristics, and, therefore, when combined with value, simply result in a neutral, market portfolio.
- **Our Perspective:** The argument that factors cancel each other out and, when combined, produce no more than the market portfolio is simply inaccurate. It represents

a basic misunderstanding of how factors work, how they interact, and how they generate alpha net of all other factor exposures. Value and momentum independently deliver excess returns and are negatively correlated (refer to Chapter 8). Value works, despite its negative exposure to momentum. Momentum works, despite its negative exposure to value. And, within a given universe, the highest value (momentum) stocks deliver the highest excess returns, while having the highest negative exposure to momentum (value) (refer to Chapter 10). Similarly, quality is negatively correlated with value, but not perfectly so. Quality is not growth. Therefore, combining quality with value doesn't bring us back to "neutral." In fact, it is well-documented that quality/profitability delivers a statistically significant alpha in a risk decomposition against the Fama-French-Carhart factors (refer to Chapter 5). It is true that the correlation structure between factors implies that when factors are combined, it may lead to reduced exposures, but not complete offsetting of exposures. And this is true for a multifactor strategy as well as an overall portfolio that combines multiple active style managers to achieve better diversification.

D. Smart Beta Is Just Active Management Rebranded and Repackaged

- **Argument:** It is well-known and well-understood that active managers load positively to certain factors and at least partially rely on positive exposures to these factors to deliver market outperformance. This means that active managers had discovered and had invested in factors that smart beta offerings seek to capture for decades. So, there is nothing new in smart beta, other than a rebranding and repackaging of traditional active management.
- **Our Perspective:** It is true that smart beta offerings exploit the same sources of excess returns (or factors) that active managers have targeted for decades. From this perspective, there is indeed nothing new in smart beta. However, the manner in which smart beta offerings aim to capture these sources of alpha is characterized by a much higher level of transparency, diversification, and implementation cost-efficiency. In our experience, these characteristics (or repackaging) are viewed by many investors as value-adding, which explains the widespread popularity and adoption of smart beta strategies (refer to Chapter 1). The term "smart beta" can certainly be viewed as somewhat confusing, and perhaps inappropriate. But it is the rebranding that the industry seems to have settled on.

E. Smart Money Doesn't Invest in Backtests

- **Argument:** Most smart beta offerings, which are new products with limited live track records, are marketed on the basis of a historical backtest. And all historical backtests invariably make a compelling case in favor of the proposed strategy. Investors should avoid investing in such strategies, as historical simulations may not be reflective of future performance.

- **Our Perspective:** This argument is more about investing in new strategies, in general, than about smart beta. If investors have governance considerations that limit their ability to invest in strategies lacking a specified period of live performance, such as three years, then they will not invest in new strategies. Beyond that, in our opinion, new strategies and backtests should not always be viewed negatively. In our experience, many investors start by focusing not on performance but on the investment process of a given strategy and the performance characteristics that can be expected from that process. A backtest may then be used to validate those expectations. Additionally, all backtests are not created equal. Investment processes that employ transparent and fully replicable methodologies should command more credibility than those that don't (refer to Chapters 8 and 10). Finally, it is also argued that new strategies deliver high returns in the initial years and may offer a first-mover advantage to early investors (refer to Chapter 16). As such, an argument can also be made that smart money does indeed invest in new strategies and backtests.

III.   SKEPTICISM REGARDING FACTOR PERSISTENCE

A.   Factors Can't Persist in Efficient Markets

- **Argument:** Simple sources of excess returns that are in the public domain are unlikely to persist under efficient markets. Such sources will be exploited by investors and their excess returns will disappear over time.
- **Our Perspective:** If factor excess returns are viewed as mispricing arising from behavioral biases of investors that can be arbitraged away, then from an efficient market's perspective, this argument may hold true. However, this argument is challenged if factor excess returns depict a risk premium. Even under efficient markets, we would expect risk premia to persist because they represent a compensation for bearing additional extra-market risks. Further, this argument is also challenged by the vast body of literature that argues that certain forms of mispricing can persist because they cannot be fully arbitraged away (refer to Chapter 3).

B.   Factor Persistence Will Be Challenged by Crowding

- **Argument:** Even if we assume that factor excess returns represent a risk premium and/or behavioral mispricing that cannot be fully arbitraged away, the widespread adoption of smart beta strategies will certainly result in much lower factor excess returns going forward.
- **Our Perspective:** It is true that if smart beta factors become highly popular, and hence perhaps overpriced, their future returns could be reduced. However, in our opinion, the capacity of typical smart beta strategies is significantly higher than traditional active strategies. And the amount of assets required to make a meaningful impact is potentially quite large. For instance, the amount of assets linked to

factors, such as value, momentum, and low volatility, has grown by multiples since these factors were first documented. Yet, the factor premia have not disappeared and have persisted over the years. Investors can also mitigate the potential impact of crowding by pursuing customized smart beta solutions, rather than "one size fits all" offerings (refer to Chapters 13 and 15).

IV. CONCLUSION

In this chapter, we have reviewed some of the various skepticisms relating to smart beta factor investing. In our opinion, some elements of the arguments being made are fair and reasonable, others less so.

CHAPTER 21

CONCLUSION

In our experience, the major appeal of equity smart beta factor investing lies in its ability to help investors structure more efficient overall equity portfolios, and achieve better investment outcomes, through various applications, such as:

- A cost-effective solution for asset owners seeking return enhancement in a low expected return environment, without increasing the allocation to equities.
- A potential solution for asset owners looking to reduce portfolio volatility, without lowering the allocation to equities.
- A replacement for and/or complement to a capitalization-weighted policy benchmark.
- A disciplined approach to alpha generation, which seeks to facilitate the basic objective of market outperformance, but with potentially greater reliability and transparency compared to traditional active management.
- A complement to active management that improves diversification benefits in a portfolio.
- An effective solution for factor exposure management and portfolio completion purposes.
- A compelling proposition for retail investors, as it combines the advantages of both active (market outperformance) and passive (low-cost, disciplined, and transparent) investing.
- A high-capacity alpha generation solution for institutional asset owners confronted with the problem of generating reasonable excess returns on a large and growing asset base.
- A systematic approach that helps investors and asset managers set appropriate expectations and maintain discipline during difficult times.
- A cost-effective solution capable of generating trading cost and management fee savings through hybrid implementation models based on licensing arrangements and index-like implementations.

Moving forward, we expect product development in years to come to further broaden the scope of smart beta investing. We anticipate continued application of factor investing in other asset classes and strategies, such as fixed income, commodities,

431

currencies, and hedge funds. We expect long-short offerings to complement the existing long-only strategies. And we expect continued integration of environmental, social, and governance (ESG) factors alongside smart beta factors.

The increased popularity and adoption of smart beta investing also poses some challenges for asset owners and asset managers. In the case of asset owners, it shifts the emphasis from manager selection to investment strategy selection, which requires forming beliefs in relation to smart beta factors, distinguishing between absolute return and relative return strategies, and avoiding short-termism in strategy selection, monitoring, and evaluation. For active managers, the primary challenge is establishing a value proposition relative to the smart beta solutions. This entails designing investment processes that deliver smart beta factor-adjusted excess returns. For instance, active managers, whether quantitative or fundamental, that primarily deliver smart beta factor payoffs, we believe, will find it increasingly difficult to maintain current management fee and asset levels. Smart beta managers also may face some important challenges. As the amount of assets linked to smart beta investing grows over time, concerns relating to factor crowding and crashes will undoubtedly become more pronounced. Smart beta managers will have to develop new, unique methodologies and customization capabilities that adequately address such concerns.

Some may argue that smart beta is a fad. We beg to disagree. In our view, smart beta is an important and useful innovation in the field of investments. It represents a structural force reshaping the asset management industry. Smart beta further broadens the tool kit and the set of strategies available to asset owners and potentially improves their ability to build more efficient portfolios that better meet their specific investment objectives and constraints. As such, we expect smart beta investing to continue to attract investor attention and assets going forward.

ABOUT THE AUTHORS

Oliver Bunn, PhD
Vice President, Goldman Sachs Asset Management

Oliver is a portfolio manager on the Alternative Investment Strategies (AIS) team within Goldman Sachs Asset Management's Quantitative Investment Strategies platform. He joined the firm in 2014 and is primarily focused on alternative risk premia and hedge fund beta strategies. Prior to this role, Oliver researched and developed equity strategy indices at Barclays. Following his master's degrees in mathematics and economics from the University of Bonn in 2007, Oliver earned a PhD in economics from Yale University in 2013 working with Robert Shiller on topics in behavioral finance. He has published research in the *Journal of Portfolio Management* and the National Bureau of Economic Research Working Paper series.

Steve Carden
Investment Director, Global Equities, California Public Employees
Retirement System

Steve is responsible for the holistic management of CalPERS' Global Equity portfolio, with specific functional responsibility for strategic asset allocation, risk management, research, and strategy development and analysis. After spending a great deal of time on quant strategy development, including the launch of a long/short portfolio and a proprietary asset allocation platform, Steve has focused much of his time over the last few years developing and implementing alternative/smart beta strategies, including the teams' move into multifactor investing.

Before joining CalPERS, Steve worked as an International Portfolio Manager at Barclays Global Investors (BGI-BlackRock) where he managed various European and EAFE portfolios.

Steve majored in finance at San Diego State University and earned his MBA from the University of California Davis' Graduate School of Management, where he has subsequently taught finance as a visiting lecturer.

Jerry Chafkin
Chief Investment Officer, AssetMark

Jerry is responsible for designing, enhancing, and managing the company's investment solutions framework and providing investment and market perspectives to advisors and their clients. He joined AssetMark in 2014, bringing to the firm more than

25 years of financial services leadership. Previously, Jerry was a portfolio manager and CEO at AlphaSimplex Group, a liquid alternatives and active volatility management specialist in Cambridge, Massachusetts. Prior to that, he was CEO at IXIS Asset Management in Boston, and spent nearly a decade at Charles Schwab in a range of leadership roles, including CEO of the asset management division. Jerry began his career at Bankers Trust Company where he spent almost 15 years in a variety of asset management roles working with institutional clients in the US and abroad. At the time of his departure from Bankers Trust, Jerry was the CEO of its Structured Investment Management business, with more than $250 billion in AUM in fixed income, quantitative equity, and asset allocation strategies. He received a bachelor's degree in economics from Yale University and holds an MBA in finance from Columbia University.

Roger G. Clarke, PhD
Research Consultant, Analytic Investors

Roger Clarke is a research consultant for the Wells Fargo Asset Management (WFAM) Analytic Investors team. He is responsible for collaborating on research ideas for the team's investment strategies and research agenda. Prior to joining Analytic Investors, Roger served as Principal and Chairman of TSA Capital Management, which merged with Analytic in 1996. Recognized as an authority with more than 30 years of experience in quantitative investment research, Roger has authored numerous articles and papers including two tutorials for the CFA Institute. He has served as a member of the editorial boards of the *Journal of Portfolio Management* and the *Financial Analysts Journal*. He also served on the faculty of Brigham Young University for more than 10 years where he specialized in investment and options theory. He concurrently serves as president of a nonprofit organization. Roger is a recipient of the prestigious James R. Vertin Award by the Research Foundation of the CFA Institute for notable contributions of research that has enduring value to investment professionals as well as recipient of the Graham and Dodd Scroll from the Financial Analysts Federation and the Roger F. Murray Award from the Institute for Quantitative Research in Finance. He earned a bachelor's degree in physics and an MBA from Brigham Young University. He also earned a master's degree in economics and a PhD in finance from Stanford University.

Hans de Ruiter
Chief Investment Officer, Stichting Pensioenfonds TNO
Associate Professor, Vrije Universiteit Amsterdam

Hans is chief investment officer at Stichting Pensioenfonds TNO. He has spent most of his career in the pension industry.

Before joining Stichting Pensioenfonds TNO, he worked for six years at Stichting Pensioenfonds Hoogovens as a senior investment manager and six years at APG as a senior portfolio manager.

Next to his CIO role at Stichting Pensioenfonds TNO, Hans serves as board member at Stichting Pensioenfonds Randstad, Investment Committee member at Stichting Pensioenfonds Van Lanschot, and as Supervisory Board member at Stichting Pensioenfonds Openbaar Vervoer. Hans is also an associate professor at the Vrije Universiteit Amsterdam and a senior lecturer at Business University Nyenrode.

Harindra de Silva, CFA, PhD
Portfolio Manager, Analytic Investors/Wells Fargo Asset Management

Harindra ("Harin") de Silva is responsible for the strategic focus of the Analytic Investors team at Wells Fargo Asset Management. As a portfolio manager, Harin focuses with the investment team on the ongoing research effort for equity- and factor-based investment strategies. He has authored several articles and studies on finance-related topics including stock market anomalies, market volatility, and asset valuation. Prior to joining Analytic Investors, Harin was a principal at Analysis Group Inc., where he was responsible for providing economic research services to institutional investors including investment managers, large pension funds, and endowments. He received a BS in mechanical engineering from the University of Manchester Institute of Science and Technology, an MBA in finance from the University of Rochester, and a PhD in finance from the University of California, Irvine.

Illian Dimitrov
Head of Growth Assets, Oak Pension Asset Management Limited
Vice President, Investments, Barclays Bank UK Retirement Fund

Ilian Dimitrov is the head of growth assets for Oak Pension Asset Management Limited, which is the in-house asset manager for the Barclays Bank UK Retirement Fund (UKRF); this circa £30 billion (Sterling) Fund is highly diversified and global. Ilian is responsible for portfolio management, manager selection, and portfolio construction of the UKRF's Growth Assets allocation, which includes public equity, private equity, hedge fund, and high-risk credit strategies. The equity allocation consists of active, smart beta, passive, and private equity strategies. The fund utilizes a significant number of external asset class specialists, with more than a quarter of assets under management invested in growth strategies.

Ilian's previous experience includes being an investment associate in the Fiduciary Management team of Fortis Investments/ABN AMRO AM (now BNP Paribas Investment Partners) based in Amsterdam.

Ilian completed MSc courses at University of Amsterdam, holds master's in finance degree from D.A. Tsenov Academy of Economics and Global Investment Risk Management certificate from Saïd Business School at Oxford University. He attained the CAIA designation in 2010.

Steven Foresti
Chief Investment Officer, Wilshire Consulting

Steve Foresti, a managing director with Wilshire Associates, is the chief investment officer of Wilshire Consulting. He is based in Wilshire's Santa Monica, California, office and heads Wilshire Consulting's research efforts, including strategic investment research and the development of asset class assumptions for use in Wilshire's asset allocation process. He serves as chair of Wilshire Consulting's Investment Committee. Throughout his tenure at Wilshire, he has worked directly with large institutional investors of all types: public- and corporate-defined benefit plans, foundations, endowments, and insurance companies. Steve has authored papers on a broad range of topics across both the traditional and alternative investment areas.

Steve joined Wilshire in 1994 and has more than 25 years of capital market experience. Prior to joining Wilshire Consulting, Steve spent nine years with Wilshire Analytics where he developed and supported quantitative attribution and risk models within the Wilshire Quantum Series of investment analytics. Before joining Wilshire, Steve worked in Morgan Stanley's Mutual Fund Division (formerly Dean Witter Inter-Capital) where he acted as a liaison between the firm's portfolio management team and sales force. He holds a BS in finance from Lehigh University and an MBA in finance and accounting from the University of Texas at Austin.

Khalid (Kal) Ghayur, CFA, FSIP
Managing Director, Head of ActiveBeta Equity Strategies, Goldman Sachs Asset Management

Khalid Ghayur is the head of the ActiveBeta Equity Strategies business within GSAM's Smart Beta Strategies platform, overseeing the team's customized, factor-based equity portfolios. Kal joined GSAM as a managing director upon GSAM's acquisition of Westpeak Global Advisors in June 2014.

Prior to joining GSAM, Kal was the managing partner and chief investment officer for Westpeak, a pioneer in the smart beta space with their patented ActiveBeta investment methodology.

Prior to joining Westpeak in 2007, Kal was the director of research policy at MSCI, in New York, where he was a member of its Global Executive Committee and chairman of the MSCI Index Policy Committee. In that capacity, Kal was responsible for MSCI's global markets and benchmarking research and new product development.

From 1994 to 2000, Kal was global head of quantitative research and strategy for HSBC Asset Management, in London, where he was responsible for the development and application of strategic and tactical asset allocation, fixed income modeling, stock selection techniques, portfolio construction and analysis, and risk management.

From 1992 to 1994, Kal was a senior quantitative analyst at Credit Lyonnais Asset Management, in Paris, and from 1987 to 1991, he held the position of portfolio manager at Union National Bank in Abu Dhabi, where he was responsible for managing the bank's UK and US investment portfolios.

Kal has served on the Board of Governors of the CFA Institute, the Board's Nominating Committee, and as chairman of the Board's External Relations and Volunteer Involvement Committee. He is also a former trustee of the CFA Institute Research Foundation. Kal was a member of the Editorial Board of the *Financial Analysts Journal* and was the founding President of the UK Society of Investment Professionals.

Kal received an MBA in finance and international business from the École Nationale des Ponts et Chaussées, Paris, and an MA and BA in economics from the University of Karachi. He is a CFA charterholder, a member of the CFA Institute, and a Fellow of the Society of Investment Professionals (FSIP). He is also a Diplomaed Associate of the Institute of Bankers Pakistan.

Ronan G. Heaney
Vice President; Head of ActiveBeta Equity Research, Goldman Sachs Asset Management

Ronan Heaney is the head of research for the ActiveBeta Equity Strategies business within GSAM's Smart Beta Strategies platform. He is responsible for investment research activities, including improving quantitative investment models and portfolio construction methodologies and identifying and testing new model components and implementation techniques. Ronan joined GSAM following GSAM's acquisition of Westpeak Global Advisors in June 2014. Prior to joining GSAM, Ronan was the director of research for Westpeak, pioneering Westpeak's patent Methods and Systems for Building and Managing Portfolios based on Ordinal Ranks of Securities. Prior to joining Westpeak in 1998, Ronan was employed by Multum Information Services, in Denver, Colorado, as a Software Architect. From 1992 to 1996, he held the position of Senior Software Developer at Swiss Bank Corporation, in Chicago. Ronan received an MS in computer science from Purdue University, where he was awarded a Fulbright Fellowship, and a BS in applied physics from Dublin City University, Ireland.

Lisa L. Huang
Head of Artificial Intelligence Investment Management and Planning, Fidelity Investments

Lisa Huang is the head of AI investment management and planning at Fidelity Investments where she leads the use of AI across the entire asset management business. Previously, Lisa was the head of investing at betterment. In her role at betterment, she helmed the quantitative research needed to make investing algorithmic. Her responsibilities include strategic portfolio construction, algorithmic fund selection, risk modeling, and tax overlay strategies. Prior to betterment, Lisa was a quantitative strategist at Goldman Sachs where she worked on risk management and built fixed income models at an internal hedge fund. She holds a PhD in theoretical physics from Harvard University and degrees in mathematics and biochemistry from UCLA.

Andrew Junkin, CFA, CAIA
President, Wilshire Consulting

Andrew Junkin is president of Wilshire Consulting and is a member of Wilshire's board of directors and Wilshire Consulting's investment committee. Andrew leads more than 90 consulting professionals who serve Wilshire's consulting clients and provides strategic leadership to Wilshire Consulting.

Andrew joined Wilshire in 2005. Throughout his tenure at Wilshire, he has worked directly with large institutional investors of all types: public and corporate defined benefit plans, foundations, endowments, and insurance companies. He has 22 years of investment experience with the last 21 years in the consulting industry. Prior to joining Wilshire, he was director of research and senior consultant at Asset Services Company where he provided advice to institutional investors. Andrew began his career as a financial consultant with Merrill Lynch in Oklahoma City. He earned a BS from Oklahoma City University, attended business school at the Price College of Business at the University of Oklahoma and earned his MBA from the Wharton School of the University of Pennsylvania. Andrew holds the Chartered Financial Analyst and Chartered Alternative Investment Analyst designations.

Petter N. Kolm
Director of the Mathematics in Finance Master's Program and Clinical Professor; Courant Institute of Mathematical Sciences, New York University

Petter Kolm is the director of the mathematics in finance master's program and clinical professor at the Courant Institute of Mathematical Sciences, New York University, and the principal of the Heimdall Group, LLC. Previously, Petter worked in the Quantitative Strategies Group at Goldman Sachs Asset Management where his responsibilities included researching and developing new quantitative investment strategies for the group's hedge fund. Petter has coauthored numerous academic papers, including four books: *Financial Modeling of the Equity Market: From CAPM to Cointegration* (Wiley, 2006), *Trends in Quantitative Finance* (CFA Research Institute, 2006), *Robust Portfolio Management and Optimization* (Wiley, 2007), and *Quantitative Equity Investing: Techniques and Strategies* (Wiley, 2010). He holds a PhD in mathematics from Yale, an MPhil in applied mathematics from the Royal Institute of Technology, and an MS in mathematics from ETH Zurich.

Petter is a member of the editorial boards of the *International Journal of Portfolio Analysis and Management* (IJPAM), *Journal of Investment Strategies* (JoIS), and *Journal of Portfolio Management* (JPM). He is an advisory board member of Betterment, member of the board of directors of the International Association for Quantitative Finance(IAQF) and of the Yale Graduate School Alumni Association (GSAA).

As an advisor, consultant, and expert witness, Petter has provided his services in areas including algorithmic and quantitative trading strategies, alternative data, data science, econometrics, forecasting models, machine learning, portfolio construction methodologies incorporating transaction costs and taxes, and risk management procedures.

Stephen C. Platt, CFA
Vice President; Head of ActiveBeta Equity Portfolio Management, Goldman Sachs Asset Management

Steve Platt is a senior portfolio manager for the ActiveBeta Equity Strategies business within GSAM's Smart Beta Strategies platform. He is responsible for portfolio management, including portfolio construction and risk management of global developed and emerging market equity portfolios and custom indexes. Steve joined GSAM following GSAM's acquisition of Westpeak Global Advisors in June 2014. Prior to joining GSAM, Steve oversaw the management of $10 billion in client assets in a variety of global quantitative investment strategies, including domestic and international long-only, enhanced index, active extension (130/30) and a market neutral hedge fund at Westpeak. Prior to joining Westpeak in 1999, Steve was cofounder and senior vice president of Cordillera Asset Management, in Denver, Colorado. Steve has more than 28 years of industry experience, including more than 27 years as an institutional quantitative equity portfolio manager. Steve received a BS in finance from the University of Colorado, Boulder. He is a CFA charterholder and a member of the CFA Institute and the CFA Society of Colorado.

James Price
Director, Willis Towers Watson

James Price joined Willis Towers Watson's manager research team in 2006 and since then has researched asset managers and investment approaches ranging from discretionary stock-pickers that invest in 10 stock portfolios based on fundamental company analysis through to quantitative multistrategy hedge funds investing in all asset classes.

As well as researching asset managers James works with asset owners helping them construct portfolios or designing bespoke strategies where existing products do not meet an asset owner's needs.

James graduated from Imperial College London with an MSci in Physics. He also holds the Investment Managers Certificate (IMC) and is a CFA charterholder.

Michael Rush, CFA
Vice President, Wilshire Consulting

Michael Rush is a vice president with Wilshire Associates and a member of Wilshire Consulting. Michael currently conducts investment research within Wilshire Consulting. He is a member of Wilshire Consulting's Public Real Assets, Private Real Assets, and DC/Record Keeping Asset Class Committees.

Michael joined Wilshire in 2001 and brings more than 20 years of industry experience. Previously, Michael worked for another consulting company and an investment management firm. He has authored papers on a broad range of topics including "Alternative Mutual Fund Strategies" and "Risk-Focused Diversification." Michael also developed the "WHIP Score," a quantitative methodology for summarizing past returns, and develops an economic quarterly review for client consumption. He holds BS and MSIA degrees from Carnegie Mellon University. Michael is a CFA charterholder.

Steven Thorley, CFA, PhD
H. Taylor Peery Professor of Finance, Marriott School of Business, Brigham Young University

Steven Thorley is the H. Taylor Peery professor of finance in the Marriott School of Business at Brigham Young University in Provo, Utah. While on academic leave from BYU, Steven served as the interim research director for Analytic Investors. Steven is a chartered financial analyst (CFA) and a co-editor of the *Financial Analysts Journal*. He teaches investments in the MBA program at the Marriott School of Business and acts in a consulting capacity for Analytic Investors. Steven is currently on the investment committees for Intermountain Healthcare, Deseret Mutual Benefit Administrators, and BYU. Steven received a BA in mathematics and an MBA from BYU, and a PhD in financial economics from the University of Washington.

Phil Tindall
Senior Director, Willis Towers Watson

Phil Tindall is a senior director at Willis Towers Watson and leads their smart beta research globally. He has developed smart beta and alternative beta solutions across a wide range of assets classes and is the lead researcher and portfolio advisor for a number of Willis Towers Watson's delegated solutions and funds. Phil has 30 years' industry experience coving a wide range of investment areas, including strategic asset allocation, liability-driven investment, and manager selection.

Phil graduated from Bristol University with a BEng in Civil Engineering. He is a CFA charterholder and Fellow of the Institute of Actuaries.

BIBLIOGRAPHY

Agarwal, Vikas, Kevin A. Mullaly, and Narayan Naik. "The Economic and Finance of Hedge Funds: A Review of the Academic Literature." *Foundations and Trends in Finance* 10, no. 1 (2015): 1–111.

Agarwal, Vikas, and Narayan Y. Naik. "Multi-Period Performance Persistence Analysis of Hedge Funds." *Journal of Financial and Quantitative Analysis* 35, no. 3 (2000a): 327–342.

Agarwal, Vikas, and Narayan Y. Naik. "On Taking the Alternative Route: Risks, Rewards, and Performance Persistence of Hedge Funds." *Journal of Alternative Investments* 2, no. 4 (2000b): 6–23.

Agarwal, Vikas, and Narayan Naik. "Risk and Portfolio Decisions Involving Hedge Funds." *Review of Financial Studies* 17 (2004).

Alford, Andrew. "Some Considerations for Investors Exploring ESG Strategies." Goldman Sachs Asset Management Quantitative Investment Strategies Publication (2018).

Amenc, Noel, Frederic Docoulombier, Felix Goltz, Ashish Lodh, and Sivagaminathan Sivasubramanian. "Diversified or Concentrated Factor Tilts?" *Journal of Portfolio Management* 42, no. 2 (2016): 64–76.

Amenc, Noel, Walter Gehin, Lionel Martellini, and Jean-Christophe Meyfredi. "Passive Hedge Fund Replication: A Critical Assessment of Existing Techniques." *Journal of Alternative Investments* 11, no. 2 (2008): 69–83.

Amenc, Noel, Felix Goltz, and Ashish Lodh. "Choose Your Beta: Benchmarking Alternative Equity Index Strategies." *Journal of Portfolio Management* 39, no. 1 (2012): 88–111.

Amenc, Noel, Felix Goltz, Lionel Martellini, and P. Retkowsky. "Efficient Indexation: An Alternative to Cap-Weighted Indices." EDHEC Risk Institute Publication. (2010).

Amenc, N., F. Goltz, and S. Sivasubramanian. "Multifactor Index Construction: A Skeptical Appraisal of Bottom-Up Approaches." *Journal of Index Investing* 9, no. 1 (2018).

Amenc, Noel, Sina El Bied, and Lionel Martellini. "Predictability in Hedge Fund Returns." *Financial Analysts Journal* 59, no. 5 (2003): 32–46.

Ang, Andrew. *Asset Management: A Systematic Approach to Factor Investing.* Oxford University Press (2014).

Ang, A., W. N. Goetzman, and S. M. Schaefer. "Evaluation of Active Management of the Norwegian Government Pension Fund—Global" (2009).

Ang, Andrew, Robert J. Hodrick, Yuhang Xing, and Xiaoyan Zhang. "The Cross-Section of Volatility and Expected Returns." *Journal of Finance* 61, no. 1 (2006): 259–299

Ang, Andrew, Robert J. Hodrick, Yuhang Xing, and Xiaoyan Zhang. "High Idiosyncratic Volatility and Low Returns: International and Further U.S. Evidence." *Journal of Financial Economics* 91 (2009): 1–23.

Arnott, R., J. Hsu, V. Kalesnik, and P. Tindall. "The Surprising Alpha From Malkiel's Monkey and Upside-Down Strategies." *Journal of Portfolio Management* 39, no. 4 (2013).

Arnott, Rob, Noah Beck, Vitali Kalesnik, and John West. "How Can 'Smart Beta' Go Horribly Wrong?" Research Affiliates (February 2016).

Arnott, Rob, and Engin Kose. "What 'Smart Beta' Means to Us." Research Affiliates (August 2014).

Arnott, Robert D., Jason Hsu, and Philip Moore. "Fundamental Indexation." *Financial Analysts Journal* 61, no. 2 (2005): 83–99.

Arnott, Robert, Noah Beck, and Vitali Kalesnik. "Timing 'Smart Beta' Stratgeies? Of Course! Buy Low, Sell High." SSRN (2016).

"A Smoother Path to Outperformance with Multi-Factor Smart Beta Investing." Researchaffiliates.com, accessed June 28, 2018, https://www.researchaffiliates.com/en_us/publications/articles/594-a-smoother-path-to-outperformance-with-multifactor-smart-beta-investing.html.

Asness, Clifford S. "Variables that Explain Stock Returns." PhD Dissertation. University of Chicago (1994).

Asness, Clifford S., Andrea Frazzini, Neils Joachim Gormsen, and Lasse Heje Pedersen. "Betting Against Correlation: Testing Theories of the Low-Risk Effect." SSRN working paper, no. 2913508 (2017).

Asness, Clifford S., Andrea Frazzini, and Lasse H. Pedersen. "Leverage Aversion and Risk Parity." *Financial Analytics Journal* 68, no. 1 (2012): 47–59.

Asness, Clifford S., Andrea Frazzini, Ronen Israel, and Tobias J. Moskowitz. "Fact, Fiction, and Value Investing." *Journal of Portfolio Management* 42, no. 1 (2015): 1–20.

Asness, Clifford S., Tobias J. Moskowitz, and Lasse Heje Pedersen. "Value and Momentum Everywhere." National Bureau of Economic Research Working papers (2009).

Asness, Cliff, Tobias Moskowitz, and Lasse Heje Pedersen. "Value and Momentum Everywhere." *Journal of Finance* 68, no. 3 (June 2013): 929–985.

Authers, J. "Is 'Smart Beta' Smart Enough to Last?" *Financial Times* (June 11, 2014). https://www.ft.com/content/808189b8-f0a9-11e3-8f3d-00144feabdc0#axzz3BVeQwvKo.

Baker, M., B. Bradley, and J. Wurgler. "Benchmarks as Limits to Arbitrage: Understanding the Low Volatility Anomaly." *Financial Analysts Journal* 67, no. 1 (2011): 1–15, 40–54.

Bank of America Merrill Lunch. "The ABCs of ESG." (2018)

Banz, Rolf W. "The Relationship between Return and Market Value of Common Stock." *Journal of Financial Economics* 9, no. 1 (1981): 3–18. doi:10.1016/0304-405X(81)90018-0.

Bares, Pierre-Antoine, Rajna Gibson, and Sebastien Gyger "Performance in the Hedge Funds Industry: An Analysis of Short and Long-Term Persistence." *Journal of Alternative Investments* 6, no. 3 (2003): 25–41.

Basu, Sanjoy. "Investment Performance of Common Stocks in Relation to Their Price-Earnings Ratios: A Test of the Efficient Market Hypothesis." *Journal of Finance* 32, no. 3 (1977): 663–682.

Basu, Sanjoy, "The Relationship Between Earnings' Yield, Market Value and Return for NYSE Common Stocks." *Journal of Financial Economics* 12, no. 1 (1983): 129–156.

Beck, J., Hsu, V. Kalesnik, and H. Kostka. "Will Your Factor Deliver? An Examination of Factor Robustness and Implementation Costs." *Financial Analysts Journal* 72, no. 5 (2016).

Bender, J., R. Briand, D. Melas, and R. Aylur Subramanian. "Foundations of Factor Investing." *MSCI Research Insight* (December 2013).

Bender, Jennifer, and Taie Wang. "Multi-Factor Portfolio Construction for Passively Managed Factor Portfolios." SSRN (2015).

Bender, Jennifer, and Taie Wang. "Can the Whole Be More Than the Sum of the Parts? Bottom-Up versus Top-Down Multifactor Portfolio Construction." *Journal of Portfolio Management* 42, no. 5 (May 2016): 39–50.

Berk, Jonathan B., Richard C. Green, and Vasant Naik. "Optimal Investment, Growth Options and Security Returns." *Journal of Finance* 54, no. 5 (1999): 1553–1607.

Berkin, Andrew, and Larry Swedroe. "Your Complete Guide to Factor-Based Investing: The Way Smart Money Invests Today." (2016).

Bhandari, Laxmi Chand. "Debt/Equity Ratio and Expected Common Stock Returns: Empirical Evidence." *Journal of Finance* 43, no. 2 (1988): 507–528

Bingham, Derek, Christopher Vilburn, Evan Tylenda, Gabriel Wilson-Otto, Hugo Scott-Gall, and Jaakko Kooroshy. "The PM's Guide to the ESG Revolution." Goldman Sachs (2017).

Black, Fischer. "Capital Market Equilibrium with Restricted Borrowing." *Journal of Business* 45, no. 3 (1972): 444–455.

Black, Fischer. "Beta and Return." *Journal of Portfolio Management* 20, no. 1 (1993): 8–18.

Black, Fischer, Michael Jensen, and Myron Scholes. "The Capital Asset Pricing Model: Some Empirical Tests." In: *Studies in the Theory of Capital Markets* (ed. Michael C. Jensen), 79–121. New York: Praeger (1972).

Blitz, David. "Are Exchange-Traded Funds Harvesting Factor Premiums?" *Journal of Investment Consulting* 18, no. 1 (2017).

Blitz, David. "Strategic Allocation to Premiums in the Equity iMarket." *Journal of Index Investing* 2, no. 4 (2012): 42–49.

Blitz, D., and P. Vliet. "The Volatility Effect." *Journal of Portfolio Management* 34, no. 1 (2007): 102–113.

Bollen, Nicolas, and Gregg Fisher. "Send in the Clones? Hedge Fund Replication Using Futures Contracts." *Journal of Alternative Investments* 16, no. 2 (2014): 80–95.

Boyadzhiev, Dimitar, Alex Bryan, Jackie Choy, Ben Johnson, and Anshula Venkataraman. Morningstar Research. "A Global Guide to Strategic-Beta Exchange-Traded Products." (2017).

Boyer, B., and K. Vorkink. "Stock Options as Lotteries." *Journal of Finance* 69, no. 4 (2014): 1485–1526.

Boyson, Nicole. "Hedge Fund Performance Persistence: A New Approach." *Financial Analysts Journal* 64, no. 6 (2008): 27–44.

Brennan, Michael J., and Avanidhar Subrahmanyam. "Market Microstructure and Asset Pricing: On the Compensation for Illiquidity in Stock Returns." *Journal of Financial Economics* 41, no. 3 (1996): 441–464

Brown, Stephen, and William Goetzmann "Hedge Funds with Style." *Journal of Portfolio Management* 29, no. 2 (2003): 101–112.

Cai, Li, and Bing Liang. "Asset Allocation Dynamics in the Hedge Fund Industry." *Journal of Investment Management* 10, no. 2 (2012).

Capaul, Carlo, Ian Rowley, and William F. Sharpe. "International Value and Growth Stock Returns." *Financial Analysts Journal* 49, no. 1 (1993): 27–36.

Capocci, Daniel, Albert Corhay, and Georges Huebner. "Hedge Fund Performance and Persistence in Bull and Bear Markets." *European Journal of Finance* 11, no. 5 (2005): 361–392.

Capocci, Daniel, and Georges Huebner. "Analysis of Hedge Fund Performance." *Journal of Empirical Finance* 11, no. 1, (2004): 55–89.

Carhart, Mark M. "Survivor Bias and Persistence in Mutual Fund Performance." Unpublished Dissertation, University of Chicago (1995).

Carhart, Mark M. "On Persistence in Mutual Fund Performance." *Journal of Finance* 52, no. 1 (1997): 57–82.

Chan, Louis K. C., and Nai-Fu Chen. "Structural and Return Characteristics of Small and Large Firms." *Journal of Finance* 46, no. 4 (1991): 1467–1484.

Chan, Louis K. C., Narasimhan Jegadeesh, and Josef Lakonishok. "The Profitability of Momentum Strategies." *Financial Analysts Journal* 55, no. 6 (1999): 80–90.

Chen, Long, Claudia Moise, and Xinlei Zhao. "Myopic Extrapolation, Price Momentum, and Price Reversal." Working paper, Washington University (2009).

Choueifaty, Yves, and Yves Coignard. "Toward Maximum Diversification." *Journal of Portfolio Management* 35, no. 1 (2008): 40–51.

Chow, T., F. Li, and Y. Shim. "Smart Beta Multifactor Construction Methodology: Mixing versus Integrating" *Journal of Index Investing* 8, no. 4 (2018).

Chow, Tzee-man, Jason Hsu, Vitali Kalesnik, and Bryce Little. "A Survey of Alternative Equity Index Strategies." *Financial Analysts Journal* 67, no. 5 (2011): 37–57.

Clarke, R., H. de Silva, and S. Thorley. "Minimum Variance Portfolios in the U.S.
Equity Market." *Journal of Portfolio Management* 33, no. 1 (Fall 2006): 10–24.

Clarke, Roger, Harindra de Silva, and Steve Thorley. "Minimum-Variance Portfolio
Composition." *Journal of Portfolio Management* 37, no. 2 (2011): 31–45.

Clarke, Roger, Harindra de Silva, and Steve Thorley. "Fundamentals of Efficient Factor Investing." *Financial Analysts Journal* 72, no. 6 (2016): 9–26.

Clarke, R., H. de Silva, and S. Thorley. "Pure Factor Portfolios and Multivariate
Regression Analysis." *Journal of Portfolio Management* 43, no. 3 (Spring 2017).

Clarke, Roger G., Scott Krase, and Meir Statman. "Tracking Errors, Regret, and Tactical Asset Allocation." *Journal of Portfolio Management* 20, no. 3 (1994): 16–24.

Cochrane, John H. *Asset Pricing.* Princeton, NJ: Princeton University Press (2001).

Cochrane, John H. "Portfolio Advice for a Multifactor World." *Economic Perspectives*
23, no. 3 (1999): 59–61.

Crain, Michael A. *A Literature Review of the Size Effect.* Florida Atlantic University;
University of Manchester–Manchester Business School; The Financial Valuation
Group. SSRN (2011).

Daniel, Kent, David Hirshleifer, and Avanidhar Subrahmanyam. "Investor Psychol-
ogy and Security Market Under- and Overreaction." *Journal of Finance* 53,
no. 6 (1998): 1839–1885.

Daniel, Kent, and Tobias J. Moskowitz. *Momentum Crashes.* Columbia Business
School and NBER, and Booth School of Business, University of Chicago and
NBER (2014).

Daniel, Kent, Sheridan Titman, and Russ Wermers. "Measuring Mutual Fund Performance with Characteristic-based Benchmarks." *Journal of Finance* 52, no. 3
(1997): 1035–1058.

Das, Sanjiv Ranjan, Daniel N. Ostrov, Anand Radhakrishnan, and Deep Srivastav.
"A New Approach to Goals-Based Wealth Management." (2018).

De Bondt, F. M. Werner, and Richard Thaler. "Does the Stock Market Overreact?"
Journal of Finance 40, no. 3 (1985): 793–805.

De Groot, W., and J. Huij. "Is the Value Premium Really a Compensation for Distress
Risk?" SSRN working paper, no. 1840511 (2011).

Dimson, Elroy, Paul Marsh, and Mike Staunton. "Factor-Based Investing: The Long-
Term Evidence" *Journal of Portfolio Management* 43, no. 5 (2017): 15–37.

Edwards, Franklin, and Mustafa Caglayan. "Hedge Fund Performance and Manager
Skill." *Journal of Futures Markets* 21, no.11 (2001): 1003–1028.

Elan, Seth. "Financial Literacy among Retail Investors in the United States." Federal
Research Division, Library of Congress Under an Interagency Agreement with
the Securities and Exchange Commission, Washington, DC (2011).

Eling, Martin. "Does Hedge Fund Performance Persist? Overview and New Empirical Evidence." *European Financial Management* 15, no. 2 (2009): 362–401.

Fama, Eugene F., and Kenneth R. French. "The Cross-Section of Expected Stock Returns." *Journal of Finance* 47, no. 2 (1992): 427–466.

Fama, Eugene, and Kenneth French "Common Risk Factors in the Returns on Stocks and Bonds." *Journal of Financial Economics* 33, no. 1 (1993): 3–56.

Fama, Eugene F., and Kenneth R. French. "Multifactor Explanations of Asset Pricing Anomalies." *Journal of Finance* 51(1)(1996):55–84.doi:10.1111/j.1540-6261.1996.tb05202.x. https://www.jstor.org/stable/2329302.

Fama, Eugene F., and Kenneth R. French. "Value versus Growth: The International Evidence." *Journal of Finance* 53, no. 6 (1998): 1975–1999.

Fama, Eugene F., and Kenneth R. French. "Dissecting Anomalies." *Journal of Finance* 63, no. 4 (2008): 1653–1678.

Fama, Eugene F., and Kenneth French. "Luck versus Skill in the Cross-Section of Mutual Fund Returns." *Journal of Finance* 65, no. 5 (2011): 1915–1947.

Fama, Eugene F., and Kenneth R. French. "Size, Value and Momentum in International Stock Returns." Fama-Miller Working Paper; Tuck School of Business Working Paper No. 2011–85; Chicago Booth Research Paper No. 11–10. (2011). Available at SSRN: http://ssrn.com/abstract=1720139.

Fama, Eugene F., and Kenneth R. French. "Size, Value, and Momentum in International Stock Returns." *Journal of Financial Economics* 105, no. 3 (2012): 457–472.

Fama, Eugene F., and Kenneth French. "A Five-Factor Asset Pricing Model." *Journal of Financial Economics* 116, no. 1 (2015): 1–22.

Fama, E., and J. MacBeth. "Risk, Return, and Equilibrium: Empirical Tests." *Journal of Political Economy* 81, no. 3 (1973): 607–636.

Feng, Guanhao, Giglio, Stefano, and Dacheng Xiu. "Taming the Factor Zoo." SSRN (2017).

Fernholz, Robert E. "Portfolio Generating Functions." Working paper (INTECH) (1998).

Fernholz, Robert E. "Equity Portfolios Generated by Functions of Ranked Market Weights." Enhanced Investment Technologies (INTECH) (1998).

Fitzgibbons, Shaun, Jacques Friedman, Lukasz Pomorski, and Laura Serban. "Long-Only Style Investing: Don't Just Mix, Integrate." *Journal of Investing* 26, no. 4 (2016): 153–164.

Foresti, Steven. *Alternative Equity-Weighting Strategies* (Wilshire Associates, 2012).

Fraser-Jenkins, Inigo, Alix Guerrini, Alla Harmsworth, Mark Diver, Sarah McCarthy, Robertas Stancikas, and Maureen Hughes. "How to Combine Factors? It Depends Why You Are Doing It." New York: AllianceBernstein (2016).

Frazzini, A., and L. Pedersen. "Betting against Beta." *Journal of Financial Economics* 111, no. 1 (2014): 1–25.

FTSE Russell. "Global Survey Findings from Asset Owners." (2018).

Fung, William, and David Hsieh. "Empirical Characteristics of Dynamic Trading Strategies." *Review of Financial Studies* 10, no. 2 (1997): 275–302.

Fung, William, and David Hsieh. "The Risk in Hedge Fund Strategies: Theory and Evidence from Trend Followers." *Review of Financial Studies* 14, no. 2 (2001): 313–341.

Fung, William, and David A. Hsieh. "Hedge Fund Benchmarks: A Risk-Based Approach," *Financial Analysts Journal* 60, no. 5 (2004): 65–80.

Garvey, Gerald, Ronald N. Kahn, and Raffaele Savi. "The Dangers of Diversification: Managing Multiple Manager Portfolios." *Journal of Portfolio Management* 43, no. 2 (2017): 13–23.

Ghayur, Kal, Ronan Heaney, and Steve Platt. "Constructing Long-Only Multi-Factor Strategies: Portfolio Blending versus Signal Blending." *Financial Analysts Journal* 74, no. 3 (2018): 70–85.

Ghayur, Kal, Steve Platt, and Ronan Heaney. "Low-Volatility Investing: Balancing Total Risk and Active Risk Considerations." *Journal of Portfolio Management* 40, no. 1 (2013): 49–60.

Goltz, Felix. "Be Serious with Equity Factor Investing!" EDHEC-RISK Institute (2017). https://risk.edhec.edu/industry-publications/be-serious-equity-factor-investing.

Graham, Benjamin, and David Dodd. *Security Analysis*. Whittlesey House, McGraw-Hill Book Co. (1934).

Graham, Benjamin, and David L. Dodd. *Security Analysis*. 6th ed. New York: McGraw-Hill (2009).

Grinblatt, Mark, and Sheridan Titman. "Mutual Fund Performance: An Analysis of Quarterly Portfolio Holdings." *Journal of Business* 62, no. 3 (1989): 393–416.

Grinblatt, Mark, and Sheridan Titman. "Performance Measurement Without Benchmarks: An Examination of Mutual Fund Returns." *Journal of Business* 66, no. 1 (1993): 47–68.

Grinblatt, Mark, Sheridan Titman, and Russ Wermers. "Momentum Investment Strategies, Portfolio Performance, and Herding: A Study of Mutual Fund Behavior." *American Economics Review* 85, no. 5 (1995): 1088–1105.

Harvey, Campbell R., Liu, Yan, and Heqing Zhu. ". . . and the Cross-Section of Expected Returns." *Review of Financial Studies* 29, no. 1 (2016): 5–68.

Hasanhodizic and Lo. "Can Hedge-Fund Returns Be Replicated?: The Linear Case." *Journal of Investment Management* 5, no. 2 (2007): 5–45.

Haugen, Robert A., and Nardin L. Baker. "The Efficient Market Inefficiency of Capitalization-weighted Stock Portfolios." *Journal of Portfolio Management* 17, no. 3 (1991): 35–40.

Hawawini, Gabriel, and Donald B. Keim. "On the Predictability of Common Stock Returns: World-wide Evidence." *Handbooks in Operations Research and Management Science* 9 (1995): 497–544.

Hawawini, Gabriel, and Donald B. Keim. *The Cross Section of Common Stock Returns: A Review of the Evidence and Some New Findings*. Wharton (1998).

Hendricks, Darryll, Jayendu Patel, and Richard Zeckhauser. "Hot Hands in Mutual Funds: Short-Run Persistence of Relative Performance." *Journal of Finance* 48, no. 1 (1993): 93–130.

Hill, Joanne M., Barbara Mueller, and Venkatesh Balasubramanian. "The 'Secret Sauce' of Hedge Fund Investing—Trading Risk Dynamically." *Goldman Sachs Equity Derivatives Strategy* (2004): 1–24.

Hjalmarsson, Erik. "Diversification Across Characteristics." *International Finance Discussion Papers*, no. 986 (2009).

Hou, Kewei, Chen Xue, and Lu Zhang "Digesting Anomalies: An Investment Approach." *Review of Financial Studies* 288, no. 3 (2015): 650–705.

Hou, Kewei, Chen Xue, and Lu Zhang. "Replicating Anomalies." Fisher College of Business Working Paper no. 2017-03-010. (2017). https://papers.ssrn.com/sol3/papers.cfm?abstract_id=2961979.

Hsu, Jason, Vitali Kalesnik, and Feifei Li. "An Investor's Guide to Smart Beta Strategies." *AAII Journal* (December 2012): 11–16.

Hsu, Jason C., Vitali Kalesnik, and Brett W. Myers. "Performance Attribution: Measuring Dynamic Allocation Skill." *Financial Analysts Journal* 66, no. 6 (2010).

Hsu, J., and F. Li. "Low-Volatility Investing." *Journal of Index Investing* (Fall 2013).

Ilmanen, Antti. *Expected Returns: An Investor's Guide to harvesting Market Rewards.* Hoboken, NJ: Wiley (2011).

Jaeger, Lars. *Alternative Beta Strategies and Hedge Fund Replication.* Hoboken, NJ: Wiley (2008).

Jegadeesh, Narasimhan, and Sheridan Titman. "Returns to Buying Winners and Selling Losers: Implications for Stock Market Inefficiency." *Journal of Finance* 48, no. 1 (1993): 65–91.

Jensen, Michael C. "Risk, The Pricing of Capital Assets, and the Evaluation of Investment Portfolios." *Journal of Business* 42, no. 2 (1969): 167–247.

Joenvaara, Juha, Robert Kosowski, and Pekka Tolonen. "Hedge Fund Performance: What Do We Know?" Working paper, SSRN (2016).

Kahn, Ronald, and Michael Lemmon. "The Asset Manager's Dilemma: How Smart Beta Is Disrupting the Investment Management Industry." *Financial Analysts Journal* 72, no. 1 (2016): 16–20.

Kahneman, Daniel, and Amos Tversky. "Judgement under Uncertainty: Heuristics and Biases." *Science* 185, no. 4157 (1974): 1124–1131.

Karceski, Jason. "Returns-Chasing Behavior, Mutual Funds, and Beta's Death." *Journal of Financial and Quantitative Analysis* 37, no. 4 (2002): 559–594.

Kat, Harry, and Helder Palaro. "Who Needs Hedge Funds? A Copula-Based Approach to Hedge Fund Replication," Working paper (2005).

Kellerer, Hans, Ulrich Pferschy, and David Pisinger. "Knapsack Problems." (2004).

Koedijk, C. G., A. M. H. Slager, and P. A. Stork. *Beleggen in systematische factorpremies, Onderzoeksrapport Robeco* (August 2013).

Lakonishok, Josef, and Alan C. Shapiro. "Systematic Risk, Total Risk and Size as Determinants of Stock Market Returns." *Journal of Banking and Finance* 10, no.1 (1986): 115–132.

Lakonishok, Josef, Andrei Shleifer, and Robert W. Vishny. "Contrarian Investment, Extrapolation, and Risk." *Journal of Finance* 49, no. 5 (1994): 1541–1578.

Leippold, Markus, and Roger Rüegg. "The Mixed vs. the Integrated Approach to Style Investing: Much Ado about Nothing?" *European Financial Management* (2017).

Leote de Carvalho, R., X. Lu, and P. Moulin. "Demystifying Equity Risk-Based Strategies: A Simple Alpha Plus Beta Description." BNP Paribas Asset Management, SSRN no.1949003 (2011).

Levy, Robert A. "Relative Strength as a Criterion for Investment Selection." *Journal of Finance* 22, no. 4 (1967): 595–610.

Liang, Bing. "On the Performance of Hedge Funds." *Financial Analysts Journal* 55, no. 4 (1999): 72–85.

Lintner, John. "The Valuation of Risk Assets and the Selection of Risky Investments in Stock Portfolios and Capital Budgets." *Review of Economics and Statistics* 47, no. 1 (1965): 13–37.

Lo, Andrew, W., and A. Craig MacKinlay. "Data-Snooping Biases in Tests of Financial Asset Pricing Models." *Review of Financial Studies* 3, no. 3 (1990): 431–467.

Lusardi, Annamaria. "Financial Literacy: Do People Know the ABCs of Finance?" *Public Understanding of Science* 24, no. 3 (2015): 260–271.

Lustig, Hanno N., and Stijn G. Van Nieuwerburgh. "Housing Collateral, Consumption Insurance, and Risk Premia: An Empirical Perspective." *Journal of Finance* 60, no. 3 (2005): 1167–1219.

Malkiel, Burton, and Atanu Saha. "Hedge Funds: Risk and Return." *Financial Analysts Journal* 61, no. 6 (2005): 80–88.

Markowitz, Harry. "Portfolio Selection." *Journal of Finance* 7, no. 1 (1952): 77–91.

Mayers, David. "Nonmarketable Assets, Market Segmentation, and the Level of Asset Prices." *Journal of Financial and Quantitative Analysis* 11, no. 1 (March 1976): 1–12.

McLean, D., and J. Pontiff. "Does Academic Research Destroy Stock Return Predictability?" *Journal of Finance* 71 (2016): 5–31.

Mossin, Jan. "Equilibrium in a Capital Asset Market." *Econometrica* 34, no. 4 (1966), 768–783.

Mulvey, John M., and Woo Chang Kim. "Active Equity Managers in the U.S.: Do the Best Follow Momentum Strategies?" *Journal of Portfolio Management* 34, no. 2 (2008): 126–134.

Novy-Marx, Robert. "The Other Side of Value: The Gross Profitability Premium." *Journal of Financial Economics* 108, no. 1 (2013): 1–28.

Novy-Marx, Robert. "Quality Investing." Working paper (University of Rochester) (2014).

Novy-Marx, Robert. "Testing Strategies Based on Multiple Signals." Working paper. (University of Rochester) (2016). http://rnm.simon.rochester.edu/research/MSES.pdf.

Parker, Jonathan A., and Christian Julliard. "Consumption Risk and the Cross Section of Expected Returns." *Journal of Political Economy* 113, no. 1 (2005): 185–222.

Patton, Andrew, and Tarun Ramadorai. "On the High-Frequency Dynamics of Hedge Fund Risk Exposures." *Journal of Finance* 68, no. 2 (2013): 597–635.

Piotroski, Joseph D. "Value Investing: The Use of Historical Financial Statement Information to Separate Winners from Losers." *Journal of Accounting Research* 38 (2000): 1–41.

Reinganum, Marc R. "A New Empirical Perspective on the CAPM." *Journal of Financial and Quantitative Analysis* 16, no. 4 (1981): 439–462.

Rosenberg, Barr, Kenneth Reid, and Ronald Lanstein. "Persuasive Evidence of Market Inefficiency." *Journal of Portfolio Management* 11, no. 3 (1985): 9–16.

Ross, Stephen A. "The Arbitrage Theory of Capital Asset Pricing." *Journal of Economic Theory* 13, no. 3 (1976): 341–360.

Rouwenhorst, K. Geert. "International Momentum Strategies." *Journal of Finance* 53, no. 1 (1998): 267–284.

Russell FTSE. "Smart Beta: 2018 Global Survey Findings from Asset Owners." (2018). www.ftserussell.com/smart-beta-survey.

Santos, Tano, and Pietro Veronesi. "Labor Income and Predictable Stock Returns." *Review of Financial Studies* 19, no. 1 (2006): 1–44.

Scherer, Bernd. "A Note on Asset Management and Market Risk." *Financial Markets and Portfolio Management* 24, no. 3 (2010): 309–320.

Schneeweis, Thomas, and Richard Spurgin "Multifactor Analysis of Hedge Fund, Managed Futures, and Mutual Fund Return and Risk Characteristics." *Journal of Alternative Investments* 1, no. 2 (1998): 1–24.

Scholes, Myron, and Joseph Williams. "Estimating Betas from Nonsynchronous Data." *Journal of Financial Economics* 5 (1977): 309–327.

Sharpe, William F. "Capital Asset Prices: A Theory of Market Equilibrium under Conditions of Risk." *Journal of Finance* 19, no. 3 (1964): 259–263, 425–442.

Sharpe, William F. "Mutual Fund Performance." *Journal of Business* 39, no. 1 (1966): 119–138.

Sharpe, William F. "Decentralized Investment Management." *Journal of Finance* 36 (1981): 217–234.

Sharpe, William F. "Determining a Fund's Effective Asset Mix." *Investment Management Review* 2, no. 6 (1988): 59–69.

Sharpe, William F. "Asset Allocation: Management Style and Performance Measurement." *Journal of Portfolio Management* 18, no. 2 (1992): 7–19.

Shefrin, Hersh, and Meir Statman. "Behavioral Portfolio Theory." *Journal of Financial and Quantitative Analysis* 35, no. 2 (2000): 127–151.

Shleifer, Andrei. *Inefficient Markets: An Introduction to Behavioral Finance.* New York: Oxford University Press (2000).

Shleifer, Andrei, and Robert W. Vishny. "The Limits of Arbitrage." *Journal of Finance* 52, no. 1 (1997): 35–55.

Siegel, Jeremy J. "The Shiller CAPE Ratio: A New Look." *Financial Analysts Journal* 72, no. 3 (2016): 41–50.

Sloan, Richard, G. "Do Stock Prices Fully Reflect Information in Accruals and Cash Flows about Future Earning?" *Accounting Review* 71, no. 3 (1996): 289–315.

Stambaugh, Robert. "On the Exclusion of Assets from Tests of the Two-Parameter Model: A Sensitivity Analysis." *Journal of Financial Economics* 10, no. 3 (1982): 237–268.

Stattman, Dennis. "Book Values and Stock Returns." *Chicago MBA: A Journal of Selected Papers* 4 (1980): 25–45.

Ter Horst, Jenke, and Marno Verbeek. "Fund Liquidation, Self-Selection, and Look-Ahead Bias in the Hedge Fund Industry," *Review of Finance* 11, no. 4 (2007): 605–632.

Thaler, Richard. "Mental Accounting and Consumer Choice." *Marketing Science* 4, no. 3 (1985): 199–214.

Thaler, Richard H. "Mental Accounting Matters." *Journal of Behavioral Decision Making* 12, no. 3 (1999): 183–206.

Treynor, Jack L. "Market Value, Time, and Risk." *Independent* (1961).

Treynor, Jack L. "How to Rate Management of Investment Funds." *Harvard Business Review* 43, no. 1 (1965): 63–75.

van Gelderen, E., and J. Huij, "Academic Knowledge Dissemination in the Mutual Fund Industry: Can Mutual Funds Successfully Adopt Factor Investing Strategies?" *Journal of Portfolio Management* (Summer 2014).

Wermers, Russ. "Momentum Investment Strategies of Mutual Funds, Performance Persistence, and Survivorship Bias." Unpublished working paper, University of Colorado at Boulder (1997).

Wermers, Russ. "Mutual Fund Performance: An Empirical Decomposition into Stock-Picking Talent, Style, Transactions Costs, and Expenses." *Journal of Finance* 55, no. 4 (2000): 1655–1695.

Whyte, A. "Asness Debunks Fama's Views on Momentum." *Chief Investment Officer Magazine* (February 7, 2016). https://www.ai-cio.com/news/asness-debunks-famas-views-on-momentum/.

Williamson, Oliver E. *Corporate Control and Business Behavior: An Inquiry into the Effects of Organizational Form on Enterprise Behavior.* Englewood Cliffs, NJ: Prentice Hall (1970).

Zhang, Lu. "The Value Premium." *Journal of Finance* 60, no.1 (2005): 67–103.

ADDITIONAL DISCLAIMERS

CHAPTER 12

General Disclosures

This material is provided at your request for informational purposes only. It is not an offer or solicitation to buy or sell any securities.

This material is provided for educational purposes only and should not be construed as investment advice or an offer or solicitation to buy or sell securities.

This material does not constitute an offer or solicitation in any jurisdiction where or to any person to whom it would be unauthorized or unlawful to do so.

These examples are for illustrative purposes only and are not actual results. If any assumptions used do not prove to be true, results may vary substantially.

Backtested performance shown is not actual performance and in no way should be construed as indicative of future results. Backtested performance results are created based on an analysis of past market data with the benefit of hindsight, do not reflect the performance of any GSAM product and are being shown for informational purposes only. Please see additional disclosures.

Simulated Performance

Simulated performance is hypothetical and may not take into account material economic and market factors, such as liquidity constraints, that would impact the adviser's actual decision-making. Simulated results are achieved by retroactively applying a model with the benefit of hindsight. The results reflect the reinvestment of dividends and other earnings, but do not reflect fees, transaction costs, and other expenses a client would have to pay, which would reduce returns. Actual results will vary.

Index Benchmarks

Indices are unmanaged. The figures for the index reflect the reinvestment of all income or dividends, as applicable, but do not reflect the deduction of any fees or expenses, which would reduce returns. Investors cannot invest directly in indices.

The indices referenced herein have been selected because they are well known, easily recognized by investors, and reflect those indices that the Investment Manager believes, in part based on industry practice, provide a suitable benchmark against which to evaluate the investment or broader market described herein. The exclusion of "failed" or closed hedge funds may mean that each index overstates the performance of hedge funds generally.

The website links provided are for your convenience only and are not an endorsement or recommendation by GSAM of any of these websites or the products or services offered. GSAM is not responsible for the accuracy and validity of the content of these websites.

This material is provided for educational purposes only and should not be construed as investment advice or an offer or solicitation to buy or sell securities.

This information discusses general market activity, industry or sector trends, or other broad-based economic, market or political conditions and should not be construed as research or investment advice. This material has been prepared by GSAM and is not financial research nor a product of Goldman Sachs Global Investment Research (GIR). It was not prepared in compliance with applicable provisions of law designed to promote the independence of financial analysis and is not subject to a prohibition on trading following the distribution of financial research. The views and opinions expressed may differ from those of Goldman Sachs Global Investment Research or other departments or divisions of Goldman Sachs and its affiliates. Investors are urged to consult with their financial advisors before buying or selling any securities. This information may not be current and GSAM has no obligation to provide any updates or changes.

Although certain information has been obtained from sources believed to be reliable, we do not guarantee its accuracy, completeness or fairness. We have relied upon and assumed without independent verification, the accuracy and completeness of all information available from public sources.

Views and opinions expressed are for informational purposes only and do not constitute a recommendation by GSAM to buy, sell, or hold any security. Views and opinions are current as of the date of this presentation and may be subject to change, they should not be construed as investment advice.

Past performance does not guarantee future results, which may vary. The value of investments and the income derived from investments will fluctuate and can go down as well as up. A loss of principal may occur.

Studied Hedge Fund Universe is not inclusive of all hedge funds in existence.

No part of this material may, without GSAM's prior written consent, be (i) copied, photocopied or duplicated in any form, by any means, or (ii) distributed to any person that is not an employee, officer, director, or authorized agent of the recipient.

CHAPTER 16

Towers Watson Limited ("Willis Towers Watson") has prepared this material for general information purposes only and it should not be considered a substitute for specific professional advice. In particular, its contents are not intended by Willis Towers Watson to be construed as the provision of investment, legal, accounting, tax or other professional advice or recommendations of any kind, or to form the basis of any decision to do or to refrain from doing anything. As such, this material should not be relied upon for investment or other financial decisions and no such decisions should be taken on the basis of its contents without seeking specific advice.

This material is based on information available to Willis Towers Watson at the date of this material and takes no account of subsequent developments after that date. In preparing this material we have relied upon data supplied to us by third parties. Whilst reasonable care has been taken to gauge the reliability of this data, we provide no guarantee as to the accuracy or completeness of this data and Willis Towers Watson and its affiliates and their respective directors, officers and employees accept no responsibility and will not be liable for any errors or misrepresentations in the data made by any third party.

This material may not be reproduced or distributed to any other party, whether in whole or in part, without Willis Towers Watson's prior written permission. In the absence of our express written agreement to the contrary, Willis Towers Watson and its affiliates and their respective directors, officers and employees accept no responsibility and will not be liable for any consequences howsoever arising from any use of or reliance on this material or the opinions we have expressed.

CHAPTER 17

This material contains confidential and proprietary information of Wilshire Consulting, and is intended for the exclusive use of the person to whom it is provided. It may not be disclosed, reproduced or otherwise distributed, in whole or in part, to any other person or entity without prior written permission from Wilshire Consulting.

This material is intended for informational purposes only and should not be construed as legal, accounting, tax, investment, or other professional advice. Past performance does not guarantee future returns. This material may include estimates, projections and other "forward-looking statements." Due to numerous factors, actual events may differ substantially from those presented.

Third-party information contained herein has been obtained from sources believed to be reliable. Wilshire Consulting gives no representations or warranties as to the accuracy of such information, and accepts no responsibility or liability (including for indirect, consequential or incidental damages) for any error, omission or inaccuracy in such information and for results obtained from its use. Information and opinions are as of the date indicated, and are subject to change without notice.

Wilshire Consulting is a business unit of Wilshire Associates Incorporated. Wilshire is a registered service mark of Wilshire Associates Incorporated, Santa Monica, California. All other trade names, trademarks, and/or service marks are the property of their respective holders.

No part of this publication may be stored in a retrieval system, transmitted, or reproduced in any way, including but not limited to, photocopy, photograph, magnetic or other record, without the prior written permission of Wilshire Associates Incorporated, Santa Monica, CA, USA, www.wilshire.com.

INDEX